ROUTLEDGE LIBRARY EDITIONS: THE VICTORIAN WORLD

Volume 19

INSTRUMENTAL TEACHING IN NINETEENTH-CENTURY BRITAIN

INSTRUMENTAL TEACHING IN NINETEENTH-CENTURY BRITAIN

DAVID J. GOLBY

LONDON AND NEW YORK

First published in 2004 by Ashgate Publishing Limited

This edition first published in 2016
by Routledge
2 Park Square, Milton Park, Abingdon, Oxon OX14 4RN

and by Routledge
711 Third Avenue, New York, NY 10017

Routledge is an imprint of the Taylor & Francis Group, an informa business

© 2004 David J. Golby

All rights reserved. No part of this book may be reprinted or reproduced or utilised in any form or by any electronic, mechanical, or other means, now known or hereafter invented, including photocopying and recording, or in any information storage or retrieval system, without permission in writing from the publishers.

Trademark notice: Product or corporate names may be trademarks or registered trademarks, and are used only for identification and explanation without intent to infringe.

British Library Cataloguing in Publication Data
A catalogue record for this book is available from the British Library

ISBN: 978-1-138-66565-1 (Set)
ISBN: 978-1-315-61965-1 (Set) (ebk)
ISBN: 978-1-138-65681-9 (Volume 19) (hbk)
ISBN: 978-1-138-65684-0 (Volume 19) (pbk)
ISBN: 978-1-315-62169-2 (Volume 19) (ebk)

Publisher's Note
The publisher has gone to great lengths to ensure the quality of this reprint but points out that some imperfections in the original copies may be apparent.

Disclaimer
The publisher has made every effort to trace copyright holders and would welcome correspondence from those they have been unable to trace.

Preface to 2016 facsimile edition

It is twelve years since the original publication of *Instrumental Teaching in Nineteenth-Century Britain* and I am delighted that it has been granted a revival as part of this series for Routledge. In the intervening time there has been a significant increase in the level of interest in British music and musicians from the nineteenth century, thanks largely to passionate advocates, including scholars, such as Nicholas Temperley and Bennett Zon, and publishers willing to break new ground, such as Ashgate.

An inevitable consequence of this growth in interest has been an increasing specialization and focus on the work and contributions of significant individuals, including performers, writers and publishers, as well as important institutions and centres of activity, many of which existed outside of London. A desire to shine a light on provincial music-making in particular has facilitated a far more holistic approach to this area of scholarship. The recent book edited by Temperley on the Loder family of Bath, for example, has chapters which cover a very diverse range of subjects, including, I am very pleased to note, a chapter on the performer, teacher and writer John David Loder, who rightly features quite prominently in the following pages. The 'Study Day' held in Bath in October 2015, focusing on 'The Loder Family and Music in Provincial Britain', is a perfect example of this trend. It is always enjoyable to return to subjects such as Loder's importance and the enduring legacy of his violin treatise, and to follow-up on leads unearthed years before. The historical study of instrumental pedagogy remains very fertile ground and I would encourage anyone interested in this area to explore it further.

Something that I have far more ambivalent feelings towards is the subject of the last paragraph of this book. Back in 2004, as a final summative thought, I was very keen to highlight the lessons that could be learned in modern times from the development of instrumental pedagogy during the eighteenth and nineteenth centuries in Britain. One of the main strands of argument presented and evidenced within the main body of the study highlighted that the benefits of music-making were felt, eventually, by all echelons of society, as pride and prejudice were gradually supplanted by a wealth of opportunity and engagement. It is always the case that the question of who gets to engage in creative opportunities within a society as a whole reveals a great deal about its priorities in general. Twelve years on it seems that there remains a very real danger that British society is destined to suffer the consequences of the self-perpetuating concept of elitism in music education. Without a reversal of this trend, then the hard-won progress made previously may well itself be confined to history.

This is not a party-political point, as successive government initiatives, such as the *Music Manifesto* (2004), the *Henley Review* (2011), and *A National Plan for Music Education* that followed in the same year, have all decreed highly laudable intentions, but no coherent approach embracing the value of music for all has emerged. We require well-trained teachers to offer young people opportunities to engage in musical activity, including singing and playing an instrument; but, crucially if the long-term future of the art is to be secured, we must also facilitate the *continued* growth in musical development, through the different stages of education into adulthood, for the benefit of both the individual and wider society. The Victorians were very alert to the potential in this and, moreover, were proactive in encouraging its application.

Those who work with aspiring young musicians know how gratifying and important this work is, and to be fair, there is a huge amount of effort going into encouraging participation and growth in certain areas. Initiatives such as *In Harmony, Sistema England*, founded by Julian Lloyd Webber and based on the Venezuelan *El Sistema* model, and the excellent work and strenuous efforts of many of our music education 'hubs' (for which funding is far from secure) are to be celebrated. But pockets of brilliance and opportunity are not enough to guarantee our musical future as a nation. There is far too much at stake to take such risks, and towards the end of 2015 we face the very real danger that generations of future musicians in all fields will be lost from certain strata of society.

When you have looked at the circumstances and repercussions of past centuries you do not relish the prospect of a return to a scenario last seen in the eighteenth century, with a music profession dominated by a select, largely predestined few and a normal level of engagement among society at large characterized by the well-heeled *ad hoc* amateur 'dabbler'.

Exeter, Devon
November 2015

To my wife
Alison
with love and gratitude

Instrumental Teaching in Nineteenth-Century Britain

DAVID J. GOLBY

ASHGATE

© David J. Golby 2004

All rights reserved. No part of this publication may be reproduced, stored in a retrieval system, or transmitted in any form or by any means, electronic, mechanical, photocopying, recording or otherwise without the prior permission of the publisher.

David J. Golby has asserted his right under the Copyright, Designs and Patents Act, 1988, to be identified as the author of this work.

Published by
Ashgate Publishing Limited
Gower House
Croft Road
Aldershot
Hants GU11 3HR
England

Ashgate Publishing Company
Suite 420
101 Cherry Street
Burlington, VT 05401-4405
USA

Ashgate website: http://www.ashgate.com

British Library Cataloguing in Publication Data
Golby, David J.
  Instrumental teaching in nineteenth-century Britain. –
(Music in nineteenth-century Britain)
  1. Instrumental music – Instruction and study – Great
Britain – History – 19th century
  I. Title
  784.1'93'071041'09034

Library of Congress Cataloging-in-Publication Data
Golby, David J.
  Instrumental teaching in nineteenth-century Britain / David J. Golby.
       p. cm. – (Music in nineteenth-century Britain)
  Includes bibliographical references and index.
  ISBN 1-84014-655-9 (alk. paper)
    1. Musical instruments–Instruction and study–Great Britain–History–
19th century. I. Title. II. Series.

MT170.G65 2003
784'.071'041–dc21

2003043745

ISBN 1 84014 655 9

Typeset by Bournemouth Colour Press, Parkstone, Poole.
Printed and bound in Great Britain by MPG Books Ltd, Bodmin, Cornwall.

Contents

Acknowledgements	*viii*
Preface	*ix*
Abbreviations	*xvi*

PART ONE

Introduction	
Music in Britain: A Social and Cultural Context	3
The Consumer Society	3
The Musician's Lot	18
Music and the Moral Dimension: 'damned if you do, damned if you don't'	27
Musical Appreciation	33
'Artistic awakening' or 'damnable flood'? The Popularity of Music and the Spread of Opportunity	36
1 Music Education and 'the Age of Improvement'	41
The Legacy of the Eighteenth Century	41
The Nineteenth Century	65
2 Instrumental Teaching	89
Instruction Methods	89
Styles and Personalities	104
Sources: General Trends	112
The Vocal Model	141

PART TWO

3 The Violin Family	145
Violinists in Britain	145
The Violin and Bow	161
Violin Technique	164
The Violin: Stigma and Solace	203
The Viola, Double Bass and Violoncello	213

PART THREE

4	Other Instruments	219
	Keyboard	219
	Wind	225
	Brass	229
	Plucked Strings and Miscellaneous	235
5	Institutions	239
	Prior to *c*.1850	240
	c.1850–*c*.1900	254
6	Conclusion: Realized Potential and Stifled Ambition	265

Appendices
1 A Chronology of Nineteenth-Century British Music
    Education   271
2 A Chronology of Principal British Instrumental Treatises,
    1780–1900   277
3 Treatises in the Chronology   305

Bibliography   *313*
Index   *347*

Acknowledgements

There are many individuals who deserve enormous thanks for assisting in various ways with this study. Inevitably numerous musicians, librarians and scholars have given generously of their time, and their assistance and advice have been invaluable. I would like to offer my gratitude in particular to Edward Higginbottom, supervisor of both my masters and my doctoral theses, Simon McVeigh, Robin Stowell, Clive Brown, Harry Johnstone, Bennett Zon, Michael Gatward, Christina Bashford and John Warrack for their comments (including a few valuable leads) and the general interest they have shown in my work. In Oxford Peter Ward Jones of the Bodleian Library, John Wagstaff of the Music Faculty Library and Hélène La Rue of the Bate Collection have been particularly helpful. Elsewhere the staff of the Royal Academy and Royal College of Music libraries, Kneller Hall, Uppingham School (particularly James Pesheck) helped to smooth the research process. Both the Woodward-Pike Trust and Sudborough Foundation deserve special mention for providing the financial assistance that enabled me to embark on my research. I must also express my sincere thanks to the extremely patient and supportive Rachel Lynch and her highly efficient and knowledgeable team at Ashgate.

I have been very fortunate in having wonderful friends who have had a very positive influence on my state of mind over the last few years. Fellow members of 'Divertimento', Charlotte Storrs, Cal Verney and Nick Parker, have been an invaluable source of support and good humour. Sincere thanks also to Malcolm Tyler and fellow staff at the Henley College.

Finally a very special and heart-felt thank you to my parents, Jill and Dave, for all they have done and the sacrifices they have made for me over the years (far beyond the call of duty), and to my wife Alison, a wonderful companion, musician and teacher. There have been times when this book has had to vie with many other demands and the patience and understanding of those around me has made it possible to see the project through.

Caversham, Reading
July 2003

Preface

It is a truth widely acknowledged that the achievements of home-grown nineteenth-century British instrumentalists gave little cause for national pride. It is my intention in this study to examine this issue in some depth and the inextricable links between trends in society and education and levels of achievement.

In recent years there has been a significant rise in interest in nineteenth-century British music history, helped in no small way by dedicated conferences and publications, including Ashgate's series of which this study forms part. In the wake of the pioneering work of Temperley and others, writers in this area no longer feel the need to justify their interest in it. England, or Britain for that matter, was no more the 'land without music' then than it is the 'land without gastronomy' today. Virtually everyone came into contact with music in one form or other. Its existence and prevalence are therefore not in question but what is of great significance are issues surrounding its role, accessibility and suitability, levels of aspiration and proficiency, concepts of taste and the origin of creative impetus. In music then as in food 'fads' today, what we find is to a great extent a pioneering assimilation of foreign ideas rather than the instigation of trends based on original thought.

This is indeed a fertile area for enquiry, particularly if professional practice and the private, 'elite' cultivation of 'art' music are viewed as just two parts of an extremely intricate patchwork of cultural activity. Any examination of nineteenth-century Britain must seek to place cultural developments within the context of unique social and economic trends. Some of the most valuable studies of the period covering the areas of music, music education and instrumental performance have kept one eye on these momentous developments. It is my intention to continue in the vein of the likes of Ehrlich, Rainbow, Leppert, Rohr, Russell, Gillett, Komlós and Herbert and use the perspective offered by a century's distance to view musical practices and the training behind them in the context of significant social and broader cultural change. Cyril Ehrlich in particular has, as an economic and social historian, brought much-needed factual information to bear on what has for the most part been anecdotal evidence and conjecture, complemented by a deep love and knowledge of music.

The historical study of instrumental (non-vocal) pedagogy is a relatively new area of research. Aspects have been touched upon by many, but this is the first dedicated study with respect to Britain. As we shall see, its neglect within the literature in many ways reflects its fortunes during the period relative to other musical and educational concerns. While professional performers and visiting or resident foreigners all have a vital role to play in the overall picture, the most significant elements are in fact the 'popular' amateur movements which occupied the middle and lower classes for much of the century. The expansion and increasing cohesion of these social groups brought a growing demand and increased opportunity for a variety of 'improving' instruction and literature. The 'elite' and 'popular' areas of musical activity have often been examined separately by different writers, but it is important to consider both here in the context of formal and informal education, as the aims and objectives, and consequently results achieved, vary a great deal between them. Some of the principal beneficiaries of social and educational reform were musicians among the lower classes. It is also important to recognize that we are often dealing with the cumulative effect of incremental change rather than large-scale, national initiatives.

My approach to the subject is predominantly historical but aspects of education theory are touched upon where relevant. It is no accident that the title to this study focuses on the 'teaching' rather than learning of musical instruments. There are dangers in adopting a 'supply-led' approach and there have been notable attempts to lead taste among different sections of society, but in the consumer age which concerns us it can be a reliable indicator of demand and learning methods. Also much of the evidence we have is related to provision rather than consumption.

One of the problems with this area is that there is little documentary evidence for the day-to-day conventions of private instruction and much group instruction, often with different aims, was delivered orally. Alongside various documentary, statistical, organological and musical evidence we are therefore dealing primarily with extant, published teaching material. My interest in this type of source was inspired by Stowell's work on the violin, my own instrument, which through postgraduate research I extended into the study of performance on the violin in England during the eighteenth and nineteenth centuries. The sheer number and variety of sources unsupported by an indigenous school of violin playing merited further investigation.

Most of the evidence for this study is taken from treatises and tutors rather than collections of musical studies and exercises without text,[1]

---

[1] The difficulty in differentiating between different types of teaching material is highlighted by Heron-Allen (1890–94, 295–7). For my purposes I have concentrated on works which place at least some emphasis on textual explanation.

and these can be divided into various groups depending on their origins and language. There are those written by foreign authors that existed at the time only in the original foreign language (French, German or Italian), some of which were published in Britain in a foreign tongue; others originally in a foreign language made available in an English translation; methods written originally in English by foreign authors; and finally those by native writers in English. The emphasis here is naturally on the sources available in English in Britain during the period and some of the most important are by foreign authors. The majority of the sources discussed in this study are housed in major UK libraries. Important collections of teaching material include those in the Royal Academy of Music and in the Bate Collection of Musical Instruments (Faculty of Music, University of Oxford), which offers many unique opportunities for examining instruments alongside relevant teaching material.

To judge the significance of individual works and their authors, native and foreign, one must consider various factors. The number of editions or versions of a single treatise are a fair indication of the popularity and influence of it and its author. With regard to British sources this is particularly relevant to translations of foreign texts. There are also a significant number of native examples in which the same or very close to the same material is reproduced under a different title, and numerous cases where the contents of a particular source are recycled and either quoted verbatim or paraphrased in later works. How different editions and versions evolve and interrelate is therefore a particularly important consideration when dealing with native sources. When comparing treatises it is important to appreciate their nature and purpose as well as technical content. In cases where this is not made clear by the author, the balance and combination of the elements (text, musical examples, possibly charts, tables, diagrams, dictionary and collection of pieces), can suggest any bias towards a specific type or level of student and the role (if any) that a teacher might play in the use of the material.

Despite the value of this material and the insights it can offer, there are many difficulties inherent in its use and a 'text-centred' approach, which the adoption of a wider contextual awareness as well as a sharper focus (such as a specific instrument and location) can help to alleviate.[2] Self-contained instructional works tell the truth of 'the kind of beauties that lie concealed under the plain notes of the scores',[3] but not necessarily the whole truth. The information presented is naturally only

---

[2] See Taruskin (1995).
[3] Boyden (1950), 37–8.

one (possibly idiosyncratic) approach and opinion at a certain point in time, which can be anachronistic as soon as the work is published.[4] As the differences between the writings of Quantz and C. P. E. Bach illustrate, there is nothing to be gained from the dogmatic application of the information in a single source as a general principle, even if it is possible to establish the time and place of origin. Other contemporary literature and repertoire, as well as the author's prominence as a teacher and/or performer and the contemporary reception of a work, including any advertisements and reviews and evidence of it being used, need to be taken into consideration. Also what was not readily available to the native instrumentalist is often of particular interest. The absence of a source, translation or specific technical direction in one place is often as significant as its presence elsewhere. Some nationalities more than others were inclined to try to put down rules for performance (even if these prescribed performer spontaneity).

It must also be borne in mind that the ephemeral nature of much of the material we are dealing with has meant that a significant proportion of it is no longer extant. Most eighteenth-century tutors for the amateur, as sources of popular melodies, were used on social occasions as well as for instruction until they wore out or the melodies were no longer popular and were then discarded. Their life expectancy, like other popular tutors from the period, was therefore short. In addition, they were usually small, thin, printed cheaply and sold unbound in soft covers for a relatively low price.[5] The survival rate is however much higher for the greater number of more substantial specimens that emerged during the nineteenth century. These were generally a more serious investment, larger in size and thickness and often hardbound. Their greater durability is also partly attributable to their content, which, rather than just fashionable tunes, often consisted of more detailed and comprehensive instructions and study material that was to be returned to repeatedly by the teacher and student.

The study of pedagogical sources has traditionally centred on performance style and technique. These insights are important, but native treatises are, as they evolve, particularly valuable (and perhaps more reliable) for the wider commentary they offer on instrumental

---

[4] The difficulty in determining the contemporary relevance of material is most evident when established and successful texts are constantly recycled, as in the case of the numerous English examples for the violin based on *Nolens volens* (1695) and Geminiani (1751). It is important to consider the motivation of the writer or publisher in including such material, which may have as much to do with convenience as with a desire to reflect the practices of the time.

[5] See Boyden (1960), 42–3, who notes that the greater survival rate of Prelleur (1731) may be due to it having been bound in book format.

teaching in this country. The surviving material of this kind is in fact the most abundant source of information we have on contemporary teaching practices, at least those amateurs and professionals making use of literary methods.[6] Also the status of musical training and the trends that dictate its provision reveal a great deal about the value that society placed on such skills. The value of the writings of Kassler is not limited to the listing of sources, as numerous insights can be gained through the contemporary critical reception of pedagogical works, an increasingly prominent and important consideration during the period.

The violin is a particularly apposite guide to society's influence on cultural trends and can be compared usefully with other instrumental groups. Since the seventeenth century, it has provoked a great number of passionate observations, both positive and negative, from contemporary commentators, and its fortunes have fluctuated wildly. The material concerning the violin therefore often gives voice to the underlying ambivalence (and resulting conservatism) evident in the attitudes towards music among individuals and British society in general during the period, and exacerbated by the in many ways 'transitional' nature of the time, and the growing awareness of the beneficial qualities of music. Increasing consumerism certainly heightened the tensions between inherent, elite conservatism and the constant arrival of the new. Innovation with a retrospective, 'respectable' slant was preferable and the potential for any broader social and moral benefits was a distinct advantage.

This and more recent research into string playing form the core of this book and have inspired the broader perspective that it represents. The central part is concerned with a detailed examination of violin pedagogy, method and content, from the period and the violin 'case-study' informs many other sections. This approach allows a high level of detail to be applied in support of arguments within a topic, the scope of which precludes comprehensive coverage of all aspects and instruments. One

---

[6] Literacy is an additional factor not to be overlooked when discussing the influence and accessibility of written sources such as these. In 1841 male literacy in England was only around 67 per cent and female 51 per cent, although both were to rise quite sharply in the remaining years of the century following direct state intervention in education. These figures are taken from Cannon (1997), 582. Royle's excellent discussion of literacy (1997: 349–55) includes similar figures for 1839, based on G. R. Porter, *Progress of the nation* (1851), 700. See also J. Barry, 'Literacy and literature in popular culture: reading and writing in historical perspective', in Harris (1995), 69–94. As with many other factors linked to opportunity, levels of literacy were naturally affected by class, wealth and location. Significantly many of the high achievers among native instrumentalists stood outside a literary tradition and, with practical concerns in mind, focused predominantly on training through experience.

only has to peruse a few volumes of the *Musical Times* to appreciate the expansion and increasing diversity in all aspects of the music market during the nineteenth century.

One of my principal aims here is to demonstrate the growth of a more serious and widespread interest in the cultivation of music in nineteenth-century Britain. The 'widespread' aspect is easily established, given the rise and proliferation of popular music education, public concerts, new repertoire, instrument sales and associated literature. In terms of the 'seriousness' of this interest we need to look at the nature of the materials more closely, beyond just their popularity, and examine markets and consumers and providers more closely.

This study and the series it forms part of are concerned with nineteenth-century Britain. There is, however, an inevitable emphasis on England, home to the bulk of the material and activity, and on London and the provinces in particular. The cultivation of music became increasingly dispersed as the period progressed, with new centres of activity developing in keeping with social and economic trends, and reference is made to Scotland, Ireland and Wales where relevant. Also the social and cultural context provided by the eighteenth century is a vital consideration in a study of this kind as many of the nineteenth-century trends and much of the material originated much earlier.

Of the three parts to the commentary the first deals with general developments and issues, the second is concerned specifically with the violin family, and the third turns to other instruments and institutional training. The Appendices offer chronologies of music education and treatises. The 'Chronology of Principal British Instrumental Treatises 1780–1900' (Appendix 2), including over 700 examples, sets out to be a representative rather than comprehensive listing. (It is referred to as 'the Chronology' in the text.) The intention is to give the reader an overview of the trends in the production of didactic material, its nature and quantity, as an indicator of extraordinary levels of largely amateur demand. These are published (rather than manuscript) sources, for the most part extant and consulted by the present writer, and are independent treatises rather than articles within periodicals, for example.[7] They qualify as 'principal' treatises as a result of their fulfilling one or more of the following criteria: by a significant author; reissued in a number of editions; translation or assimilation of foreign text(s); influential, unusual or innovative; listed in contemporary and/or recent secondary literature. The period covered extends back to 1780 in order to include significant 'transitional' examples (in terms

---

[7] Other types of study material and associated repertoire as well as texts on organology are listed in the Bibliography.

of expressive priorities, organological trends or pedagogical developments). Due to considerations of space this is a short-title listing referenced in the main text by '[author's surname] (Chron., [year])'.[8] For ease of reference this is complemented by an alphabetical listing by instrument. Primary sources which fall outside the time-span of the Chronology or have proved impossible to date, as well as predominantly 'theoretical', vocal and foreign-language works, appear in the Bibliography.[9] This instructional material (and repertoire) and separate secondary texts are referenced using '[author] ([year of publication])'.

It is inevitable in light of the previous work I have undertaken that there is perhaps an English, string and early nineteenth-century bias in the Chronology and Bibliography. Nevertheless every effort has been taken to include the 'principal' examples for each instrument. I apologize in advance for any glaring omissions and would welcome any additional leads.

The 'Chronology of Music Education' (Appendix 1) includes main events, publications and initiatives with a direct or indirect influence on the development of British music education, formal and informal, during the 1800s.

---

[8] While this listing is more comprehensive than anything previously attempted in its combination of length of period and range of instruments covered it has not been possible to include full publishers' details and prices, length, dimensions and locations (full details for violin sources are given in Golby (1999b), vol.2). Comprehensive coverage of all these elements in a single volume would be a welcome and valuable addition to the literature but this is a separate and substantial undertaking.

[9] The Chronology (Appendix 2) presents the foreign material under entries for English translations in order to place it in its proper historical context relevant to Britain. This is not to deny, however, that some individual sources may have been available and consulted in their original language before an English version was available. Edward Heron-Allen's personal collection of violin sources (RCM Library) certainly contains many original foreign examples.

Abbreviations

ABRSM	Associated Board of the Royal Schools of Music
AM	*Acta Musicologica*
CPM	L. Baillie, ed., *The Catalogue of Printed Music in the British Library to 1980*, 58 vols (London, 1981)
DNB	L. Stephen, ed., *Dictionary of National Biography*, 63 vols (London, 1888–1900)
EM	*Early Music*
Grove 1	G. Grove, ed., *A Dictionary of Music and Musicians*, 4 vols (London, 1878–90)
Grove 2	J. A. Fuller-Maitland, ed., *Grove's Dictionary of Music and Musicians*, 5 vols (London, 1904–10)
Grove 3/4	H. C. Colles, ed., *Grove's Dictionary of Music and Musicians*, 5 vols (London, 1927/40)
Grove 5	E. Blom, ed., *Grove's Dictionary of Music and Musicians*, 9 vols (London, 1954), supplementary volume (1961)
Grove 6	S. Sadie, ed., *The New Grove Dictionary of Music and Musicians*, 20 vols (London, 1980)
Grove 7	S. Sadie and J. Tyrrell, eds, *The New Grove Dictionary of Music and Musicians*, 2nd edn, 29 vols (London, 2001)
GSJ	*The Galpin Society Journal*
ISM	The Incorporated Society of Musicians
JAMS	*Journal of the American Musicological Society*
JRMA	*Journal of the Royal Musical Association*
M&L	*Music and Letters*

MQ	*The Musical Quarterly*
MR	*The Music Review*
MT	*The Musical Times*
MW	*The Musical World*
PPR	*Performance Practice Review*
PRMA	*Proceedings of the Royal Musical Association*
QMMR	*Quarterly Musical Magazine and Review*
RAM	The Royal Academy of Music, London
RCM	The Royal College of Music, London
RCO	The Royal College of Organists, London
RMA Research Chronicle	*Research Chronicle*, published by the Royal Musical Association
RMCM	The Royal Military School of Music, Kneller Hall

Pitch Registers, Keys and Editorial Method

Middle C is abbreviated as c^1. The violin is therefore normally tuned to g, d^1, a^1, e^2.

With reference to keys, upper-case denotes major and lower-case minor (i.e. A = A major and a = A minor).

Passages of text that appear in quotation are given as they appear in the original version and original spellings and punctuation are retained. Any annotations to quoted material appear in square brackets. Translations of foreign texts are my own unless otherwise stated.

PART ONE

INTRODUCTION

Music in Britain: A Social and Cultural Context

The purpose of this chapter is to outline some of the main issues that permeate the later discussions of music education and instrumental pedagogy. It is concerned principally with contemporary attitudes towards music and the consequences of these on patterns of provision and consumption. The link between social and cultural trends and the demography of demand is self-evident but nonetheless important to stress.

The Consumer Society

As Britain rose to prominence from the early eighteenth century as the centre of world commerce, characterized by its unrivalled economic and industrial growth, it fostered a society with an exceptionally mercantile character. A by-product of and to a large extent the motivation behind consumerism was of course inequality. The resulting concern for status, conspicuous wealth and social emulation on the part of the individual and among the upper and expanding middle classes as a whole preserved and further enforced the all-important class distinctions swept away elsewhere by the revolutionary climate. Rather than democratic power to the masses the greater opportunity and emancipation produced by the nation's unrivalled wealth (particularly in the area of education) were determined and in many cases limited by the agenda of the privileged. Those in positions of power, financial and political, were given the means to protect their own interests and maintain a fiercely hierarchical structure to British society.

Music, like most things, was therefore a commodity, to be bought and sold. As the focus moved away from the court and a professional infrastructure was slow to materialize, the fortunes of those who depended on music for their livelihood rested on the characteristically fickle tastes of a fashionable society eager to exert its status. Although professional musical activity remained centred on the London season for much of the period, the growing number of large towns and accelerating industrialization in general provided numerous other centres for the cultivation of metropolitan pleasures aided by improving transport and communications networks. Conspicuous consumption of culture and material goods took place within the home and in public, epitomized by the importance and development of keyboard instruments and the early appearance of the public concert and music society. The obvious result of the new market possibilities in music was new opportunities for performers, teachers, instrument makers and publishers. There were, however, significant negative effects to this level of commercialism in the cultural sphere.

Naturally consumerism placed the concert-goer and amateur performer, composer or critic in a position of great power and their voracious appetite for the well-trained and 'exotic' foreign musician exacerbated the position of the already lowly and generally overshadowed native professional. Foreign professionals, such as Cramer and Salomon, often had control as impresarios and soloists leaving native performers with at best a supporting role. In an environment where for many the importance of music lay in what it could do for the social status of the consumer rather than any intrinsic value it might have, it was far preferable to be seen to appreciate it from a safe distance in opulent surroundings. Why dedicate a great deal of time that could be better spent to its practice and risk public humiliation when others could be paid to provide the service? Such opinions among high-born gentlemen were promoted for a significant period through the writings of Chesterfield and others (see Chapter 1), and many middle-class men were keen to emulate their conventional wisdom.

It was not just that musicians were hired to perform for their social betters (hardly a new concept), but that a huge gap opened up between the status and musical standards of amateurs and professionals, with the native musician the lowest in status and below foreign professionals in terms of standard.[1] We find, after a relative honeymoon period in terms of the practice of instrumental music among affluent amateurs and the rise of public or semi-public concerts during the late seventeenth and early eighteenth centuries (reflected in the numerous pioneering

---

[1] An attempt to settle on definitions in this area raises certain significant difficulties and insights. Professionals, career musicians, sought (if often without success) to earn their living primarily from music, usually on a full-time basis, whereas the amateur undertook their activities without expectation of or desire for remuneration, although some may have been received (such as prize money, for example). The semi-professional, an increasingly important category in the nineteenth century, was engaged in some temporary or part-time employment, for which teaching was particularly suitable. However there are numerous grey areas, particularly between amateur and semi-professional, and it soon becomes evident that in addition to financial rewards we must also take intentions, aspirations and standards into account.

publications of Playford and others), a growing disparity between amateur and professional achievements.[2] It is evident from Burney,[3] pedagogical sources and the repertoire as a whole that as we approach the middle of the eighteenth century the professional (particularly solo) repertoire progressed far beyond the capabilities and, more importantly, aspirations of the amateur instrumentalist. As technical demands increased and the proficiency of the gentleman amateur remained largely static, the new solo repertoire became almost exclusively the preserve of professionals, and then mainly the pioneering foreign virtuosos.[4] Native musicians, struggling to earn the respect of their social betters, often found themselves performing the works of Corelli and Handel rather than Vivaldi and Haydn. In many cases it was not until the middle of the nineteenth century that new (but still conservative and retrospective) foreign instrumental styles and repertoire achieved sufficient approbation to stand alongside those of the eighteenth century and inspire higher amateur aspirations. The new music was therefore generally consumed by audiences rather than practised among amateur instrumentalists for a significant period.

Ambivalent attitudes towards music in certain quarters in Britain during the eighteenth and nineteenth centuries allowed social conventions and prejudice to temper evident enthusiasm and even passion for the art. Music as an 'intellectual' pursuit became far more respectable for the gentleman than the 'mechanical' skill of performance (see Chapter 1). Rather than the audience identifying with and respecting the skills of the paid performer and teacher, even aspiring to them, and thereby increasing the pool of talent and lending status and the incentive to innovate to the artist, it became all the more important for those with consumer power to maintain and even increase the distance between themselves and the provider. Besides promoting a desire to cling on to outdated compositional models and

---

[2] The English concert tradition, stretching back to Thomas Britton and his series (1678–1714), began with a mixture of amateurs and professionals performing on a small scale (see Fiske and Johnstone, eds (1990), 32–3). At this time rich amateurs, such as Lord Edgecombe, would even travel to Italy to study (see Edwards (1989), 330). In addition to financial support, this more supportive environment provided native musicians during the early eighteenth century with the confidence to be innovative and take risks, as demonstrated by the exploits of William Corbett ($c.1675$–1748) (see Edwards, 1989).

[3] See for example Burney (1776–89), vol.4, 642.

[4] New compositions of all types, not just solo, appear to have exceeded the capabilities of most male amateurs. See Edwards (1968–9) and Fiske and Johnstone, eds (1990), 332–3. The 'accompanimental' role of the violin in numerous compositions and arrangements from the late eighteenth and early nineteenth centuries can be seen to cater for these modest aspirations (see Chapter 2).

styles, this division created a 'them and us' mentality between consumer and practitioner, audience and performer. Native musicians' social status, regardless of their (generally lower-middle) class, was extremely low.[5]

The situation described above gave rise to the durable trend of musical ambition (particularly in the practical sphere) being inversely proportionate to social status (judged by gender as well as wealth and class), or, put simply, those with the greatest opportunity being the least willing to take advantage of it.[6] This is especially true around the period 1750 to 1850, when the exclusivity of British society and the resulting divisions between amateur and professional, male and female, and native and foreign were particularly evident and proudly retained. With musical aspirations naturally related to the prospects, social and financial, it offered, parents of high social birth, preoccupied with status and exclusivity, stifled any latent musical talent and ambition, and so perpetuated low amateur standards while attracting the best foreign musicians into their circle. Moreover they often placed what they perceived as their greater 'refinement' above the 'manual skill' of 'boorish tradesmen', thereby preserving division and exclusivity through technical mediocrity.[7] Although always imperative and desirable for professionals to mix with amateurs and music-lovers in lessons and music societies, for example, there was little 'crossover' between the two groups. The popularity and longevity of the concerto grosso among music societies, with the hired help forming the concertino group and the amateurs the ripieno, exemplifies the division. Meanwhile future performers and teachers continued to be educated haphazardly and inadequately. Professional training, particularly for men, continued to rely on traditional methods and family networks, resulting in little capacity for expansion and collective influence. The amateur, as both director and consumer, remained in control even at the RAM and later institutions, supposedly the sharp end of professional music education in Britain.[8] Some musical skill was acquired by women who wished to

---

[5] Adam Smith's comments of 1776 further illustrate this point (quoted in Ehrlich (1985), 76, and Towse (1993), 1–2). Amateurism retains its high status in light of the 'discredit' of being employed in such an activity. Financial reward is only necessary 'recompense' for the stigma attached.

[6] See also Ehrlich (1985), 93 and 95 regarding the lack of aptitude and taste among the higher echelons of British society, the 'perceived distinction between social eminence and professional competence', and the arrogance that gave rise to a certain proud ignorance of music. Perhaps common contemporary British attitudes to the learning of foreign languages, again originating in a perceived lack of incentive, are not so different.

[7] See Gillett (2000b), 337ff.

[8] See Ehrlich (1985), 228–9.

become 'domestic teachers' or governesses for the wealthy, but their efforts were seldom 'truly beneficial'.[9]

The longevity of these trends and the emphasis on the consumer rather than the influential protagonist did not bode well for nineteenth-century British music. The vicious circle of low standards and neglect rather than the necessary achievement and expectation was a recipe for disaster. Fortunately other areas of activity offered a brighter future, as the nature of the consumer continued to relate to the level and extent of amateur participation. We therefore find significant improvements in the status of music and consequently in the standards achieved with the rapidly increasing breadth and depth of activity. Most notable and of great importance to the sphere of instrumental practice are those 'boom' areas of the 'popular'[10] music movement, represented chiefly by middle-class women and lower-class men, who, in their different ways, offered a means of narrowing the amateur/professional divide. It is of course significant that in both cases the release of musical potential on such a scale came partly in response to the adversity and constraints experienced at the hands of the male ruling classes. The arrogance and complacency common in high society that stifled the potential of native professional music therefore gave rise to huge demand and creative energy (within certain confines) among these 'oppressed' groups. There is an important tension here that will be frequently encountered in this study, between the freedom sought by those in search of practical music-making and the control exerted by those eager to direct this demand in ways beneficial to them. Music therefore came to be perceived as 'useful' on both a personal and social level.

Following chapters will discuss these and related issues in greater depth but it is important to identify the essential points concerning the expansion of the market for instrumental music. If we continue with the argument that the high social status of the consumer of culture in Britain bred division between audience and performer and limited aspirations as a result, it is possible to highlight the reversal of this trend as the market for practical music-making among amateurs diversified. This was the continuation of earlier trends but on a much larger scale, particularly after around 1850. The huge increase in the consumption of music and practical instruction among the middle classes, particularly among girls

---

[9] See Kassler (1979), 877 and 1165.
[10] Here and throughout the study 'popular' refers to that which is consumed and practised by large numbers of people. This definition, concentrating on the numbers involved rather than any specific style or genre, is roughly in keeping with the use of the term by Russell (1997: 2) and Scott (2002: 545) and acknowledges the consistency of repertoire between different types of group and performance contexts.

and young women, marked an important step forward for the quantity of instrumental practice among amateurs. The situation also improved with some of the new secondary-school education offered to boys during the second half of the nineteenth century (see Chapter 5). As we shall see, pioneering pedagogues and fellow promoters of music's cause in various fields attempted to direct this enthusiasm in directions beneficial to the art and the profession as a whole and nurture more enlightened attitudes in both appreciation and participation.

The female market continued to expand rapidly and many women, encouraged by the burgeoning specialist institutions and some schools, took the opportunity to enter the profession, predominantly, as Victorian society demanded, as teachers rather than performers. Significantly, their domestic and school pupils were generally from their own or a similar social class. Music therefore became a rare respectable source of income, most often on a temporary, premarital basis. Although high standards could be and were achieved and amateur performance was becoming ubiquitous on a wider range of instruments, the limits male society put on the range of activities open to most women continued to restrict their musical achievements and therefore aspirations. The focus for them when turning from consumer into provider was necessarily on music as a source of financial reward, either directly or as a valuable commodity in the marriage market, and as an (albeit temporary) outlet for self-expression and emancipation. Little attention was paid to music's inherent value and, it being 'unseemly' to become truly proficient, low standards were perpetuated through poor training, diploma 'fever' and a market reaching saturation point. We therefore find in such 'genteel' areas a predilection for 'chaperoned mediocrity'.[11] This is a wonderful phrase, encapsulating the common and enduring contemporary issues of conservatism, safety, and adherence to convention that were of great importance to those for whom appearance and respectability were so vital. Public performance was still to be consumed rather than participated in for most women. Teaching was (and is) one of the more secure and regular sources of income for a musician and the rapid spread of cheap and easily accessible lessons offered by large numbers of women seriously threatened the livelihood of the career musician. The army of women teachers finally forced the profession into action in various (generally unsuccessful) attempts to restrict this 'weed' of semi-professionalism and so protect its own interests.[12] In this area during the later nineteenth century, when demand was unprecedented and attitudes were much

---

[11] Ehrlich (1985), 115.
[12] Ibid., 131. See also Gillett (2000b).

more positive, the disappearance of the amateur/professional divide was perhaps not in the interests of the profession. Greater opportunity was effectively cancelled out by competition.

This type of semi-professionalism, based on temporary earning potential and part of middle-class consumerism, is distinct from that practised by our second group of musicians. The depth as well as breadth of opportunity increased and the lower-class popular movements came to be the great musical success stories of the age. Although partly the products of middle-class fears and concerns for social order, they are proof of what the British were capable of given the opportunity to fulfil their musical potential. Free from the social 'baggage' of their social superiors, men of the skilled working classes were able to take charge and establish, through the medium of the brass band in particular, a hugely effective infrastructure that placed the emphasis firmly on technical excellence and the music itself. The scope for escaping and transcending the problems of urbanization, and also (particularly later in the century) for receiving some financial reward, were also factors, but these were overshadowed by musical concerns and the appetite for group public performance rather than individual private teaching.[13] Essentially teaching, as in the professional sphere and along similar lines, was a means to an end rather than an end in itself. Audiences and performers from the same communities displayed remarkable levels of enthusiasm, application and dedication.[14] Along with the music itself those engaged in such activity were appreciated and respected by their peers. For the first time participation in practical music-making offered a significantly large group of people outside the profession the prospect of improving rather than risking their social standing. The market had diversified and opportunity descended to the point where the musician could be perceived as a role to aspire to rather than deride, creating a far healthier musical environment that went some way towards reversing the vicious circle of low expectation and neglect. The net result was standards often comparable to (and even exceeding) those of professional musicians. In this sense the amateur/professional divide was blurred through sustained effort to the point of irrelevance,

---

[13] See Mackerness (1964), 130 and Russell (1997), 279 and 284–5.

[14] Russell's exemplary study (1997) effectively conveys the love of music and the extent of self-sacrifice entailed among the lower orders. These elements were of course by no means exclusive to them, but the evidence is consistent with what one might expect in that dedication and application akin to that of professionals were far more common among those amateurs otherwise regularly employed who filled their leisure hours with music. This contrasts with those for whom music was merely another recreational pursuit, rather than a means to significant personal achievement, and 'drudgery' was to be avoided (see Gillett (2000b), 330).

rather than, as in the case of the large number of women teachers, temporarily and quite easily crossed. By focusing on new areas of and audiences for performance they also avoided, unlike women teachers, infringing on existing professional interests. In fact they provided employment for professional band trainers as well as instrument makers and publishers.

Placing the emphasis on conspicuous musical excellence, displayed through public performance and competition, rather than income or solace, led to far more success stories over a longer period. These priorities, based on genuine enthusiasm and need rather than whim and fashion, proved much more sustainable and secure. The Industrial Revolution, source of the means as well as the incentive for this success, therefore had a vital part to play in the musical 'renaissance' commonly observed during this period. The rise and variegation of popular music were crucial factors in the removal of the straitjacket of social convention that continued to govern practical music-making in other areas.

Popular music-making during the period demonstrates the latent potential in British society for active participation in practical music rather than passive appreciation and also shows that when the status of consumers and providers converge the cultural environment they inhabit becomes far more supportive and is able to feed off itself. Activity 'grew out' of certain strata of society rather than being imported. Positive role models emerged and incentive replaced stigma, enabling both sides, supply and demand, to thrive within the same community. The broadening of opportunity meant that there was much more to be gained than lost, socially and financially, through the cultivation of music among significant numbers of those outside the traditional professional networks. The result was an explosion of activity, with potential standards limited only (if significantly) by the desire to see and the willingness to appreciate success from within the peer group.

Some parts of British society were destined to remain reluctant to embrace music (in particular instrumental performance) as a worthwhile pastime let alone occupation for themselves. Their view of the value of music and therefore their demands for musicians remained 'utilitarian and culturally impoverished'.[15] However, the role that music could play in encouraging a civilized and respectable use of recreation time among the lower orders was increasingly recognized as the nineteenth century progressed. It is evident that the perception of music's 'usefulness' and 'moral' value among the intelligentsia, including social reformers and

---

[15] Ehrlich (1985), 112.

industrial philanthropists, changed with a growing awareness of its potential social benefits, particularly as far as the urbanized lower classes were concerned. The potential benefits of this greater market diversity for music itself (lagging some way behind on the list of priorities) were the concern mainly of music specialists. Writers, critics and pedagogues were keen to encourage higher appreciation and standards, especially among literate middle-class amateurs, with the fortunes of native professionals partly in mind. The lower classes were not in need of this encouragement, although a largely shared repertoire despite different media reflects the continued presence of middle-class ideals as well as the ability of quality music to transcend social boundaries.

As our period comes to a close we can see new trends in amateur consumerism that had an important influence on the status of music and musicians within British society. Although some things progressed very little (especially for the professional), improvements on the eighteenth-century situation came, in varying degrees, in terms of both quantity and quality. In addition to greater and more enlightened consumption among existing groups there was the introduction of new lower-status areas of activity in which supply and demand were based on common interests and priorities to a far greater extent.[16] We should of course also not overlook the importance of cheaper tools and services in offering greater accessibility to musical activity and so decreasing the role played by a large disposable income and high social status.

As a postscript to this section assessing the role of consumerism and the harmful divisions it created in British culture, it is interesting to view the different situations around the British Isles and beyond. London, a major cultural centre with all the trappings of conspicuous wealth among the upper and aspiring middle classes, naturally contrasts sharply

---

[16] It is interesting to look at the area of vocal music in this context. For various reasons discussed in greater detail below, the vocal movement enjoyed wider-ranging success as far as 'semi-professionalism' is concerned than the instrumental sphere. Long-standing amateur traditions and the spread of sight-singing among both adults and children provided training, and numerous choral societies provided opportunities for amateurs to achieve high standards in public performance (see Caldwell (1999), 236). Crucially the focus was on musical standards rather than financial incentives and, like other forms of 'popular' music, success depended on ideals of fellowship and discipline. Moreover, in contrast to most instrumental practice, the activity involved the cooperation of a relatively large cross-section of society (middle and lower classes, men and women) as well as a broad geographical spread. Brass bands retained their male working-class membership and the middle classes sought to preserve the 'genteel' areas for themselves for much of the nineteenth century. It is interesting to observe the popularity of the violin among middle-class women when the piano became within the reach of the lower classes (see Chapter 3).

with the cultural environment of the industrial midlands and north of England. These extreme examples illustrate the argument that this disparity is evident in the different relationships between amateur and professional musicians, with levels of wealth and consumerism in communities inversely proportionate to amateur ambitions. It is ironic if understandable that the very 'professionalism' of London's musical culture should promote such negative attitudes to the status and standards of native music-making. Its unchallenged supremacy as a commercial and cultural centre in many ways made it atypical, at least as far as native trends are concerned. There was little need or desire for serious amateur participation in London,[17] but as we move further from the capital and reliance on the consumption of professional music diminishes we find an increasingly vibrant amateur tradition and a far greater number of success stories among native instrumentalists.

This is an area for further research but recent studies of specific areas of Britain have revealed a happier alliance and blurred distinction between amateur and professional musicians, who were willing and able to respond to a less vociferous (if perhaps more sincere) demand for music within the smaller and more closely knit community.[18] Amateur performance, rather than passive appreciation or instruction as an end in itself, achieves a higher level of importance. The affluent middle classes of the eighteenth century take an active role in secular musical life, using cathedral musicians and professionals for occasional 'stiffening'. A music society such as that founded in Edinburgh was based on amateur strength and talent with only some additional support.[19] Naturally the level of professional input relates to the extent to which the activity is a commercial enterprise. Bath and Dublin, for

---

[17] Russell (1997, p.57) refers to London's 'stunted' amateur music tradition.

[18] I draw the reader's attention in particular to a number of articles in *EM* (November 2000), covering aspects of music in Halifax, Colchester and Scotland (by Cowgill, Holman and Nelson respectively), as well as the contributions of Ehrlich (1985), Russell (1997), McCalman, ed. (1999) and Bashford and Langley, eds (2000).

[19] Scotland, possibly because of its relative isolation, enjoyed an independently vibrant intellectual culture and a progressive approach to the provision of basic education. Greater numbers of prominent instrumentalists and teachers travelled to Edinburgh as a result of improvements to the transport system and there was a proposal to establish a music school in 1816 (see G. F. Graham in Kassler (1979), 402–3). However, an earlier appetite for serious study among amateurs, in the absence of easily accessible high-quality practical instruction, is perhaps suggested by the number and quality of pedagogical publications published there during the eighteenth and early nineteenth centuries, including examples by Bremner and Pasquali. The Corri family were also important music publishers in Edinburgh as well as London. The same can perhaps be said of Bristol during the early nineteenth century, where the likes of Howell were issuing instrumental teaching material with the increasing number of more ambitious amateurs in mind.

example, played host to prominent performers prior to economic decline, whereas the general bias within the provinces was distinctly amateur (and therefore often conservative in terms of repertoire). The number of professional musicians naturally increased in towns, such as Leeds and Birmingham and later Liverpool and Manchester,[20] with a growing population and market for concerts, lessons and accompanying paraphernalia. Amateurs and semi-professionals did however continue to play an important role in performances in these places well into the nineteenth century, although the balance shifted as commercialism and the 'acquisition of metropolitan pleasures' came increasingly to the fore.[21] It is also worth noting that native professionals found increasing opportunities outside the capital, where foreign dominance was deeply entrenched, and that musicians with an amateur background, in particular brass players, became an important element in provincial orchestras, such as that founded in Manchester by Charles Hallé.[22] Recent studies have also revealed the potential and appetite for music of amateurs in other areas, including Belfast, Dublin and Wales, where the emphasis was less on consumption than participation and less on foreign visitors than home-grown talent.[23] Conservatoire-trained, 'semi-professional' women also enjoyed greater opportunities as performers and promoters of music in these less commercial areas and still more outside major cities.[24]

It is also interesting to extend this discussion of the amateur/professional divide beyond British shores. Those cultural centres where conspicuous consumerism was not such an overriding characteristic and concern show evidence of the importance of serious amateur involvement, through patronage, appreciation and participation, in achieving high professional standards.[25] Middle-class consumption of largely professional instrumental concerts was much slower to take off in Paris and Vienna than in London, allowing vibrant amateur performing traditions, such as high-status amateur orchestras,

---

[20] See Ehrlich (1985), 22–3 and 62–4.
[21] Ehrlich and McVeigh in McCalman, ed. (1999), 248. Although the prevalence and standard of amateur singers ensured the financial viability of the oratorio as a genre, the amateur chorus/professional orchestra dichotomy is worth highlighting.
[22] See Russell (1997), 280.
[23] Including Johnston (1996); Johnston (2000), 228; Pine and Acton (1998), especially 12–32; and Herbert (2000b).
[24] See Gillett (2000b), 327–8.
[25] Ringer, ed. (1990) provides useful surveys of musical trends in various cultural centres during the early nineteenth century. There is also Rainbow (1990) on music education, Weber (1975) on social dynamics and the consumption of music and, of course, various useful entries in *Grove 7*.

to retain their significance for longer. Although London's public 'concert culture' and professionalism were later emulated at similar levels elsewhere, 'discriminating, or at least interested, continental audiences and managements'[26] were already firmly established. While Britain was laying the foundations for prolonged underachievement and lack of influence in mainstream musical developments, other cultural centres were investing in their future through both professional training and a much higher level, in terms of status and standard, of amateur participation. It is evident and of course logical that levels of bourgeois wealth and status were inversely proportionate to musical ambition on a national as well as personal level for a significant period. From the early eighteenth century comparisons were drawn between Italy and France as places for 'listening and learning' and England for 'earning'[27] and England's 'musical lethargy' was seen in contrast to 'music's native soils', namely Germany and Italy. Germany was able to boast widespread music education 'in the common reading and writing schools, even in small Villages', and in 'kinds of musical Charity-schools' at a relatively early stage.[28]

It is of course no coincidence that the most successful players and schools of performance and the flow of musical styles and figures imported into Britain accordingly match trends in music education and professional development on the continent.[29] We therefore find a succession of well-developed playing and pedagogical traditions, supported by sophisticated and skilled amateur participation, emanating from Italy, Austro-Germany and France.

Italy was naturally a centre of musical excellence during the seventeenth and eighteenth centuries, a position assisted and promoted by famous teachers and teaching institutions which influenced systems and plans elsewhere, including in Britain, during the eighteenth and nineteenth centuries. Professional training through academies and conservatoires encouraged by the state, in Naples, Venice and elsewhere, formed highly durable and influential models and a teacher/pupil lineage based mainly on oral rather than written pedagogy which sought to guide rather than restrict performer freedom.

German methods, practical and written, were often more

---

[26] Ehrlich (1985), 74.

[27] Comments by Johann Mattheson from 1713. See Careri (1993), 9.

[28] These are the observations of the German writer W. Steetz in his music treatise (1812). He reserves particular scorn for British male amateur flautists and violinists (see Kassler (1979), 979).

[29] Discussion of the most prominent and influential playing styles in British instrumental pedagogy follows in subsequent chapters.

prescriptive, but, as in Italy, the continued importance and proactive approach of the court, both supportive and demanding, in Berlin and Mannheim for example, created similar centres of musical excellence and an array of brilliant 'exports' and famous names.[30] In addition the amateur musicians of Berlin, through the Musikübende Gesellschaft (founded in 1749) for example, collaborated with professionals in their music-making in 'semi-public' settings as well as the royal orchestra.[31] The 'moral and social agency of music'[32] continued to flourish in Germany into the nineteenth century with the demise of the court's influence and the consequent spread of musical activity throughout society. The provision of education was fundamental to Germany's success, with universal elementary instruction complemented by conservatoires that nurtured talent.[33] Publications such as the *Allgemeine musikalische Zeitung* (issued in Leipzig from 1798) reveal a mature market at a relatively early stage for serious music journalism among professional, musically educated readers.

Musical activity in imperial Vienna was dictated by the elite (non-artisan) amateur. The 'near universality of musical training among the middle class'[34] and the large number of 'serious musical institutions, religious and secular'[35] allowed Viennese society to nurture local genius rather than establish a professional 'concert culture' and commercial marketplace for music. The founding of the Gesellschaft der Musikfreunde in 1814 brought together 'elite' amateurs of various types as well as an increasingly broad base of active musicians, which supported and sponsored music, including the conservatoire, and achieved a great deal in its own right.[36] The strength and durability of this musically literate and discerning elite involvement elevated music, particularly instrumental music, to a prestigious position. Its association with 'the aura of noble birth and cultivation' allowed future generations

---

[30] In the case of Berlin and in contrast to the situation in London during the eighteenth century, Frederick II exerted a great deal of control from on high with positive effects on the state of music education there. See J. C. Baird, 'Introduction', in Agricola, ed. and tr. Baird (1995), 2 and 5–6.

[31] See Ringer, ed. (1990), 109 and 116. The performance of amateurs in 'semi-public' contexts, perhaps similar to late seventeenth-century England, suggests the importance of serious participation over and above conspicuous, passive consumption.

[32] Mackerness (1964), 169, quoting George Hogarth.

[33] See Hughes and Stradling (2001), 29.

[34] Weber (1975), 96.

[35] D. Beales, 'Vienna', *Grove 7*, vol.26, 559.

[36] Its contribution to the first performance of Beethoven's Ninth Symphony in 1824 is a notable example. The professional bias of the Philharmonic Society, who had commissioned the work, could not prevent the 'disaster' of its British premiere under Smart's direction in 1825 (see Ringer, ed. (1990), 216).

of Viennese to 'link the cultivation of music with high social status and refinement'.[37] This cultural environment therefore set a very different example for the middle-class agenda than was commonplace in Britain and demonstrates how status and standards could complement each other at the opposite, high-achieving, end of the spectrum. Such an environment, conducive to high standards among the highest echelons of society, provided a figure like the acclaimed pianist Moscheles with 'pupils of the highest rank'.[38] Also, the bias towards a 'private, aristocratic taste' promoted a highly 'polished' style of performance[39] that was not challenged by 'popular' demands and outside influences to the same extent experienced in more commercial arenas. The cultivation of instrumental music among amateurs remained the norm in Vienna into the 1850s, around the same time that a large number of lower-status amateurs were beginning to blur the distinction between themselves and professionals in public performance in Britain.

Paris can perhaps be seen to sit somewhere in between this level of amateur participation and London's emphasis on the consumption of professional music, allowing much greater scope for the participation of the 'low status public'[40] at an earlier stage than Vienna but also offering significant state support and an infrastructure to realize potential among professional performers.[41] Without wishing to paint the Parisian scene as Utopian during this extremely unstable period in French history, it is significant that this balancing of amateur and professional musicians' interests during the early nineteenth century coincided with the rise of pioneering and hugely influential instrumentalists of the French school, many of whom came to Britain in search of fame and fortune. The Conservatoire, established in 1795, was undoubtedly hugely successful in the formation of schools of instrumental performance which were codified in authoritative texts. Britain was unable (or unwilling) to reconcile amateur and professional interests until much later in the nineteenth century (and then only in some specific areas), by which time the ship had effectively sailed. Fétis, who makes many pertinent comments on music education in particular in his writings, places

---

[37] L. Botstein, 'Vienna', *Grove 7*, vol.26, 560. See also J. Rink in Samson, ed. (2002), 55–86.

[38] Wylde (1882), 20–21.

[39] See Komlós (1995), 147.

[40] Weber (1975), 97. The influence of music teaching in Parisian *commune* schools and public singing classes on methods employed in Britain is discussed below. Also, the Bourbon Restoration 'led to a flourishing of amateur music-making' (Ringer, ed. (1990), 42).

[41] See Ehrlich (1985), 39 and 50, on the favourable circumstances of Parisian professionals and Mackerness (1964), 185, on French state subsidies for opera.

England 'at the bottom of the scale' in his London letters when comparing music in different European countries.[42]

High levels of amateur involvement and achievement in instrumental music-making are also evident further afield during this period, including in Moscow and St Petersburg[43] and various parts of the United States of America, such as Boston and Philadelphia, where there was often a shortage of highly trained musicians.[44] Vernacular traditions with a strong moral emphasis, nurtured by part-timers, received widespread approbation in the young, forward-thinking cultural environment of the USA, and music was seen to offer a great deal to both the individual and society.[45] It was therefore able to achieve a status generally far higher than that common in societies preoccupied more with social conventions and exclusivity. Although British influence loomed large, neglect was less pervasive and established and there were genuine attempts to promote music, through societies, teaching institutions and the widespread cooperation of amateurs and professionals.[46]

The status of the amateur relative to the professional musician, or audience to performer, is fundamental to the subject of instrumental teaching, as it affects levels of appreciation and participation, which in turn are important indicators of the value placed on music for its own sake. Communities in which there was less emphasis on commercial concerns and the consequent division between supply and demand (Vienna being a prime example) were therefore more nurturing of high standards among and a happier relationship between elite amateur and professional (or potential professional) musicians. The British social elite were relatively apathetic and complacent as far as music was concerned and a predilection for professional music did not equate with a similar respect for professional musicians. The general impression is that, outside Britain, music was something to participate in rather than just consume for a longer period. It was taught, appreciated and practised as a matter of course, and with the higher status associated with the subject came a more obvious respect for the musician's skills. The improved

---

[42] These were originally published in Paris in 1829. See Kassler (1979), 350–51.

[43] See Ringer, ed. (1990), 252–4.

[44] Ibid., 260–65. The level and extent of amateur demand for written instrumental instruction is illustrated by American editions of texts originally published in Britain, including examples by Geminiani from the eighteenth century and Langey from the late nineteenth and early twentieth. Many texts published in North America are listed in Brown (1886).

[45] Ringer, ed. (1990), 268.

[46] Ibid., 272. However if the violinist Brodsky's experiences are anything to go by there are signs that towards the end of the nineteenth century, in New York at least, 'art for art's sake' came second to commercial concerns (see Zaltsberg (2002), 526).

British institutions of the later nineteenth century still struggled to achieve their goals and compete with the perceived 'advantages' of foreign study.[47]

Burgeoning and eager lower-status communities, outside London, promoting indigenous, 'popular' traditions, managed during the mid- to late nineteenth century, prior to the slump in their economic fortunes, to counterbalance many of the harmful effects of earlier amateur music-making in Britain. An additional important boost to the standing of music and the musician within British society and a powerful incentive for amateurs and professionals to join forces with a common goal in mind came with the rise of nationalism. As Britain's economic and territorial dominance began to slide, culture and its potential to influence perceptions of the national identity came increasingly to the fore. For the first time there was a degree of urgency and consensus in society's attitude to arts education, albeit a whole century behind France. The assertion of 'Englishness' (if not 'Britishness') sought to lessen the German dominance of the music industry, musicology and profession at the time,[48] and educational institutions as well as publications such as Grove's *Dictionary*[49] played an important role in the control and dissemination of a national identity.[50] Music had a recognized political significance and, although a long time in coming, by the second decade of the twentieth century the acceptance of native musicians had become more widespread.[51]

The Musician's Lot

The status of a product within certain communities tends to equate with their corresponding view of the producer. With respect to eighteenth- and early nineteenth-century Britain the groundbreaking work of Rohr (1983), McVeigh (1993) and others has helped to paint a now familiar picture of low status, often poorly educated native musicians, even relatively eminent figures, contrasted with the fortunes of their 'exotic' foreign colleagues. These harmful, self-perpetuating stereotypes had obvious consequences for levels of proficiency. This section will

---

[47] See Gillett (2000a), 201.

[48] See Crump (1986), 165–7. There is evidence of German complacency and even the 'decline' of musical instruction in German schools at this time of progress in British music education. See Rainbow (1989a), 39–40.

[49] See Dibble (2001).

[50] See Dodd (1986), 3. The 'popular imperialism' of the music hall also played its part. See Russell (1997), 164.

[51] Galloway (1910), 7.

highlight a few issues relevant to the training of native instrumentalists. This is a fertile area and there is still much information to be gleaned from general contemporary literature as well as specialist musical texts of the time.

Having already established the importance of amateur demand in the cultural environment of Britain it is important to stress the nature and detrimental effects of this consumption on the part of the elite amateur and those wishing to emulate their social position. At an early stage the formation of ideals of 'good taste' by native connoisseurs from the foreign delicacies on offer was not only convenient but also assigned exclusivity and status to their chosen representatives with which native talent, even if in possession of distinctive and favourable qualities, could not compete.[52] The superior musical training and general education of foreign musicians as well as their perceived exoticism and refinement of manners afforded them great artistic and social prestige, enabling them to infiltrate the highest levels of polite society.[53] British 'xenophilia' in music,[54] extending back to the court of Charles II, peaking in the eighteenth century and still in evidence today, therefore had at least as much to do with the desire to flex consumer muscle and create a hierarchy of taste and culture as any high ideals. Such favouritism naturally provoked resentment among the musicians themselves and such an unhealthy dependency was vulnerable to political trends and the consequent ebb and flow of foreigners.[55] Also, as we shall see, the resulting 'melting pot' of imported styles, modern and anachronistic, caused problems when it came to the writing of didactic texts and the promotion of a coherent approach to instrumental performance in Britain.

It should not be forgotten, however, that this level of foreign superiority existed within a generally unsympathetic and testing environment for the artisan musician. Even the foreign visitors found it difficult to earn a living from music in this fickle consumer society.[56] Geminiani and Viotti became seriously involved in the art and wine

---

[52] The prominence of foreign instrumentalists in comparison to their native counterparts in eighteenth-century Britain is clearly evident in Burney's writings among others.

[53] See Temperley (1999), 11 and 14.

[54] A term increasingly in vogue since Temperley's 1999 article.

[55] Foreign players formed the 'bedrock of London's orchestral concerts' and their absence revealed severe weaknesses among native instrumentalists (see McVeigh (2000), 162). The mass exodus of refugee performers had a detrimental effect on the orchestra of the Philharmonic Society (Ringer, ed., (1990), 212).

[56] Even eminent foreign musicians' earning capacity was far below that of successful lawyers and doctors (see Ehrlich (1985), 49 and 130).

trades respectively. Although this was without great success in both cases, they obviously considered the risks worth taking.

Britain did of course export instruments, particularly pianos, reflecting its strong manufacturing base and flair for things scientific and mechanical; but foreign influence in terms of performance was predominantly a one-way street and native musicians were considered very much second best. This is demonstrated by consumer preference when it came to prestigious appointments. Then, as now, often the most lucrative engagements for a musician were the private teaching of wealthy amateurs and performances at private gatherings. Foreign musicians therefore enjoyed their favoured role in this type of employment. They found it far easier to exhibit the required business acumen while still being perceived as 'gentlemen'. As Mendelssohn observed, this was a vital combination in the commercial and social climate of the time.[57]

The result was that 'polite' society monopolized the efforts of the best instrumentalists, both as teachers and performers. The less affluent but more ambitious individual or specialist institutions were seldom able to secure their services. As well as individual appointments, foreign talent reigned supreme in more far-reaching cultural decisions. Limited state intervention in music education, primarily vocal training from the mid-nineteenth century onwards, continued to promote the flawed, French-inspired, Hullah-Wilhem system while overlooking superior indigenous methods.[58] Once again, a lack of consensus and standardization undermined the effectiveness and cause of British music education.

Despite tales of hardship and misery among musicians in general, humble native instrumentalists were at a distinct disadvantage for the whole of the eighteenth and much of the nineteenth century, particularly in consumer-led, 'elite' areas of activity. They were forced to curry favour in a society obsessed with status and class, in which music and those who cultivated it were not accepted as a matter of course (let alone respected) as inherently valuable. Flattery, personal deference and conservatism, particularly in a counter-revolutionary climate, were the order of the day when musicians were dealing with clients, be they audience or pupil, from the upper echelons. The dedication of compositions and treatises was an obvious means of soliciting further employment. The cultivation of music was not only lacking genuine support from those in influential positions, but, moreover, it was often actively talked down and stigmatized among 'gentlemen' who associated it with their view of low society. Musicians were servants who provided

---

[57] See McCalman, ed. (1999), 245.
[58] See Rainbow (1989a), 25–8 and Chapter 1 for further discussion.

amusement for the privileged classes and saved them from the horrors of self-degradation. Music was never to detract from more 'worthwhile' pursuits.

These damaging and hugely influential views were compounded during the late eighteenth and early nineteenth centuries when the role of musicians in the church diminished further in favour of the secular opportunities offered by the theatres and pleasure gardens,[59] particularly important outlets for British talent. The contempt and disdain for musicians continued as they struggled to discard notions of their 'social uselessness, narrow education, unrefined manners, and immorality'[60] and break the vicious circle of low expectation and low achievement. The situation was not going to improve spontaneously, although at least one writer of the time, while acknowledging the 'degenerate state of the art in England' and the 'present dearth of native musical talent', believes that 'to patronize a bad production of any kind, is to destroy one of the strongest motives to improvement'. The native musician must motivate himself to improve and therefore earn the right to patronage: support is therefore 'the *consequence*, not the *cause*'.[61] With no infrastructure or even will to assist with training and promote higher standards on a large scale (see Chapter 2), and with views such as this expressed in a dedicated music journal, it is evident what a struggle the ambitious young musician with modest means faced during the period.

It hardly needs saying that music was not an attractive profession for the social elite and children (particularly boys) of the upper echelons of society required (and probably still require in many cases) any musical exploits beyond superficial 'amusement' to be sanctioned by respectability-conscious parents. The potential detrimental effects of serious application, to mind, body and soul, were expressed in fairly vivid terms over a long period,[62] and strong family opposition often stifled musical ambition, particularly when there was scope to choose a different, perhaps less arduous, career path. Throughout the nineteenth century amateurs of the higher social orders maintained their desire to remain separate to 'the common herd of paid musicians'.[63] Even musical families were not optimistic about the prospects of a musical career in a cut-throat marketplace and such a heritage was not widely envied.[64]

---

[59] See Rohr (1983), 31.
[60] Ibid., 33.
[61] J. Gatie, 'English music', MW, 2 (1836), 177–8.
[62] See Ehrlich (1985), 8–9 and 44. A comment on Mozart's pupil Thomas Attwood distinguished between his grasp of 'musical science' and his possession of 'the well cultivated understanding of a *gentleman*' (ibid., 41).
[63] Gillett (2000b), 338.
[64] Ehrlich (1985), 174.

Samuel Wesley (1766–1837) for one, in possession of an unusually thorough musical education, was not encouraged by his father to become a professional musician.[65] Also, once established in a musical career, many 'sought approval by leaving it'.[66] In addition it was essential for a musician to be versatile in order to earn a living at different times of the year or as fashions changed, to follow the money and become a 'jack of all trades', rather than gain experience in one or two areas (or on one or two instruments) and fulfil potential. The demand and expertise required to specialize and achieve acclaim in any singular branch of the art, in the same way as the foreign competition, were slow to arrive, which of course had a further impact on standards and any potential challenge to foreign dominance. Even relatively eminent figures, such as Sir William Parsons (the first professional musician to be knighted), William Crotch and James Hook, were forced to cast their net very wide, including trading, tuning and repairing instruments, in order to earn a living. It is all too significant that Parsons received his title (in 1795) on the basis of the 'score of his merits' rather than the 'merits of his scores'.[67] George Smart, a highly adept social climber as well as similarly versatile musician, was knighted in 1811.[68] It is true, however, that elementary teaching retained (and retains) a fundamental role in the musician's financial status.

Prior to the huge increase in 'semi-professionalism' and cheap labour during the nineteenth century, those who sought to earn a living primarily from music were usually male, career musicians and the products of family or local professional networks. There are many examples of single families dominating different aspects of musical activity in certain localities and creating in effect 'closed shops'. In large commercial centres, such as London, there is likely to have been a paucity of candidates with the means or inclination to enter the performing or teaching professions.[69] Elsewhere there was probably a greater emphasis on a reluctance to encourage competition. This was a more important consideration when pupils were generally from the same peer group rather than wealthy dilettantes. The insecurity and low status of native musicians, denied access to the most lucrative posts and

---

[65] See Olleson (2000), 25.

[66] Ehrlich (1985), 42, who highlights Dr Burney and Sir George Smart as figures over a period of more than a century who achieved social standing primarily on the basis of their non-musical achievements. Similarly the undistinguished Gresham professorship offered greater opportunities for social rather than artistic advancement and Frederick Ouseley, as a baronet and priest, was ensured respect as music professor at Oxford.

[67] Brown and Stratton (1897), 312.

[68] See 'Royal honours through the century' in Scholes (1947), vol.2, 735.

[69] See Ehrlich (1985), 6 and 74–5.

forced to accept the drudgery of teaching incredibly long hours in private practice and in schools for their bread-and-butter income, made them wary of each other and outsiders.[70]

The lack of respect or opportunities enjoyed by musicians in some other countries[71] therefore encouraged isolation in the artist, which in turn served only to exacerbate and prolong their difficulties. Low status and lack of respect were destructive additions to the artist's inherent alienation from society, which was a potential source of creativity in more open-minded cultural environments. The profession displayed little evidence of collective influence or mutual support and so were ineffective in initiating change or protecting their own interests in the face of the threat from growing numbers of semi-professionals. Consequently, as a matter of principle and self-preservation, they were often reluctant to share 'trade secrets' and suspicious and defensive when it came to initiatives to train musicians in groups (such as Logier's keyboard classes) or institutionally.[72] Effective material for written instruction was also considered a danger to teachers' livelihoods rather than an important complement to good teaching practice. The true value of a publication could be lost if 'masters', fearful 'their mysteries should be revealed', sought to discredit it. Insecurity and the resulting self-interest encouraged them 'to lead on a scholar, in the course of two or three years, to the knowledge of what they might, upon a plain, easy, simple principle, accomplish in a few weeks'.[73] Far from inspiring higher standards, the fear of competition therefore held the progress of musical appreciation back among both amateurs and professionals, with instruction given most willingly to those who had little interest in musical proficiency and so posed the least threat. The precarious nature of the profession engendered such myopia.

In keeping with their general predicament and priorities, when provision was made for musicians it tended to be in the form of benevolent funds (such as the rather exclusive Royal Society of Musicians or the New Musical Fund for non-Londoners) rather than initiatives to improve training and supply.[74] Later action, through

---

[70] Leppert's 1985 article discusses the low status of native teachers, with little choice but to tolerate poor pay and conditions. Even the relatively famous and successful Dr Burney had 55 years' teaching of up to 14 hours a day (see p. 150).

[71] It is interesting to compare the early training and encouragement afforded Moscheles with that experienced by most native musicians (see Wylde (1882), 17, 28 and 57).

[72] See Rainbow (1981).

[73] See Kassler (1979), 773.

[74] The Royal Society provided vital financial aid for musicians who suffered financial hardship and poor health, such as the ill-fated instrumentalist and music publisher William Napier (c.1741–1812).

professional associations and trade unions, paid greater attention to the control of supply than the quality of training. The unfortunate characteristics associated with the musician proved very hard to shake off. The lack of collective effort had obviously made the promotion of professional identity and self-respect all the more difficult, thereby playing into the hands of those with low opinions of musicians and their skills. The new unions could at least attempt to rectify this situation.

Relative success stories among British musicians during the eighteenth and early nineteenth centuries tended to come in areas where there were greater opportunities to shine and emerge from the shadow of foreign dominance. Less common instruments with less scope for domestic and other recreational use and therefore amateur interest and published repertoire[75] (although perhaps with a greater ceremonial role) could offer greater potential to native performers. Wind and brass instruments, rather than the keyboard or violin, for example, were not prone to the same level of imported excellence given the limited demand from amateurs and the professional concert scene. This situation assisted native musicians in some 'elite' areas, in which foreign competition could be a positive rather than dominating force.[76] In some cases, such as Sammartini's influence on native oboists (the Vincent family for example), a raising of standards and expectations was complemented by the necessary potential to participate (and specialize) and achieve some level of eminence in the field. This is in contrast to the violin and Geminiani's influence, for example, where significant efforts and progress in some areas did little to raise the general status of native violinists in a climate that continued to favour and rely upon foreign talent. Eminent foreign players were crucial to the successful performance of Beethoven's string quartets during the 1840s.[77] Although the amateur market offered far fewer teaching opportunities for wind and brass players (at least prior to later widespread expansion), foreign visitors appear to have been happier to cater for professional needs when this was not at the expense of attending the rich dilettante. Even so family contacts and professional networks remained of great importance and a life of poverty was an all too real prospect. Even Sir William Sterndale Bennett, who enjoyed crucial and equally rare foreign (particularly German) esteem, faced the pressures of an inadequate income.[78]

---

[75] Capel Bond was unusual in having his concertos for wind instruments published (see Fiske and Johnstone, eds (1990), 210).

[76] Military and brass band musicians would of course later benefit from this situation.

[77] See Bashford in Bashford and Langley, eds (2000), 89 and 108.

[78] See Ringer, ed. (1990), 228.

The native musician did receive support and encouragement from some individuals who were often linked to the profession in some way but were not career musicians as such. These well-needed allies were enthusiasts who, responding to the middle-class appetite for music journalism and public lectures, realized the importance of the amateur in determining the fortunes of the profession and sought to direct public taste and attitudes in a constructive and beneficial manner. The lectures of Edward Taylor, for example, a civil engineer by profession and champion of amateur music, were highlighted for their 'bold and biting remarks on the tendency of fashion in this country to despise and neglect its native musical produce, and to lend a willing ear only to the productions of the newest and weakest of foreign composers'.[79] Richard Mackenzie Bacon was an influential ally and identified, among other things, the importance of improving the general education of native musicians in achieving wider acceptance and respect in light of the manners and refinement associated with their foreign counterparts.[80] Circumstances and methods of instruction had fuelled criticisms of the value of the subject by allowing this situation to arise and persist, much to the dismay of sympathetic observers. The 'artisan' professional musician, locked into apprenticeship or similar arrangement from an early age and required to earn money from music as soon as possible, in many cases fell between those whose general formal education was catered for (if at all) by voluntary schools of various types and those of more privileged circumstances who were taught at home and later at school and university. Significantly those groups of instrumentalists who would have had greater access to more general (if still limited) formal education before turning to or alongside music as a serious pursuit, such as female middle-class and male lower-class amateurs and organists, achieved a certain level of acceptance and respect. Organists, like singers, also benefited from established platforms for performance and teaching.

Educating musicians beyond the immediate demands of their profession was, however, only partly the solution. Conventional wisdom had long promoted the harmful dichotomy between the gentleman amateur scholar/theorist and the lowly musician devoid of a liberal education and, even if successful, proficient merely in a 'mechanical' and 'commercial' art without inspiration or genius.[81] But at least there were

---

[79] Comment on lectures given in 1835. See Duckles (1981), 489.
[80] See Kassler (1979), 546.
[81] The writings of Davy (1787), Graham (1816), Jarrold (1819), Horncastle (1822) and Bacon (1829), among others, are significant in this respect (see Kassler (1979), 267–8, 402–3, 546–7, 559, 583 and 1129). See also Duckles (1981), 483, Ehrlich (1985), 44 and Chapter 1 below.

a growing number of observers vocal in their objection to this division and degradation of the performer's skills and aware of its detrimental effect on the general level of musical proficiency and taste in Britain.[82] The idea of a specialist academy for the training of musicians was proposed on many occasions, but a continued preoccupation with the traditional view of musicians among powerful upper-class amateurs was, when it finally arrived, destined to limit its effectiveness (see Chapter 5). Purely musical attributes, like the subject itself, were considered of insufficient importance in themselves and therefore extramusical factors, relating to status and respectability, continued to play a very important role even in professional training.

It is evident that the situation facing native career musicians was in most cases not conducive to effective systems of training and accreditation and therefore promoted mediocrity rather than excellence. The lowly position of the native professional, whether performer, composer or teacher, is virtually constant throughout the momentous changes witnessed during the period: a situation demonstrated by their almost incidental role in any of the major developments discussed in this study and the general impression of Britain as 'the Great Un-Musical Power of Europe'.[83]

With the expansion of education and institutions inevitably came new opportunities, but there were also new groups of consumers joining the ranks of the profession with relative ease. This would not have been such a problem if general standards had been higher. There must have been, potentially at least, a relatively good living to be made for native performers of a high calibre. Unfortunately the social and cultural environment had not produced many. In truth the nature of the profession had changed very little since the eighteenth century and the concerns of the amateur still held sway. Perhaps the best time for native performers in general had been the second and third quarters of the nineteenth century, when amateur, middle-class demand for teachers and performers had increased substantially, alongside the promotion of musical appreciation by various pioneering individuals. At the same time there was little 'drift' between amateur and professional status, as music was still considered an unsuitable and unpromising career among those with access, even if amateur participation was more widely and seriously practised. As a result, although society's view of music and musicians continued to be somewhat ambivalent, there was a rise in

---

[82] Some other individuals concerned with the elevation of music and musicians in Britain around the middle of the nineteenth century are highlighted in Ehrlich (1985), 42–4.

[83] Rainbow (1981), 45.

their fortunes. The producer came to be valued alongside the product, which was inextricably linked with perceptions of its 'usefulness' and its respectability.

Aside from the fortunes of the beleaguered professional, the increasing presence and acceptance of music at the 'grass-roots' level, including in schools of various types, as the nineteenth century progressed was fundamental to and indicative of the musical recovery of the nation. Amateurs and semi-professionals in the popular sphere and working-class communities in particular, faced with the possibility of climbing the social ladder, created and nurtured to a much greater extent their own opportunities for supply and demand based on mutual support and appreciation. Music in this area was therefore much less vulnerable to whims of fashion and codes of convention. The relative security nurtured positive developments, among both local communities and society as a whole, which in turn realized artistic potential to a much greater extent than had previously been possible or even perhaps desirable. Positive attitudes towards music in the 'popular' sphere were self-fulfilling in the same way as perceptions of inferiority had been in 'elite' areas.

Music and the Moral Dimension: 'damned if you do, damned if you don't'

Morality and class are two inextricably linked issues which are never far away in this (or any other) discussion of nineteenth-century British history. They are of particular relevance to trends in education, permeating patterns of provision and consumption at all levels, from the proliferation of the mechanics' institutes to Arnold's Rugby, during a period of notorious sanctimonious puritanism. In British, particularly English, education, what was taught needed to be justified on moral and/or utilitarian grounds. The Puritan legacy and resulting distrust of the art meant that music was seen to comply with these criteria only as opportunity spread and, as a consequence, the tide of opinion began to change.

Prior to the late nineteenth-century writings of individuals such as Haweis and the wider appreciation of and belief in music's inherent worth, music – and instrumental practice in particular – struggled to establish itself as moral per se. This was in no small part due to the common views of musicians and the circumstances of their trade discussed in the previous section. One may even assert that greater currency was given to the view that music was intrinsically immoral, a virtue-sapping, hedonistic pursuit, in the light of the number of derogatory connotations it suffered as an increasingly secular art with dangerous 'sensual' overtones. For music to be perceived as wholesome, improving and beneficial, it was therefore necessary for its associations and the activities that accompanied it to be considered in a far more positive light.[84] Vital extra-musical considerations could work to instrumental music's advantage; but, denied the advantages of vocal practice (such as the possibility of a devotional or 'moral' text or acknowledged practical and health benefits), other factors had to come into play.

Involvement in practical music-making within the secular sphere was increasingly accepted in certain areas,[85] as the huge expansion of earlier practices and concerns was impossible to resist. The middle classes, preoccupied with the emulation of their social betters and the acquisition of all-important 'respectability', incorporated instrumental music into their lives as a means of occupying their time generally within the privacy of their own homes. This was of course, in continuation of eighteenth-century convention, a case of men prescribing the acceptable place of music within female society. Its important role in the marriage market was assured for a long time to come, but, as opportunity spread and the stern controls on its practice were weakened somewhat, the role that music could play in women's lives on a personal level was seen to shift. A new focus on the 'delight' of music, its expression and sensuality, was, however, at odds with its accepted qualities in relation to discipline, morality and the intellectual.[86] The danger that the lady could be 'corrupted' through a too serious application in the study of the arts was not a new phenomenon.[87] Such a conflict and the continued criticism of self-expression and restriction of ambition could only be detrimental to the development of performance skills.

Gentlemen of the highest social orders continued to find difficulty in reconciling musical performance with a worthwhile use of their and their male offspring's time. Young gentlemen from the expanding middle orders, however, though still mostly 'dabblers', found greater encouragement and demonstrated greater proficiency in light of their closer proximity to professionals in terms of class and social status.

---

[84] H. J. Pye, writing in 1807, claims that 'music can have no moral effect, but it certainly possesses other powers that have' (see Kassler (1979), 860).

[85] Religion did however become an important 'template' for the discussion of music. See Zon (2000), 99.

[86] Burgan (1989) has much of interest to say on this subject and the 'deeply ingrained English moral tone-deafness' (ibid., 64), highlighting in particular the contrast between George Eliot's emphasis on the need for the expression of deep feeling and the convention of music as a feminine social grace.

[87] See Kassler (1979), 783.

Writers and journalists, now more of a chorus than a few solo voices, promoted music as 'improving' (if not 'moral' as such) and there was much greater access to public performances. It is also significant that the religious and moral (rather than musical) education of career musicians was increasingly considered and catered for (although it remained very much at the mercy of financial considerations).[88]

Instrumental performance was accessible to a much greater number of people across a much wider cross-section of society who were more willing to consider it a potentially 'improving' rather than damaging (socially and/or financially) activity. With incentives to promote and consume in place, perceptions of secular, instrumental activity changed, although, with conventional wisdom still in evidence and a continued challenge to more positive attitudes, there remained an uneasy acceptance of the practice of instrumental music among those with leisure time and a disposable income. An enduring, deep-seated spirit of puritanical philistinism could only serve to suffocate innovation and progress among native musicians.

The most far-reaching development in terms of the perception of instrumental music and its largely unqualified acceptance was the provision of access to the lower orders.[89] This trend fitted perfectly into the proliferation of secular education and the complementary drive towards material progress. The prospect of further urban-industrial growth and the corresponding potential for highly damaging social unrest provided both the means and incentive for the provision and consumption of popular musical idioms. The fear of the 'barbarous' masses and a fervent desire to redeem them from 'wholesale mental and spiritual degradation'[90] had a direct effect on the direction of provision in education, above and beyond the issue of market potential. The cultivation of 'art' music, vocal and instrumental, among lower-class children and adults, was therefore considered of benefit to reformers and employers as well as the practitioners, and as such it could be perceived as 'useful' and 'productive' (such vital contemporary considerations),[91] beyond any functional or devotional context. Musical performance acquired an 'intellectual' as well as moral quality within this changing social structure and beyond the 'protective shield'[92] of the

---

[88] See Ehrlich (1985), 84 and 86.

[89] Russell, Mackerness, Rainbow and Gillett have all made important contributions on this subject that do not require lengthy repetition here. Comments of particular interest have been concerned with the promotion, among both adults and children, of social betterment, moral health and temperance through music itself and also the training and travel it often entailed.

[90] Mackerness (1964), 147.

[91] Hughes and Stradling (2001), 3; and McCalman (1999), 151.

[92] Russell (1997), 188.

church. Church musicians may not have had a comfortable living and often needed to supplement incomes with outside teaching, but they had at least enjoyed a moral status by association and relative to their secular colleagues.

Figures in positions of influence were keen to make use of music as a social tool, acknowledging its passifying, civilizing effects as part of 'rational recreation'.[93] Writers such as Hogarth were quick to highlight its ability to improve the mental state and social habits of the individual, rich and poor, and provide 'relaxation from toil' and relief from 'the demoralizing effects of a crowded population, fluctuating employment, and pauperism'. He also noted the role of some employers in promoting, encouraging and paying for musical associations and instruction.[94] Of course the potential 'humanizing' and restorative effects of music had long been appreciated,[95] along with its direct application in therapy of various kinds and association with charitable concerns for the benefit of society's disadvantaged in a wider sense. There was an established role for music, at home and abroad, in institutions and plans concerned with charitable work and education. These movements in late nineteenth-century Britain also afforded women an unusually prominent and public role as performers and as singers in particular.[96] But the most significant changes came within the general, increasingly urban context, in which the 'elite' found it much easier to perceive the performance of music as worthwhile for the lower orders than for themselves and could benefit indirectly from their activity.

The long association of music with 'haunts in which melody was the handmaid of vice'[97] naturally gave rise to some ambivalent feeling regarding its influence among the working classes.[98] But, more importantly, these traditions highlighted an existing audience, appetite and even enthusiasm for the art among this expanding group, offering the potential for its influence in both national and local schemes of adult education and schools, if only its context could be elevated. A powerful agent with the ability to touch the emotions, for better or worse, there was therefore great scope for music to be perceived as a vehicle for

---

[93] D. B. Scott (2002), 558.

[94] Hogarth (1838), vol.2, 273–4. See also Elbourne (1980), 64–6; Ehrlich (1985), 66–8; and Chapter 5 below.

[95] See for example Kassler (1979), 117, 139–41, 222–3, 814–15 and 1192.

[96] See Gillett (2000a), 40–62; and Ehrlich (1985), 52. Such 'useful' work outside a domestic setting naturally encouraged higher standards of performance in many cases.

[97] Mackerness (1964), 152.

[98] There is certainly a 'complicated relationship between music, morality and ale' (Elbourne (1980), vii–viii), with musical activity able to both complement and resist the influence of ale depending on the context. See D. B. Scott (2002), 559.

morality rather than vice. The dual role of music philanthropy in this context, as a means of control and containment as well as emancipation, was essential to its success and the proliferation of interest and opportunity in this area during our period. Education, itself a double-edged sword in the hands of Kay-Shuttleworth and others, was a vital means of imbuing the middle-class moral agenda among the urban labouring class. Affording music a moral dimension enabled and justified its use as a controlling force beyond the home. It became a very useful weapon (despite some persistent reservations, including Sunday performances and opera) in an evangelical age. Its unifying and passifying qualities were naturally most evident and therefore encouraged in group, 'popular' practice, rather than individual, largely 'elite' and self-gratifying recreation. Group training and performance promoted discipline and a belief in the value of cooperative action which were enhanced by the inherent 'inventiveness and determination' of the lower classes.[99]

The issue of morality was therefore prominent in the thinking and activities of the (mainly middle-class) pioneers of vocal education among adults and in schools. Reformers and educationalists, such as Kay-Shuttleworth, Hullah, Mainzer, Curwen and their disciples, applied what they had gleaned from continental texts and public singing classes to the British market. A desire to 'save' the masses and bring social and work benefits through music was a powerful motivation. The vocal art and the training associated with it retained its superior position relative to instrumental performance and enjoyed (albeit mainly moral rather than financial) support from the state for its practice among adults and children. Following on from the initial impetus, to improve the singing of congregations in church,[100] there was an appreciation of the wider social, group benefits in formal education and recreation that this useful, rewarding (and relatively cheap) form of music-making could offer. A variety of initiatives to provide vocal training touched tens of thousands of people, especially working-class children and adults. Religious institutions became a key training ground for the fellowship and discipline of the choral movement. A movement such as Methodism epitomized the alliance of singing and devotion. The value of choral worship was later realized in the new Victorian boarding schools, which played an important role, along with the writings of Haweis and others, in achieving a broader acceptance of music among the middle and upper classes and among boys in particular. Music was to be harnessed for its potential improving effects on the moral health of the individual and

---

[99] See Russell (1997), 198 and 273.
[100] Rainbow (1981), 40.

society at large.[101] A genre like the oratorio provided the means of satisfying devotional and musical, sacred and secular needs. It went some way towards reconciling what were often seen as conflicting interests within a consumer society as well as crossing class, gender and geographical boundaries.

Morality and taste went hand in hand, and therefore, in the British cultural climate, the alliance of music and poetry as well as intellectual simplicity and sobriety were placed on a moral pedestal.[102] It is no surprise that figures such as Handel and Mendelssohn should be so admired in this and other areas, both of whom enjoyed what amounted to musical deification. Purity and balance, rather than excess and novelty, were important ingredients of musical style as well as personal character. Conservatism largely determined the critical (if not always popular) success of repertoire and performers and was itself perceived as Christian by Haweis and his followers and remained an important element in the drive towards a musical 'renaissance'. It is important to remember that middle-class support for working-class music was imbued with conservative values which the resulting activity largely reinforced.[103]

The growth and changing dynamics of consumer demand in an overtly moralistic and utilitarian age allowed music to change its role fundamentally in the eyes of the state and reforming individuals. From being perceived as the villain it was increasingly viewed as the ally of moral perpetuity, encouraging rational recreations rather than dangerous pursuits. Acceptance, promotion and proliferation of musical activity came as music itself was seen to produce far more positive effects than purely musical results. Music as an agent of redemption rather than damnation had been very much a minority view during the preceding century, when the majority of practitioners were from the privileged classes. It was given moral credence and so actively encouraged by middle-class reformers, thereby helping to create and realize its potential among those 'boom' areas occupied by lower-class men and middle-class women. A propaganda victory for the cause of music was achieved through the singing class, choral society and brass band in particular and an increasing range of (often shared) repertoire.[104]

---

[101] See Hughes and Stradling (2001), 6–8; and Caldwell (1999), 320.
[102] See Kassler (1979), 862.
[103] See Russell (1997), 285–92.
[104] Russell (1997), 228. The music halls, although increasingly respectable mass entertainment, had an additional function in providing a focus for much of the criticism previously aimed at music in general. See Russell (1997), 83ff., for a detailed discussion of the music hall and its repertory.

Although this did not preclude snobbery and derogatory comments concerning the artistic value of working-class efforts[105] and was not necessarily helpful to the cause of lower-priority areas (such as career musicians and creative innovation), it did enable much greater access to and acceptance of music as a worthwhile pursuit among British society as a whole. The later moral climate and 'declining religious observance' promoted a greater emphasis on 'art for art's sake' and a keener acceptance of other, emerging, leisure pursuits.[106]

Musical Appreciation

Playing a musical instrument captured the imagination of a significant proportion of the British population during the nineteenth century. Although more exclusive than singing in terms of the required equipment, technique and sometimes notation involved, it was an activity enjoyed by a rapidly increasing number of amateurs as the period progressed. However, this was of course only one way of gaining some degree of musical appreciation. Associated literature and the experience of live performance also became more accessible and influential as a result of the greater opportunity and demand and music's important role in Victorian social reform. As the appreciation of music spread and deepened, the acceptance of the art was further enhanced.

Writings on musical subjects became more pervasive and increased their sphere of influence alongside more accessible printed music, the publication of a greater variety of pedagogical material and instrument manufacturing on a large scale. Written music criticism was naturally aimed at the respectability-conscious middle classes, and the growing number of publications and journals dedicated to or offering coverage and discussion of musical events and developments cater for these literate classes and their predominantly amateur, if increasingly well-informed, interest in the subject. The greater market diversity and increasing affluence of the 1820s onwards gave rise to a plethora of publications, from specialist journals, catechisms, and dictionaries, to the music criticism in daily newspapers and the programme notes of Ella, Grove and others, and the further proliferation of 'practical' music

---

[105] See Russell (1997), 7–10. It is all the more significant that 'cheerful condemnations' (ibid., 8) of working-class taste often came from those (such as Haweis) wishing to promote music as morally beneficial. They found no difficulty in distinguishing between music's social role and its intrinsic qualities, which were supposedly of much greater concern to themselves, as part of the 'intellectual' higher orders.
[106] Ibid., 296.

theory. We should also not forget the complementary phenomena of the public lecture, accessible to the whole range of middle-class society, and bodies such as the Musical Institute of London and later the (Royal) Musical Association, which undertook and promoted the scholarly study of the 'art and science' of music.

Much of this literature complemented the attendance and appreciation of live public performance as well as its cultivation within the home. The early and rapid expansion and proliferation of British concert life, in keeping with consumer demand, is widely acknowledged, as is the relatively elite character of most audiences during the eighteenth century.

The concert life of nineteenth-century Britain retained its exclusivity in many cases, seeking to present the best performers to audiences of the highest social distinction possible.[107] This was still, after all, where the most lucrative and mutually beneficial social connections could be nurtured. The Philharmonic Society, itself a promising early nineteenth-century sign of professional independence and a significant contribution to the appreciation of new repertoire, did not begin selling tickets to the general public until 1841. Around this time, as the commercial potential of large-scale events was realized and access consequently increased (the demise of the exclusive Concerts of Ancient Music came in 1848 after more than 70 years), a penchant for intimate, semi-private, pioneering chamber music series emerged, including string quartet and solo recitals. Small-scale performance was therefore brought out of the home but was allowed to retain its audience exclusivity beyond the masses and, in many cases, even professional musicians.[108] Musical standards were undoubtedly raised through the presentation of often new and challenging repertoire and (at least on the surface) higher levels of appreciation. The music was to be listened to and understood, assisted by programme notes and the study of pocket scores. These aids assisted comprehension and therefore, it would seem, critical acceptance. Such a stage demanded far more than the affluent amateur performer could offer. It also precluded most native professionals judging by Ella's penchant for top-class foreign artists for his Musical Union (1845–81).[109]

---

[107] Christina Bashford has contributed valuable work on 'elite' repertoire and reception and the activities of John Ella in particular.

[108] See Bashford in Bashford and Langley, eds (2000), 211. The performance of chamber music did eventually offer some women the opportunity to fulfil their artistic potential (see Ehrlich (1985), 160).

[109] Ella was criticized for his strong preference for foreign talent although he did campaign for higher standards of training for British musicians and music education in general and for financial support from the government (see Bashford in Bashford and Langley, eds (2000), 213).

Elite and elitist performances in London's West End present us once again with the marriage of affluence and professionalism, hand in hand with a distinctly male leadership and foreign bias, which was increasingly in evidence in prosperous communities like Manchester and Liverpool. These emerging centres of professional musical activity did, however, offer greater performing opportunities to both conservatoire- and brass-band-trained native musicians and also seem to have been more willing to recruit their audiences from a broader cross-section of society than the capital.

There was of course a huge latent demand for good music waiting to be tapped and, as we have seen, a growing desire to harness its power for the good of society. Consequently the educational angle played a large part in many public-performance and municipal initiatives. Pioneers and philanthropists in this area, taking advantage of increasing population density, sought to attract and educate the masses through 'art' music in particular. Publishing firms were quick to identify the marketing potential and often sponsored performances.[110] The active appreciation of music among the middle orders, a large and diverse category, was a truly populist movement, encouraged by the spread of good-quality, affordable live performances. Professional (and some good amateur) orchestras as well as brass bands brought music to the people up and down the land, from the industrial north to Bournemouth, and, assisted by new advancements in communication and transport, were able to tap demand and musical potential in previously neglected areas. Charismatic figures such as Louis Jullien brought entertainment and enlightenment through both light and cerebral repertoire to the provinces and the 'one shilling public'. The founding of the Monday Popular Concerts and new venues such as St James's Hall, the Crystal Palace and Queen's Hall further aided the dissemination of 'art' music and the People's Concert Society cast its net even wider in order to provide concerts and instruction for the working classes.[111] Even the curriculum in formal secondary education broadened in many cases, with music's traditional superficial or purely functional role and focus on vocal music enhanced by a greater emphasis on practical instrumental music. Familiarity with the masterpieces of the art was also encouraged through performance within schools and the attendance of public concerts.[112]

Amid this general improvement in the level of musical appreciation among society at large, itself a spur to higher standards and greater

---

[110] See Mackerness (1964), 177.
[111] See Gillett (2000a), 48.
[112] See Rainbow (1989a), 34–6.

participation among amateurs in their homes, the lower orders once again displayed a voracious appetite, dedication and practical bias that many of their social superiors preferred to keep behind closed doors. The consumer potential among this group could not be ignored and, combined with characteristic public participation and corresponding ambition, it bore fruit in choral festivals and brass band contests, such as those staged at the Crystal Palace. As highlighted earlier there was a moral justification for the public presentation of the efforts of the lower classes and, though this was the 'people's music' with performers and audience, supply and demand, as one, the concerts and musical societies generally provided the middle classes with opportunities to 'promulgate their ideology'. Their presence was often conspicuous in the backing, audience, repertoire and even performers.[113] There was a great deal of common ground between the core repertoire of all kinds of ensemble and performance contexts, with opera and oratorio, for example, featured at both ends of the social spectrum. Ensembles such as brass bands therefore presented a remarkably catholic selection of repertoire to their audiences.[114]

The arrival and spread of the gramophone and radio broadcasts during the following century allowed the appreciation of music and its performance within the home without the need for practical involvement. Although perhaps detrimental to the health of live music in the long term, these innovations, alongside the efforts of conductors such as Beecham, Boult and Barbirolli, promulgated higher standards of performance and a better-informed public. They played an educational role that the competitive music festival had previously filled on a much smaller scale. The eradication of the ignorance and therefore mediocrity which had fed on itself within the music profession and had been propagated among the middle orders by large numbers of poorly qualified music teachers was long overdue.

'Artistic awakening' or 'damnable flood'? The Popularity of Music and the Spread of Opportunity

This Introduction has set out to outline some of the main trends in the development of music in British society during the eighteenth and nineteenth centuries. It is a story of expansion and diversification, as music-making and appreciation increased rapidly in line with new incentives to provide and exploit opportunities in this area. Before turning

---

[113] Russell (1997), 44 and 215–17.
[114] See ibid., 9–11, 192 and 228ff.

to the specific role of music education in these changes, we should, having established the importance of amateur consumerism, look in a little more detail at the nature of these expanding markets and areas of popular interest among self-conscious groups. The oxymoronic nature of this growth and diversification is alluded to in the heading to this section[115] and has a direct bearing on varying levels of musical success in 'boom' areas.

Investigations into the marketplace for music in Britain during this period, led by Ehrlich, have revealed an increase in the supply of professional musicians far beyond population growth.[116] The scale of supply and demand is of course only part of the story and Ehrlich's figures[117] support the empirical evidence of a huge increase in those offering their services as musicians and women teachers in particular. Also from the first half of the century London was joined by the midlands and north of England as key centres of musical activity and therefore employment. Community-based music provided fertile ground for development in areas with increasing population density, replacing small, perhaps stagnant pools of native talent. All in all music was cultivated and appreciated by a greater proportion and cross-section of society as the century progressed.

New movements in music education, work-based, institutional and self-help, are featured in subsequent chapters, but it is important to highlight the role of industrialization and mass-production in bringing cheaper, more accessible (including hire-purchase schemes) and easier-to-play instruments to the masses. These were of course complemented by a corresponding growth in the provision of practical tuition, supporting materials (such as Novello's cheap music editions) and public performances. As raised above, morality and profits, opposite sides of the industrialization coin, went hand in hand in providing both the means and incentives for the promotion of music throughout society. Further assistance from economic development came in the form of increasing incomes and literacy, designated leisure time, and greater social and physical mobility. The strong consumer bias of the British cultural scene presented interested parties from early in the century with opportunities to encourage more serious amateur interest and participation in music. Whether social or musical, the potential benefits to social reformers, philanthropists and (up to a point) those in musical circles, prompted schemes to attract and educate the public and consolidate existing interest.

---

[115] Both descriptions appear in the same paragraph (p.125) of Ehrlich's seminal 1985 work.
[116] Ehrlich (1985), 51ff.
[117] Ibid., 235ff.

Naturally the most successful efforts were those led by the political and economic pioneers of the time. They were concerned with quelling any potential dissent while motivating the swelling labouring classes, the 'engine' of the economy, and set about harnessing music for this purpose. Developments affecting the middle classes were largely at the mercy of market forces and the male agenda, while a downtrodden music profession amounted to less than the sum of its parts. There is therefore little surprise attached to the contrasting achievements of middle-class women and working-class men (chiefly represented by the teacher and bandsman respectively), who adopted crucially different positions in between the career musician and amateur 'dabbler' in terms of financial reward and artistic achievement. Neither of the two groups was widely credited with intellectual sophistication during our period, and as a result they were both directed towards practical disciplines which offered them a means of temporarily transcending their environment. They had far more to gain from music as a 'rational recreation'[118] than their social superiors and so entered into it with greater diligence; but those in control were still able to limit activity, whether within the home or workplace, to suit their own interests. Although there was a crucial change in the balance of perception, with a huge increase in the numbers of those who viewed musical talent as a potential source of freedom rather than as a 'snare to be shunned' in the pursuit of business,[119] there was therefore still a strong element of control from above in both cases. The extent to which this control stifled musical aspirations among the two groups determined the musical standards achieved and so their success in narrowing the amateur/professional divide for the better. Naturally there was a much greater likelihood of achieving high musical standards in situations where both artist and audience valued music's inherent qualities rather than concentrating on its wider social connotations.

In fact one can discern the scope for success and even the scope for enjoyment from the prevailing tone of the primary and secondary literature surrounding both areas.[120] Put simply, lower-class male musicians were free to excel within a predominantly amateur, mutually supportive context. Initiatives here which reconciled supply and demand (including matching young men with well-crafted brass instruments) were far more self-perpetuating and durable than those responding to the whimsical demands of the individual or attempts to change deeply entrenched attitudes. Activity was often linked to the workplace rather

---

[118] Ehrlich (1985), 65.
[119] Dubourg (1878), 193–4.
[120] Compare Gillett (2000a) and Herbert (2000a), for example.

than focused on the purchasing of leisure and all the inequalities that entailed. The popular music movement among the lower classes in fact did more than anything else to help break down the social barriers between performers, audiences and amateur activity, thereby reversing a trend evident from the second quarter of the eighteenth century. Although the support from social superiors was in effect a controlling force, it was one that actively initiated and encouraged practical involvement in music: a true 'awakening'. If some autonomy and freedom to experiment were sacrificed in the process, these concessions allowed the movement to prosper in a commercial environment. It was a trade-off that provided working-class music with the assistance and protection and therefore organization and efficiency that the 'mainstream' professional could only dream of. The prevailing 'unification of taste and repertoire',[121] imbued by middle-class involvement and state elementary education, dealt a blow to traditional rural folk music, but a 'sub-industry'[122] was generated around the new movement to the benefit of the wider community. Bandsmen made the most of their opportunities and although the role of the working-class woman in musical activities was primarily supportive and 'offstage', cheap instruments (particularly pianos) eventually provided a possible outlet in addition to the choir.[123]

In contrast to the intervention affecting the working classes, the restrictions experienced by many middle-class women sought to limit certain musical activity and ambition, thereby concentrating their efforts in areas where standards went largely unchecked and the career professional was most vulnerable. Such activity, the consequence of a relatively sudden release of pent-up, latent demand into a specific area (a true 'flood'), was mainly detrimental rather than helpful to the cause of native music and the native musician. Talent was tapped but far from maximized among 'genteel' society. Nevertheless a great deal of literature offering musical instruction, in journals and elsewhere, appeared in response to the demand during the last quarter of the nineteenth century,[124] altering the balance of music criticism as mainly middle-class men writing for their own kind.

Civilian, military and volunteer bands and choral societies form part of a 'discovery of possibilities'[125] in music at this time. They had an important social as well as public function outside the traditional

---

[121] Russell (1997), 7.
[122] Ibid., 179.
[123] Ibid., 11–12.
[124] Gillett (2000a), 98–9.
[125] Caldwell (1999), 321.

professional 'art' music sphere and their 'usefulness' extended beyond the needs of the individual consumer. Truly popular movements involving public performance were initiated, allowing musical training to become more than an end in itself at the same time as developing moral fortitude. It was of course much better for the musicality of the nation to have professional standards among amateurs rather than professionals of an amateur standard. The idea of amateur musicians keen to perform and achieve had been evident much earlier on the continent and represented by the social elite downwards. A groundswell of popular activity in Britain contributed in a large way to the 'renaissance' in its musical fortunes and prominence. The professional musician benefited from the impact of technology and war during the early twentieth century, along with the role of 'art' music in nationalism and the protection of interests through more effective union activity. However the role of the amateur remained (and remains) fundamental to the British music scene, even if easier access may have bred greater passivity than is evident in popular movements and the incentives behind them during the nineteenth century.

CHAPTER ONE

Music Education and 'the Age of Improvement'

If we now turn to issues concerned specifically with music education, we can see how the prejudices, concerns, desires and ambitions discussed in the previous section manifest themselves in aspects of supply and demand. It is perhaps surprising that the subject of music education has not been more widely studied, particularly in view of its ability both to reflect and determine the changing fortunes of music and its role in society. It is after all education, both formal and informal, that determines how culture is provided and consumed. Investigations into the subject have, in keeping with contemporary priorities, focused mainly on the spread of vocal practice and training, in formal education and recreation, among adults and children and the importation of foreign models.[1] The story to tell is far more self-evident than in the case of instrumental practice. As highlighted in the previous section, the roles of the amateur and of those forging and responding to burgeoning amateur activity are crucial to the British musical scene.

The Legacy of the Eighteenth Century

We have already established the importance and longevity of eighteenth-century trends and so it seems appropriate to outline this legacy of continuity and change as a suitable context for our period, which has been seen by many historians to represent a major step forward in a number of ways.[2] This section highlights several important 'binaries' which have a particularly important relevance to the cultivation of music during the eighteenth century and continue to affect the

---

[1] The series 'Classic texts in music education' (Aberystwyth, 1982–91), general editor Bernarr Rainbow, is typical in omitting instrumental works but featuring important contemporary British texts in other areas such as singing, education and biography by authors such as Curwen, Mainzer, Crotch and Baptie. Cox (1993) similarly reflects contemporary concerns in concentrating on the involvement of the state in the provision of vocal training in schools.

[2] For example Briggs (1959/R1979), from the title of which the phrase 'the age of improvement' is taken.

cultivation of music in the nineteenth. They therefore resonate through the second section and subsequent chapters.

Discussion of these binaries adds to our understanding of this period as one which, characterized by neglect and a lack of musical ambition among the majority of society's movers and shakers, ensured that the underachievement of British music and musicians in many cases continued for a significant period. Education in general during the period was regarded by the state as a means of social control, with people, adults and children, educated according to their lot in life, which was largely determined by class and gender rather than ability or potential. Naturally the 'station' of the individual was most easily determined at either extreme of the social spectrum and this is reflected in the structuring and priorities of formal education during the period (church and charitable schools on the one hand and home tuition, public schools and universities on the other).

It was not until towards the end of the nineteenth century when lower-order power became irresistible that education became a force for emancipation and social mobility on a large scale.[3] Wealth (in the case of the upper and some middle classes) or family connections (for the lower and lower-middle classes) were most often required to take the first steps. This was particularly the case during the eighteenth century in a profession such as music, which, as we have seen, suffered a great deal not only from neglect but also from efforts to preserve its low status.[4] Brewer observes that almost any other passion for art, including a love of poetry and letters or even sketching and drawing, was considered more reputable than an obsession with music.[5] Music was

---

[3] See Briggs (1994), 16, and Strong (1998), 413–15. Other particularly useful general surveys of education in Britain and England in particular during the period include Woodward (1962), 474–501 and 560–61; Trevelyan (1978); Morgan (1984), 448–9 and 488–91; May (1996), 92–100, 155–65 and 239–46; and Royle (1997), 349–403 and 438–44. See also the useful summaries provided by D. Taft, 'The Victorian Education' at the website www.gober.net/victorian/reports/schools.html (searched 8 August 2001).

[4] In addition to Rainbow's series of edited texts, important studies of general music education in England during the period include Rainbow (1967 and 1989b) and various articles in Scholes's treasure trove (1947). Chapter 4 of Rohr's thesis (1983) discusses the different educational routes for musicians during the period, primarily the chorister and university route, apprenticeship, private lessons, study in Europe, and military training, which are all touched upon at various points in the present study. See also Ehrlich (1985); Fiske and Johnstone, eds (1990); Beedell (1992); Cox (1993); Brewer (1997); McCalman, ed. (1999), 161–70; Caldwell (1999), especially 548–53; and various articles in *Grove 7* (2001). Some attention is paid to music education in Scotland in Farmer (1970). A *Chronology of Nineteenth-Century British Music Education* can be found as Appendix 1 in the present study.

[5] Brewer (1997), 560. Even other performance arts such as acting were held in higher esteem.

irrelevant or, at best, a tangential concern to most, and musicians were merely the purveyors of entertainment that could be purchased and dispensed with at will by those with money and leisure time. Music did not have the high intellectual status it enjoyed on the continent.[6] Practical music, at least, was regarded more as a sensual pleasure than as stimulation for the mind.

Considering these associations, it is not surprising that the acquisition of musical skills does not feature prominently in education at this time, particularly in the case of young men.[7] Musical standards were low in the boarding schools for girls and boys, and the standard and status of music education is demonstrated by the frequency of criticisms and the often satirical treatment of music masters.[8] One does not have to delve too deeply to discover that the ingredients of success in education, particularly those related to opportunity and expectation, are sadly lacking in many instances. The all-too-common scenario of the ill-educated music teacher instructing the unmotivated student is certainly a recipe for disaster[9] and the desire to maintain the amateur/professional divide ensured mediocrity across the board. If popular music movements eventually blurred the distinction and if the association with low society and 'dissolute habits'[10] subsided over time, financial considerations continued to discourage many potential 'career' musicians, especially instrumentalists, for a significant period.

The Battle of the Sexes

The music profession in Britain was dominated by men until the second half of the nineteenth century, when the wave of female teachers shifted the balance in their favour.[11] Nevertheless men were long to be

---

[6] See Temperley (1999), 10 and 13–14.

[7] See Brewer (1997), 532. Leppert (1988, in particular pp.51–70) provides a very useful discussion of upper-class music education, for men and women, in eighteenth-century England (pupils, teachers and methods), and related sources.

[8] See Leppert (1988), 53.

[9] If we examine the table of positive and negative influences as provided in Pitts (2000, p.5), it is evident that factors affecting provision during our period at both national and local levels limited access and the acceptance of new ideas, thereby compromising the effective use of available resources. Contemporary pressure made 'critical engagement' with ideas, resources and curriculum innovations, on the part of consumers and providers, very difficult. Improvements later in the period were linked to enhanced status and higher expectations at both local and national levels.

[10] Kassler (1979), 44.

[11] See table in Ehrlich (1985), 235. Conscious of encouraging competition, male teachers tended to charge male pupils twice as much as women prior to the huge expansion of the later nineteenth century (see Kassler (1979), 877).

considered the most suitable vehicles for musical and in particular instrumental public performance.[12] The methods of training the professional instrumentalist (see following chapter) dictated that it was men from established musical families who most often achieved the standards and exposure required as performers. Women often achieved a relatively high level of proficiency as amateurs, but, despite some notable exceptions (few of which were instrumentalists), the flowering of musical talent, even among 'semi-professional' teachers, was brief and inconsequential in the vast majority of cases. The teaching and learning of musical instruments among women was a largely self-perpetuating and isolated process, with greater social and economic than purely musical significance.

Instrumental performance played a generally tangential role in the lives of well-to-do male and female amateurs. Social conventions demanded that talent and passion for the art as a practical discipline be stifled to varying degrees in most cases. If its value was limited then its study was subject to restriction, a fact borne out by contemporary writings, teaching material, repertoire and iconography.

Gentlemen were amateurs in the literal sense as 'lovers of the arts', but any serious ambition as such (let alone professional aspirations) was frowned upon within and outside the home. Young men of good birth during the eighteenth century were certainly open to criticism if there was a danger that they were becoming too attached to the study of music, thereby exposing themselves to bad company and substituting 'useful' business and study for skills of little value beyond the hired musician. The now notorious views of the Earl of Chesterfield,[13] following on from those of John Locke and widely circulated in print, certainly exacerbated the situation by relegating music to 'last place' in the gentleman's list of accomplishments with little or no intrinsic value, at least beyond the playfulness of infancy.[14] Such comments confirmed and promoted in particularly strong terms the general feeling among fashionable circles that a too eager involvement in the performance of instrumental music, free of the 'protective shield' often held out to music by religion,[15] was harmful rather than beneficial to the interests and personal development of the gentleman. Chesterfield, who took an active interest in musical matters, commented with particular virulence

---

[12] See Gillett (2000a), 6. It is of course significant that the vast majority of college students towards the end of the century were women, directed towards teaching, whereas men continued to dominate the student orchestras (see Weber in Bashford and Langley, eds (2000), 309).

[13] See Caldwell (1999), 91.

[14] See Kassler 1976 and 1979, including 696–7.

[15] Russell (1997), 188. See also Kassler (1979), 1107.

on 'fiddling' and 'fiddlers' in particular and the need for the young gentleman to be 'protected' from the generally negative effects of a conventional music education. Men of fashion did not require a great deal of convincing and it was left mainly to a few lowly musicians and others with a professional interest, such as Philpot (Chron., 1766: 4), and a few clergymen to go against the grain of mainstream contemporary opinion and promote music as a wholesome alternative to 'expensive Diversions' such as gambling and drinking.

Influential figures such as the music journalist Richard Mackenzie Bacon later identified the crucial importance of and set about improving attitudes towards music and standards among amateurs and removing the deeply ingrained negative (if not subversive) connotations. His strategy, designed to portray music as a pursuit beneficial to all, focused on raising the public's opinion of the musicians themselves through a concern for their liberal education as well as on a rejection of the opinions promoted by Chesterfield and others.[16] The fact that he felt the need to highlight Chesterfield in particular over 35 years later in 1820, and that the reply of Lord Suffield in 1823 was, despite some musical accomplishments of his own, perhaps even more extreme in its criticism of music than Chesterfield himself, demonstrates the persistence of these views and the extent of the struggle for musicians and the serious cultivation of music to gain respectability among the higher orders at this time.[17]

It could be said that for much of the eighteenth and nineteenth centuries the activities of aristocratic amateurs, rather than inspiring serious interest in music, served only to undermine the status of native professional musicians and promote poor standards. In some cases, such as with Chesterfield and Suffield, the ferocity of the criticism perhaps serves to hide a necessarily private passion. The efforts of some members of high society and the aristocracy do suggest greater dedication, but many were still at pains to display apathy and accounts of great proficiency among these circles are rare. The dedication of musical and pedagogical works[18] must be considered in light of the musician's need to receive and retain patronage. Achievements could seldom have compared favourably with those of the continental nobility. However

---

[16] Kassler (1979), 39ff., contains useful summaries of Bacon's writings from this period, including (as 'Vetus') those 'On the character of musicians', 'On the objects of musical education', and 'Music as a pursuit for men', all from *QMMR* (1818–20), of which he was editor. The Revd Charles Davy had expressed similar views during the 1770s and 1780s (see Kassler (1979), 266–9). See also Beedell (1992), 111–12.

[17] Kassler (1979), 44–5. This situation was not unique to England as Graham's reflections on opinion in Scotland demonstrate (ibid., 402ff.).

[18] See Edwards (1989), 322.

the involvement of the social elite in a certain musical activity could, as the efforts of the Prince of Wales on the cello show, greatly raise its status and reputation.[19]

Opinions of practical music-making among polite society therefore ranged from an uneasy ambivalence to unashamed hostility. A 'scholarly' interest on the other hand, focusing for instance on the long-standing mathematical principles of music theory, was considered far more respectable and very much the preserve of the gentleman amateur rather than the professional musician.[20] There is no denying the huge amount of amateur musical activity during the period (Chesterfield does not disprove this), but, through self-imposed and other ceilings on ambition, there was undoubtedly a great deal of damage done over a significant period to the standing of practical music-making among men of the higher orders. As a result the instruments they made their own, particularly the flute and violin, similarly suffered in terms of proficiency and esteem.[21]

Musical ambition continued to be stifled as long as the social standing of the professional musician remained far below that of the amateur. The all-important social aspirations of the upper echelons of the 'middling sort'[22] preserved the amateur/professional divide. The further descent of opportunity and access during the nineteenth century was essential to enable dramatic changes in how music and its value were judged and the removal of stigma from its serious study. As we shall see, the surge of new middle-class consumers and entrepreneurs promoted higher standards among young male instrumentalists and the achievements of the lower orders further enhanced the range of instruments and standard of activity undertaken by male amateurs.

Ladies born into wealthy families were, in contrast to their male siblings, actively encouraged to undertake the study of a keyboard or plucked string instrument as part of their 'useful', formal education. As discussed above, such skills were not just for casual amusement and became valuable currency in the marriage market; but, alas, that is as far as they went in most cases. In keeping with mainstream native thinking

---

[19] As discussed by Harvey (1995, particularly pp. 139–42 and 302), the cello appears to have been the favoured instrument for amateur players among the aristocracy and consequently enjoyed a much higher status than the violin. In fact, Potter refers to it being 'highly cultivated in this country' and even expresses a preference for 'the tone produced by the performers in this country' ('Companion to the orchestra ... No.III', *MW*, 4 (1837), 180). The cello's higher status is also reflected in the pedagogical material published for it (see Chapter 3). See also Kassler (1979), 1107.

[20] See Kassler (1979), 1107, Duckles (1981), 483 and the discussion below.

[21] See Kassler (1979), 979.

[22] See Morgan (1984), 395.

during the period, music was significant and valuable only in so far as it complemented or assisted with something else in line with what the male agenda considered suitable. Men were able to exercise a great deal of control over an activity that was essentially practical, domestic and focused on the individual and they continued to limit the possibilities for emancipation offered by music.

With their intellectual freedom limited, women were directed towards the lower-status, 'mechanical' aspects of the art rather than encouraged to undertake theoretical study.[23] Also the time devoted to it was to be in proportion to its value to the individual. The daughter therefore, although able to display greater dedication than the son, was not to be seen to get carried away with her musical studies and display great dexterity,[24] let alone aspire to any public role beyond perhaps entertaining family and guests.[25] Given the strong moral dimension, it was the industry and application that were sought rather than 'superior talents'.[26]

This was not a recipe for success, with the disinterested and untalented forced to endure the instillation of genteel behaviour and discipline that music was seen to provide, while those with real ability and ambition had their aspirations effectively capped by an unavoidable if slowly rising glass ceiling.[27] The potential for female musicians to

---

[23] See Kassler (1979), 1108. Written material intended for the keyboard instruction of young ladies was extremely popular during the nineteenth century although many could also double as 'theory' primers for adults (for example, ibid., 1018). It was, however, unnecessary for women to 'enter into the Minutiae of the Science', as they only needed to know enough musical 'grammar' in order to perform (ibid., 772, 774, 791 and 1080). Sources from the late eighteenth and nineteenth centuries set out to provide this. The women who undertook the intellectual appreciation demanded by Ella's male-led Musical Union were notable exceptions.

[24] Conduct books for the ladies of the time promoted modesty and an avoidance of vanity or 'show' (see McCalman, ed. (1999), 463–4). Kassler (1979) discusses numerous examples which allow practical music its place in the education of the young lady while warning against over-indulgence and serious ambition.

[25] The option of taking on pupils or becoming a musically proficient governess in a private family or at a female boarding school was naturally not an option for the ladies of high (or perhaps even polite) society. The number of female music teachers, a crucial factor in the delivery of musical tuition, grew in line with levels of middle-class activity and demand, with the piano serving as a powerful symbol of consumerism and allied prosperity.

[26] Burgan (1989), 52. This is a particularly valuable article dealing with the important if strictly circumscribed nature of music in the lives of women during the period. 'Even when women's musicality is presented as an avenue for her autonomy in society, its depiction is strained and unconvincing' (ibid., 60).

[27] There is a huge amount of evidence for the restriction of musical ambition among ladies. Numerous contemporary writers, male and female, consider art as an

significantly raise standards among amateurs, appreciated by many contemporary writers on music, was therefore undermined, and the shackles of social convention were seldom strained let alone broken until the First World War.[28] Nevertheless with the huge popularity of choral societies and instruments such as the violin, there was increasing scope for 'respectable' amateur and semi-professional practice.

The number of women requiring musical tuition continued to rise in line with the expanding and socially ambitious middle classes (reaching saturation point by the end of the century), but the increasing demand for largely limited and often superficial musical skills did little to raise standards and the status of the private or school-based music teacher.[29] In order to avoid any risk of sexual impropriety fathers were keen to hire elderly teachers often beyond their best or required the student to rely on often inadequate written teaching material.[30] When some musical proficiency (often modest, sometimes much more) had been acquired by whatever means, and it had served its purpose with the lady attracting a husband, then it became largely surplus to requirements, at least as far as the man was concerned.[31] However it could be used within the married home in order to reinforce the political aspects of domesticity and therefore the conventional roles of the sexes in society. The most popular repertoire of the time, such as the 'accompanied' sonata, gave the female, seated keyboardist the bulk of the musical material while allowing the male violinist or flautist to stand and appear 'soloistic' with his treble line at the same time as having little to play of consequence.[32]

The presence of practical musical tuition in schools and the home and opportunities to practice and perform in private did however promote

---

embellishment to life which must take on a very minor role following marriage lest it become a corrupting force (see Kassler (1979), 783, 842, 910 and 1167). Those with a more favourable view of the art, such as Bacon and Hogarth, lamented how the musical potential of young ladies was often neglected (ibid., 43–4 and 519).

[28] See Ehrlich (1985), 188.

[29] Some forward-thinking individuals, including Charles Dibdin, proposed solutions to the problems posed by teaching large numbers of students in a short space of time, especially in ladies' boarding schools (see Kassler (1979), 276–9, 282–3 and 1018). Unusually, Sarah Spence, a governess, issued her own piano and thorough-bass tutor (c.1810) (Kassler (1979), 961).

[30] Improvements to the quality of teaching material in response to inadequate or non-existent practical tuition are discussed in following chapters.

[31] It was very rare for women of a certain class to marry male musicians.

[32] Arthur Devis's painting *Gentleman and lady at a harpsichord* (1749) (reproduced in Leppert (1988), 182) captures perfectly this assignment of roles, with music as a visual metaphor for 'marital fidelity and domestic bliss' (ibid., 183). The husband, standing, hands his wife, seated at the harpsichord, the music with which she is to 'accompany' him on the violin.

far greater proficiency among female amateur musicians than their male counterparts. The sheer number of dedicated articles and journals intended for girls and young women demonstrates the extent and level of the demand.[33] Although the efforts of Thring at Uppingham and other pioneering initiatives were significant steps forward in terms of both appreciation and vocal and instrumental practice among middle-class boys, it is worth noting that 'the academically slanted, examination haunted grammar schools for boys generally failed to admit music teaching' until the Butler Education Act of 1944.[34]

The conventions governing the instruments acceptable for the different sexes, along with patterns of consumption and provision in general, remained to a large extent in place throughout the period, at least until the end of the century and the emergence (with male approval) of female bowed string players and (to a much lesser extent) wind players. Men of a certain class continued to pick up the violin, cello and flute and only later sat at the keyboard, while the lower-middle- and working-class male thrived on the new and improved designs for wind and brass instruments in particular and the exacting demands of both military and civilian bands as part of a physically strenuous and increasingly structured way of life. A 'shackle' to avoid therefore became 'the Heavenly science'.[35] There was far greater incentive to encourage the continuation of musical study into adolescence and adulthood in these areas, providing scope for steady and sustained progress and the prospect of self-improvement and perhaps even financial reward. In a low-status area such as practical music the potential returns naturally increased as opportunity descended and there was therefore a much greater inclination to participate rather than merely to consume and be seen to appreciate from a safe distance. We should remember that although music rose in status as an area worthy of consideration with beneficial effects, even among some well-to-do men,[36] musicians were (and still are in many ways) far from being seen on a par with other professionals. It was unfortunate for the progress of British music that the most powerful in society, wealthy men, were for a significant period the most reluctant to engage in the performance of music and view it as intrinsically valuable. Its long-standing associations with sensuality, sentimentality and effeminacy ruled it out for many. It was for lower-status groups to realize, in line with the extent of the opportunities on offer, its potential as a means of transcending environment and consequently raise standards.

---

[33] See Gillett (2000a), vii (n. 2).
[34] Rainbow (1989a), 41.
[35] Mackerness (1964), 130.
[36] This transformation is also evident in Victorian fiction (see Burgan (1989), 66).

Theory or Practice; Science or Art?

Expanding on a point raised in the previous section, the division between 'practical' and 'theoretical' music was an important consideration in contemporary commentary, particularly that concerned with the appropriateness of different forms of music education for each sex. This is a necessarily brief treatment of a complex issue,[37] but, essentially, the preservation of the traditional and relatively high status of music as a science allowed male amateurs to justify their own musical interests while demeaning those of their female counterparts. The proficiency of instrumental performance among amateurs was an inevitable victim of this situation as the relatively serious practical and instrumental preoccupations of the seventeenth-century amateur and the correspondingly pioneering texts (such as those famous examples issued by Morley and Playford) were overshadowed by more purely 'intellectual' concerns during an increasingly socially mobile and mercantile age. In short the intellectualization of music was detrimental to the cause of instrumental performance, which could give rise to dangerous 'irrational passions'.[38]

Given that the provision of education in general during the period was very much based on the individual's station in life, music was, as we have seen, learnt by men and taught to women with different priorities in mind. The practical, 'mechanical'[39] aspects of the art usefully occupied the time of ladies who could then 'cash in' these skills when seeking a husband, whereas the gentleman, perceiving such skills to be below them and of little material worth, sought a self-consciously erudite, 'scientific' approach from an early age. It is therefore possible to perceive a change of emphasis in pedagogical and other sources from theoretical to practical in keeping with a rise in consumption and

---

[37] Kassler (1979), including introduction, is an invaluable and authoritative source on many aspects of this subject and individual texts and writers. See also Kassler, 'The science of music to 1830' in *idem* (2001), 165–200, for excellent background to the position of music in various intellectual traditions. Other useful studies include Herissone (2000); Gouk (1999) on seventeenth-century English sources; and Zon (2000), in particular chapter 4, 'Musicology through science', 115–78, and his exploration of scientific metaphor in nineteenth-century music history. The need for a mutual understanding and balance between theory ('text') and practice ('act'), and therefore theorist and practitioner, in music remains an important issue and is a central theme in Taruskin's illuminating writings (1995). They are after all sister pursuits rather than rival gods.

[38] Brewer (1997), 532.

[39] 'Mechanical' was often used as a pejorative term with respect to music, particularly with reference to the manual performing skills of artisans and women, in contrast to the work of the liberal intellectual, and those musicians or styles which placed dexterity above 'science' or 'art'.

participation, particularly among the middle and lower classes, and the proliferation of 'romanticism' as a means of facilitating human expression.[40] There was an increasing awareness of and tension between the science/theory and art/practice divide during our period, which, in keeping with broader trends in early modern aesthetics and music criticism, witnessed the transition from a mathematical to an inspirational basis for music. This is perhaps most readily apparent when comparing the scientific, intellectual emphasis of Hawkins with Burney's concern for the subjective appraisal of 'contemporary musical taste'[41] and his subsequent influence on Busby and Hogarth.

The definitions of 'theory' and 'practice' must be considered carefully as each divides further into its constituent parts. The theoretical study of music includes 'speculative', mathematical and geometrical elements (drawing on Pythagorean number theory, the monochord and music's place in the *quadrivium* of the liberal arts as well as 'acoustical fact'),[42] whereas practical, 'applied' aspects incorporate the rudiments of harmony and composition as well as performance. As such, *musica practica* or practical music theory itself has a significant and long-standing theoretical bias relating to musical grammar and rhetoric with the study of performance (and with it instrumental technique) forming just a small and evidently inferior sub-set. A corresponding hierarchy was applied to contemporary musical literature, from theoretical and historical works down to instrumental tutors. We only have to think of the most enduring British tomes and writers from the period to see this hierarchy at work.

Gentlemen of the eighteenth and early nineteenth centuries, such as Chesterfield, could buy in to the pioneering scientific spirit of the times and develop their musical interests through the study of harmony and counterpoint, often with a leaning towards the conservative, 'ancient' style and with only limited reference to existing 'real' repertoire.[43] The art of composition and with it the composer therefore had widely recognized academic and 'scientific' credentials, as exemplified by the achievements of amateur enthusiasts such as John Marsh and the requirements of Oxbridge doctorates in music at the time. An anxiety concerning music's intellectual status is evident through much of the later university provision and its concentration on speculative and theoretical

---

[40] Rousseau's focus on 'the secret but powerful unison between music and the passions' was gradually accepted in Britain (see Kassler (1979), 910).

[41] Fiske and Johnstone, eds (1990), 414, part of a valuable survey of contemporary music literature.

[42] Ibid., 411.

[43] Ibid., 412–13; and McCalman, ed. (1999), 309.

elements.[44] Significantly the Gresham Professorship, despite its poor reputation and ineffectiveness, allowed the more respectable 'scientific' face of music to stand alongside divinity, astronomy and geometry.

Naturally the art of performance, with its human and subjective bias, and the performer himself were considered of a much lower status in comparison. Those high-status amateurs who did have a serious interest in practical music and mixed in musical circles often had their status assured through other professional accomplishments, such as Thomas Gainsborough and those clergymen who encouraged music-making within their communities. British pedagogical sources, inevitably always a step behind the continental examples they later assimilated, turned to music theory of various types during an era when others (especially respected German musicians/writers) had moved on to a detailed coverage of expressive, professional or advanced amateur performance and related instrumental issues. In addition to numerous dedicated theoretical writings by mainly amateur musicians[45] and a variety of devices and inventions, this is also evident in those numerous British elementary instrumental tutors which, reflecting their target audience (generally wealthy gentlemen) and the writers'/teachers' survival instincts, have scant regard for the fundamentals of technique but cover subjects such as temperament in intricate detail. Many commentators have looked at the large number of eighteenth-century sources concerned with instrumental instruction and concluded that the market was buoyant and healthy. Buoyant certainly, but the nature of many of these instrumental methods from the second decade to the end of the eighteenth century reveals demand and levels of amateur proficiency to have been largely stagnant (see Chapter 2). It is no coincidence that 'scientific' and 'valuable' often appear together in reviews,[46] particularly with reference to what is of 'use' to the gentleman scholar. An ambitious if largely self-taught student such as the young William Crotch struggled to find sufficient grounding in the 'gamut' and 'fingerboard' as a result of the attitudes of his 'learned mentors'.[47] In contrast to continental views of and sources dealing with instrumental performance, serious musical activity per se was not seen as a complement to 'intellectual progress'.[48]

---

[44] See Rainbow (1981), 33.

[45] See Kassler (1979), including 'index of genres and subjects', 1314–39, which illustrates the paucity, in terms of both volume and detail, of material concerned specifically with music performance and professional issues relative to theoretical, mathematical and speculative subjects. Pickering (1990), 365ff., also reflects the relative comprehensiveness of theoretical works.

[46] See for example Kassler (1979), 933.

[47] Ehrlich (1985), 36.

[48] Mackerness (1964), 151.

The relatively high status of the theory of harmony, counterpoint and composition in general, the 'manly' musical concerns dependent on logic and scientific justification, continued through the crucial transitional period of the late eighteenth and early nineteenth centuries, alongside the burgeoning and irresistible market for lower-status practical music-making. It is therefore easy to see how a discipline such as thorough-bass could become such a prime concern during this transitional process, uniting the theoretical (masculine) and performance (feminine) elements within the practical 'science' and offering a compromise between science and art, codified principles and inspiration and genius. Numerous British pedagogical texts from the period focus on the subject, both relatively advanced and comprehensive and less ambitious examples (see Chronology).[49] The combination of theory and practice is often stressed in the titles of such works.[50] As a result thorough-bass, as an only partly performance-based skill, receives relatively serious treatment and paves the way for the more comprehensive, practically biased instrumental (and particularly keyboard) tutors of the nineteenth century. Its unification of theory and practice (if only as a necessary adjunct to the 'advanced' study of composition and criticism)[51] was therefore a positive trend in terms of standards. The door was open for a dramatic shift in the balance between the two elements, and therefore between composers and performers, within and between pedagogical works.[52]

This period, with changes in the dynamics of the target audience and the concerns of teachers and writers, witnessed an irresistible shift in emphasis from theory to practice and therefore from passive appreciation to active participation and self-expression. The new consumers, particularly middle-class women, children and the lower classes, were far less preoccupied with the need for erudite concerns, theory and terminology, to elevate mere 'mechanical' skill. Issues of literacy and access in general often precluded such concerns and for them performance skills had intrinsic merit and worth. Many wealthy and influential gentlemen were happy with this situation as they saw these groups as incapable of the serious scholarly, rational application demanded of their own 'advanced' amateur interests.[53] Studies of the

---

[49] Rameau's theories in particular influenced British thorough-bass treatises and made the subject more accessible through a 'simplification' of harmonic theory (see Fiske and Johnstone, eds (1990), 411–12).

[50] For example Lillycrop (Chron., 1826).

[51] Crotch's thorough-bass tutor (Chron., 1812 and 1826), for example, was a means of learning composition, even if the pupil was unable to perform the result (Kassler (1979), 236).

[52] See Kassler (1979), 746, 882 and 884.

[53] See Kassler (2001), 195–6.

physics and physiology of sound still occupied the time of many gentlemen and there was a great penchant for the emulation of scientific methods and analogies in cultural fields.

The increase in the number of practising instrumentalists was a positive step, but the preservation of the practical/theoretical gender and class divide in terms of attitudes and teaching material was set to produce numerous amateur performers without the required theoretical knowledge to progress, thereby further perpetuating the division. Some serious writers on music in Britain, such as Kollmann, Hodges and Worgan, identified a 'trivialization' of music through the eighteenth and early nineteenth centuries, brought about by a neglect and dilution of serious theoretical enquiry and teaching in favour of trivial practice and amusement. The improved 'practical' native treatises and translations of the period were seen as a way of reversing this decline. They sought (like their continental models) to effectively combine and balance 'science' with 'art'; the requisite technical dexterity and theoretical knowledge with suitably 'tasteful' expression; 'ancient' with 'modern'; and student with teacher, in order to form a rounded, practical musician, especially for the benefit of young performers.[54] It was now also the time for well-educated (and therefore predominantly foreign) professional musicians, such as the prolific Bemetzrieder[55] and keyboard pioneer Logier, to produce these works in much greater numbers and cater for expanding markets (see Chapter 2).

It was judged far easier (but nonetheless challenging) among musical

---

[54] See Kassler (1979), 664-5 and 878. Even so it is worth noting that most instrumental sources throughout our period, in contrast to modern 'sound before symbol' theory (see Pitts (2000), 5), first present notation and other rudiments (in relative detail) in order to allow the subsequent presentation of practical concepts. The vast majority of contemporary writers of instrumental works display little concern for developing an aural or even more general musical awareness before the instrument is picked up. This is consistent with the desire of many native writers to satisfy the demand for quick (and largely superficial) results in return for minimum effort. This is, however, less the case with the more substantial and detailed continental works which became increasingly prevalent in translation and influenced later, more serious native works (see following chapter). Nevertheless most instrumental teaching methods (then and now) tend to separate theoretical and performance elements. The limitations of the written form need to be complemented by effective practical instruction if high standards are to be achieved, regardless of the period. The most honest and effective written works stress this fact and urge the consumer to seek such guidance. Significantly, in light of their proven effectiveness and subsequent modern methods, the approaches of sight-singing pioneers Sarah Glover and John Curwen were based, like speech, on 'deducing theory from practice, rather than practice from theory'. Teaching methods were therefore designed to complement those teaching and being taught and the desired practical outcome (see Rainbow (1989a), 29–30).

[55] See Kassler (1979), 67–84.

reformers and perhaps offered potentially greater returns to promote serious music education among some men than attempt to justify an explicitly intellectual angle in the education of large numbers of existing female amateurs. Significantly many nineteenth-century instrumental tutors continue to allude to 'scientific' principles in their titles although the content shifts in favour of music as a practical, performance-based discipline. The constitutions of both the Musical Institute of London (from 1851 to 1853) and its successor the (Royal) Musical Association (from 1874) made a virtue of uniting artistic and scientific concerns while maintaining the distinction. Although not the norm in nineteenth-century secondary education, the combination of music's imaginative and intellectual facets also appealed to pioneers such as Edward Thring at Uppingham, who sought to promote participation as well as appreciation.[56] There is a growing tendency in much nineteenth-century music literature for theoretical concerns to be presented as the means to a practical end, involving actual compositions (rather than abstract examples) that were to be performed and/or listened to. Writers such as Grove, Prout and Tovey are representative of this important popularizing trend. In a further unification of disciplines late nineteenth- and early twentieth-century instrumental treatises often introduce a physiological element into the theoretical and practical equation.

The traditional theoretical/scientific and practical/artistic divide between the music education of men and women and different classes and the consequent unhelpful disparity in their status were to remain important factors so long as the different social roles and characteristics of the sexes and classes continued to be enforced.[57] Unsurprisingly, when it came to professional musicians, budding (predominantly male) composers enjoyed a higher status and greater support than performers (such as from the Society of British Musicians) and tended to receive more effective, dedicated instruction from institutions such as the RAM. An academic bias allowed music some hard-won respectability. Influential figures in musical circles, from Burney to Smart to Grove, sought and found social and intellectual status outside practical music-making. Instrumentalists, amateur and professional, remained the poor relations in terms of status and education despite the reassessment of

---

[56] See Rainbow (1989a), 34.

[57] Some progressive learning theorists of the twentieth century identified effective education with 'whole-person learning': that which seeks to combine the logical, left-brain, 'male' (commonly required in schools and colleges) and intuitive, right-brain, 'female' processes. The gender traits of theory and practice naturally apply far beyond musical disciplines (see C. Rogers, *Freedom to learn for the 80s* (Columbus, Oh., 1983), 20).

their 'usefulness' in social and cultural terms. For many, accomplishments as a performer were of little worth in themselves. Beyond the ambitious lower classes, the military and some church musicians, all of whom sought musical training with a definite purpose in a utilitarian environment, innovation and experimentation were tempered in the practical (particularly instrumental) sphere. Meanwhile 'academic' and erudite compositional styles continued to prosper in the church and concert hall.[58] Hogarth (1830), remarkably perceptive even with the benefit of hindsight, made the link between a preoccupation with 'acoustics and antiquities' and a dearth of 'great' musicians.[59]

Vocal and Instrumental

The hierarchy of musical activity established in the eighteenth century also raises a disparity within the practical sphere. In general singing appears to have been practised (rather than just appreciated) among a much wider cross-section of society and enjoyed higher standards and reputation than instrumental performance, at least until the end of the nineteenth century. There are of course practical reasons why this should be so, but we should also consider a range of social and musical factors.[60]

There is a wealth of evidence to suggest the high status and respectability afforded professional singers (and singing teachers) relative to the majority of their instrumental colleagues, even if the music profession as a whole was held in some disrepute. Italian singers in particular were revered and rewarded accordingly.[61] Naturally they benefited from the popular perception of the singer themselves being the 'instrument', the voice 'formed and tuned by God himself',[62] without the type of impure, human, mechanical 'enhancement' required by any instrumentalist. Beautiful voices were associated with appealing, refined artists and, combined with its inherent convenience and potential for religious and moral texts and associations within both sacred and recreational contexts, the vocal art was practised with enthusiasm

---

[58] It is significant that the Union of Graduates in Music, established with the aim of protecting the value of university degrees in the face of false qualifications, was made up of 'men of the organ-loft and classroom, not the concert-hall, and still less the theatre' (Ehrlich (1985), 136 and 140).

[59] Kassler (1979), 523.

[60] Useful summaries of various aspects of the vocal field during the period can be found in the writings of Rainbow, Scott, and Russell (1997). Later sections of the present chapter look at popular vocal practice in more detail.

[61] See Ehrlich (1985) and Towse (1993).

[62] See Kassler (1979), 1053.

among both genders and all classes. Its capability to combine the separate effects of words and music in a form of expression greater than the sum of its parts received wide recognition and approval. Singers and singing were able to connect with the populace in a way that much abstract, consciously elitist instrumental music could or would not.

Song was enjoyed in public and in private (or in contexts somewhere between the two), with the eighteenth-century gentleman demonstrating a great fondness for the conviviality of the glee and catch clubs, which often had distinguished members in musical and other fields, and domestic part-song singing in general. A certain pride was taken in the success of such group music-making and pedagogical sources reveal a more serious interest on the part of amateur (particularly male) vocalists than their instrumental equivalents. The long-standing analogies of the 'instrument-sensuous' and the 'vocal-intellectual', with the instrumental therefore 'the more inherently musical of the two elements', may, in keeping with the preceding discussion, have contributed to this disparity.[63]

A large number of texts concerned with vocal practice were published during the period.[64] Moreover many of these, from Galliard's translation of Tosi (1742) onwards, were more substantial and ambitious than contemporaneous instrumental examples. These offered insights which enabled native amateurs to attempt to emulate the Italian *bel canto* style they heard in public, rather than just providing a few tunes and basic rudiments for the purpose of casual, mainly private amusement. In addition to Tosi's important (if retrospective) work, nearly a decade prior to Geminiani's violin treatise and a long time before the more advanced works for keyboard instruments and translations of mainstream instrumental texts, we have important examples published in Britain by such well-known and respected names as Billington, Corri, Nathan and García (see Bibliography), aside from seminal sight-singing texts and examples by women.

As the nineteenth century witnessed burgeoning musical activity of all types, vocal practice led the way in many contexts as a result of its relative accessibility and potential for 'improving' associations as well as recognized physical benefits. Practitioners such as the upper-class female amateur vocalist, more 'songbird' than 'siren' opera singer, were seen to possess a 'wholly beneficent influence'.[65] However, as discussed above, music and morality were most easily reconciled within the vocal

---

[63] See Zon (2000), 196, citing J. Rowbotham, *A history of music* (London, 1885).

[64] Toft (2000: ix) cites 101 tutors promoting the technique of expressive singing in England between 1780 and 1830.

[65] Gillett (2000a), 36–7.

traditions of the church and the lower orders, where settings of texts that promoted religious fervour and temperance found their natural home. Consequently vocal training provided the opportunity to increase the provision of music in the elementary curriculum. Many members of the clergy were also active amateur musicians and/or writers, such as William Hughes (d. 1798) and William Dechair Tattersall (?1751–1829), who promoted the use of vocal music within the church and the home 'to excite a laudable Zeal throughout the lower Orders'.[66] Nonconformists warned against the 'degeneration' of sacred music into 'sensual delight' as opposed to its intended function of assisting 'the soul in the worship of God';[67] but vocal music had far less to fear in this respect than instrumental practice, with its hedonistic, 'worldly' connotations derived from its prominent theatre, pleasure garden and dancing contexts. The place of 'impure' instrumental music within the church was slow to gain universal acceptance, although mechanical improvements to the organ did aid its use following the demise of the amateur church bands.[68]

The explicitly moral tone of the tonic sol-fa movement, intended in part to aid the devotional fervour and standard of congregational choral worship, extended to both sexes and ensured its presence in lower-class elementary and adult education. It is a prime example of music acquiring moral and broadly beneficial associations and therefore achieving widespread acceptance. The position of vocal music and vocal training was in fact enhanced as the century progressed and new respectable avenues of activity, including the early music revival, emerged.

Choron's Parisian model (1817–30), providing singing classes for workers and their children, was developed by James Kay (later Sir James Kay-Shuttleworth), who also focused on popular song with 'improving' texts as a positive force within society. Such rare government-sponsored support, with a moral agenda based on the merit of song, was the force behind Hullah's classes based on Wilhem's system, which struck a chord and cultivated high standards of vocal accomplishment at an early stage among 'workhouse boys'.[69] From then on, as vigorous public demand and singing 'mania' took hold, involving tens of thousands of pupils, other protagonists and (superior) methods came to the fore, eager to promote singing's positive effects on body, mind and soul. The proliferation of Mechanics' Institutes also contributed to the spread of singing classes.

---

[66] N. Temperley, 'Tattersall, William Dechair' in *New Grove 7*, vol.25, 121.
[67] Scholes (1934), 350.
[68] Herbert (2000a), 146.
[69] Rainbow (1989a), 22.

Significantly, sight-singing pioneers such as Glover and Curwen had close personal ties with the church, and religious institutions were intrinsic to the spread of vocal proficiency and the choral movement. This was able to expand on its firm manufacturing foundation, with, like the band movement, demand, opportunities and appropriate training in place. Classes and genders mixed in the amateur choruses, often performing to great acclaim with a professional orchestra. Again, like the bands, there was a strong competition element focused on standards rather than remuneration, even if competing choirs tended to have a lower-status clientele.[70] Contemporary evangelical and puritanical thought, heightened by declining religious observance and the continued rise of 'secular' instrumental performance, objected to the concept of 'oratorios for amusement' until the late nineteenth century.[71] The 'musical simplicity' and 'generally high moral tone' of the unaccompanied choral part-song thrived in this environment.[72]

There was also, beyond convivial, extra-curricular pastimes involving instrumental music, directed and purposeful choral activity at university and in the (particularly newer) public schools for girls and boys, often nurtured by the organist professor/music master.[73] Although generally not the formal class teaching of the lower-class elementary level, this tuition helped to create the lasting traditions of the school concert, chapel music (ancient public schools continued to employ a professional choir), the school song and house-singing.

The vocal art retained its superior status over largely abstract instrumental music and continued to flourish throughout society, in church, school, the concert hall, music hall, tavern and home, where it often had a 'useful' and perhaps even philanthropic role to play. Far more easily reconciled with puritanical utilitarian ideals in most contexts, song had the power to transcend 'the limitations of an English culture mired in commercialism and caste'.[74] Meanwhile instrumental tuition, devoid of any significant state assistance and wider public approbation, had to look after itself and remain on the fringes, within schools and elsewhere, particularly among wealthy male students. It had to wait for the various popular movements of the nineteenth century and the introduction of instrumental classes into state schools during the early twentieth century to come within the grasp of the lower orders (and then predominantly men) in a significant way.

---

[70] Russell (1997), 255.
[71] See Scholes (1934), 353.
[72] Caldwell (1999), 236.
[73] See Rainbow (1981), 31 and 42.
[74] Burgan (1989), 66.

Instrumental tuition and performance were better suited to the age and relative wealth of boys and girls in secondary education than singing when music instruction was made available; but vocal practice had proved its suitability in elementary schools and had long demonstrated the power to bring classes, genders and ages together in a variety of public contexts across the country.[75] Instrumental practice on the other hand had the tendency to be divisive or represent division. In addition the expressive art of singing has remained a reliable foundation and arbiter of 'taste' with respect to many general musical principles and expressive instrumental techniques since the first advanced instrumental tutors of the eighteenth century.[76] It now seems natural that the pupils who received formal vocal and aural training during their elementary education before they potentially took up an instrument (generally lower-class young men at this time) should achieve the most in musical terms. The importance of sound ear-training at an early stage for all young musicians including would-be instrumentalists only came to be realized fully during the twentieth century, through the methods of Kodály and Orff, for example.

In a continuation of earlier trends and attitudes, the primary musical beneficiary of developments in mass education during the nineteenth century was the vocal art. As traditionally the more readily acceptable face of practical music-making in Britain, it was far more easily reconciled with the age's moral, social and utilitarian priorities. Instrumental music rose from a far more lowly position by association and in some relatively isolated (albeit influential) areas as new markets and opportunities arose. The following century saw a greater integration of vocal and instrumental tuition in all schools, replacing the elementary/secondary and corresponding class divide, and consequently a rise in standards. In modern times the playing of instruments has overtaken singing in terms of its prominence within schools and the publication of pedagogical and critical texts.

Conservatism and Innovation

During our period the concept of 'good taste' impacted significantly on both the critical evaluation of repertoire and performance traditions.[77]

---

[75] See Rainbow (1989a), 38. College- or university-trained specialist music teachers in independent secondary schools (not grammar schools for boys at this time) were often organists and therefore instrumentalists themselves.

[76] See 'The Vocal Model' in Chapter 2, which examines the influence of vocal delivery on instrumental performance.

[77] See the 'Good Taste' section of the following chapter for more detailed reference to specific styles and performance models.

Naturally it was closely connected with issues of class, gender and morality. The influence of the wealthy gentleman amateur and his predilection for high-status theoretical enquiry and 'academic' styles discussed above equated 'good taste' with conservatism in many cases. The more 'human', expressive, inspirational and openly virtuosic styles, often associated with rapidly developing instrumental performance and technique, were therefore discredited by many of society's most powerful consumers and patrons. The coexistence of such contrasting styles during this transitional process in the melting-pot of British culture naturally resulted in a level of tension and ambivalence. This was especially the case when many of the most influential voices looked to the past while new repertoire, instruments and traditions were struggling to find a footing in the hub of commercial activity. The focus on consumption rather than provision in high-status areas created complacency and stagnation in place of any progressive impetus.

Patterns of consumption that took shape during the eighteenth century allied intellectual superiority and morality with an essentially conservative, 'tasteful' approach to performance. This was particularly the case with respect to instrumental music and its greater potential for harmful, secular associations. The 'safety' of Corelli, Geminiani and Handel, for example, allowed them and other representatives of the 'ancient' style to become yardsticks of taste and decorum, with a recognized intellectual pedigree, that formed points of reference for a prolonged period. Many pedagogical sources published in Britain (Geminiani's violin treatise among them) have a tendency to bring together old and new, or 'ancient' and 'modern' stylistic elements. Conflicting principles are not easily reconciled within a written work frozen in time, whether serious or trivial, and consequently it is seldom a marriage made in heaven. Examples from eighteenth-century works often appear in nineteenth-century texts and some progressive authors, such as Marsh and Barthélemon, make a point of stressing the need to study and perform both ancient and modern styles in order to form a rounded musician.[78]

The 'ancient versus modern' debate in eighteenth-century English music, represented by Hawkins and Burney respectively, was an

---

[78] Of particular interest is Marsh's *A comparison between the ancient and modern styles of music, in which the merits and demerits of each are respectively pointed out*, anonymously printed in the supplement to *The Monthly Magazine*, 2 (London, 1796), 981, which is reprinted in Cudworth (1955). See Young (1994) for further comment on Marsh. Also an important issue in music education, Barthélemon expresses similar sentiments in his treatise (see Chron., 1790: i–ii). Jousse's drawing together of both 'ancient' and 'modern' elements in his treatises (Chron., 1805 and 1811) is discussed in following chapters.

important factor in the existence of diverse and fluctuating musical styles.[79] The 'ancient' style and its relative simplicity came to represent the moral and intellectual, while the complexity of the 'modern' epitomized the trivial and corrupt.[80] In this environment there was little scope for progress through experimentation among native artists and 'sanctioned' foreign musicians. Novelty was more likely to result in failure than success. Even a highly respected composer of the 'ancient' school such as Geminiani could experience failure if his works (such as his Opus 7 concertos) were deemed too experimental, and when he reworked his compositions it was often to simplify them to make them more playable among amateurs. Generally he advocated the doctrine of 'good taste', which made indelible virtues of beauty and refinement.

Many figures rose to prominence at least partly through their allegiance to the 'traditional', including Henry Smart's valued insights into performing conventions for Handel arias (passed on to singers such as Henriette Sontag and Jenny Lind), and his son Sir George Smart's avoidance of the organ pedals even when they were commonly employed. Crotch was also heavily influenced by and influential in promoting (though not exclusively) earlier styles and writings (particularly those of Charles Avison). Musicians eager to infiltrate high society naturally had to comply with their conventions, which often involved a strong allegiance to older styles of music.

Music that excited the emotions and captured the imagination of the populace was also much in evidence. There was no shortage of novelties arriving in Britain from abroad in search of fame and fortune. The new virtuosic style, represented by figures such as Vivaldi, Boccherini, Haydn and Pleyel, was popular among English audiences, but it was viewed by some as frivolous and contrary to the seriousness exemplified by Corelli's works. Writers such as North disapproved of attempts to dazzle the listener, and preferred to cite Corelli as the ideal model.[81] His works continued to occupy a lofty aesthetic position long after they had gone out of date stylistically, exemplifying 'good taste' while the commercial marketplace increasingly sought novelty and virtuosity. Even Burney, a staunch advocate of the new instrumental style, admitted the classic appeal of Corelli and the 'grace and elegance' of his compositions.[82] Significantly Hogarth states that 'if ever this divine music [of Corelli] is thrown aside and forgotten, it will be the

---

[79] See Irving (1999) for a detailed study of this issue.
[80] See Kassler (1979), 862, 1081 and 1108.
[81] See Weber (1992), 85–8.
[82] Burney (1776–89), vol.2, 443–4. See also Grant (1983), 206–10.

most unequivocal sign of the corruption of taste and the decay of music in England'.[83]

Throughout the period discussed here the upper classes and connoisseurs alike take pride in affirming their appreciation of refinement and subtlety in performance, often distancing themselves explicitly from excess and display for its own sake and returning to anachronistic styles and models. It is common to find English musical commentators judging musicians accordingly, as in their rejection of the antics of the violinist Lolli and their stern criticism of the desire 'to surprise the ear' rather 'than to please the judgement' and display 'execution' rather than 'expression'.[84] Blatant virtuosity is treated with suspicion and often amounts to 'charlatanry', whether paraded by foreign or native musicians. Accordingly the later, famously virtuosic feats of Paganini could achieve commercial and popular success while in receipt of severe critical disapproval.

This highlights the importance of the distinction between popular and critical taste and success, again a means by which the high-status consumer and compliant critic were able to apply a hierarchy to aspects of musical practice. These were, after all, judgements based on what this type of consumer felt comfortable with. University-educated amateurs destined for business or the professions were happy to continue performing and appreciating repertoire with which they identified, technically and musically (such as Corelli and Handel) rather than look to newer continental developments. The relatively elementary technical demands of these works therefore ensured their longevity as much as their role as icons of good taste. Also scholars of music often relied heavily on their expertise in the 'ancient' style in order to achieve their 'scholarly' status and university qualifications. The Exeter musician William Jackson wrote in 1791 that 'we are not certain that our present musical doctors and graduates are *quite up* to Haydn yet', although 'the public are so unanimous in applauding'.[85] In the vibrant cultural environment of Britain this division, allied to the high-status amateur/professional divide, further exacerbated the reluctance to embrace innovation. In such an environment the Concert of Ancient Music could remain an influential force on the side of conservatism up until 1848, 'insulated' from middle-class appetites and representing the power of the social elite to hold 'the cultural reins'.[86]

As we have seen, vocal music was superior to instrumental in its

---

83   Hogarth (1838), vol.1, 154.
84   J. Warton, 'Simplicity', *The World* (28 June 1753), 138–9.
85   Kassler (1979), 579.
86   McCalman, ed. (1999), 244–5.

ability to gain widespread acceptance. Works such as Handel's *Messiah* and Mendelssohn's *Elijah* were able to succeed from a popular, critical and moral perspective and so achieve an iconic status up and down the country and among men and women of different classes. There was also a great impetus for the creation of new choral works which were then performed to a high standard. The majority of these works, however, reinforced conservative values and, as in Methodism, achieved their success largely through the alliance of musical sobriety and an explicitly moral context.

It is also important to recognize the penchant of the middle classes (excepting perhaps those who subscribed to the Philharmonic Society) to emulate the tastes of their social superiors. In turn we find the further 'filtering down' of conservative repertoire and attitudes to the music-making of the lower orders. This came primarily through the financial and organizational involvement and support offered by the middle classes and their music societies and educational reforms.[87] Such support bred innovation in terms of what was achieved for standards of instrumental performance in Britain rather than through repertoire. We should remember that music was encouraged among the lower classes and women, in choirs, bands and the home, as a 'calming' influence. The sharing of 'high art' repertoire (and with it a literate musical culture) among both the social elite and the masses, music widely considered as inherently 'good',[88] served to reinforce the status quo prior to the Edwardian era. This was to the detriment of vernacular and often more spontaneous traditions. By the same token 'inappropriate' repertoire was seen as subversive.

Conservative tendencies and the corresponding distrust of modernity were indicative of broader social concerns and fears. Repeated reference to past, tried and tested models and methods served as a weapon against moral corruption. This was, as discussed above, epitomized by excess, in musical terms 'surface dexterity'[89] or 'mechanical' display. In violin playing the refined classicism of Viotti and Spohr (and still Corelli) acted as a long-term (until the end of the nineteenth century) antidote to the perceived excesses of the new virtuosity (see Chapter 3). Spohr himself wrote that 'the established thing is regarded here as holy and untouchable', the English in general 'being the most wretched slaves to etiquette'.[90] This was a situation not harmful to Spohr's own fortunes if it did hold progress back in some areas.

---

[87] See Russell (1997), 185, 286, 290–91, 297, 302 and 304; and Herbert (2000), 58. Russell has much of interest to say on the reinforcement of conservative elements within English culture throughout the nineteenth century.

[88] Herbert (2000), 33.

[89] Burgan (1989), 63.

[90] Letter of 1820 to William Speyer, quoted in Carse (1948), 319.

Unsurprisingly considering its heritage, the repertoire promoted by the RAM among potential professionals was for a long time generally retrospective.[91] The canonization of musical classics at the heart of the culture and institutions such as the RAM, which allowed the nobility to remain as arbiters of taste and purveyors of opportunity, further consolidated and instilled traditional attitudes. Hence even though the names changed, the essential qualities and virtues of those promoted as consummate artists and suitable models for native musicians during the period remained largely intact.

Along with the 'chaperoned mediocrity' among the female bourgeoisie we find widespread 'chaperoned conservatism' among society at large. With one foot in the past Britain's most significant musical contributions came in the form of music histories and, later on, editions of early music. The foundation of the Sacred Harmonic Society in 1832 and 'historical' recitals[92] demonstrated and helped to engender a large audience for early music through performance as well as publication. Although, once again, this is something that the spread of opportunity and corresponding new markets helped to change. Increased access, resulting in a less status-conscious, appreciation-biased approach, allowed the possibility of sustained popular and commercial success in the face of stern critical disapproval. The popularity of new musical idioms among new, much less exclusive and increasingly musically literate audiences, was a positive step in terms of the acceptance of innovation. Lower-status groups, particularly the working classes, had greater freedom to embrace the new in some cases and use it to their advantage, such as the development of new instruments and technique, thereby further aiding access and ease of participation. The tentacles of conservatism, however, spread far and wide and novelty was always vulnerable to the wrath of the higher orders and puritanical thinking. It was one of a number of arguably negative attitudes that originated in eighteenth-century Britain and retained their potency into the nineteenth.

The Nineteenth Century

The preceding discussion highlights the musical legacy of the eighteenth century as one that gave rise to an overriding ambivalence in terms of the worth and role of music within British society. In essence the cultivation of an ambitious and innovative instrumental performance

---

[91] See Weber in Bashford and Langley, eds (2000), 314.
[92] Rowland (2001), 6.

tradition was a low-status concern compared to the 'scientific', conservative interests of well-to-do men or vocal performance, both of which owed a great debt to safe, past glories, as represented by Handel in particular. Serious instrumental practice was very much the poor relation fit only for the hired help. There was little opportunity or incentive for British musicians to forge ahead with new ideas and respond enthusiastically to hugely significant developments elsewhere.

When progress was made during the following century it came most noticeably via the new 'boom', high-volume areas of primarily amateur activity, where large numbers of practitioners could, to varying degrees, use music as a means of transcending their environment. As mentioned previously this activity, expanding rapidly from the 1830s onwards, was seen to benefit society in general and so received widespread support and provision of various kinds. Where acceptance of performance as a worthwhile pursuit was more equivocal this support and provision depended far more on the initiative of the individual, both provider and consumer. Instrumental practice more often than not fell into the second category. Proficiency beyond 'modest accomplishment' came as a welcome by-product of an overdue release of potential in both cases.

State Laissez-faire *and the Status Quo*

There is insufficient space here to provide an in-depth investigation into the relationship of the state to the provision of music education. Nevertheless some general comment is required in a study of this kind. The overriding impression is, in keeping with eighteenth-century precedents, that state involvement had little to do with music's inherent worth but was rather concerned with harnessing its wider social benefits in order to maintain the status quo and encourage compliance. This was to be done in return for minimal investment from the world's richest country. Consistent with 'elite' preoccupations and music's continued low status there is a distinct absence of sustained and systematic intervention and support until national interests are challenged at the end of the nineteenth century. Once again the professional's interests are of little concern.[93]

Regarding patterns of provision we see, as emphasized in Rainbow's writings, the spread of vocal practice among working-class children in elementary schools and adult singing classes prior to the expansion of instrumental provision in new, middle-class secondary and then elementary education. In each case (but particularly instrumental

---

[93] Ehrlich (1985), 69.

teaching) the involvement of the state is minimal compared with continental neighbours; but until the last few decades of the nineteenth century this was true not just of music but of education in general. The reluctance of the state to play its part and invest in education was highlighted by progressive thinkers such as William Wordsworth:

> O for the coming of that glorious time
> When, prizing knowledge as her noblest wealth
> And best protection, this imperial Realm,
> While she exacts allegiance, shall admit
> An obligation, on her part, to *teach*
> Them who are born to serve her and obey;
> Binding herself by statute to secure
> For all the children whom her soil maintains
> The rudiments of letters, and inform
> The mind with moral and religious truth,
> Both understood and practised, – so that none,
> However destitute, be left to droop
> By timely culture unsustained; or run
> Into a wild disorder; or be forced
> To drudge through a weary life without the help
> Of intellectual implements and tools;[94]

The state remained reluctant to intervene as the religious establishment and Dissenters of various kinds and their rival monitorial systems competed for children's souls.[95] The church was loath to concede to politicians on such a fundamental issue and Nonconformists favoured church- rather than state-led education lest the Church of England should dominate. Religion, the 'keystone' of education, was therefore in some ways 'the bar to its progress',[96] although it did succeed in giving music a moral and therefore an enhanced status in some contexts. The result was a 'diverse non-governmental patchwork of popular educational programmes', reaching about half of the country's children and providing an 'extremely narrow or haphazard' curriculum.[97] The rate of progress was still painfully slow as apathy steadily gave way to reluctant action. The year 1833 saw the first state grant for education, the appointment of the Committee of Council on Education (with James Kay as secretary) followed by the appointment of school inspectors in 1839; but the grant of £20,000 a year was in real terms a 'pittance'[98] and governmental reforms generally lacked conviction.

---

[94] W. Wordsworth, *The Excursion* (1814), bk. IX, 292–308.
[95] McCalman, ed. (1999), 168. More progressive inclinations were to be found in Scotland and Ireland than in England and Wales (see pp. 163 and 653).
[96] Trevelyan (1978), 455.
[97] McCalman, ed. (1999), 653.
[98] Trevelyan (1978), 455.

The expansion of the scope and accessibility of education as 'self-improvement' in England is a central feature of the age, to which the huge increase in printed material covering a whole range of subjects and the proliferation of public libraries contributed in no small way. Provision responded to both existing and potential demand from those sections of the urban working and middle classes determined to achieve intellectual, social and moral advancement. As discussed above, the reform of popular education in general brought music teaching (singing) back into the school curriculum. Its position and the amateur choral societies which thrived on it were entirely harmonious with the unmistakable moral and utilitarian agenda of middle-class educational reforms. Vocal music in particular was seen to foster desirable characteristics in the young of the lower orders.

However, scepticism and many deep-seated prejudices remained higher up the social ladder[99] and it might have been a very different story without the involvement of James Kay, who was willing to occupy the somewhat precarious ground in between the church and the state. With an awareness of continental precedents (including Pestalozzian theory) he subsequently promoted music as a useful tool in enforcing the priorities, and responding to the dangers, of the age. Nevertheless the 'obligation' to teach referred to by Wordsworth was not felt on the part of the state in the case of music until much later in the nineteenth century. Kay was in a position to offer moral support and governmental approval, but, as in the case of the singing classes for practising teachers at Exeter Hall, he did not necessarily have access to the required finances. Also the involvement of the state, inexperienced in such matters, could be a mixed blessing and counter-productive. It was not necessarily placed to have music's best interests at heart, as demonstrated by its long-term support for Hullah's flawed sight-singing system (based on Wilhem) in favour of Curwen's more sophisticated and appropriate method (indebted to Glover).[100] However, in an area of acknowledged importance as far as the nation's wider interests were concerned, such as military music, intervention was relatively swift and effective in the form of the government taking over the running of Kneller Hall in 1867, just ten years after it had opened.[101]

As the dominance of the church and associated tensions receded a little, the state's role in the provision of education finally increased. If not to

---

[99] See Woodward (1962), 474; and Briggs (1994), 336–8 and 521–3.
[100] Mackerness (1964), 156.
[101] Turner and Turner (1996), 32. It is worth comparing this with Ehrlich's statement that the 'Government's first serious attempt to accept responsibility for the training of civilian musicians came in 1944' (1985: 228).

everyone's liking, the Forster Education Act of 1870 made school attendance compulsory to the age of 12, providing 'Board' schools to fill the gaps left by the various voluntary institutions.[102] Curwen's superior tonic sol-fa soon came into its own in the new schools,[103] although enthusiasm for and knowledge of music and its instruction were certainly not universal among opinion-formers or Her Majesty's (largely public-school educated) inspectors for that matter.[104] As helpfully highlighted by Cox, music education in schools struggled to find its place in the curriculum even after Forster's 1870 Bill.[105] Forster himself, keen to identify with the connection between music and its new-found morality, sought to rectify the omission by tackling the thorny issue of inspection and implementing financial incentives. Schools were fined for not teaching vocal music from 1872 and, in an improved system, were rewarded for satisfactory teaching from 1874. The efforts of enlightened individuals and 'public pressure'[106] gave vocal music an official position in state elementary education.

John Hullah, himself a passionate advocate of the civilizing qualities of music within the working-class environment, was appointed the first Government Inspector of Music in Schools for the United Kingdom in 1872 (to 1881).[107] It is significant if unfortunate that he was appointed only on a year-by-year, part-time basis and was to focus his attention on the teacher training colleges rather the schools themselves.[108]

---

[102] The largely anti-democratic Prime Minister Lord Salisbury for one appears to have been disdainful of such efforts to educate the lower orders beyond their predetermined station and regretted advances made by education since Forster's Act. He saw little point in the education of the working classes extending beyond the 'three Rs' to include 'French, pianoforte playing and trigonometry'. Salisbury was also keen to defend the interests of the church, including Voluntary schools (see A. Roberts, *Salisbury: Victorian titan* (London, 1999), 818–19). It is interesting that special reference is made to the rise of piano playing as instruments became more affordable but no reservations are expressed concerning singing.

[103] Rainbow (1989a), 31–2. Its use continued into the early decades of the twentieth century.

[104] Mackerness (1964), 159; and Ehrlich (1985), 70. Albert, prince consort, was a notable exception but died before his love of and support for music and the arts could reach fruition and influence real change. It is also worth mentioning that professional musicians, as well as the upper classes, had misgivings about educating the lower orders and the ambitions this might encourage.

[105] Cox (1993), 19–21. Cox provides many useful insights into music's place in state education from this period into the twentieth century. See also Russell (1997), 51–3.

[106] Cox (1993), 23.

[107] Hullah identified (if failed to reconcile) the contrasting interests and needs of amateur and professional training in music, requiring inclusivity and exclusivity respectively (see Ehrlich (1985), 92–4). This was a particularly significant and difficult problem for cash-starved music colleges to grapple with (see Chapter 5).

[108] Ibid., 21.

Nevertheless Hullah's appointment was a significant symbol of improvement, and moves to establish a belief in the inherent worth of practical music-making among society at large and create a serious and coherent approach to music education in Britain had received a substantial if long-overdue boost. At long last some meaningful state support had arrived and an increasing number of people were seen to be taking pride in a knowledge rather than ignorance of music.

Private Enterprise and Philanthropic Zeal

The delivery of education primarily through a variety of voluntary elementary and public secondary schools prior to the 1870 Act illustrates the fact that a great onus was placed on the initiative and circumstances of the individual provider and consumer. If vocal practice enjoyed at least some support on a national level in Britain, innovation and impetus were still largely dependent on a few individual pioneers, such as Curwen: amateur musicians whose efforts began as 'pockets' of social work. Most of the advancements in instrumental practice and pedagogy made during the nineteenth century were necessarily individual and private initiatives, devoid of even this level of state sponsorship and support. In this context the individual amateur consumer remained particularly powerful, creating the market for practical instruction and written teaching material.

Many individuals responded to the demand for musical instruction and, motivated by self-interest, loftier musical or social aspirations, or both, attempted to fill the gaps. The result was a flourishing informal, largely auto-didactic educational infrastructure. This was particularly useful among the 'middling sort' who did not have access to the instruction offered at either end of the social spectrum as a matter of course. However, from a medium- to long-term perspective, as attested to by Fétis (1829), 'the freedom that left to individuals the power to promote their own pursuits was not favourable to the arts in England'.[109] In truth, a close to ideal balance between specialist input and state support was, at least in the case of music, much more likely to be found beyond Britain's shores. The absence of leadership by example and a coherent strategy for music education based on a belief in its inherent worth left the future of music at the mercy of fluctuating social, cultural and economic trends that were largely determined by those very neighbours and rivals.

In the professional sphere the inability of native musicians to form

---

[109] Kassler (1979), 351.

themselves into an effective and influential body until late in the nineteenth century hindered the formulation of standard guidelines for training methods and agreed levels of technical accomplishment. Given the continued lack of security through autonomy or monopoly control, the professional's interests were inevitably selfish and short-term. They were forced to comply with the amateur consumer/connoisseur's generally conservative agenda (even at the RAM), leaving little scope to lead taste and instigate reform. The consistency of styles and expressive priorities in the face of experimentation referred to above was one consequence of this situation, as was a series of failed attempts to establish an institution for the training of professional musicians (see Chapter 5). The individual therefore reigned supreme not just in the amateur sphere, as one might expect, but also in the area of professional training. The emphasis on the amateur's ability to pay continued in cash-starved specialist music institutions during the whole of the nineteenth century, and, remarkably, amateurs also had to be accommodated by the unions when such initiatives were eventually taken.[110]

If individuals earning their living in whole or in part from music had next to no influence in polite society as native instrumentalists, there was, in the marketplace outlined above, at least some potential for recognition and influence through the provision of musical instruction, particularly in the form of public lectures and the publication of written texts.[111] Names such as Bishop, Goodban, Hamilton, Kemp, Kollmann, Langey and Loder, who we will encounter again in subsequent chapters, were able to rise to prominence as writers, 'compilers' and translators of pedagogical texts for a variety of instruments. There were particular niches to be carved out in catering for ladies' instruments and through texts that complemented the expansion of practical instruction. Some, but by no means all, contributors were also trained music specialists and/or prominent performers. Those who were writers in a broader context naturally had less to fear from any threat of competition.

The power of the pen was often the musician's mightiest weapon and the sphere of influence of these individuals could be surprisingly wide, even before the amateur Grove's famous dictionary. N. B. Challoner's keyboard tutor (1st edn, c.1808) had sold nearly nine thousand copies by 1824; Thomas Howell from Bristol produced a wide range of pedagogical material, much of which was tried out on his eldest daughter, including keyboard works and various musical 'games', and took out patents for improvements to musical instruments; Jean (John)

---

[110] See Ehrlich (1985), 145ff.

[111] Some relatively prominent figures in this area receive entries in biographical dictionaries such as Bingley (1814) and Sainsbury (1824).

Jousse, a French refugee at the time of the Revolution, settled in London as a teacher and writer on music and contributed numerous compilations, translations and editions of didactic works on music, including a very popular keyboard tutor (12th edn, 1830); and R. W. Keith, from a family of professional musicians, wrote and published examples for violin, keyboard, guitar and German flute, and made and sold musical instruments.

An enterprising figure such as J. B. Logier was able to tap into the especially lucrative market for keyboard instruction in Ireland, Scotland and England and attract passionate disciples and critics (chiefly professional musicians fearful of competition and saturation) in equal measure. Spohr, a valuable ally, was among the supporters of his methods and Logier was effectively vindicated by widespread application. In fact his influence, through writings, inventions and classes, extended beyond the British Isles and also into the twentieth century.[112] As practical skills were increasingly sought, the demand for 'mechanical' assistance grew (despite continued negative connotations in some quarters) and Logier's 'gamut-board' and 'chiroplast' were aimed at young children and the blind as well as intended for the correction of bad habits that ladies might already have acquired. Other pedagogues, including Eager, used the Logier system and it inspired similar innovations, such as Hawker's 'hand-moulds' for the keyboard, which also contributed to the general popularizing trend. There was therefore increasing scope for musical creativity to be taught alongside the basic rudiments.

Lecturers such as Crotch reached out to the public and influenced taste and criticism among performers and concert-goers of the bourgeoisie. This medium also proved effective for progressive musical pedagogues such as Dibdin, Fétis and Kemp.[113] New concert activity, including August Mann's entertainments at the Crystal Palace (where George Grove was secretary), attracted a wider audience and had a corresponding entrepreneurial spirit attached. Louis Jullien's extensive tours entertained and instructed audiences, including the lower and lower-middle classes, up and down the country. Such efforts resulted in the serious presentation of high standards of performance for possible emulation among a much greater proportion of the population and a leadership of taste based on the inherent worth of the music itself.[114]

The voracious appetite of the lower orders for practical music and active participation allowed much greater scope for musicians to forge

---

[112] See Kassler (1979), 719, whose entries on Logier contain much useful information.
[113] See Kassler (1979), 279–80, 349–50 and 625–32 respectively.
[114] See Russell (1997), 76–81; and Musgrave (2000), 189–90.

taste and effect change among large numbers of willing recipients. After all, music had a recognized place in the classroom as well as working-class society as a whole far beyond what even the most progressive of the more exclusive secondary education could achieve. As well as those figures already highlighted who strove to promote vocal music, there were also important innovators who contributed to the growth of the brass band movement, such as the Distin family, Enderby Jackson and later John Henry Iles. In addition to those who approached lower-class participation from the musical angle, devising and regulating strategies often with serious participation in mind, there were inevitably also influential individuals and municipal bodies whose agendas were primarily social and perhaps even philanthropic.[115] Money from manufacturing was used to sponsor festivals, and pioneers such as Robert Owen, John Strutt and Samuel Greg identified and were sympathetic to the social value of and appetite for music and, of crucial importance, sought to match supply and demand within their schemes for the education and 'improvement' of workers.[116] The importance of these figures amply demonstrates the difference they made to ordinary people's lives and the enthusiasm with which new musical opportunities were acted upon within local communities. Cheap published music (especially from the 1840s onwards), new and/or cheaper instruments and instrument makers' hire-purchase schemes (often initiated alongside practical instruction), and new journals were among other initiatives which identified market opportunities and consequently also helped to bring music within the reach of the masses.

In light of the trends discussed above it is not surprising that what we find is a history focused on the incremental, collected influence of numerous relatively minor figures and small-scale innovations responding to demand and the retention of certain social conditions, rather than on a small number of major pioneers able to dictate taste and attitudes within an environment conducive to dramatic change. Within a more evolutionary than revolutionary climate, instrumental practice, for the practical and social reasons already highlighted, retained an elitist rather than popular bias for far longer than the vocal art, the achievements of certain working-class communities being notable exceptions. Where such a focus on individual consumption was in evidence it served in many cases only to reinforce the prejudices and ambivalence as well as the highly variable standards of the past. The job of salvaging instrumental music in particular fell to those opportunists

---

[115] See Gillett (2000a), 34 and 38; Russell (1997), 42; and Ess in Temperley, ed. (1981), 139.
[116] See Mackerness (1964), 129–30; and Russell (1997), 26–7.

who either identified the situation as being detrimental to national culture, or, more often, saw the potential financial and social rewards in a rapidly expanding and increasingly diverse market-place. The extent of the appetite for music among the new markets is demonstrated by the speed with which it was consumed when access was gained, even if the standing of British music was not always the beneficiary.

The 'Tabooed' Art

This is a necessarily brief sojourn into an area of immense scope, the intention being to view music within a broader cultural context. Generally speaking, the performance arts, music, drama and dance, were accredited a low status in comparison to literature, sculpture, painting, drawing and architecture, and music (particularly instrumental practice) appears to have sat at the bottom of the pile within the performance arts 'curriculum'.[117]

There are certainly many issues at play here, including the respectability of the environments and venues within which the art was appreciated and practised, the time and effort required to gain some degree of proficiency, the scope for noticeable (audible) error, as well as the all-important appropriateness of the physicality involved and the corresponding emotions and passions associated with its practice. The same social conventions and attitudes which were counter-productive in the case of music therefore gave its sister art forms the advantage.

It is especially interesting to compare the fortunes of fine art and fine artists with those of music and musicians during the eighteenth and nineteenth centuries. The contrast with music is immediately apparent as we observe the interrelated presence during the late eighteenth and early nineteenth centuries of leading British protagonists (Gainsborough, Reynolds, Constable and Turner for example), support (moral and financial) for advanced training and cultivation through the Royal Academy of Arts (founded in 1768), and respectable amateur pursuits. There is in fact evidence to suggest that the status enjoyed by

---

[117] Brewer's comments (1997: 560) referred to earlier in this chapter apply here. The term 'tabooed' is taken from Arthur Sullivan's reference to 'the hitherto tabooed art' of music in his affectionate obituary tribute to the painter Frederic Leighton, president of the Royal Academy of Arts, who had initiated the welcoming of music in the 1890s (see Gillett (2000b), 325–6). Interesting insights can be found in L. Lipking, *The ordering of the arts in eighteenth-century England* (1970) and J. Opper, *Science and the arts: a study in relationships from 1600–1900* (1973), and contemporary texts such as Anon., *The polite arts, or, a dissertation on poetry, painting, musick, architecture, and eloquence* (1749) and T. Robertson, *An enquiry into the fine arts* (1784). See also McCalman, ed. (1999), 250–60.

fine art was higher at all levels, from artists of international stature to its value and level of expertise among the dilettanti, and that effective long-term strategies and their associated bodies concerned with serious artists and their work existed happily alongside fickle and vain commercial concerns. We are not surprised to note that Chesterfield, writing in 1749, considered a 'taste of sculpture and painting' as 'becoming, as a taste of fiddling and piping is unbecoming a man of fashion'.[118] Naturally the former, along with literature, had a greater intellectual pedigree and did not present the same risk of 'bad company'.[119] Accordingly the need to enforce the amateur/professional divide was less eagerly felt.

Expanding on this foundation of respectability sketching, drawing and painting in particular were practised and consumed as fashionable and affordable pursuits by increasing numbers of middle-class men and women as the nineteenth century progressed. They, like music, were able to profit from market trends, but they were also free of many of the social conventions and prejudices that held music back (and correspondingly made fewer gains through the changes in perception that the possibilities of lower-class cultivation could offer). There were native figures of both artistic and intellectual stature, such as Reynolds, who inspired emulation from a 'morally and culturally elevated position'[120] and the institutions they were often part of had serious intentions and led by example. Both a knighthood and an honorary Oxford doctorate were bestowed upon on the 46-year-old Reynolds in 1759, 36 years before the musician William Parsons received his knighthood for sheer volume rather than distinction of efforts.

For those desperately trying to breathe life into a fledgling RAM (see Chapter 5), the funding of the Royal Academy of Arts, a prime exhibition space as well as teaching institution and a 'home' for the British school, was a constant annoyance. It also came far closer to the ideal of being actively patronized by the state while being run by professionals who could promote new art rather than merely endorse the aristocratic preference for the work of 'deceased foreigners'.[121] To further exacerbate the disparity the National Gallery was established in 1824. It is significant that Walmisley's failed plan for an academy of

---

[118] Kassler (1979), 973. See also Leppert (1985), 135.

[119] Conduct books such as Miss Maria Edgeworth's *Practical education* (2nd edn, London, 1801), written for middle-class infants and young girls and boys, placed music (and other arts) below literature in the hierarchy of subjects in education due to their lack of intellectual (in favour of 'mechanical') content (see Kassler (1979), 307–10).

[120] McCalman, ed. (1999), 252.

[121] McVeigh (2000), 152–3.

music, in association with the Philharmonic Society, should have aimed 'to give a standing to professional musicians equivalent to that enjoyed by painters associated with the Royal Academy'.[122]

In the absence of professional musicians of significant standing the fortunes of music were ultimately dependent on levels of interest and achievements among amateurs. Quantity and quality were united more often as the century progressed and figures of prominence and even eminence came to the fore and were listened to when they campaigned on music's behalf. Sir Arthur Sullivan for one espoused in 1888 the essential purity of music and therefore its superiority over painting and sculpture.[123] However, in the case of painting, role models and high-status advocates had been in place for a far longer period. Landscape painting in particular provided numerous celebrated models for emulation and drawing had an important role to play in the furthering of scientific enquiry. Also women, if 'typically amateur watercolourists rather than professional practitioners in oil',[124] enjoyed greater scope for the respectable public exposure of their creativity than was the case with musical performance. Their work, a tangible item, could be displayed while they were not and the subject matter could still be of a private, intimate nature in keeping with required modesty and domesticity. Increasing numbers of peripatetic drawing masters, including some artists of merit, brought serious study into the homes of aristocratic and middle-class girls.[125]

The correlation already discussed between amateur and professional achievement, status and standards, is in evidence in all areas of creative endeavour. It is striking how much more favourable the situation was regarding painting than music and consequently how much kinder history has been to artists than musicians. Without comparing their relative merits it is apparent how artists were in a much better position to achieve more. Musicians can perhaps be forgiven for having resented their fine artist counterparts[126] and it is significant that musicians often

---

[122] Kassler (1979), 1043.

[123] Mackerness (1964), 189.

[124] McCalman, ed. (1999), 256.

[125] The exhibition at the British Museum in 2000 entitled 'A noble art: amateur artists and drawing masters c.1600–1800' revealed high levels of achievement (and corresponding levels of practical instruction and complementary teaching material) among amateur artists from the upper and upper-middle classes. It is naturally far more difficult to assess musical achievements without similar surviving evidence, but contemporary accounts, repertoire and teaching material all suggest that they were valued less even if they reached similar heights on occasion. It should be remembered that high levels of technical accomplishment in music, among men and women, were often frowned upon in certain circles. Proficiency in drawing was far more respectable (see Burgan (1989), 54).

[126] Ehrlich (1985), 122.

looked to other art forms in order to achieve a wider recognition. If Gainsborough was serious about his musical endeavours, Burney certainly gained more status from his literary career, as did Crotch (also a successful painter).

As a respectable group activity promoting social identity and engendering cooperation, sport, and particularly cricket (with its amateur/professional division of labour),[127] perhaps had a similar role among the upper and upper-middle classes to music among the lower orders. The competitive dimension to music, important in the success of popular movements, manifested itself in elite education in the form of house-singing. As the respectability of music rose in line with its moral status and role within society, particularly towards the end of the century, and wider participation was encouraged as a consequence, the industrial working class increasingly turned to previously public-school sports as a source of entertainment.

New Horizons

It is easy (and in many cases no doubt essential) to view the burgeoning of musical activity in nineteenth-century Britain within a context of continued restriction and prejudice with accordingly limited progress. It is nevertheless important to give genuine innovation and progress, which often sought to unite quality and quantity, the credit it deserves. As we have seen this was often, but by no means always, found in purposeful, new and therefore largely 'stigma-free' initiatives involving a captive and genuinely enthusiastic audience. Given the power of private enterprise and, despite enormous demand and potential, the minimal involvement of the state in education already identified, there was huge scope for enlightened (and opportunistic) individuals to improve significantly the profile of music and musicians. Changes in the dynamics of amateur consumption facilitated expansion, diversification and changes in the role of music in society; but the standing of the professional musician and the attitudes of opinion-formers needed to be tackled if music was to be seen as more than a means of controlling the masses or as an essentially trivial pursuit.

The enforcement and protection of the amateur/professional divide remained a potent force despite the division being temporarily crossed or blurred to the point of irrelevance by the 'semi-professional' accomplishments of middle-class ladies and lower-class men respectively. The continued bias against music as a practical pursuit worthy of serious

---

[127] Cannon, ed. (1997), 259 and 884.

attention among upper-class and upper-middle-class gentlemen undermined the status of the profession. It did not become an employment option outside the traditional circles until it came within the sphere of those for whom it represented a step up rather than a significant drop on the social ladder.

The evidence of foreign successes (and later lower-class achievements) demonstrated the importance of an ambitious and supportive amateur foundation in cultivating professional excellence. It was essential for music to be seen as a completely separate issue from the need to earn a living. Gentlemen who viewed it as an escape from drudgery rather than as a snare and as a discipline requiring participation and appreciation rather than mere consumption would sanction its use beyond its current limited role among wives and daughters.

The strenuous efforts of R. M. Bacon, through his writings and other means, to refute the traditionally derogatory, Lockean views pedalled by Chesterfield and others and consequently raise the public estimation of the music profession have been referred to above. It is worth reiterating here that he was one of the first to identify the fundamental role of the amateur in determining the status of music and musicians in Britain and to set about harnessing this influence. The amateur was in a unique position in being able both to reflect and promote (high and low) levels of appreciation and practical music-making, and Bacon was all too aware of the effects of generally low amateur standards. The middle classes, proactive in searching out education and self-improvement in general, offered new horizons.

If not a chorus of disapproval there were increasing numbers of dissenting voices provoked by the state of education in Britain and England in particular and some, usually linked to the profession in some way, championed music's cause and had some collective influence through their writings and campaigns. Extra-musical associations, both positive and negative, were of vital importance both to providers and consumers and, given the utilitarian climate, these were initially isolated figures promoting to some degree music for music's sake within a secular context. There were prevalent and well-established reservations, but some acceptance and sympathy came with increasing numbers of eager consumers. Music's domestic and social function had far wider relevance than in the eighteenth century and efforts to improve the training of both amateurs and professionals were intended to aid the musicality of the nation in general and refute claims that music (particularly instrumental performance) was 'derogatory to character, both as becomes a man and a gentleman'.[128] It was essential that music acquired

---

[128] From 'Vetus' [R. M. Bacon], 'Music as a pursuit for men', *QMMR*, 2 (1820), 7–14.

this 'improving' dimension. To a certain extent they succeeded and, by helping to increase the accessibility and nurture a broader acceptance of music at all social levels, the foundations for the 'renaissance' (and 'flood') later in the century were laid. Unsurprisingly there were still instances of the musical ambitions of young gentlemen from prosperous backgrounds being stifled at home and in school, but, as in the case of E. H. Fellowes, there was scope for them to rise to prominence given sufficient tenacity.[129]

Bacon's desire to see musicians educated properly was only one (if a very important) way of rejuvenating and bolstering native talent. As the nineteenth century progressed, writers, with increasing frequency and vehemence, noted and deplored the dominance of foreign musicians and the consequent lack of support for native talent. Some, acknowledging that the situation was detrimental to the standards of native performers but aware of the tastes of the concert-going public, emphasized the need to match the achievements of foreign musicians, so as to compete successfully with them. Fewer sought to discourage their presence.[130] Also the founding of the Philharmonic Society in 1813 by the pick of London's instrumentalists signalled a new desire on the part of professional musicians to lead musical taste and assert their intellectual superiority over their social betters. In contrast to the Ancient Concerts[131] the appeal was to the middle classes, increasingly prominent and discerning consumers of music. The RAM was founded as a means of enabling native talent to compete with the foreign visitors. A flawed conception from day one as well as a victim of circumstances, it undoubtedly failed in this regard. When limited protection did arrive later in the century in the form of professional regulation (through the ISM, the Union of Graduates in Music and other similar bodies),[132] the greatest threat to the livelihood of the career musician came from the army of 'semi-professionals', mainly female music teachers, infiltrating the ranks and armed with meaningless or even false paper qualifications.

The encouragement of higher amateur standards was an important tactic among music's most vocal supporters. The effect (if not the

---

[129] Ehrlich (1985), 71–2 and 138. The initiative of the boys themselves at Harrow to invite John Farmer to teach piano is also worth noting (see Rainbow (1989a), 34). Real progress was indeed being made if boys of the upper-middle class, traditionally raised to scorn music, were actively seeking out opportunities to learn it.

[130] See Anon., 'Sketch of the state of music in London', QMMR, 5 (1823), 241–75. Some comments are made with specific reference to the violin (p. 265) and the importance of the Royal Academy (p. 266). See also E. Hodges, 'On the objects of musical study', MW, 1 (1836), 150.

[131] See Weber (1992); and Palmer (1997), 122ff.

[132] Ehrlich (1985), 133 and 136.

explicit motivation) was a narrowing of the amateur/professional divide in terms of both standards and attitudes, a divide which would have widened further with the technical demands of the new virtuosic age. Aware of the influence of the literate amateur and their increasing interest in musical matters, musicians used dedicated journals and articles as well as teaching materials as a platform to foster the appreciation of music and emphasize the importance of good training. One only has to look through the pages of Kassler (1979) to become aware of this trend in early nineteenth-century music journalism and contrast it with the concerns of most eighteenth-century contributors. The previous reluctance to publish serious and effective teaching material, through the lack of an obvious sizeable market and a consequent fear of competition, was replaced by a much greater range of study aids in the nineteenth. Indeed as the nineteenth century progressed, the volume and quality of written material concerned specifically with music dramatically increased, indicating a burgeoning interest and a desire to foster more positive attitudes. The interests of the profession were still the prime concern but now, as a result of the increasing opportunities, these were best served by directing rather than merely following taste.

In response to the need to nurture the amateur and potential professional in the absence of any other system, specialist journals adopted a more critical approach to the training of musicians and pedagogical publications in particular. Titles such as *The Quarterly Musical Magazine and Review, Harmonicon* and *The Musical World* provided the profession with the means to enforce some quality control. A journal such as *The Musical World* was 'calculated, from the cheapness of its form, to draw increased attention to musical matters'.[133] Teaching material was reviewed and judged on its effectiveness rather than by the name attached to it and increasingly the most effective tuition of middle-class amateurs was seen to require a combination of practical and written instruction (see Chapter 2). Highly respected writers such as Hogarth, Worgan, Young, Graham, Kemp and Relfe promoted music education as 'a valuable object of enquiry'.[134]

The tension between the theoretical/logical and practical/instinctive disciplines was still in evidence and distributed largely along gender lines, especially with increasing numbers of female performers. The need to teach performance more effectively led to the combination of complementary theoretical and practical aspects within sources which

---

[133] Hogarth (1838), vol.2, 273.

[134] Kassler (1979), 524. There is much of interest in these two volumes on the individual significance of the writers listed above and many others.

also served to reverse an inclination towards superficiality that was identified as particularly damaging to the cause of native music and musicians.[135] Music needed to be a serious subject, intellectually as well as recreationally, if it was to be taken seriously and quantity without some quality would do little to raise approval and status. For the first time there was an attempt to identify the 'right way' of studying music for amateurs and professionals and perhaps even facilitate a progression from the former to the latter if desired.[136]

A firm theoretical grounding was essential for all and for young amateurs, the majority of music students, there was a special need for a combination of 'brevity, perspicuity, and a close connection of its component parts' as well as 'relevant' instruction.[137] Accordingly there was a greater desire for teaching material to be progressive, accessible and comprehensive, covering all varieties of style (including 'ancient' and 'modern'). In addition mechanical skill and tasteful expression were both required of the true artist and the finer points of performance were to be gleaned from the appreciation of accomplished performance. This was increasingly offered to a wider audience by the tours of Jullien and others.

As well as advice on effective practice there were also campaigns on behalf of individual instruments, including 'The rise and progress of ...' series of articles in *QMMR* in the 1820s and volumes such as Dubourg's study of the violin. In the first of the *QMMR* series concerned with the violin[138] it is admitted that 'musicians have been held far lower in the scale of artists than any other class', but it is believed that 'the profession is every where rising in character and estimation'.[139] Writers outside the

---

[135] There was sometimes a greater 'scientific' bias in works intended for the gentleman, such as J. Macdonald's violin and cello tutors, which purposefully set out to present 'useful' knowledge.

[136] Kassler (1979), 1183.

[137] Ibid., 880, quoting John Relfe in 1819, a respected teacher of piano to professionals and amateurs (including the poet Robert Browning). Relfe was active in promoting the effective teaching of music with a practical rather than theoretical bias. He advised the Philharmonic Society on the subject in 1818, which was then considering the establishment of a music school.

[138] *QMMR*, 3 (1821), 439–52; 4 (1822), 52–8 and 444–9; 5 (1823), 325–30; 7 (1825), 42–57.

[139] *QMMR*, 3 (1821), 440. The market for a wide range of literature on the violin continued to expand during the rest of the nineteenth century, including periodicals and articles and examples for and by women. Series of cheap tutors such as 'Alliance Musicale' and the 'Philharmonic Edition', and those issued by Novello, Boosey, and Hawkes & Son among others, allowed a much wider dissemination of good-quality teaching material. Such developments could only help to raise standards, and by 1889, although native violinists were generally still unable to demonstrate the brilliance of the imported artist,

music profession also promoted higher aspirations. Charles Dickens (son-in-law of George Hogarth) was critical of music's traditional role in female education. Rather than 'an ornament for lightheaded husband-hunters' it should be thought of as an important practical endeavour and means of expression, to be 'used in conjugal mutual support'.[140] In reality the activities of the lower classes perhaps came closer to this ideal, although George Eliot also identified the communal powers of musical performance which could be realized by the duet in a domestic setting. There was, however, little value in 'surface dexterity'.[141]

A diverse amateur market took shape which attempted to cultivate higher ambitions and a deeper understanding, covering all standards and the full, expanding range of instruments. This differed from the concern of most continental sources, which continued to concentrate to a large extent on mainstream, professional practice on certain instruments (and provide Britain with its models in this area) until much later in the century. The result was that a previously rare and muted view of music, which, when of 'an elevated character', was of real benefit to both the rich and the poor and served to 'soften and purify the mind',[142] became increasingly credible during the nineteenth century and was expressed by numerous musicians and non-musicians alike.[143] Training methods improved alongside public taste (even if 'obsolete practice' was still common)[144] and there were many positive steps, such as W. E. Barrett, the editor of the *Musical Times* (originally *'and Singing Class Circular'*), also becoming an inspector of music in schools and training colleges (1871 to 1891).[145]

The methods employed further down the social scale and their

---

there had been an 'astonishing' improvement in the 'rank and file' (P. David, 'Violin-playing', *Grove 1*, vol.4 (1889), 298–9). New periodical publications such as *The Strad* (beginning in May 1890), intended expressly for both amateurs and professionals, *The Violin Monthly Magazine* (1890–94) and *Violin Times* (1893–1907), involving distinguished writers such as Eugene Polonaski and Edward Heron-Allen, were born out of the popularity of the instrument and the serious attention paid to the different subjects connected with it.

[140] Burgan (1989), 54–6.

[141] Ibid., 62–3.

[142] Hogarth (1838), vol.2, 273.

[143] The spread of a belief in the arts as 'crucial to the nation's economic prosperity and moral progress' was aided by Henry Cole and the Committee appointed by the Society for the Encouragement of Arts, Manufactures and Commerce in 1865 to enquire into the state of music education at home and abroad (see Ehrlich (1985), 88).

[144] Ehrlich (1985), 192.

[145] Rainbow (1989a), 37. The arrival of the Music Teachers' Association in 1908 was an important if overdue development which promoted progressive ideas relating to the teaching of music in schools (ibid., 41).

outcomes naturally had a far more practical than literary bias. The task was in fact far easier as it was to a large extent merely a case of tapping into latent enthusiasm and talent. If dissenting voices had promoted music among the well-to-do, its potential moral and utilitarian qualities (especially through military bands and those associated with the Volunteer movement) were readily apparent among the lower orders. Although there was greater freedom to focus on the inherent qualities of music among lower-class consumers, it was therefore not a case of music for music's or amusement's sake in the eyes of the intelligentsia. Moves in this area were therefore in keeping with mainstream political opinion (if not always supported by required action and finances).

As the status of music-making improved in the estimation of opinion-formers and the public at large, its presence in the curriculum, whether in private or in schools, received wider support. Vocal practice was, as we have seen, the initial and perhaps chief beneficiary, but instrumental performance also gained from this trend.[146] Given its lowly position, improvements in this area were signs of significant change. Amateur activity such as northern brass bands offered rather than threatened opportunities for professionals, who often provided help and guidance.[147] There were real opportunities, including performances for concert societies and competitions, to gratify musical aspirations as well as entertain within supportive communities. Later, when band-trained amateurs moved into the professional sphere, it was because they alone possessed the levels of proficiency demanded by the new repertoire which short-term priorities and ad hoc professional training methods had failed to produce. Their threat to professional livelihoods was therefore born out of sheer ability rather than opportunistic employment.

The range of musical activity in Britain was far wider towards the end of the nineteenth century than it had been at the beginning, as a result of individual initiatives and a change in the groundswell of public opinion. It now involved both men and women of a relatively wide social spectrum active in a variety of vocal and instrumental music. However despite the significant inroads made by the middle and upper classes, the real catalyst came from the mid-nineteenth century onwards through the spread of opportunity to those lower-status groups for

---

[146] If not a literary tradition to the same extent as middle-class education, vocal training in schools and singing classes for adults and children still required effective and coherent texts for use by the teacher. The combination of Sarah Glover's singing method and Pestalozzian educational theory in Curwen's practical approach provided a suitable guide. See Rainbow (1989a), 29–30.

[147] Russell (1997), 238.

The 'Flood' and Popular Music Education

Before turning to specific aspects of instrumental pedagogy this short section is concerned with the circumstances of those areas of popular musical activity which expanded rapidly from the mid-nineteenth century onwards. The familiar issues of gender, class and morality are all in evidence and expansion came in those areas which successfully managed to reconcile all three and develop systems of music education alongside. As outlined in the Introduction, whether this was welcome growth or a counter-productive 'flood'[148] depended to a large extent on the motivation for provision and consumption and the importance of the music itself, vis-à-vis other factors, in each case.

The consumption of music among middle-class amateurs, both male and female, during the nineteenth century preserved many eighteenth-century aesthetic and socio-economic priorities within the context of huge expansion. The choice of instruments for the different sexes remained much the same, although the rise of female violinists and male wind and brass players were significant developments (see Chapters 3 and 4). Levels of demand, if not always discriminating, created a great variety and depth of musical practices and affordable supporting materials (and qualifications), vocal and instrumental, elementary and advanced.[149] In some ways the extent of this demand loosened the grip of the higher orders on culture and education; in other ways it strengthened it by prompting sweeping reform and large-scale initiatives.

Given the inclination there was scope for music to become much more than a form of recreation for many accessing it for the first time. It is important not to underestimate the importance of the 'diverse, vibrant culture of radical self-improvement'[150] and the extent to which Victorian individuals would discipline themselves in the interests of education. Once music was accepted into the fold as morally sound in

---

[148] As mentioned in the Introduction, a term used to great effect in chapter 5 of Ehrlich (1985).

[149] Henry Fisher's pioneering book on *The musical profession* (1888) is careful to describe the diversity of amateur musicianship, from the accomplished to the incompetent (see Ehrlich (1985), 121–2). New instruments, such as concertinas, accordions and melodeons, offered novel opportunities and attracted a great deal of attention among the lower and middle classes.

[150] McCalman, ed. (1999), 654.

an increasingly secular and consumerist society (further aided by the increasing acceptance of pleasure and entertainment per se),[151] it was natural that its fortunes would improve substantially.

In the case of the higher (middle to upper) orders, however, music's status remained, inevitably, limited by the male agenda and a strong female bias. There was some new-found emancipation within this context, with increased scope for semi-professionalism and activity outside the home (including the role of female musicians, and violinists in particular, in amateur orchestras). Nevertheless standards are invariably linked to incentives and, although some music education was desirable for ladies, excellence in this area usually went unrewarded. This was true of the whole period, despite remarkable advances in the education of young women and girls in general. We have already highlighted the 'unseemly', 'empty' nature of 'mechanical' display, the negative connotations attached to 'conscious artists',[152] and the longevity of the tradition of 'genteel accomplishment' within the home and in schools.

The story of late nineteenth-century expansion in middle-class music is therefore more a tale of quantity than quality. Although standards did rise in certain areas, the philosophy behind it remained focused on the means rather than the end, the teaching of music largely for its own sake perpetuating mediocrity. There was little prospect of long-term artistic or financial gratification. The scope for financial reward, which had to compensate for the lack of status and esteem, obviously diminished as competition continued to rise. With an increasing number of unmarried women in society some looked for a career in music, but most often it offered a stopgap prior to marriage, after which many would sacrifice their work and freedom for relative financial security. The music was almost incidental, merely allowing entrance into paid work, which was itself often not conducive to the promotion of high artistic principles and a genuine love of the art.

Higher amateur aspirations generally remained, at least in the long term, amateur, and so while provision for amateur consumers improved, professional training remained poor or biased towards the amateur. The market, based as it was largely on middle-class consumerism, was vulnerable to outside pressures and whims of fashion. Also, as discussed above, the fact that it was very easy for (often female) pupils to become teachers (and therefore for demand to become supply) was not only generally harmful to the interests of the (often male) career professional but encouraged unsustainable levels of expansion. Ultimately the demise

---

[151] Russell (1997), 17.
[152] Burgan (1989), 53–4, and Rainbow (1989a), 36.

of domestic music-making and the services associated was an inevitable result of the new convenience and ease of access offered by new technology, the gramophone and BBC in particular.[153]

Vocal music offered one of the few opportunities for respectable female public performance. There was of course a widely recognized moral dimension to much of this activity, from singing classes to the competitive festival movement and its similarly educational bent, which made a rare consensus possible. The popularity of choral society and the oratorio itself owed a great deal to their inherent sacred/secular ambiguity. This is demonstrated by the sheer numbers and diversity of performers and audiences. It is also important to recognize the existence of an in-built training infrastructure for the choral tradition, stemming from the home to the school, church or chapel choir or perhaps tonic sol-fa society. The success of this system, with its own performance demands already in place, was much in evidence during the nineteenth century and remains relevant up to the present day.

There is, however, evidence here also of standards being inversely proportionate to social standing. The luxury of 'gentility' higher up the social scale, in education and practice, generally resulted in lower standards, and competitive choirs, like bands, tended to have a narrower social mix in favour of the working classes.[154] A disparity in sight-singing capabilities of 'high' and 'board' school students was also observed.[155] Naturally school music thrived most noticeably in areas with an already vibrant amateur culture. Amateur successes were therefore more commonly found in Yorkshire than London.[156]

Our discussion so far has aimed to show that the progress of music among the 'sons of toil' was far more rapid than among the 'lettered' classes.[157] Both sides of the industrialization coin conspired in music's success, which grew out of and offered a relief from the new social landscape, and allowed it to become an important part of the framework of society. What we find is a concentration of groups of people of the same class, raw materials and production methods combined with a real sense of community spirit and social identity. There is much evidence of 'the hearty appreciation of effort in the direction of increased excellences',[158] which in many ways sums up the philosophy of popular music. The nurturing of musical ability and the

---

[153] Ehrlich (1985), 208–9 and 212.
[154] Russell (1997), 255.
[155] Rainbow (1989a), 37.
[156] Russell (1997), 57.
[157] Mackerness (1964), 197.
[158] Russell (1997), 277.

provision of 'openings from within'[159] are essential characteristics of the movement, the success of which depended on not leaving activity to chance and the 'closed shop' of the profession. Another important ingredient was that the practitioners were working-class men. This ensured a vital level of autonomy within the communities themselves and greater freedom to realize potential than in more 'genteel' areas.

If the band movement was more insular and isolated than its vocal equivalent, this appears to have been a strength as it managed to solve its own problems relatively easily.[160] Training methods, often moving from the home straight into the band,[161] focused on public performance standards rather than polite, sheltered and largely self-gratifying accomplishment. The increasing ease of travel and the celebration of local achievements provided specialized tuition and equipment which continued to contribute to the relative inaccessibility of 'elitist' instrumental practice further up the social scale. To the great benefit of the standard and status of British music-making, essential tools and training were now accessible and directed towards the potential high achievers rather than mere 'dabblers'.[162]

Various organological developments aided and were in turn spurred on by the new demand for instrumental music, particularly in the expanding, male-dominated wind and brass areas. These had hitherto been largely neglected by upper- and middle-class men and were not considered appropriate for women until much later in the century. Instruments suitable for wind/brass bands therefore grew in popularity alongside the more informal 'fiddle and flute' music, and there was also a great increase in the playing of the piano with the circulation of cheap instruments.[163]

The bias of lower-class music in favour of instrumental performance perpetuated respectable musical standards and often much more. Financial reward was possible but community status and self-esteem were more important. In any case all of these in a discerning environment required success and high standards. Payments to soloists and trainers still placed music at the forefront of concerns and rewarded high levels of proficiency. The 'pyramid' structure, common to all effective and systematic pedagogy, was allowed to form, providing incentives for ambition, dedication and high artistic ideals. Without a reliance on financial reward there was a resistance to many market pressures.

---

[159] Ibid., 282.
[160] Ibid., 175.
[161] Ibid., 260.
[162] See Herbert (2000a), 4, 18, 143, 171 and 306–11.
[163] Russell (1997), 180–81.

Despite long-term neglect and the lack of a professional infrastructure and coherent strategy for music education, the appreciation of music increased dramatically during the nineteenth century among virtually the whole of society and all genres. Whether through participation, informed listening or both, encouragement came from individual figures and initiatives which traded on a strong belief in the beneficial qualities of musical activity. Popular music education in terms of the large-scale descent of opportunity to the lower orders certainly does not equate with low standards, particularly when viewed alongside the 'proud dabblers' of the previous century.[164]

---

[164] Leppert (1985), 158.

CHAPTER TWO

Instrumental Teaching

The intention here is to examine the means of teaching and learning musical instruments within an environment which, as outlined above, encouraged largely ad hoc, rather systematic provision. Although attention is paid to the violin as a representative example of social and cultural trends and attitudes, individual instruments and practitioners will be dealt with more fully in following chapters.

An important consideration when approaching these issues is the paucity of contemporary accounts of the music lesson, the 'nitty-gritty' of what was actually taught or learnt from the perspective of the pupil or teacher. In establishing who taught whom, how, and where, we often have to form a general impression or gain insights from secondary evidence emerging from the use of the surviving teaching material itself or fictional (often satirical) accounts of the music lesson. It is interesting to consider why this should be so beyond the material just not surviving. From the point of view of the provider and advanced pupil or potential professional there was a reluctance to divulge 'trade secrets' in a highly competitive environment. For the higher-status pupil, why take the trouble to record the details of musical tuition if, indicative of the general importance of music and therefore the music lesson within their lives, there was little concern for diligent application in the lesson or at home? Nevertheless private diaries and correspondence are potentially valuable sources of information on this subject (particularly as more 'ordinary' people gained access to private instruction) once they are identified and their significance assessed.

Instruction Methods

Apprenticeships

In contrast to the high-status church music careers, which traditionally followed the cathedral chorister/university route, those embarking on a secular career as a singer or instrumentalist were generally trained through apprenticeships or (less often) private tuition. The intricacies of the apprentice system during this period have been discussed elsewhere.[1] However, it is important to note that even under the best conditions it had serious shortcomings as a form of training for a musical career. So much depended on the abilities and professional connections of the 'master', which were often not equal to the task of instructing the apprentice in all the necessary areas of music and introducing them to the profession. To 'study' with the same musician for five to seven years (even if he was conscientious and competent) was naturally restricting and opportunities to perform informally with other musicians were limited. Even so, any opportunity to gain practical experience through participation was likely to have been more useful to the aspirant than the actual tuition offered. Burney, formally apprenticed to Arne, learned as a copyist of his master's music and as a violinist at Vauxhall Gardens. Arne, however, took Burney's fees and there was little time for any formal instruction. There was also little concern paid to the general, formal education of the student, the damage of which figures like Bacon later struggled to repair.

Notwithstanding its shortcomings, within a generally insecure environment for musicians, the apprenticeship system did offer the profession at least some means of regulating entry and activity. This anti-competition element suited musicians' short-term interests, but such a closed shop, often focused on family ties, was counter-productive. Despite a few success stories, such as the Vincent family of eighteenth-century instrumentalists, stagnation ensued. This of course played into the hands of the upper orders' conservative and foreign-biased cultural agenda.

The massive expansion of consumption and therefore access during the nineteenth century naturally introduced something closer to free trade into the music profession, as greater financial benefit was to be had from divulging musical knowledge than from protecting trade secrets. Increasing numbers of proficient but strictly amateur gentlemen were a great asset to a profession eager for social acceptance; but, as discussed previously, when the incentive to earn some money from music and consequently challenge traditional professional livelihoods reached large numbers of (generally female) students, this freedom of information became a problem. Attempts were then made to introduce safeguards that would limit 'semi-professionalism'. Once again opportunities and freedom of choice often came to those who were reluctant or unable to take full advantage of them.

---

[1] See Rohr (1983), 154–8; McVeigh (1993), 183–5; and C. Brooks, 'Apprenticeship, social mobility and the middling sort, 1550–1800', in J. Barry and C. Brooks, eds (1994), 52–83. Further discussion can be found in Ehrlich (1985), 37, 77–8 and 239–40 ('Articles of Apprenticeship, 1860'); and Fiske and Johnstone, eds (1990), 10.

A positive development was the involvement of pioneering individuals without a direct musical lineage in the forging of public musical taste. For example John Ella, long associated with the elite Musical Union, did not come from a family of musicians and was apprenticed to his baker father in addition to taking violin lessons and developing a wide range of social and business skills. It is tempting to associate these circumstances with Ella's unusual social and economic success for a native musician.[2]

Unsurprisingly, considering their greater concern for high musical standards, the activities of the lower orders gave rise to a more balanced system of music education than their social superiors. This was delivered through both formal education and 'hands-on' practical experience. Serious amateur activity was based around working communities, in which musical training had a recognized and important role to play as part of both formal education and as a complement to vocational training and the workplace. The family also played a vital role in a philosophy which was geared towards 'learning by doing' through practical experience rather than motivated by a desire to restrict other potential aspirants. Among the lower-class amateurs we can therefore observe something closer to continental practice, such as in Italy,[3] in which family ties, the passing of expertise (often as well as an instrument and position) down the line in the form of a type of practical apprenticeship, is based on a continuity of excellence.[4] Crucially, in both cases moral and financial support was forthcoming, whether through court or similar appointments or the wider community, thereby facilitating rather than discouraging collaboration and healthy competition.

In a similar way to the training of church and military musicians (and in contrast to the opportunities offered by the early RAM) activity was purposeful. Success bred success, with examples of achievement within the peer group as well as from some outside professionals suitable for emulation. Incentives were in place to give generously of expertise and encourage progress, thereby further increasing the demand for professional input. Also much could be learned through 'osmosis', the collective effort and discipline of the group (whether a band or the wider community) and resulting performance experience playing a vital role in the formation of the musician and an appreciative audience. After all, music formed an intrinsic part of the lives of the individuals concerned rather than a small part of general education kept at arm's length as a private, individual study.

---

[2] See Bashford in Bashford and Langley, eds (2000), 196–7.
[3] See Ringer, ed. (1990), 175–6.
[4] See Herbert (2000a), 144; and Russell (1997), 221 and plate 9.

In short this was a proactive system which encouraged the sharing of knowledge. It thrived on expansion and competition rather than the desire (albeit natural in the climate) to restrict both. There was a definite drive to improve taste and proficiency rather than merely reflect and cater for existing levels through a 'genteel' tradition focused on the individual teacher and/or written material. Where music had a function, approaches to instruction and performance reflected this.[5] There was a need for training to be effective and proficiency to be gained in the shortest possible time, in marked contrast to the luxury of leisurely application and consumerism over many years with no real musical aims. This is exemplified by the effectiveness of the formal musical training offered the military bandsman, a lamentably rare concept in British music education of the period.

In essence the apprenticeship system endured by aspiring professional musicians was not dissimilar to aspects of the training experienced by many lower-class amateurs. However, the systems in place in working-class communities were characterized more by the advantages than the evident disadvantages outlined above. They managed to create a supportive infrastructure which was based on a desire for success and a genuine love of the art rather than a fear of failure in a highly competitive and downtrodden profession. It is important to note that musicians active in the amateur sphere, of whatever class, were far more likely to have access to the expertise of leading practitioners than their professional counterparts. What they did with the opportunities on offer is naturally where class enters the equation.

Self-Instruction and Private Tuition

The apprenticeship system was not relevant to the growing and increasingly influential body of musical amateurs, who, depending on their circumstances, made use of self-instruction manuals and (their authors hoped) possibly outside practical instruction. During the eighteenth century private lessons outside the apprenticeship system catered primarily for amateurs in search of civilized recreation. The modest ambitions of this group, often content with self-instruction, combined with the often poor state of the teachers and their teaching

---

[5] The church/cathedral organist provides a good example of the unity between functional music and its associated, structured training methods. Besides a liberal education the organist was often able to hone his skills through regular church services and the necessary provision for rehearsals. This framework offered relative security and, in some cases, a standing from which to influence activities outside the church. Later on there was also potential in independent secondary education (see Chapters 4 and 5).

methods, ensured low standards from the beginning of the century.[6] Few potential career musicians had access to private tuition. It required that there was a teacher in the area, and, as Rohr has observed,[7] it was not until well into the nineteenth century that musicians worked in provincial England (especially outside cathedral towns) in any great numbers.[8] In London, teachers (particularly Italians) were able to specialize in one or two instruments, but elsewhere the demand was insufficient for this to be financially viable in most cases. Therefore teachers offered their services as liberally as possible, with obvious consequences for standards of instruction and proficiency among their students.[9] Regardless of location the budding instrumentalist was also unlikely to have been able to afford private instruction. In addition to the cost of the lessons, there was the lack of income during the years of study to consider. In most cases foreign study, popular among some ambitious amateurs during the late seventeenth and early eighteenth centuries and aspiring professionals during the nineteenth century, could only be afforded by the relatively wealthy students of middle-class families. However, until the end of the nineteenth century in the area of 'art' music, this did offer more prestigious teachers and institutions and, significantly, a higher status for the recipients when they returned.[10]

Another factor affecting access to practical instruction was, as already highlighted, fear of competition on the part of the teacher, particularly in places where demand was limited and unlikely to expand. Music masters working in schools and in private suffered poor working and social conditions and the desire of some performers to protect their livelihoods by keeping their trade secrets to themselves was, if understandable in this environment, detrimental to the profession as a whole. Musicians were more than happy to travel to teach the wealthy, influential amateur and his offspring with little musical ambition, advertising their services through benefit concerts, tutors, handbills and trade cards (also popular among teachers of fine art), newspapers and journals.[11] The poor, ambitious student living in a relatively remote location was, although perhaps the most needing and deserving of such instruction, the least likely to have access to it. Moreover throughout the period the lack of opportunity among native musicians and the fierce

---

[6] See Roger North, 'Hints about Music', quoted in Weber (1992), 85.

[7] Rohr (1983), 158.

[8] Ehrlich (1985) is naturally full of valuable insights into the proliferation of musical tuition and associated materials within a broad social and economic context during our period.

[9] See 'Music teachers and social borders' in Leppert (1988), 56–61.

[10] See Wessely (1913), 5.

[11] Leppert (1985), 141.

competition it prompted seriously hindered the emergence of a cohesive and mutually supportive profession that would be in a position to influence change.[12]

Studying with a relative was the obvious solution to many of these problems, allowing, in addition to tuition, much easier access to often scarce and expensive instruments and (hopefully) a conducive home and professional environment. Therefore in addition to teaching the children of affluent men and perhaps an apprentice or two, musicians' pupils were quite often their own children, thereby saving money and still gaining the professional credentials. This situation, with family connections such an enormous advantage and forming part of an oral rather than text-based tradition, further exacerbated the closed shop tendencies of the 'trade', with succeeding generations of the same family continuing to dominate an area of expertise in a certain location.[13]

Much like today, the reality was that almost all musicians were, out of choice or necessity, also teachers and had to pursue other areas of musical activity. Violinists were no exception and during the eighteenth century there was much money to be made by eminent instrumentalists teaching the violin to gentlemen. Also, because it did not involve public performance, teaching was one of the few completely respectable and remunerative forms of musical employment open to women. Naturally the best performers (if not always the best teachers), who were predominantly foreign, sought to attract their pupils from the wealthiest and most influential among society and satisfy their demand for recreation and status. Giardini, a prominent and influential figure, had a number of gentlemen violin pupils and taught singing and the harpsichord to ladies, in addition to his more serious students and his morning *academia* at which his students performed.[14] There is no violin treatise in English by Giardini,[15] but, reflecting the extent of his influence as a teacher of dedicated violinists, he is viewed by Burney as the successor to Geminiani's violin treatise (1751) and is later credited with

---

[12] See Dubourg (1878), 215; and Stolba (1968–9), 40. Wilhelm Cramer's apparent reluctance to teach Samuel Wesley (see McVeigh 1989; 113, and 1993: 184–5) suggests that the fear of competition also spread to some eminent foreign visitors.

[13] This was also the case with violin making (see Harvey (1995), 88–9). Rohr's 'biographical catalogue of 6,587 musicians' reveals that 'about three-quarters of professional musicians' fathers were also professional musicians' (1983: 49–50). My own contributions to the *New Dictionary of National Biography* (Oxford University Press, due for publication in 2004), which cover over 150 individual musicians from the eighteenth and nineteenth centuries in most areas of the profession, reveal the same trend.

[14] See McVeigh (1989), 119, 155 and 201–3.

[15] There are 'three very short instruction manuals for harpsichord, cello and violin' surviving in manuscript in Italian libraries (McVeigh (1989), 189).

'having reformed, or rather founded, a school for the violin in England'.[16]

Entering rich households to play and teach provided musicians with unique opportunities to, as Ehrlich puts it, 'cross frontiers of wealth and class' and attain some prosperity and a relatively high social status.[17] Indeed the most successful teachers enjoyed a higher status than orchestral instrumentalists within the secular branch of the profession.[18] However, teaching constituted a much less secure existence for most. The large numbers of unlicensed or poor performers and teachers who operated as professional musicians continued to undermine the status of the profession. Consequently, native aspiring musicians with modest means were at best left to gain their expertise from relatively unqualified teachers with little or no practical experience and/or from written material, which was itself often inadequate. There is little evidence of the seriousness of application demanded elsewhere by the likes of Quantz, for example, who recommends four hours' practice a day for the beginner, with one hour a day resulting in slow progress.[19] An abundance of teaching material generally illustrates low aspirations and expectations in terms of both technical proficiency and critical judgement.[20] The predicament of teachers led to 'the musical plunderings of the least talented of students'.[21] Greater attention was paid to areas with some 'intellectual' credibility, such as composition, which created an unhelpful environment for instrumentalists, performers and teachers. It is significant that during the eighteenth century it appears that practical instruction was most often sought and given in the female-dominated areas of keyboard practice and singing.

The nineteenth century, along with increasing leisure time, disposable incomes and a desire for self-improvement, witnessed a significant growth in the demand for musical instruction, particularly among middle-class families requiring private music lessons for their daughters. The eighteenth-century tradition of self-instruction, reflected in the majority of sources from the time, appealed to the privileged in society and imposed a culture of self-sufficiency on the majority, severely limiting progress. It appears that during the eighteenth century the

---

[16] *Harmonicon*, 5 (1827), 215.

[17] Ehrlich (1985), 31.

[18] See 'Letter on the character of musicians', *QMMR*, 1 (1818), 286; and Rohr (1983), 296–7.

[19] See Quantz, ed. Reilly (1966), 118; and Lawson (2000), 66.

[20] Leppert (1985) paints a dismal picture indeed of the teaching of music to the upper classes, of both sexes.

[21] Ibid., 149. Pitman's *The miseries of the musick-masters* (1815) attests to many of the difficulties faced by music teachers (see also Kassler (1979), 843).

supply of teachers, especially in London, exceeded demand, even in the case of the most popular keyboard, violin and flute.[22] Instruments and tuition became more affordable for the middle-class beginner with leisure time and a disposable income, and with changes in the nature of the consumer came new approaches to teaching. This naturally resulted in new opportunities for native teachers, particularly as more consumers were concerned less with the status offered by a foreign virtuoso than with the actual learning of the instrument. However with the profession suffering from a general lack of cohesion for most of the century, there were no safeguards in place to ensure standards and competence among those who responded to this increased demand. By the 1820s, it was observed that:

> the demand for instruction is now so great, that everyone presumes to satisfy it, and, as little discrimination is used in the selection of teachers, persons are often employed who are totally unqualified for the task which they undertake ... Almost every performer on the violin, violoncello, double bass, or flute, will now give you lessons on the piano forte or in singing.[23]

This was nothing new, as Stevens's recollections of 'superficial' violin teachers (after his few lessons with Barthélemon in the 1770s) testify.[24] Some questioned the value of instructing so many amateurs and 'young ladies'.[25]

What we find in the nineteenth century is an increasing number of teachers (of variable and unregulated quality) responding to demand, rather than eminent figures protecting their 'trade secrets' for themselves and their offspring. Private tuition was given to an increasingly large number and wide spectrum of amateurs, with professionals continuing to rely mainly on the systems discussed above. Prior to the huge rise of semi-professionalism among female music teachers during the last quarter of the nineteenth century, the expansion of music instruction provided musicians with new markets but, at least until opportunity descended further, limited risk of competition. Earning potential outweighed fear of competition until the market became saturated. However, if there was anything approaching a honeymoon period it was short-lived and, with the heightened competition for pupils and the economic strains caused by the Napoleonic wars, the amount of money

---

[22] Leppert (1985), 144.
[23] 'Musical tuition', *QMMR*, 7 (1824), 306–7.
[24] See Argent (1992), 17–18.
[25] See E. Hodges, 'On the objects of musical study', *MW*, 1 (1836), 87–8. See T. Carrighan, 'Letter to the editor', *MW*, 1 (1836), 152–4, for the objections of a 'humble amateur' to this view.

to be made from teaching declined generally from around the turn of the nineteenth century.[26] It appears that the better teachers in London were able to charge a basic fee of one guinea per lesson by the mid-nineteenth century.[27] For many others outside the capital it was probably much less. Crotch charged amateurs one guinea but, significantly, taught professional pupils for only 15s. a quarter.[28] It was easier to differentiate between the two at this stage and they wanted very different things from practical instruction. Crotch appears to have based his charges on ability to pay (there was a similar disparity with regard to admission to Logier's lectures),[29] whereas Relfe, who taught the poet Robert Browning, charged professional male pupils, a greater threat to his livelihood, twice as much as female pupils.[30]

Like their eighteenth-century counterparts they had to teach to survive, regardless of their enthusiasm for the job, and the drudgery of elementary teaching was experienced by even relatively eminent figures. John Barnett, a friend of Dragonetti and an opera composer and singing teacher in Cheltenham from 1841, refers to the 'quackery and charlatanism' of other singing teachers and confesses that 'I give my lessons mechanically, I think of the half guineas, my wife and children, and I become as mechanical as my lessons'.[31] In the 'Life of Domenico Corri', prefaced to his *The singer[']s preceptor* (1810), Corri states that 'the cultivation of pupils, to which I have devoted chief part of my time, is an employment attended with much anxiety, and too often productive of but little satisfaction to a master'. In addition to a want of talent and application Corri also observes that:

> The profession not being followed by the most wealthy part of the community, for the purpose of public exhibition, there are few therefore who can afford the expence [sic] of instruction from a good master; and some of those who can allow this expence, frequently form public engagements before they are sufficiently competent to such situations. If the rules of this treatise, with the assistance of lessons given, *viva voce*, are considered adequate to

---

[26] See McVeigh (1989), 142–3.

[27] On fees charged for music lessons see Rohr (1983), 293; Ehrlich (1985), 78 and 174; Leppert (1985), 155ff.; McCalman, ed. (1999), 614; and Bashford and Langley, eds (2000), 29.

[28] Ehrlich (1985), 37.

[29] Pine and Acton, eds (1998), 25 and 27 n. 130. Aside from Logier's influence in Dublin this work (particularly pp. 25–32) contains much useful information on the expansion in music education, supply and demand, in Ireland during the nineteenth century in keeping with trends elsewhere.

[30] Kassler (1979), 877.

[31] Quoted in Palmer (1997), 55, who also discusses Dragonetti's teaching activities (pp. 86–8).

> form a singer, the failures cannot be attributed to the master ... I also continue to take young persons as apprentices, to qualify them as public professors, or as private tutors.

Such evidence suggests that, much to the dismay of serious pedagogues, the legacy of neglect ran very deep indeed and the activities of many native musicians working during the period served only to confirm the frequent criticisms of their worth and ability. Consequently there were very few native instrumentalists of a sufficient standing in the musical community to inspire the next generation and provide an incentive to attain some proficiency in the face of the limited opportunities on offer. Poorly qualified teachers and unambitious pupils were never going to promote high artistic ideals.[32]

In the case of the violin Spohr was largely responsible for filling this gap. His direct influence as a teacher, however, was greater than it might have been. Although there were many more students with a greater seriousness of purpose in the nineteenth century, there remained numerous 'dabblers' who wished to gain social kudos rather than expertise from their teacher, and Spohr offered the ideal combination of personal and musical attributes. Wealthy parents still preferred to engage the services of male teachers and prestigious connections were a bonus. Spohr was inevitably drawn towards the rewards offered by the wealthier but less ambitious pupil,[33] but he still managed to offer generous assistance to many gifted native violinists who came his way.[34] Nevertheless with the failure of any teaching institution to secure his services and the rarity of his public performances in England, it is evident that his skills, and those of many major figures, were inaccessible to many of the most deserving and promising practitioners. Little had changed in this respect. His treatise was therefore the main source of information on his ideas for the majority of interested parties, and the longevity of this work, the number of English translations, editions and derivatives, suggest that the demand was great. It is a testament to his popularity and reputation that he was able to influence violinists and performance style in England to the extent that he did.[35] The English musical environment made it far easier for Spohr's influence to be felt at the grass-roots level through his treatise rather than his

---

[32] See Kassler (1979), 987.

[33] See Brown (1984), 142; Ehrlich (1985), 45–6; and Kolneder (1998), 387. Prominent and successful musicians and teachers, such as Smart and Steibelt, also gained a great deal from mixing in the circles of high society (see Ehrlich (1985), 42, and Kassler (1979), 939 and 981).

[34] See Golby (1999b), vol.2, appendix II, 226.

[35] See Dubourg (1878), 182.

teaching and performing activities.³⁶ His pupils and succeeding generations influenced by his example who were active in England later in the century benefited from closer contact with teaching institutions, including both schools and music colleges (see Chapter 5).

Spohr promoted higher standards of performance and more positive attitudes towards the violin among amateurs and professionals alike. The native writer Dubourg also reflects a genuine interest in the subject from the 1830s onwards. While appealing to the multitude he promotes a more serious approach to instrumental pedagogy among his readers. He acknowledges the failings of an English musical education (1878: 249) and stresses the need to improve standards among amateur violinists. In addition to highlighting the need to increase the amount of private practice and choose written material carefully, he points to the fundamental role of the teacher (1878: 247). If a standard is to be achieved that is anything better than insulting to an instrument as challenging as the violin, the 'Master' is required to assist over an extended period. In the case of female pupils, the master's lessons could be complemented by the governess's supervision of practice.³⁷

This greater seriousness of purpose, promoting a move away from if not abandonment of casual self-instruction and parental disinterest, is reflected in the growing proliferation of written methods and materials during the period which, in line with much earlier continental examples, recognize and accommodate the fundamental role of practical instruction. Innovative early nineteenth-century teachers and writers, such as Jousse, Keith and Howell, responded to the demands of an increasing number of parents (and elements of the music profession) in providing works which cultivated more effective methods both within and outside of the lesson. These (often native) musicians, who were perhaps better pedagogues by virtue of being below the top flight of performers, were able to prosper in less saturated but still affluent areas such as Bath, Bristol, Edinburgh and Glasgow. This progressive trend is evident in sources ranging from short handbooks and pamphlets to substantial and comprehensive treatises. This is particularly true at a relatively early stage in the case of keyboard instruction, where the master–pupil scenario among well-to-do girls and women was already well established. The rise of written material to complement and supplement (rather than replace) the work of the teacher, including in their absence, was a healthy and prudent development in both musical and commercial terms. The inherent failings of the treatise without the addition of practical guidance and demonstration were, as technical

---

36 See below for a discussion of the role of Spohr's treatise at the RAM.
37 Kassler (1979), 1145. See Coggins (Chron., 1815) in Kassler (1979), 204–6.

demands rose dramatically, increasingly appreciated among the expanding consumer base.

Crucially, in many cases at least, expectations were now significantly higher and there was a greater willingness to receive new ideas and look for advice on good teaching practice. A new concern for effective pedagogical method, often assisted by parental involvement, sought to integrate the theoretical and practical methods discussed above.[38] Eventually a range of sources across a variety of instruments allowed and catered for a progressive if not entirely systematic approach and assisted both the student and teacher alike in one-to-one and group, private and institutional contexts. Of course self-instruction still had a role to play and there was a substantial market for 'dual-purpose' publications.[39] It is also important to recognize that the bulk of the market for instrumental instruction, even in the case of keyboard tutors, remained directed towards the 'meanest capacity' for much of the period.[40] Increasing numbers of treatises, however, in line with the greater availability of continental examples in translation, attempt to cultivate higher standards of proficiency from around the 1840s onwards (see the following section and Chronology).

Advancements in instrumental pedagogy during the nineteenth century, aided by improved transport and communications infrastructures, affected quantity as well as quality. By the end of the century, in line with a huge (if often undiscriminating) demand for cheap lessons, teachers dominated the music profession and self-employed teachers (mainly women teaching girls elementary piano privately at home) became the largest single group of professional musicians. As Fisher (1888) observed, the music profession became predominantly a teaching and consequently a female profession. Teachers of earlier generations had taught, generally out of necessity, as part of their musical lives, while perhaps eager for performing opportunities. During the second half of the nineteenth century a career as a music teacher, albeit curtailed, became the sole aim and an established position within a school, which may have made a supplementary charge for musical tuition, could offer relative security. Recent studies have shown that the increase in the number of people, primarily female teachers, earning their living from music during the nineteenth century in Britain was rapid and far exceeded the increase in population.[41] The expansion in the area of performance, still dominated by men, was on nothing like the

---

[38] See Kassler (1979), 324 and 648.
[39] See Schneider in Kassler (1979), 920–22.
[40] Kassler (1979), 408.
[41] See Ehrlich (1985), 52–3, 70 and 235–6; and Herbert (2000a), 31.

same scale. Competition among teachers, particularly those catering for the potential for income offered by the most popular instruments among the general population, resulted in derisory rewards for tuition. The army of female music teachers, including the 'daily governess', often suffered great hardship while purveying low standards.[42] Despite this, the prospect of some financial reward and independence and a rare career opportunity (of sorts) for the spinster in the form of 'genteel' employment appealed 'even to girls of lower or scant talent'.[43]

Teachers' advertisements, reminiscent of the eighteenth century, often encompassed a number of skills and services, including instrument hire and tuning. From the pupil's point of view instruments and sheet music, as well as tuition, became much cheaper and more accessible, if often at the expense of quality. It was certainly detrimental to standards that, in contrast to the cultivation of music among the lower orders and military bandsmen, the emphasis was very much on teaching rather than performance and that there was little crossover between the bulk of teachers and performers. Male musicians were left without a vital source of income and women teachers without the necessary rigours of public scrutiny. Inevitably the foundations laid were generally poor and the follow-up provision, such as that offered by the music colleges, necessarily prioritized financial rather than musical considerations and, accordingly, examinations and certificates rather than direct tuition.[44] This 'teaching to the test', even if it did set higher standards for those who taught music as one of many subjects (such as the all-round governess), was no way to engender a love of music and raise the status of music teachers.[45] Attempts to register 'bona-fide qualified' music teachers, excluding amateurs and 'part-timers', and so set certain standards were too little too late and proved ineffective.[46] Once again we encounter a cycle of low standards and neglect among the expanding profession and polite society with a huge market and 'an ever-expanding army of importunate teachers' supported only by the fragile pillars of consumerism and 'social emulation'.[47] A collapse in demand was inevitable.[48]

The ill effects of a swift transition from closed shop to a free-for-all flood could have been avoided if neglect had not been so long term and

---

[42] Gillett (2000a), 9–10.
[43] Ibid., 107 and 189.
[44] Ehrlich (1985), 118–20.
[45] Gillett (2000a), 209.
[46] Ibid., 132.
[47] Ehrlich (1985), 68, 70–71 and 104.
[48] Ibid., 209–11.

safeguards had been put in place to regulate admission to the profession while encouraging serious amateur interest. Much could have been gained if earlier initiatives to learn from continental models had been allowed to prosper. As we have seen, continental methods, whether consciously or not, were most commonly utilized with respect to the training of lower-class amateurs and where musical interests were of greater relevance. In such cases the involvement of able amateur instrumentalists, conductors and trainers could be a hugely positive force for themselves and their local communities in that, even if the principal motivation was financial, established professional livelihoods were not always at risk in the same way as within 'genteel' amateur circles and effective collaboration was possible.[49]

Even though the state eventually played a role in the provision of education for the masses, for the upper classes music and the violin in particular retained many of their unfortunate associations. Even when performance on a musical instrument became a vehicle for morality and personal improvement it remained and could be no more than a refined form of recreation for the majority of young men who moved in social circles above those usually associated with professional musicians. Boys of 'good family' were still directed away from music (often in favour of classics and mathematics) particularly if they showed promise or interest. This is illustrated by the case of the 'well-born' E. H. Fellowes, who was unable to take up Joachim's offer of violin lessons and was allowed to practise on his Amati violin and Tourte bow only when he returned from school in the holidays.[50] The idea of the 'Society amateur' or 'dabbler' as a 'a godsend to teachers but a hindrance to art' continued to the end of the nineteenth century and led to increasing discontentment among native musicians.[51]

Institutions and Group Tuition

More detail on musical and specifically instrumental tuition offered through the growth of dedicated and other institutions can be found in Chapter 5, but it is nevertheless important to comment here on the provision of instruction beyond the one-to-one system. Increasingly

---

[49] The Halifax-based D. H. Sugden, a fustian cutter prior to becoming a teacher of a variety of instruments, appears to have been an accomplished player and popular teacher despite being self-taught. In 1817 he charged a 'guinea a quarter for 1 lesson a week & a guinea & a half per quarter for 2 lessons per week' (see Cowgill (2000), 569). See also Russell (1997), 172, 229 and 281–2.

[50] See Ehrlich (1985), 71–2. The promotion of music in some boys' schools is discussed in Chapter 5.

[51] Gillett (2000b), 336.

during the nineteenth century musical instruction in groups and classes occurred, as we have seen, within the vocal sphere and among lower-class communities as well as some fortunate aspirant professionals encouraged to emulate the well-educated foreign visitors. The ambivalence of the higher orders naturally encouraged a liking of solitary or at least semi-private instrumental activity. The lack of a training infrastructure and financial support outside the family, military and lower classes could mean a very lean existence for even first-rate artists, particularly performers on instruments which did not attract large numbers of amateurs or students in general.[52] Professional musicians, left to sink or swim, were seldom equipped for the challenges they inevitably faced. The activities of wealthy amateurs and professionals, the confines of Kneller Hall excepted, were therefore both concerned in most cases with the individual and self-interest and in the absence of a common philosophy and coherent strategy institutional centres of musical excellence would struggle to emerge. We should remember that the burgeoning of music colleges in Britain and the desire among prospective teachers to acquire paper qualifications was down to willingness to cater for amateur consumerism rather than professional demand. Success was most commonly found where general diversification and market growth had brought specialization, such as at the Royal Military School of Music or the fairly small-scale College of Violinists.

Despite this, some entrepreneurs and musical innovators, spotting huge potential for demand and financial reward in some areas, did provide for group/class instruction within an amateur instrumental and 'genteel' context and helped to improve musical appreciation among amateurs along the way. Independent of both the state and church, a figure such as Logier saw the suitability of the piano for group teaching and tapped into latent demand among middle-class girls and their status-conscious parents. Logier's classes during the early nineteenth century, assisted by converts (in varying degrees) such as Burrowes, Cutler and Eager[53] achieved enormous influence and success, aided a great deal by the 'chiroplast', intended to assist teachers to 'advance their pupils much more rapidly'.[54] The threat to other teachers' livelihoods was not appreciated by many, but Logier's methods, in addition to being a clever commercial venture, were a positive step in attempting to 'eliminate some of the drawbacks associated with private tuition'[55] and offering an alternative to the over-worked and

---

[52] See Humphries (2000), 24, on the fortunes of the horn player Henry Platt.
[53] See Kassler (1979), 137–8, 247 and 304.
[54] Ibid., 704–12.
[55] Mackerness (1964), 174.

demoralized boarding school music master. In a similar vein Sophia Dussek Moralt's piano academy in Paddington opened in around 1812 and a number of tutors were published for schools and families.[56] The examples for schools could save the master's limited time and guide the provision of class instruction. Instrumental instruction, involving individuals and groups and specialist teachers, became a more common feature in secondary education, for girls and then boys, as the century progressed and eventually found its way into the elementary curriculum. The interests of lower-class instrumentalists had of course been taken care of in other ways prior to this development.[57]

Styles and Personalities

Native and Foreign

Prominent performers, composers, pedagogues, theorists and their methods will be discussed in following sections, but if we look at this group as a whole it is apparent that there is a dominant foreign element in most cases. We have already discussed the British predilection for the convenience, status and exclusivity offered by overseas talent. Accordingly the evolution of pedagogical method as well as technical and expressive priorities and models in British sources of various kinds (including the instruments themselves) most often betrays a delayed reaction to continental developments. The most influential of these tended to be those brought over by the visiting or resident pioneers themselves or their disciples which were sympathetically received (and employed) by wealthy patrons and accepted critically. The nature of instrumental teaching, based on individual provision and consumption rather than institutions and the large-scale nurturing of talent, placed great emphasis on such influence. Burney's record of prominent native and foreign performers is testament to the extent of this foreign dominance, particularly in areas of great demand, during the eighteenth century.[58] Handel was chosen as the teacher of Princess Anne, daughter of George II, and the case of the respected keyboardist and teacher Joseph Kelway, quickly replaced in his position at court following the arrival of J. C. Bach, shows that even when one existed a native virtuoso was easily displaced by a distinguished foreign visitor.

---

[56] Kassler (1979), 1018 and 1074.
[57] See photographs of family, school and village groups in Graham (1997), 87 and 90 and Russell (1997), plates 8 and 9.
[58] Burney, ed. Mercer (1935), vol.2, 1008.

Nevertheless native talent, when not forced into becoming a jack of all trades and picking up the scraps discarded by continental talent, did rise to the surface in some cases during the eighteenth and nineteenth centuries and not just in the less competitive provinces. Examples include the oboist William Parke, the cellist Robert Lindley, the Harpers on the trumpet and Robert Sidney Pratten and Joseph Richardson on the flute. Rather than native artists supplanting the foreign competition, this was often in less popular areas of activity, where foreign brilliance was less conspicuous and was not monopolized by the demands of the social elite. Consequently, in some cases opportunities arose for home-grown talent to blossom under the guidance of a foreign master. In marked contrast to the fortunes of the bulk of native instrumentalists, expectations were therefore sometimes higher and positions of importance, even eminence, were possible. Generally speaking, however, it was native singers who captured the concert-goers' imagination. With respect to music education the figures connected with instrumental pedagogy are certainly less well known and celebrated today than those connected with the sight-singing movement, but they also played an important role in the cultivation of more enlightened attitudes.

'Good Taste'

When examining the assimilation of continental trends, a pervasive characteristic of British music history, it is vital to look at the nature of the choices and the motivation behind them. The idea of 'good taste' has a fundamental role to play here. One might expect this to be a highly subjective concept, but in the case of British critical reception it takes the form of a virtually objective evaluation of high artistic ideals and one is struck by the consistency with which these ideals are critically applied during the whole period. As raised in Chapter 1 ('Conservatism and Innovation') their essential character is derived from the 'refined' and 'sober' qualities of tried and tested repertoire by composers such as Corelli and Handel and later composers and performers who exuded similar qualities both through their music and personally. A cultural environment in which consumer power held sway, in addition to a legacy of ambivalence among the wealthy with respect to the value and role of music, led to the patronage of conservatism in many cases and a pervasive distrust and delayed acceptance of innovation. The continuous influx of new artists and styles into the vibrant and transient cultural centres of Britain, and London in particular, and the public appetite for novelty prompted the social elite and some influential musical connoisseurs to become even more entrenched in their attitudes. After all, greater accessibility and democracy merely increased the desire among the wealthy intelligentsia to use their consumption of culture as a means of distinguishing themselves from the populace. The challenge of the new, public virtuosity of the early nineteenth century further exacerbated this resistance to change and the anachronistic nature of any native contributions. The safety of the old masters allowed a certain class of amateur to offset some of the negative connotations and any further 'corruption', maintain the distinction in taste and aspirations between themselves, the lower orders and professionals, and so justify their own involvement to themselves. The longevity and nature of the Academy of Ancient Music is evidence of this belief and its demise points to the blurring of such distinctions as opportunity and activity spread.

There was little incentive for native or even resident foreign musicians to stand at the cutting edge of musical developments, although some visitors did exploit their freedom to cash in on the unique public concert scene and their novelty value before retreating back to the continent. Critical reception was reluctant to show appreciation of the perceived excesses of others and thereby restricted progress. Risk-taking, spontaneous virtuosity impressed but did not receive admiration, in contrast to some other cultural centres[59] and the experimental mentality of Britons in some other areas. Rather the emphasis, out of desire and necessity, was on the selection and emulation of appropriate foreign models. As already mentioned, some enlightened (and commercially astute) writers did seek to represent both the 'ancient' and 'modern' styles.

The impact of these and other trends on the teaching of musical instruments was that the models chosen for emulation, through the success and critical reception of individual teachers, performers and writers, were generally conservative. Endorsed practice was often retrospective if not 'obsolete' and music colleges were no different.[60] Exceptions did come in areas where demand and innovation (including organology) were sufficient for new approaches to take hold. Keyboard instruments, first harpsichord and then piano, in particular benefited from their fixed place in the 'respectable' household and the relatively high expectations resulting from female, dedicated practice and a recognized role for the teacher.

Social dynamics played a significant role in establishing whether approaches to certain instruments were firmly conservative or relatively progressive. As mentioned in Chapter 1 ('The Battle of the Sexes') the popularity of the 'accompanied' sonata from the late eighteenth century

---

[59] See D. B. Scott (2002), 551.
[60] Ehrlich (1985), 192 and 223.

onwards, particularly in a domestic context, illustrates the typically contrasting aspirations and freedoms of amateur keyboardists and violinists (or flautists) which were determined along gender lines. This was a favoured genre in England even after more 'equal' sonatas by mainstream composers entered the repertoire. Of Domenico Corri's 21 keyboard sonatas from the early nineteenth century, 13 were published with an optional accompaniment and some, such as Thomas Carter's Op. 3 (1774), were marketed as accompanied keyboard sonatas despite the violin part being essential. They were also often included in keyboard and thorough-bass treatises which demonstrates their potential pedagogical as well as performance role within the home.[61] The more virtuosic solo continuo sonatas were popular among amateur music societies which were in a position to hire in professionals, but were beyond most amateurs for domestic use, at least the average amateur male 'soloist'. Examples emanating from Austro-German centres generally appear to have demanded a great deal more proficiency and independence of the non-keyboard instrumentalists.[62]

It is of course significant that Viotti's violin concertos, which in many ways bridge the gap between the contributions of Mozart and Beethoven in the form, were published in London as piano arrangements a long time before they appeared in their original form. We can assume that there would have been very little market for such modern repertoire among male amateur violinists at this stage, although their ability to offer a middle path between the 'classical' and new virtuosic expressive ideals did make them very popular in England. Viotti as a pivotal figure managed to 'astonish' audiences while also receiving praise for 'something infinitely better': awakening 'emotion', giving 'a soul to sound', and leading 'the passions captive'.[63] His works, particularly the violin duos, became acknowledged teaching tools (see following chapter), but naturally not until amateur proficiency had caught up and long after mainstream developments had moved on. The Beethoven Violin Concerto, long neglected on the wider European stage because of its lack of sensation and bravura, was also 'rediscovered' in England and championed by foreign and native artists throughout the rest of the century. Despite Beethoven's 'canonic' position it is perhaps unsurprising that approval and understanding of the challenging late quartets were less unified and slower to materialize.[64]

Music criticism was long to be a male-dominated area and, prior to the

---

[61] See Kassler (1979), 942; and Kidd (1968).
[62] See Komlós (1995), 86–7, 89 and 93. See also Gillett (2000a), 90.
[63] *London Morning Chronicle* (10 March 1794).
[64] See Bashford (2000), 96, 102, 107 and 112.

more professional specialists and dedicated journals of the early nineteenth century, its appearance (aside from music histories) in journals and elsewhere was often down to amateurs who earned their living by other means. Dilettante priorities therefore imbued mainstream critical opinion, but we should also not ignore the penchant of the British for novelty, especially that from abroad. Although this tended to equate with superficiality, charlatanism and quackery in the eyes of the critics, who wished to be seen promoting conservative and 'softer' approaches to performance, the growing mass of the concert-going public was often more receptive. We therefore find an important distinction between critical and popular taste. This perhaps manifested itself most notably in the range of prominent foreign violinists active in major commercial centres.

An almost mythical figure such as Corelli provided a valuable benchmark for the critics. He represented the antithesis of the mechanical virtuosity of 'pipers and fiddlers' and gained a great deal of intellectual credibility as a result.[65] The longevity of Corelli's fundamental position in British violin playing, through his own works and those of his disciples and their pupils, provides an important context for nineteenth-century attitudes towards musical expression.[66] The musical and personal qualities he epitomized, such as mildness and modesty, were emulated and lauded throughout the eighteenth and nineteenth centuries. His works enjoyed widespread popularity for performance and teaching in London and the provinces, particularly among amateurs, although it must be said that most violin tutors of the eighteenth century, including the 'Prelleur' model (see below), fall short of even Corelli's technical demands in their aspirations. He inadvertently contributed to the amateur/professional divide with respect to violin playing. Corelli's 'ease and simplicity'[67] represented in many respects the zenith of amateur violin playing for much of the eighteenth century and only later became, along with some of his disciples, the ideal model for a sound foundation in violin playing before moving on to more advanced (but equally 'refined') repertoire. It is no accident that he is repeatedly viewed as the originator of all that later developed that was worthwhile and enduring in violin playing.[68]

---

[65] See Hodges (1836), 40–41.

[66] See Golby (1999b), vol.1, 16ff. for detailed discussion of Corelli's legacy with respect to the violin. Valuable work has been done on the reception of Corelli in England, in particular Edwards (1976) and Weber (1992: 77–89), who summarizes contemporary and more recent thought on this subject. See also Allsop (1999) and, with particular relevance to the violin, Johnstone (1996) and Zaslaw (1996).

[67] Burney (1776–89, ed. Mercer 1935), vol.2, 444.

[68] See Spohr (Chron., 1878), 174; David (1889), 291 and 299; Dubourg (5th edn, 1878), 245–7; and Hogarth (1838), vol.1, 145–78.

Geminiani, a Corelli disciple, inherited his master's status and, despite some particularly progressive if idiosyncratic approaches to violin playing (see below and the following chapter), contributed to the longevity of the 'ancient' style. His 'reheatings' of his own works were generally simplifications, appealing to conservative amateurs, and more individual, innovative elements, which broke with the Corellian tradition (such as in his Op.5) were much less successful.

The continued focus on such performance qualities in the critical and pedagogical literature directed popular taste (whether consciously or not) away from the frivolity and excess personified by Paganini. Writers such as Hodges, following in the tradition of C. P. E. Bach and others, sought to draw attention to

> the superficiality of this vain-boasting, self-complacent age, which prefers sound to sense, and would rather have its ears tickled with an empty nonsensical air or wanton ballad, than to have the noblest passions and affections of the heart acted upon, stirred up and brought into full force and play, by the sublime efforts of talent, taste and genius; concentrated, if it were possible in the productions of an archangel.[69]

The rejection of virtuosity as a sign of good taste naturally struck a chord with traditional hierarchy of musical study, focusing on logic and reason rather than mechanical display as a means of stirring 'noble' passions. It is interesting to note that Crotch, a truly prodigious and hugely influential individual, was of the opinion during the 1820s that 'a composer need not play an instrument at all'.[70]

The popularity of Prince Albert and associated Teutonic erudition around the mid-nineteenth century provided an ideal backdrop for Spohr and Mendelssohn, both German, conservative but masterful figures at home with English polite society. In this environment and assisted by the festival movement, Handel became a unifying, adopted national symbol of morality and refinement.[71] Spohr's ability to combine the already 'approved' and enduring elements of the earlier Italian, French and German schools proved highly successful. He managed to attract widespread admiration and become a model for emulation among increasing numbers of middle-class amateurs who, though still respectability-conscious, were eager to achieve a great deal more than previous elite groups and received encouragement from musical connoisseurs. The works of Spohr and Viotti to a lesser extent provided

---

[69] Hodges (1836), 149.

[70] Kassler (1979), 236.

[71] See K. Ellis in Samson, ed. (2002), 365. Naturally Wagner had to wait a further few decades to achieve widespread popularity and acceptance.

'safe' and respectable incentives to improve. Their critical success, built as it was on the firm foundation of 'good taste', was far more enduring than the popular success achieved by some prominent names. In fact Spohr's qualities were essentially 'anti-popularist', but his erudite and sober music, if 'too good for the people',[72] was exactly what the connoisseur required. The inherent exclusivity of critical taste is of course not confined to this particular period, although the emphasis on consumption and assimilation at this stage in Britain focused attention on the critical evaluation of what others had created. In the absence of a 'quest for a national voice'[73] until economic dominance was at risk, canonic tendencies with very little original input ensued, the continuation of a 'native' violin school along 'Corellian' lines being just one example.

The huge popular success enjoyed by Paganini came from his immense stature as a great and pioneering violinist in performance. Spohr transcended this virtuosity, and critical approval (amounting almost to deification) of him as a pedagogue and composer came, as in the case of his eighteenth-century equivalent Geminiani, through limited exposure on the concert platform but effective promotion among the literate community and an identification with the all-important concept of 'good taste'. Through treatises and other texts musical taste became as much a literary as an aural phenomenon and as such the cerebral, almost logical element became of vital importance. Geminiani and Spohr both represented retrospective, learned qualities that the consumer was eager to be identified with. The potential of texts such as treatises to afford their purchasers 'good taste' by association alone, perhaps akin to today's 'coffee-table book' mentality, makes it dangerous to assume that the popularity of a treatise equates with its proper use on a large scale. Geminiani's curious example certainly demonstrates a desire to appeal to a market that would have little interest in its many subtleties and complexities.

Many other foreign figures who managed to promote similar expressive priorities, including Moscheles, Joachim and Mendelssohn, enjoyed comparable levels of success. Mendelssohn perhaps exceeded even Spohr's achievements in his critical reception and popular success, not least through his even more popular oratorios and the usefulness and respectability of middle-class participation they embodied. In contrast, the prominence and influence of the 'London School' of piano playing and manufacture, largely down to the opportunities offered by industrialization, an expanding amateur market and the public concert

---

[72] Gillett (2000a), 47.
[73] J. Samson, 'Nations and nationalism' in *idem*, ed. (2002), 598.

scene, did allow far more virtuosity and generally more extrovert approaches to keyboard performance. Clementi's new legato style and the power and increased range pioneered by Dussek (of whom Spohr was critical), for example, made a significant contribution to the development of Romantic piano music. However they were astute enough to develop a repertoire of teaching pieces distinct from those for their own professional performance and issue effective, progressive pedagogical works suited to the burgeoning amateur market (see Chapter 4) and, in the case of Clementi (Chron., 1801), incorporate 'lessons' by earlier as well as contemporary composers.

It is apparent that unhelpful divisions of various kinds are present in many aspects of British musical culture during the period. With regard to 'taste' the disparity between conservative and innovative, critical and popular naturally put writers of pedagogical texts, especially during the transitional late eighteenth-, early nineteenth-century period, in a difficult if not impossible position. Those who did not choose to recycle previously approved instructions ad nauseam (apparently a minority) needed to reconcile these frictions while taking account of changing aesthetic and expressive ideals. The evolution of the instruments themselves and different reactions to these organological developments on the continent itself (such as to the introduction of valves on the horn in Germany and France) added yet another dimension and sometimes prompted a middle path (see Chapter 4). The long-standing 'pasticcio' tradition, from as early as the time of Playford, of creating 'new' tutors through the piecing together of material from various others, continued to appeal to many with varying levels of sophistication (including Jousse), although the result was often an ineffective, contradictory or, at best, confusing mixture. The most successful contributions were complete translations of mainstream foreign texts (such as Tosi and Spohr) which were able, through their length and authority, to present a coherent if seldom up-to-date approach to performance. It is also worth noting those elementary native 'handbooks' which could offer a detailed and progressive precursor to these translations.

The nineteenth century witnessed increasingly serious, even 'scientific', approaches to the learning of musical instruments. In this respect perhaps image and social respectability per se receded slightly as genuine self-improvement and education came to the fore; but nevertheless 'good taste' still played a significant role in the selection of teaching material among British consumers.

Sources: General Trends

The abundance of music-teaching material published during the eighteenth and nineteenth centuries in Britain tells a fascinating and valuable story of expansion and diversification as consumer demands changed in line with the expansion of the middle classes in particular. Both consumers and providers heightened their aspirations, albeit within the often strict parameters set down by social convention. This section sets out some of the main trends in the development of this material as discerned from the dozens of examples, taken as a representative sample, studied so far (see Part 4). It concentrates on sources for the violin in order to present a consistent, coherent context, and while some issues are particular to this instrument, the dramatic change in its fortunes during the period as a whole makes it a valuable indicator of underlying trends.[74]

The treatises discussed here are a symptom of the general educational scene, their numbers and scope reflecting the lack of state provision and a coherent system for music, and specifically the neglect of instrumental tuition. For many beginners they were the only means of learning an instrument and for others a necessary complement to the often inadequate private tuition discussed above. Again eighteenth-century trends provide an essential context for our period.

During the eighteenth century in Britain tutor books appeared in abundance and, responding to demand, were often written with the highly influential adult amateur in mind. The vast majority were intended for self-instruction and merely satisfied the demands of these 'dabblers' for easy and fast results.[75] This form of instruction appealed to the gentleman with no serious musical ambition, avoiding deference to and potential embarrassment in front of the socially inferior music master. It was also cheaper for the man to provide for the spouse and child than private lessons and greatly reduced the risk of any sexual impropriety between teacher and pupil.[76]

The sources themselves have little worth as a means of achieving proficiency on an instrument. These small pamphlets provide little more than the basics of notation and fingering (in about twelve pages of text)

---

[74] More detailed discussion of the individual violin treatises, their context, structure and contents, and associated literature can be found in Golby (1999b). Other valuable listings of a variety of instructional material from the period include Brown (1886); Simpson (1966); Warner (1967); Kassler (1979); and Pickering (1990).

[75] See Leppert (1988), 68. 'Adult music education and self-tutoring manuals' (ibid., 67–70) is a useful summary of the issues surrounding these works.

[76] See Fiske and Johnstone, eds (1990), 5.

and, by far the most substantial part, an anthology of dance tunes and popular airs. Success is judged by the number of tunes learned rather than by any concept of general proficiency or musicianship. This format is common to literally hundreds of British examples from the seventeenth century, through the eighteenth and into the nineteenth, for a wide variety of instruments.[77] This was obviously a buoyant market, and the numbers and the nature of these publications kept prices low (often one shilling and sixpence) for the whole of the eighteenth century in comparison with private tuition. However, access to instruments remained restricted and generally expensive, which prohibited the active participation in music for the majority of society without wealth and/or family connections.

British elementary methods written at the beginning of the eighteenth century (or even earlier) often provide the model for works published much later, with little modification or revision. This is particularly evident with regard to the violin. In line with the decline of the viol and the growing popularity of the violin, an extremely vibrant 'do-it-yourself' movement in violin instruction emerged in Britain during the eighteenth century.[78] Many of the works issued in response to this demand were, out of convenience and complacency, based on the same model for well over a century.

The seminal source was *Nolens volens* (1695). During the late seventeenth century the English violin method was pioneering as a genre and provided the self-taught amateur with insights into contemporary practice. Unfortunately most English contributions on the subject did not progress from this level and the late seventeenth-century models laid down by Playford and others for over a century. They stood still, satisfying only the limited demands of the gentleman 'dabbler' (the principal target audience), while those on the continent substantially developed the instrument and its capabilities and published tutors to reflect these changes.[79] The *Nolens volens* model lived on through at

---

[77] In addition to instruction books and primers on instrumental technique there were also examples concerned with music theory and harmony. Rohr (1983: 315) refers to 'two hundred [and] seventy-two musicians, including fifteen women, who were employed as composers, teachers, and/or performers' who wrote such books on a range of subjects during the period, most of which were of limited pedagogical value. See also T. McGeary, 'Music Literature', in Fiske and Johnstone (1990), 408.

[78] See Boyden (1965), 244–7.

[79] Although Lenton (1693) has in turn been established as a model for *Nolens volens* (see Boyd and Rayson (1982)), it is significant that *Nolens volens* is a considerably simplified version of Lenton. By including only a small amount of text and numerous simple tunes, *Nolens volens* managed to exploit the large market provided by the amateur 'dabbler' for easy repertoire and remain in print, in various forms, for well over a century.

least 30 English elementary works published for the violin and used by amateurs up to and including part V of Prelleur's work (1731),[80] a tutor with which Geminiani has often been wrongly associated, and the various publications derived from Prelleur (including Crome (c.1740) and Rutherford (c.1750)). These also include the numerous supposititious works bearing Geminiani's name that continued to be published after his death and into the nineteenth century (including examples from 1770, 1775, 1792 and 1800).[81]

The use of the Italian's name is justified only in so far as his table of embellishments and some fingering exercises and bowing instructions (very different from the equivalent passage in Prelleur and subsequently prominent in many nineteenth-century English sources) taken from his 1751 violin treatise appear in these works.[82] Whether out of ignorance or for commercial reasons Geminiani's role in these posthumous attributed works, which differ slightly although they promote very similar levels of proficiency through their collections of pieces, is less prominent than the title-pages give him credit for. By using elements from Geminiani's advanced work (1751) they gain an association with a name that represents musical 'good taste' and respected teaching practices, which in turn gives credibility to an anachronistic and retrogressive model. They do not reflect Geminiani's general approach to the violin, but do assure his name of prominence well into the nineteenth century in England.[83] What Geminiani did for violin tutors the prominent virtuoso 'Mr [J. C.] Fischer' did for equivalent works for the oboe.

Lenton, an altogether more serious and comprehensive affair written by a professional violinist, appears to have been pitched above the level of the market and consequently appeared in only two editions. The failure of a more substantial and detailed tutor no doubt discouraged other writers from producing more advanced material until the demands of the market had changed.

[80] For details and references see Golby (1999b), vol.2. See also Kolneder (1998), 291 and 317 and, in particular, Sharpe (1999). Boyden (1965) discusses technical details in the early English sources and their context between 1650 and 1700 (pp.247–84) and 1700 and 1761 (pp.356–494).

[81] See Boyden (1952), ix–xi for an important evaluation of the methods associated with the Italian.

[82] See Boyden (1952), x–xi. The original source of the embellishments is the Italian's *Treatise of good taste in the art of musick* (London, 1749).

[83] The body of treatises associated with Geminiani illustrates how the perception of the influence of an individual can be distorted and also demonstrates that the date of a treatise is often no indication of its stylistic bias or pedagogical method. The use of material from Prelleur by nineteenth-century writers in English is probably inadvertent and due to the prevalence of these supposititious works promoting Geminiani as the author of this material.

The numerous sources derived from *Nolens volens* contain minimal teaching material and so are tutors only in the loosest sense. Most consist of little more than fingerboard charts, the rudiments of notation, a dictionary of musical terms, a table of ornaments, followed by a collection of short, elementary pieces (usually airs and dances). Significantly the fingerboard charts (folding inserts) are highly complex in relation to the rest of the contents, detailing an extensive range and unequal semitones. These elements are not taken up elsewhere and such a conspicuous 'mathematical' element would seem to be appealing to the intellectual concerns of the male consumer outlined above (temperament was an area of great interest for eighteenth-century British music theorists). Despite claiming that they are 'compleat', the most fundamental aspects of technique are described in insufficient detail in these publications or are omitted completely. The lack of consistency and complementary material between the text, fingerboard charts and the music in the sources derived from Prelleur is one of their idiosyncrasies and consequent failings as instruction manuals. This lack of integration is not surprising considering the popular nature of the pieces included, and these examples serve only to emphasize the wide gulf between the technical standards of the amateur and the professional violinist during the eighteenth century and the level of most written instruction at this time and the demands of the core repertoire, which only professionals or dedicated amateurs with the assistance of private tuition could have attempted with any degree of success. This incongruity also applies to the similarly complex and detailed (as well as plagiarized) ornament tables. Most mainstream continental sources restrict ornamentation to accomplished masters, prescribing sparing use and suitable discrimination,[84] and again this level of detail is completely out of place in works of this kind. However, such 'borrowings' probably appealed more to the gentleman than other technical details concerned with the mechanics of instrumental technique or artistic performance. Clearly comprehensive supplementary instruction would have been required if the reader was to learn anything of value from these works.

It is quite remarkable and a testament to the appetite of the amateur as well as a reflection of low standards that the substantial part of a treatise, originating in 1695, could have passed between a variety of different publishers and been reprinted in 1813 as *The entire new and compleat tutor for the violin*. This is more than half a century after the publication of Leopold Mozart's pioneering *Versuch* (1756), in which the text is by far the most important element. It is also indicative of the

---

[84] See Lawson (2000), 69, on Türk's discussion of the matter.

general standard of British treatises at this time in comparison to continental examples that Quantz (1752) is able to incorporate what is in effect a detailed violin method into a treatise on the flute.[85] Similar works for other instruments are numerous throughout this period and offer convincing evidence of the limited standards among the dilettanti. Well into the nineteenth century many native treatises continued to focus on technique only to the extent to which it was necessary to play the favoured repertoire, rather than, as in the case of continental examples, the knowledge required to form a rounded musician.

The continued promotion of self-instruction, at odds with opinion in more enlightened circumstances,[86] through these publishers' 'reheatings' not only perpetuated low standards among those who, out of choice or necessity, made use of it, but it also undermined the status and stifled the provision of serious instrumental tuition for those with more ambition. This market provided little incentive for the writing of more comprehensive and effective instruction methods. However some sources from the eighteenth century demonstrate a demand, albeit relatively small at this stage, for more sophisticated violin instruction among more serious amateurs and budding professionals and material to complement practical instruction.[87] The more progressive specimens from the eighteenth century have been overlooked as a body of works and crucially for the present discussion they are the precursors of many nineteenth-century British sources. They require much greater dedication on the part of the student and aspire to higher technical standards. Also these tutors are in most cases the work of foreign figures writing in English or their native disciples whose names appear on the title-pages. Their status and relative security allowed them to rise above the fear of competition that characterized the activities of the majority of native musicians. This market expanded during the nineteenth century, providing greater opportunities for native musicians and writers, but from an early stage the contribution of the native writer was confined mainly to observation and assimilation rather than original thought.

Ways in which these tutors are more ambitious include an attempt to

---

[85] See Stolba (1968–9), 114ff.

[86] Löhlein (1774), cited in Straeten (1911), 243.

[87] The emergence of more serious works to aid the learning of the violin is mirrored by the contemporary literature for some other instruments, particularly the flute (see Powell (1996), 5–9). The situation regarding the cello appears to have been different. As referred to earlier, it was taken more seriously by the aristocracy, and, with no part of Prelleur (1731) to plagiarize, it appears that more valuable pedagogical works were issued in England at an earlier stage than in the case of the violin. See Heron-Allen (1894), 343; Walden (1998), particularly 26–33 and 300–301; and Stowell (1999), 224–5.

ally the text and often more advanced musical content to a much greater extent in a drive towards increasingly effective pedagogy. Crome's tutor (1740 and 1765), a popular work for around half a century, is indebted to part V of Prelleur, but often provides more detail than the original or the other works derived from it. It uses the dialogue/catechism format to imitate the private lesson,[88] remarks on the difficulty of the violin and its popularity among 'young Gentlemen' (1765: 1–2), shows concern for the 'young Scholar' (p.5) and a desire to provide a 'good Foundation' for 'the two Fundamentals of Musick; Tune and Time' (pp.1–2), and, perhaps most significantly, the short pieces Crome includes are often scored as duets or used as lessons to complement and consolidate the instructions in the text.

Comment should be made here on the character of Geminiani's 1751 treatise itself.[89] This work is unique in the eighteenth and nineteenth centuries as an instrumental treatise originally published in English that has international significance and contains principles that have contributed to the modern approach to the instrument. At first glance it does appear strange that the first advanced violin treatise, designed principally for existing or potential professionals, should be published in England, the home of the proud gentleman amateur. However it is easier to understand when one considers that the author was not only resident in this country but also an Italian disciple of Corelli, whose seminal role in violin playing and qualities of taste and refinement in performance were appreciated in Britain throughout the eighteenth and nineteenth centuries. Geminiani continues the Corellian tradition in his treatise by placing taste before display and technique as the servant of expression. Also it is one of the relatively few advanced violin treatises by a native of Italy, the birthplace of the instrument and where the well-established master–pupil approach and oral tradition of instruction made such publications less essential. The absence of such a tradition in eighteenth-century England and the popularity of self-instruction created, in contrast, a much greater demand for a treatise which claims to provide 'All the Rules necessary to attain to a Perfection on that Instrument' (title-page). Even though most of the material in the treatise would have been beyond the requirements of the dilettanti, they may have bought it for its status as the work of an influential and respected foreign violinist and as a sign of their 'good taste'. The title itself, with its echoes of Prelleur part V, may have been an attempt to appeal to the gentleman-

---

[88] The 'virtual' lesson was also usefully employed by Domenico Corri in his 1810 singing treatise.

[89] Careri (1993: 171–9) provides a useful discussion of the general contents of the treatise.

amateur market. When established in Britain, Geminiani may have spotted his opportunity to publish a work begun in Italy (judging from the Italian text on the music plates) and intended for a more advanced market.

The content of the treatise (discussed further in Chapter 3) is an odd synthesis of material without the systematic thoroughness and technical detail of Leopold Mozart's work (1756). The twelve compositions and many of the examples are undoubtedly advanced for a published violin method, irrespective of country, but the text (even though Geminiani is almost generous with words compared with his other treatises) provides insufficient explanation and leaves too much to be inferred from the music itself. Also, despite the advanced character of a great deal of the treatise, it descends to the level of a fingerboard chart (Example 1A) and directions for violin and bow holds (examples 1B and C). The fingerboard chart is far simpler than that in Prelleur and those examples derived from it, and would seem to represent a token gesture towards the concerns of the dilettante market. In keeping with this hypothesis this initial part of the treatise is immediately followed by scales using the fourth finger and up to seventh position (example 1C (1a–7a), p.1), even though the student is advised not to 'meddle with' the bow until the seventh example (text pp.2–3). When the use of the bow is allowed for the first time (Example 7, p.5), the player is confronted with an exercise equally demanding for both hands. A huge range of string-crossings is immediately required, some of which cover all four strings. There are no easy rhythm exercises to ease the player in and nurture confidence.

The contents of Geminiani's treatise, reflecting the tensions inherent in British culture already highlighted, are therefore a curious and not altogether convincing juxtaposition of the basic and the advanced, with the former added, it would seem, in the interests of attracting the widest possible readership. This makes the work not only anomalous but also very difficult to use in practice without the assistance of a teacher to apply the basic principles espoused in the text to the examples and pieces.[90] Therefore in addition to its use as a text for the apprenticed student and his master, it may have influenced the more dedicated amateur to study with a professional, rather than rely solely on self-instruction. A treatise intended solely for an advanced/professional market was not at this time (and for a significant time to come) a viable option and the success of Geminiani's work was ensured by its pedigree rather than its usefulness.

---

[90] The fact that it is not particularly user-friendly, especially for young pupils, is commented on in the *Advertissement* to the updated edition published in Paris in 1803 (see Careri (1993), 174) and by Philpot (1766) in the context of his own treatise (see below).

Regardless of its failings as a pedagogical work, the influence of Geminiani's treatise is of great significance in British violin playing as well as a vital part of the whole picture of violin performance. Despite its nod towards the fingering chart, its modification of the rudiments/airs format in favour of a more progressive integration of theory and practice, precept and example, looks towards the nineteenth century. At the end of the nineteenth century, influential writers still considered it 'of the greatest interest' as 'the only direct evidence of Corelli's method and principles'.[91] It prompted among some forward-thinking individuals a more serious and systematic approach to British violin pedagogy and published tutors generally. In addition to contributing to the contents and credibility of the hugely popular tutors derived from Prelleur discussed above, it directly influenced the progressive works of several of Geminiani's pupils, in particular Robert Bremner, an important publisher and writer, and Stephen Philpot.

Philpot, one of the King's musicians, was a pupil of Michael Festing who had been taught by Geminiani. Although indebted to Geminiani, Philpot's treatise (1766) is pioneering as a work explicitly for 'young beginners' and 'scholars' (title-page and p.5) and in its use of text and musical examples to the complete exclusion of separate compositions, as is characteristic of Leopold Mozart and many continental and nineteenth-century sources. The comments in the Preface to the treatise describe the origins, purpose and structure of the work and exemplify its seriousness. Philpot highlights the lack of a 'rational Treatise upon this Subject' and the consequences of this for standards of performance, as well as the difficulty of Geminiani's work for children or young beginners (pp.4–6). Literally 'An introduction' to 'the art of playing on the violin', it prepares the ground for Geminiani's treatise and attempts to compensate for its failings with the limitations of the British market in mind.

The text is complemented by the musical examples, which include scales, exercises, and, along the lines of short études, short pieces in binary form with explicit technical aims. Thorough-bass is supplied for the accompaniment and fingerings and some bowings are added. The author also suggests how other instruments and parts can be introduced, and how the 'Assistance of a Master' is required for the best results and to surmount 'Difficulties' (pp.13–14). This is in complete contrast to the numerous 'Prelleur-derived' examples which, wary of limiting their potential readership, give the impression that such assistance is unnecessary.

---

[91] David (1889), 292.

The work of an active teacher (p.5), Philpot's treatise is therefore a far more effective and comprehensive *teaching* tool than anything previously published in England (or after for a great number of years), and is designed to assist the master and student alike. The progressive and systematic content is far less self-consciously 'scientific' (exemplified by the previously incongruent treatment of temperament) in favour of an effective blend of theory and practice along the lines of mainstream continental texts from the mid-eighteenth century onwards. The recommendation of his anonymous 'friend' reflects its success in achieving its aims, in spite of the subject not appearing particularly 'promising' (p.2) at first sight.

This is an important and ground-breaking source: the work of a descendant of the Corellian school, which displays a genuine concern to develop young native musical talent and achieve higher standards among English violinists. Perhaps an equivalent figure for the flute and oboe would be J. Wragg (Chron., 1792 and 1804). James (Chron., 1826) offers a more detailed native flute treatise for the nineteenth century, although it remains far less comprehensive than earlier continental examples. The British market did remain largely amateur after all.

Unfortunately for native musicians Philpot's treatise, although significant as a pedagogical work and despite the appearance of some of his directions in works by Jousse and related sources, was not the beginning of a reversal in the violin's fortunes. A consistently low standard among players other than professionals remained the status quo, prior to the much more serious involvement and achievements of the middle-class amateur during the nineteenth century. However some other sources reveal a steadily increasing desire on the part of professional musicians and connoisseurs to produce teaching material of a much better quality and encourage better standards among violinists, often relying on well-established foreign names. Burney promoted the theories of Tartini (1771), which retained their popularity well into the nineteenth century, and the various tutors by the Belgian Gehot (Chron., 1780, 1784 and 1790), which, despite the trend towards specialization, often reflect earlier priorities (as exemplified by Playford) in providing guidance for a vast array of (up to 35) different instruments. Nevertheless the technical content is often more ambitious than in the case of earlier general treatises. The last of these sources (*The art of bowing*, extracted from Chron., 1784) is in effect an étude, making use of a theme and 30 progressively more difficult variations to help develop left- and right-hand technique. The theme and variation form was ideal for study material and was evidently popular in England throughout the period. Also the treatise of Barthélemon (Chron., 1790), an important teacher, performer and writer, is ambitious technically, although it is intended 'for the improvement of the lovers' of the violin among the 'PUBLIC' (title-page and pp.i–ii). The progressive examples and six 'capricios' provide the main substance of the work, and the relatively small amount of text demands that the teacher should play at least some part in its use. Similarly Tashanberg (Chron., 1796) makes use of quite demanding fingering and bowing exercises for the more advanced player. New, progressive pedagogy often focused on not just a single instrument but also increasingly on individual aspects of instrumental technique, such as fingering or bowing, for example, rather than general concerns related to composition such as ornamentation. There were also increasing numbers of independent publications which offered separate guides to the essential 'rudiments', such as Clarke (1830).

The emergence and growth of a market for effective practical musical instruction during the period, as belief in music as a 'science' diminishes, is a significant development in British music education. It highlights a more serious interest on the part of many beginners and, born out of this demand, a greater willingness among performers and critics to encourage higher standards of proficiency and resist continued foreign dominance. For example Relfe (1819) reflects a desire to provide more people (primarily amateurs) with grounding in the basic rudiments of music through written material. This desire for knowledge among the literate classes was of course not confined to music, and the market for these guides in all sorts of subjects grew as the century progressed and the consumer base increased in size. Music, however, had more ground to recover than most areas of interest and still had no established role in mainstream education. Despite their limited scope relative to many continental examples, these publications, assisted by developments in the technology of printing, therefore contributed a great deal to the enhanced appreciation of music among the multitude and, by benefiting both the teacher and pupil, eventually led to improvements in the general standard of amateur participation.[92]

Various factors contributed to the effectiveness and success of these methods other than their numbers and, for reasons highlighted previously, it was probably keyboard tutors which took the lead in the greatest numbers.[93] Higher aspirations demanded a different approach

---

[92] This is suggested by the reference (most likely by the violinist John Ella) to the 'vast number' of good musical amateurs 'whose acquirements average above those of the professors (even the imported ones)' (*The Athenaeum*, 3 (1830), 442). See also Haweis (1881: 513), who refers not only to the intolerable adult amateur but also to the 'fine violin amateur', whose playing is as enjoyable as, 'perhaps more than, that of many professional artists'.

[93] Pasquali's thorough-bass treatise (see Chron., 1810), containing 'practical

to the eighteenth-century 'compleat' tutor, which was only complete as far as the superficial demands of the 'dabbler' were concerned. In contrast, the more sophisticated elementary works from the eighteenth and nineteenth centuries aim to provide a firm foundation in order to enable progression to the more advanced stages and methods, and therefore form just one part of an increasingly integrated and progressive approach. This is reflected in their greater concern for introducing the young beginner to the art, who would naturally have had a greater chance (and probably desire) to become a proficient musician than the mature, prejudiced gentleman. Some sources state explicitly that they are for the younger market,[94] whereas many others appeal to the wider readership but are conceived with accessibility in mind. The new breed of tutor, even if based largely on old principles, takes its responsibility to teach far more seriously and takes care to make the learning process 'both easy & agreeable'.[95] Paine's treatise (Chron., 1815), which includes a young gentleman pupil in the illustration on the title-page and other references to the young beginner, demonstrates a desire to encourage violin playing on a large scale and ease the widely acknowledged difficulty of the instrument through devices for practice such as the 'Bow Guide', 'Patent finger-board' (pp.13 and 47), and 'Mute violin' (p.48). Thomas Busby saw 'progressive' lessons as a way of 'smoothing' the 'path to improvement' among juvenile pupils[96] and numerous publications promoted musical 'games', toys and devices in order to promote good practice among children and save valuable time in schools by assisting both the student

---

instructions', was particularly successful. Originating in 1757 it appeared in at least three British editions and, remarkably, a foreign translation (see Kassler (1979), 818–20). It tapped into the more demanding, diligent female market and, once again, made the most of its author's Italian heritage and associated kudos. Pasquali was associated with Geminiani and the Scot Robert Bremner, an influential opportunist who played his full part in disseminating both Italians' works as well as his own. Another work worthy of note is P. A. Corri's piano tutor *L'anima di musica* (Chron., 1810), one of the most comprehensive of the time, which shows a real concern for the teaching of young students and has a practical emphasis although essential theoretical background is not neglected. It was reissued in 1822 and a popular, abridged version (*Original system of preluding* (c.1812)) was itself reprinted on several occasions (see Kassler (1979), 220). Also Goodban's catechism (Chron., 1814) is an attempt at an integrated approach involving pupils, teachers, parents and schools.

[94] Including Philpot (1766) and later Keith (Chron., 1813), Sanderson (Chron., 1825) and Honeyman (Chron., 1885), which demonstrates in many ways a more advanced and serious approach to progressive instruction, involving parents, pupil and teacher. Challoner (Chron., 1825) is designed with schools in mind as well as for use in the home.

[95] Hack (Chron., 1835), title-page. See also the title-page of Goodban (Chron., 1810). Thomson (Chron., 1840) also makes it clear in his introductory remarks that his desire is to make 'the path as easy and agreeable to the Amateur as a correct and proper knowledge of the Instrument will admit' (p.1).

[96] Kidd (1968), 42.

and the teacher.⁹⁷ Such developments aimed at increasing accessibility naturally reduced the scope for the 'intellectualization' of the art. Market forces therefore shifted the focus on to the 'use' rather than the 'philosophy' of sound.⁹⁸

Another essential development during the period was a shift in the balance between self-instruction and practical tuition. The teacher is naturally fundamental in effective instrumental instruction and these more serious teaching tools often reflect this and incorporate their role in the form of duos and general advice. It is only natural that a progressive writer such as Philpot, who seeks to encourage young native talent, should stress the importance of the 'Master' and endeavour to provide him with guidance (1766: 13–14). This is also true of Bremner (1777: iv), another Geminiani pupil, and Jousse (Chron., 1811: v, xx, 1, 45 and 55). However this later example expresses the desirability of practical tuition but also acknowledges that it may not always be possible for those 'residing in the country' (p.1), and therefore provides fingering for the exercises. Similarly his earlier treatise provides extra assistance for the pupil 'who has not the assistance of a Master' (Chron., 1805: 6). Paine (Chron., 1815), like Crome before (1740 and 1765) and Hamilton (Chron., 1835)⁹⁹ and Thomson (Chron., 1840) after, uses the dialogue format to 'imitate' the structure of a lesson. He considers a master necessary in order to learn most effectively from the treatise and 'gain a foundation' (p.v), but (no doubt with accessibility in mind) stresses that 'the greatest attention' is given to 'Country Orders' for his works (p.48).¹⁰⁰

Therefore while these works promote written material as a complement and not an alternative to practical tuition (livelihoods as well as musical standards were still at stake), they are realistic in acknowledging that this ideal is not always possible for many to achieve, particularly in the early nineteenth-century musical environment discussed above.¹⁰¹ Many nineteenth-century examples however urge the

---

⁹⁷ For example see entries for R. M. Blagrove, Butler, Goodban, Howell and Worgan in Kassler (1979). There was also an evident demand for material to teach music to the blind (see Cheese, ibid.).

⁹⁸ Kassler (1979), 665.

⁹⁹ Also the 'deficiency of verbal instruction is amply supplied' by Präger's 'little Catechism' (Chron., 1830) according to Hamilton (Chron., 1835, 15th edn (1883), 33).

¹⁰⁰ A review of Blagrove's method (Chron., 1827) also highlights the reality of practical instruction being inaccessible to many aspiring violinists, and the consequent need for an alternative.

¹⁰¹ Bertini's system for 'all music instruments' (Chron., 1830) purports to cater for those without access to a master or even an instrument. See also Purdy (Chron., 1858), which attempts to alleviate the difficulties experienced by self-taught beginners.

reader to consider the teacher indispensable and operate as progressive teaching and learning aids rather than purely 'self-help' tutors for the amateur.[102] The transition from sources encouraging self-sufficiency to those promoting practical instruction reveals a great deal about the changing dynamics of supply and demand taking place around the turn of the century.

Challoner (Chron., 1825: 9) advises those without a teacher, but adds that 'it is by no means recommended, as a good Master may in a very few Lessons teach his Scholar infinitely more than this, or any other Book ever published upon the same subject'. This view is also shared by Hack (Chron., 1835: 52). Thomas Howell of Bristol, a pupil of Busby and an important figure in nineteenth-century instrumental pedagogy, stresses the importance of the teacher (Chron., 1825: 1) as an integral part of the learning process, required to demonstrate and direct the application of the principles in the treatises.

Howell's improvements to forms of written instruction were inspired by the dearth of systematic and accessible specimens, a situation especially evident in the case of the violin. His treatises avoid popular airs and aim to reflect contemporary practice and repertoire more closely than those that consciously protect 'trade secrets' and so discourage real progress. He was aware of a demand for more effective and progressive examples, particularly from parents on behalf of their children, which would not only cover the fundamental aspects of technique succinctly and aid practice in the master's absence but also promote the essential role of the teacher. With the key elements documented for easy reference the teacher was in a much better position to demonstrate and illustrate the finer points of technique with complementary material and independent repertoire.[103] Such works therefore helped to improve the quality and effectiveness of practical instruction in often less than ideal circumstances. The more serious eighteenth-century continental treatises had set a valuable precedent in offering assistance and wisdom to both students and teachers.

Spohr's treatise, which aims to complement practical tuition and assist the teacher (see Chron., 1843: i–iii), came to the fore in England at a time when written instruction and the greater technical requirements of all kinds of music forged an increasingly important role for the teacher.[104] Also, as standards improved and the demands

---

[102] Thomson's comments (Chron., 1840: 1) on the importance of a 'qualified and conscientious' teacher from the outset for the amateur violinist are based on Spohr (see for example Chron., 1843: I). See also Kassler (1979), 68.

[103] See Chron. (1825: 1) and Sainsbury (1824), vol.1, 379.

[104] See also Anon., 'Elementary treatises', QMMR, 2 (1820), 100–101.

increased, the practice of an individual teaching (and writing about) several instruments became less common in favour of specialization. Spohr's work was ideal for the specialist violin teacher and he was able to exert a strong influence over the tuition given by others, particularly at an advanced level. Henry Holmes's edition of Spohr's treatise, continuing the intentions of the original, is explicit about the role and importance of the teacher (Chron., 1878: iv). Similarly his 'Supplement' to this edition (c.1880) is intended to aid learning 'in the intervals of the master's instruction' (title-page).

Spohr's is one of the increasing number of mainstream violin (and other instrumental) methods by foreign authors that found a market and appeared in Britain during the period amid burgeoning amateur demand. Most became available (in whole or in part) in an English translation, but, in contrast to versions in other languages, this was often many years after the original and frequently in an abridged form.[105] The exceptions in the case of the violin are the two most influential treatises in Britain in their respective periods: Geminiani (1751), which originally appeared complete in English, despite its foreign author, and later appeared in French and German translations and made its way to North America; and Spohr (1832), which was given a complete English translation the year after its original publication, prior to several other versions.[106]

In spite of some attempts at more advanced material by British (and particularly English) writers, the most significant violin treatise in England from the early 1830s until the early twentieth century is the

---

[105] See Mozart (Chron., 1812), Rode et al. (Chron., 1823), L'abbé le fils (Chron., 1828), Campagnoli (Chron., 1830), Spohr (Chron., 1833) and Baillot (Chron., 1884). No complete translation of Baillot's work (1835) appeared until 1991, although, in keeping with the higher status of the instrument, the cello method of Baillot et al., also adopted by the Paris Conservatoire, appears to have enjoyed greater prominence in England (see Chron., 1832). In addition these abridgements, presumably for commercial reasons, often focused on excerpts applicable to performers in general rather than the specifics of technique.

[106] Although not a treatise as such Tartini's 'Lombardini' letter (1770) was also available in English very soon after the original source, and the extent of its influence is demonstrated by its frequent reproduction throughout the nineteenth century. Tosi's singing treatise (1723) appeared in Galliard's (inaccurate) translation in 1742 and 1743. The market for an advanced vocal work in England was evidently already in place by this stage, although it should be mentioned that the treatise itself was, even in 1723, in essence conservative and that Agricola's additions, which in effect brought Tosi 'up to date', did not receive a complete English translation until 1995 (see Agricola, tr. Baird (1995), 1–38). Hummel's piano treatise, translated into English very soon after its original publication (Chron., 1829), was particularly popular as a result of its promotion of 'classical' refinement in performance (see Chapter 4) as well as its effective pedagogical method.

example by Spohr. His unrivalled appeal, popularity and influence in this country during the period have been discussed previously, and there is nothing in the native pedagogical sources prior to the translations of Spohr's treatise to suggest that this work would not be accepted and approved wholeheartedly. In fact the conservative and often old-fashioned content of many native examples reflects an approach to the instrument and a lack of authority that makes Spohr's method and performance style ideally suited to this environment. As discussed above, the need to expand the scope of teaching methods and publish materials of a more ambitious nature had been identified long before Spohr's treatise was available in Britain. Spohr did, however, provide the British with, in a single volume, the ideal template of style and taste in violin playing for the advanced student. Its foreign origins and the qualities associated with its author gave it the authority and prestige that allowed, finally, Geminiani's treatise to be superseded.

Although Spohr's work, like his performance style, shares its stylistic heritage with the early French violin school of Viotti (represented also by the abridged English translations of Rode *et al.*), it still encompasses many advanced techniques in unprecedented detail for a violin treatise published in England. The author therefore manages to present well-established technical principles which are challenging to native violinists but do not exceed the all-important boundaries of taste and refinement. An emphasis on greater virtuosity, as represented by Guhr's account of Paganini's performing style (1829), would have been unrealistic and even counter-productive among the vast majority of British violinists at this time.

Spohr's treatise was well known before Bishop's translation in 1843, courtesy of the accurate and virtually complete translation by Rudolphus.[107] As mentioned above, this is an unusually prompt complete English translation of a continental work. The value of the Rudolphus edition has not been fully appreciated, with the Bishop and Holmes versions receiving what little attention the English editions of Spohr's treatise have hitherto enjoyed. Contemporary reviews and advertisements reveal its prominence during the 1830s and the important contribution it made to English violin pedagogy, including the promotion of Spohr's refined style among both professionals and amateurs.

John Bishop's faithful and complete translation of the treatise

---

[107] All of the sections are present, but the text is not always complete. The original plates and musical examples are faithfully reproduced, and there is an additional plan dividing the bow into different sections which are referred to in the text and examples (p.15 and plate C, fig.V).

appeared in 1843, endorsed by the author himself and the RAM, and was dedicated to Edward Taylor, a close friend of Spohr in England. Dubourg makes frequent mention of Spohr's method and the Bishop translation in particular, including its accession to the RAM Library and some reviews (1878, *Appendix*, pp.3–4).[108] In addition to illustrating the high esteem in which the work was held, references in a publication as significant as Dubourg's must also have contributed in some way to the continued popularity and widespread use of the treatise later in the nineteenth century. Although advanced it is recommended in the chapter devoted to amateurs (after the importance of scale practice and the use of Corelli's solos has been stressed), along with some of Spohr's individual suggestions (1878: 243–7). It is also fitting that the author refers to the essential role of the teacher (p.247) and the essential requirement for all players that purely musical qualities are placed above display, whether achieved or merely attempted (p.244). In keeping with these sentiments Dubourg's 'Friendly advice to the young amateur' (p.253) provides a miniature lesson in verse, incorporating directions in bowing and stressing once again the value of Corelli, along with the unsuitability of aspiring to the extremes of Paganini.

It is significant that the periodicals of the time reveal a relatively fierce competition between the Rudolphus and Bishop editions of the Spohr treatise.[109] This competition, in combination with price reductions,[110] was naturally to the advantage of the consumer and marked the continued importance and greater accessibility of Spohr's theories among both serious amateurs and professionals.

The longevity of Spohr's influence is evident from the Henry Holmes edition of the treatise (Chron., 1878). This contains various additions and amendments that demonstrate some differences of approach and a desire to include some aspects of technique that Spohr chose to distance himself from when compiling the original work, most notably springing bowings and harmonics (see Chapter 3). There is also an 'Editor's Preface' (p.iv) and 'Editor's Appendix' (pp.217–24) and updated illustrations and directions for posture and the violin and bow holds. This new edition demonstrates that by the final quarter of the nineteenth century even the British considered it expedient to reflect some of the innovations of the more virtuosic style cultivated during the era of Paganini.

---

108 It should be noted that the *Appendix* to Dubourg (1878) was added by the same John Bishop.
109 Selected advertisements and reviews are presented in Golby (1999b), vol.2, 106–7, 115 and 137–8.
110 See 'Correspondence: Spohr's violin school', *MW*, 18 (1843), 85.

However, while Holmes accepts more elements of the 'brilliant school' than Spohr, he takes care to differentiate between this and the loftier, more refined style. The numerous additions to the translation are presented in a smaller font and are therefore differentiated in an honest and explicit way from the main body of Spohr's text, which is translated faithfully. Consequently this edition is more complete than the original but the substantial part of the work remains faithful to the practices of Spohr, supplementing them without discarding any of the original material. Many of the additions are not concerned with technique, but add text and musical examples to guide the teacher and to make the progression of learning a more gradual process. There is more information on how to teach and how to practise the contents of the treatise with suggestions for repertoire to complement it (Chron., 1878: 40, 78, 100, 174 and 193), catering for, significantly, both the *bravura* and refined, 'classic' styles, and various ages, aspirations and abilities. With the editorial contributions clearly marked, the treatise becomes more systematic and thorough.

In a similar vein Ferdinand David combines 'the sterling qualities of Spohr's style with the greater facility and piquancy of the modern school',[111] which reflects the eclecticism that is increasingly evident in instrumental teaching during the second half of the nineteenth century and into the twentieth. David, a prominent and highly influential teacher and writer (see Chron., 1874), promoted Spohr's approach to the violin in England, passing on his ideas to such important pedagogues as Wilhelmj (Chron., 1898) and Joachim (1902–5).[112]

The importance and prominence of Spohr's violin treatise in nineteenth-century England is firmly established. However, its use as a teaching tool is another issue and an important consideration when considering the range of material for the violin and other instruments published in this country. W. C. Honeyman wrote a number of anonymous violin tutors during the second half of the nineteenth century, including *The young violinist's tutor* (Chron., 1885).[113] It is interesting for a number of reasons, including its use of exercises by Loder and the progressive attitude it shows towards written pedagogy generally, and particularly for its comments on Spohr and his school. Honeyman stresses the need to acquire 'a thorough knowledge of the system of bowing elaborated by Spohr and David in their great schools

---

[111] F. Hiller, 'David, Ferdinand', in *Grove 1*, vol.1 (1879), 433–4. See also Brown (1984), 213.

[112] The influence of Spohr on figures such as Ries (Chron., 1876) and Hering (1909) should also not be overlooked.

[113] His writings and life are discussed in Harvey (1995), 177–80.

of Violin playing' (p.3), but is also conscious of the need to provide 'a stepping-stone to the standard Violin Tutors' (p.4). Spohr, as a central figure in English violin pedagogy, receives special consideration and criticism under the title 'Spohr and the Young' (p.4). No book is better than Spohr's for 'the advanced student and professional player', but 'no book could be worse' for the 'young Violin player' (ibid.), although Honeyman concedes that Spohr was aware of his own lack of experience when it came to elementary instruction (ibid., based on Chron., 1843: iii). It is significant that the shortcomings of Spohr's work are highlighted in this way, especially by a native (in fact Scottish) violinist and writer, and that similar (if less defamatory) criticisms had been made by Philpot with regard to Geminiani's treatise, which held a similar position in the sphere of advanced violin instruction during an earlier period.

Similarly Holmes is careful to point out how the method is of use to amateurs but its primary purpose is for 'the intended Sons of Art' (Chron., 1878: iv). Wessely comments on how Spohr 'progresses far too rapidly' and omits all 'leggiero' bowings, but considers the work still to be of value, particularly if combined with other material (1913: 9–10). Cobbett's additions to David's *Grove 1* article (1910: 330), which appear to have informed Wessely's thoughts, stress the importance of the Spohr treatise and its legacy, faults and omissions accepted, and the continued relevance of the directions for certain aspects of technique.

There were also various spin-offs based on the original Spohr treatise, reflecting its popularity (long after the author's popularity as a composer had waned) and a desire to increase its accessibility to less proficient or less wealthy players.[114] Haddock's tutor (Chron., 1895) is a specific attempt to provide progressive and thorough instruction, using material from Spohr's method in particular.

Also it is significant that the works of Campagnoli, an important figure in violin pedagogy in his own right, have a role to play in relation

---

114 These include the 'Musical Bouquet' editions (published in London, probably during the 1860s) of *Spohr's Violin School, in a condensed form, as a practical exposition of the art of Violin Playing for the use of Students, either with or without a master. Price 2s. 6d.*, and *Spohr's Hand-book for the Violin, with numerous Studies and Exercises, and a selection of 40 Melodies. Price 1s.* Also echoing the treatment that Geminiani received during the eighteenth century, some works use Spohr's name to market old material. An interesting example is *Spohr's celebrated instructions for the violin, containing a variety of progressive examples, on the various styles of bowing and fingering, for the use of amateurs & professors, to which is added thirty six favorite [sic] melodies ...Price 10/6* (London, [1854]). This work includes material from Spohr's treatise but presents it in the traditional rudiments/airs format. It also incorporates directions which originated in Jousse's assimilation (?1805) of Prelleur part V, Geminiani and Philpot discussed below.

to Spohr. Campagnoli's publications on the violin, the most substantial of which was in preparation at the end of the eighteenth century, were popular in Britain throughout the nineteenth century and into the twentieth (see Chron., 1830 and 1856). His popularity in England is not surprising given that Spohr praised his playing, while considering his method 'antiquated'.[115] In fact Campagnoli's approach to the instrument became an important part of the more systematic approach to violin pedagogy and was identified by important native figures as presenting a solid foundation for teaching. More importantly it offered a 'stepping stone' between the elementary stages and the advanced pedagogical and technical level achieved by Spohr. Some works, such as Thomson (Chron., 1840), incorporate the writings of both Campagnoli and Spohr. Also in addition to his translation of Campagnoli's treatise (Chron., 1830), Hamilton's popular *Catechism* (15th edition, 1883) is based largely on the technical principles espoused by the Italian, quoting some passages almost verbatim (see Chapter 3). Hamilton also recommends many of Campagnoli's other pedagogical works.

The approach of some writers to Spohr's treatise during the second half of the nineteenth century is also evident with respect to other established texts. The revised and enlarged edition of Loder's treatise (1911), a testament to the sustained popularity of the method among 'beginners and teachers alike' (p.3), highlights the weaknesses of the first part of the original treatise, making various additions to the original format (including diagrams), in an attempt to provide more detailed and systematic elementary instruction. Also Reed's edition (1934) of Tours's treatise (Chron., 1874) recognizes that 'the early stages need to be treated in greater detail and illustrated by more copious examples than was thought adequate by the author of the book', which, 'like many other Violin Methods and Tutors of its time', devotes 'too little space to the bow and its technique' (Preface, p.3).

During the nineteenth century the market for instrumental tuition broadened and there was a tendency for tutors to be published in places other than London or to be associated with specific regions. Prominent figures and families were able to dominate the market in those areas, it being easier to make an impact outside the capital. For example Howell's works (Chron., 1825 and 1829) were an important influence in Bristol, Honeyman (Chron., 1880 and 1885) was able to satisfy demand in Scotland as well as England and numerous examples were published in Dublin. Also although Loder's treatises were published in London (Chron., 1824 and 1842) and he taught at the

---

[115] Straeten (1933), vol.2, 48.

Royal Academy of Music, the Loder family were very prominent and long-established in Bath,[116] which must have encouraged the use of these texts locally.

The developments we have discussed so far have been in the area of pedagogy rather than technique, as this is where the English writer was able to make a significant contribution. With this emphasis on the development of pedagogy itself it is not surprising that many of the writers who produced teaching material for the violin were not violin specialists (or even violinists in some cases), but rather specialists in material for gaining proficiency in various musical skills. For example names like Goodban, Jousse, Keith, Challoner, Howell, Hancock, Rimbault and later Langey produced a number of works on various subjects which reflect the appetite for learning music and a growing demand for effective elementary teaching material during the nineteenth century. Two of the most important figures in this respect, whose translations, revisions and original material are well represented in the Chronology, are the aforementioned John Bishop[117] and James Alexander Hamilton.[118] Some works feature both writers and incorporate additions that Bishop made to some of Hamilton's publications after his death (see Chron., 1835). There was a definite shift away from anonymity (despite the use of prominent names on the covers) in favour of authors, including women, using their works to advertise their services as teachers. This was of course in keeping with the increasing demand for practical instruction rather than a reliance on self-instruction.

The rise of mass consumption, far more distanced from the artists themselves than had previously been the case, encouraged the proliferation of such specialists and the appropriation of discernment via a third party. Although not unknown earlier, during the early decades of the nineteenth century, as writing about music became a more specialized and professional pursuit, reviews of pedagogical works such as treatises became more concentrated in magazines and specialist music

---

[116] See 'Loder', *Grove 6*, vol.11, 119–22.

[117] Bishop (1817–90), an organist in Cheltenham, made 'contributions to the literature of music, and especially to that of the violin' that 'are numerous and of masterly excellence' (Heron-Allen (1894), 49).

[118] Hamilton (1795–1845) was born in London, the son of a dealer in old books, and was largely self-educated before becoming a professor of harmony and composition. In addition to works for the violin, other tutors (often using a common format) include examples for the piano, organ, double bass, cello and singing. Although evidently industrious Hamilton appears to have been neither temperate nor provident, selling 'to the publishers, for a few pounds, the copyrights of a large quantity of musical works, which ... might have kept him in affluence' (Heron-Allen (1894), 143–4).

journals and advised the amateur and professional alike.[119] A more critical attitude is evident as the need was identified, at least by a few, to raise the standard of native instrumental performance and rescue it from terminal decline. An article in the 1820 edition of *QMMR* includes a commentary on the nature of 'elementary treatises' in general (pp.100–103). Apart from asserting the vital role of the master and proposing the idea of preliminary instruction from the 'mother or governess', the passage expresses the need for more effective methods of 'instilling' information, with text and music complementing each other and presented progressively, in place of 'popular airs'. It therefore builds upon the views expressed and material published by some of the more progressive eighteenth-century writers such as Philpot, who sought to improve the content and presentation of such works. The desire for 'a positive determinate series of lessons', as opposed to a disorganized collection of disparate parts, is designed to facilitate quicker progress and produce a more sound technical foundation.

Having already established the vibrancy of the British musical environment during the early part of the nineteenth century and the coexistence of contrasting styles of composition and performance and different stages of organological development, it is easy to appreciate how an authoritative, coherent approach to performance would struggle to emerge. In areas where demand was sufficient to warrant only a small number of seminal texts, some even by native writers,[120] this was not such a problem, whereas in the case of more popular instruments among literate amateurs, such as the violin, writers not in a position to issue full translations of foreign works were often faced with making a choice or presenting a compromise between conflicting expressive priorities and prominent practitioners. Either way (the piano excepted) the bias was most often in favour of the conservative and retrospective, even allowing for the inherent qualities of treatises in general. With no native 'school' or paternal figure, there was little alternative but to draw on the most prominent imported styles and it is unsurprising that many authors and publishers presented, whether explicitly or not, anthology or amalgam-style works.[121]

---

[119] These publications also provided reference material of their own, as in the case of the 'Lexicon' of musical terms in the *Harmonicon* (see Kassler (1979), 1120), which was able to offer 'standardization' to a certain extent in the absence of consensus and coherence elsewhere.

[120] Including the Harpers for the trumpet and Lazarus for the clarinet (see Chapter 4).

[121] See Hamilton (Chron., 1833), Anon. (Chron., 1880) and J. R. Lafleur & Son's successful 'Alliance Musicale' series. It is important to acknowledge the vital role of continental models and developments in inspiring a variety of methods in native music education during the period, including the sight-singing movement, and the process of synthesis and assimilation that often ensued.

In the case of British violin playing the theories of Geminiani and Spohr were, between them, able to provide guidance and some degree of consistency over a period of a century and a half.

The tendency to assimilate rather than create is evident from Jousse's early treatise (Chron., 1805). This is the work of a French writer catering for an English market, and much of its content is rooted in the eighteenth century and especially in the theories of Geminiani and his followers. For example his discussion of the violin hold (p.8) combines the comments of Prelleur part V (1731: 2), Geminiani (1751: 1–2) and Philpot (1766: 6), and the instructions for the bow hold and 'Directions for playing' (p.8) owe a general debt to Geminiani (1751: 2) and Philpot (1766: 6). Numerous other sources make use of these directions in this or a similar form (sometimes with additional material), including Goodban (1810: 15), Keith (1813: 12), Challoner (1825: 6), Hack (c.1835: 11), West (?1840: 4), Bates (1845: 7–8), Anon. (1846: 29–30), Dean (1852: 1) and Hancock (1853: 5–6).[122] Like Jousse some English writers, such as Wybrow (Chron., 1858) and Haddock (Chron., 1895), published works that were explicitly based on the most important foreign sources. For example Wybrow's directions for the violin and bow holds in 'New and complete instructions for the Violin' (ibid., Chron., 1858: 1) take passages from Campagnoli, Rode et al. and Spohr (he also makes use, without acknowledgement, of material from Prelleur part V and Geminiani (pp.7 and 9)). This is also true of Hamilton's double bass treatise (Chron., 1833), and his *Catechism* (see below) is based on foreign material and recommends key publications although it is not explicitly an amalgam.

The more substantial violin treatise by Jousse (Chron., 1811), dedicated to J. P. Salomon, expands substantially on the basic components used in the earlier work. It has many idiosyncrasies and reflects the heterogeneity of violin playing in England during the early part of the nineteenth century. Evidently intended for the more serious student (including 'Young learners' (p.55)) and requiring the guidance of an 'intelligent' and 'judicious Master' (pp.v and xx), this work draws upon various foreign methods (spanning over half a century) and is both progressive and retrospective in its approach. Jousse, although a prominent and successful pedagogue, did earn himself a reputation for adorning his name with 'borrowed honours'.[123]

Jousse laments the neglect of the instrument 'by English gentlemen'

---

[122] See respective Chronology entries. The treatises of Bates and Hancock are both very close relatives of Jousse's early work.

[123] Kassler (1979), 819. This comment was made in 1815 with reference to his 'new' version of Pasquali's successful thorough-bass treatise.

and the lack of a suitable English method (p.v). As Philpot had done more than 40 years earlier, he notes the unsuitability of Geminiani's tutor (1751) for the early stages, but does include it (along with the works of L. Mozart, L'abbé *le fils*, and Rode *et al.*) in the list of works that have contributed to his own theories (p.v).[124] Another connection with Philpot's treatise is chapter IV of the Introduction (pp.xix–xx), which, in a similar manner to the earlier work (1766: 3–6), refers to the 'Requisites in an Artist' as 'Genius, Taste and Application'.[125] The section that follows ('What kind of Music should be practised by the Student', p.xx) includes works by Corelli, which are important for 'forming the hand of a young practitioner'; Tartini's 'Art of Bowing'; and Kreutzer's Studies, 'just imported from Paris'.[126] The author has not 'swelled' the treatise with 'Airs, or Elementary pieces' (p.v) but includes a second part which contains exercises with a second violin accompaniment for the master. The exercises demand a range up to the modern ninth position (although 'Young learners' need not go beyond fourth or fifth (p.55)) and include examples for double stops in thirds, sixths, octaves and tenths. As in Loder's treatise published later (Chron., 1841: 43–63), Jousse recommends (p.1) that the exercises are used progressively to complement the directions in the first part of the treatise.

The more frequent use of the duet in nineteenth-century British instrumental treatises is an important development, continuing the trend set by the more progressive eighteenth-century examples, such as those by Crome (1765), Tessarini (1765) and Philpot (1766). The duet has always had an important place in pedagogy, but until the nineteenth century its role in native sources is less prominent compared with foreign examples, particularly Löhlein (1774). With the role of the teacher increasingly integrated into teaching material, it becomes an important element in treatises and some independent compositions by influential figures such as Jousse, Howell, Challoner and Loder.[127]

---

[124] In addition to Philpot's comments Jousse also uses material by Robert Bremner without acknowledgement.

[125] Goodban is also keen to point out the importance of 'Practice and Application' (1810: i).

[126] Straeten (1911: 276) comments that 'it is interesting to see that some of these never ceased to be "daily bread" for violin students, while others were lost sight of for a time – as, for instance, many of the works of the old Italian school – yet have returned to their former position quite recently again'.

[127] Challoner (Chron., 1825) includes duos for the pupil and master or for two pupils to practise together 'in Schools &c'. He also published separately 'Progressive duets op. 7' (advertised on p.20 of the treatise), which were designed to 'succeed the Lessons hitherto given'. Hack's treatise (Chron., 1835) also advertises his own duos, with fingering and

Howell refers to the advantage of duet practice, 'with a steady performer to accompany' (probably the teacher), in helping the student to keep 'strictly to the time, and well in tune' (Chron., 1825: 38), and Loder (Chron., 1841: i) uses it to add interest to the study of technique and help with rhythm. Spohr is quick to acknowledge the value of duet practice (Chron., 1843: iii) and uses the genre extensively in his treatise for exercises and examples of repertoire.[128]

The duet remained an important element in violin treatises during the rest of the century, including works specifically for beginners such as Honeyman's tutor (Chron., 1885). In addition to assisting with technical matters, the duet also promoted greater informality in the relationship between teacher and pupil, which was a more attractive proposition to children and the increasing number of amateurs from the lower orders of society than it had been to the more pretentious eighteenth-century gentleman.

Jousse's work (1811) and that of John David Loder (1824) are mentioned in a review of a translation of the method by Rode et al.[129] The review begins with praise of the French and their desire to promote a systematic and standardized approach to instrumental pedagogy, and then recommends, for different reasons, the Jousse and Loder examples. Jousse assimilated the principal foreign influences of the last 60 years, but Loder, over a decade later, produced something more original. A rare creature: an eminent English violinist associated with the Philharmonic Society, he was in a far better position than most native musicians to venture into this area. In fact from the 1820s until the early twentieth century his work became the most important and pervasive native violin treatise, enjoying a large number of different editions and versions and widespread popularity among students and teachers, amateurs and professionals (see Chron., 1837: i, and Chron., 1841: i). By the late 1820s it was viewed as one of two 'standard violin tutors before the public', the other being a translation of the method by Rode et al.[130]

The different Loder editions are largely consistent, but there are slight changes in the exercises used in the second, third, and fifth editions. They demonstrate an increasing desire to provide more comprehensive elementary material and progressive examples (including duos) for the

---

bowing, to complement his instructions, and Sanderson (Chron., 1825) adopts the duet scoring for his technically demanding theme and variations for 'amateurs & young professors'.

[128] A *Supplement to Spohr's violin school*, compiled by Henry Holmes (c.1880), provides piano accompaniments for the exercises, which are transcribed from the original second violin part.

[129] *QMMR*, 6 (1824), 527–31.

[130] *QMMR*, 10 (1827), 405.

early stages, and so integrate the teacher to a greater extent. The Carrodus edition of Loder's treatise (Chron., 1884), copies of which are in the RAM Library, is almost identical to the third edition, save for references to the modern second and third positions and a glossary of musical terms. There is in fact no evidence of any input from Carrodus, although, as professor of the violin at the National Training School and then the RCM, the use of his name in connection with a work like this would no doubt have given it greater credibility 60 years after its original publication.

Despite the popularity of Loder's work there are no directions for, or diagrams of, the playing posture or the violin and bow holds until the last edition (1911). The role of the teacher is therefore fundamental if this method is to be used effectively from the early stages. The omission of such details from this work and Loder's short treatise on bowing (Chron., 1842) may have been fully intentional, but may also reflect the author's position as a prominent performer and teacher rather than a specialist writer of instructional works, like J. A. Hamilton and T. Howell, for example. The novelty of a relatively prominent English performer publishing teaching material says a great deal about British pedagogy and the status of native musicians compared with their continental counterparts.

Thomas Howell may indeed be considered an innovator in the field of instrumental pedagogy in Britain. Although he was not the first to present new ideas and was not a prominent performer, his approach is significantly more advanced, both in the extent of the technique presented and in its concern for pedagogy, than any previous native writer. The progressive integration of detailed text and music (original exercises akin to contemporary repertoire) is in marked contrast to the earlier use of the rudiments/airs format. Howell's approach is referred to in the introductions to several of his works[131] and in reviews.[132] A review of his *Original instructions* (published in Bristol in 1825 and dedicated to Nicholas Mori) also reveals how treatises came to be critically assessed on their effectiveness as teaching tools, their clarity, accuracy, relationship to practical instruction, and on how accessible they were to the less wealthy student.[133]

A review of this particular treatise in *Ackermann's Repository of Arts*

---

[131] See *Practical instructions* ... (Chron., 1816: 1, and Chron., 1825: 1).

[132] For example *QMMR*, 2 (1820), 101–3, and *QMMR*, 9 (1827), 262.

[133] *QMMR*, 7 (1825), 507. Crouch's cello treatise (Chron., 1824), although by this stage unexceptional, was praised in a review for its ability to rise above 'dry technical rules and examples' and engage with 'the mind of the student', giving a 'philosophical view of art' (*QMMR*, 7 (1825), 232–6).

(Nov. 1825) reflects Howell's genuine efforts towards raising the standard of instrumental and especially violin pedagogy in England:

> As regards the advice and instructions peculiar to the Violin, Mr. Howell's work shews, not only that he is master of his subject, but that his pen is guided by a clear and methodical intellect. In concluding, we shall only express a hope, that the pains taken and the zeal displayed by Mr. H. will meet with the reward they deserve; and that his labour will contribute its mite in rescuing the queen of musical instruments from the neglect which he so feelingly and so truly deplores.

Howell's violin treatises (Chron., 1825 and 1829) display a genuine concern for the systematic development of technique. Taken as a whole they present general information on the instrument and carefully constructed exercises, often scored as duets, to help develop both right- and left-hand technique. They represent a definite step forward in the teaching of the violin in England.

When the 'Prelleur part V' model finally died out during the first half of the nineteenth century, many writers responded to the demand for more sophisticated instruction and the more critical and discerning approach to written methods. Numerous sources from the whole of the nineteenth century (and into the twentieth) reflect the eighteenth-century model, with text and musical examples (including the gamut) combined with a relatively large collection of short pieces.[134] However the old format is often modified to cater not just for amateur 'dabblers' but also beginners with greater aspirations. There is more text of a lucid, coherent nature, sometimes with illustrations of the posture and violin and bow holds, combined with pieces and exercises which complement the written instructions. These are often duets arranged progressively and by key and preceded by a 'Prelude' or similar introductory piece. Also Challoner (Chron., 1825), whose work is designed to prevent 'unnecessary trouble to the master' (title-page), gives helpful general advice on intonation, rhythm and practising, and discusses issues as they arise in the examples. There is a great deal of helpful advice on the selection and maintenance of the instrument, bow and fittings in Hack's substantial and detailed work (Chron., 1835). The airs are incorporated into the main body of the work to illustrate the principles discussed in the text.

Among the new breed of elementary treatise is Hamilton's *Catechism*

---

[134] For example, in the Chronology, Jousse (1805); Goodban (1810); Keith (1813); Challoner (1825); Blagrove (1827); James (1830); Hack (1835); Thomson (1840); West (1840); Bates (1845); Anon. (1846); Farmer (1847 and 1903); Hamilton (1850); Dean (1852); Hancock (1853); Wybrow (1858); and Anon. (1880).

(Chron., 1835) for 'beginners' and 'the young violinist' (15th edition (1883), 28 and 81). A popular, cheap (1s. in 1883) and durable work, it uses the question and answer format and no independent compositions, and makes use of material from Campagnoli (?1797), Leopold Mozart (1756) and Baillot (1835). The result is relatively comprehensive and detailed, and, if no teacher is available, a suitable tool for self-instruction.

Various low-cost publications from the 1840s and 1850s were issued with the intention of encouraging the beginner violinist and presenting the reader with a range of general information on the instrument.[135] Henry Farmer's violin treatise is one of the most important elementary works in English from the nineteenth century. It enjoyed unrivalled popularity and longevity, with editions spanning over half a century (Chron., 1847). Taking into account its format of brief text (with gamut and finger charts) followed by a substantial collection of exercises and short pieces, this work could be considered an updated version of Prelleur part V for the 1800s. However there are new features, including more detailed directions and an illustration for the posture and violin and bow holds (with the text partly derived from Spohr), and more comprehensive and progressive exercises, for left and right hands (including double stopping and third position), following a sequence of keys. Similarly Wybrow's treatise (Chron., 1858) is generally retrospective in its presentation and content, but it does include a page of 'Preludes' in different keys prior to the collection of airs (p.12).

These are generally more serious methods for self-instruction or (preferably) to complement practical tuition than what was previously commonplace: actual 'primers' rather than supposedly 'compleat' methods. The number in existence suggests an increasingly buoyant market during the nineteenth century. Also in contrast to their predecessors, these examples form just one important part of a more progressive approach to instrumental pedagogy. The more sophisticated elementary material has the intention of providing a solid technical foundation before the introduction of more advanced material.[136] In the

---

[135] Aside from the large, hard-bound translations of continental works, native treatises were not prohibitively expensive during the period. Their role in attracting students would have made this an imprudent move. In fact they became cheaper, with, for example, a c.1802 tutor issued at the same price in 1830 (Kassler (1979), 1057) and a c.1817 edition cheaper than the c.1810 version (ibid., 1074).

[136] Of course, many inadequate examples of 'quick and easy' teaching material continued to be published during the period, which were neither complete nor scientific despite their claims. This 'superficial quackery' (Hodges (1836), 39) was no doubt harmful to the livelihood of teachers and the status of musicians. Also there remained a market for 'old-style' general tutors, such as Tansur (1746), partly derived from the writings of

case of children there was support for the idea of parents assisting and providing tuition in the basic rudiments before a teacher was employed. The parents would gain their knowledge through written tutors before passing it on to their offspring.[137] The quantity of material had never been a problem but now the market had expanded to demand a greater diversity of material and with it much of a higher quality.[138]

An abundance of elementary material for the learning of the violin appeared in England during the rest of the century, particularly from the 1870s onwards (see Chronology). Most of these sources are the work of native writers who were able to satisfy the huge demand for this kind of work as the fashion for playing musical instruments and the quest for self-improvement and respectability spread throughout society.[139] The potential for publishing instructional material for a wide variety of instruments was realized by increasing numbers of music publishers, both relatively new and long-standing. Firms who were particularly active include Boosey, Hawkes & Son (publisher of Langey's numerous late nineteenth-century tutors), Metzler, Bates, Cocks & Co. ('Modern methods' and 'Modern tutors'), Addison & Hodson, Chappell & Co. ('Popular instruction books' series, 1858–70), Longman & Co., Novello and Lafleur & Son ('Alliance Musicale' series). Numerous authors took the risk of publishing their own works. It was also far from a new idea for music publishers, often also manufacturers or sellers of instruments, to issue 'house' tutors.[140] Even in areas where the emphasis was traditionally on an oral tradition, openings were exploited for written material.[141] However as far as teaching material for the advanced violin

---

Playford and in its eighth edition by 1830, although its continued popularity can be partially explained by its suitability 'as a textbook for school children' (Kassler (1979), 1001–2).

[137] See 'Elementary treatises', *QMMR*, 2 (1820), 100–101.

[138] The delayed expansion of amateur demand in other countries and its impact on instructional material is an issue warranting further investigation. Given their much stronger position at an early stage in terms of mainstream, professional developments in many cases, it is tempting to foresee a trend in the opposite direction, with greater diversification bringing with it a dilution of quality and experimentation. Nevertheless strong foundations and high levels of discernment were already in place.

[139] See Ehrlich (1976: 97) for comment on the importance of 'social emulation' in the proliferation of cheap lessons and learning manuals and the promotion of the piano in Victorian society.

[140] See Kassler (1979), 1130–31.

[141] For example *Wright and Round's Amateur Band Teacher's Guide and Bandsman's Adviser* (1889) was a popular publication (see Herbert, ed. (2000a), 294–5), although the market for home-grown teaching material appears to have remained small in this area and foreign instruction manuals were used by British brass band players more for their musical exercises than stylistic commentary and as a complement to the 'aural and communal learning process' (ibid., 300).

student is concerned, catering for the accomplished amateur and aspiring professional, as we have seen, the scene continued to be dominated by famous, well-established foreign names, with one or two innovative native examples.

A more enlightened and critical approach towards pedagogy demonstrates that the large numbers of elementary works discussed above were not only filling a gap in the market but also responding to a real need among amateurs. After all there was now more money to be made and other benefits to be had from the spreading of knowledge than its retention, and native writers were becoming well practised in presenting the early and intermediate stages in an effective way using material and principles gleaned from elsewhere. Treatises targeted more effectively at beginners (including children) and intermediate players provided the means necessary to progress on to the more advanced methods.[142] To a much greater extent than previously sources were targeted at and defined by different levels of technical proficiency rather than at certain 'types' of consumer. Their effectiveness had been vastly improved even if their content, prior to the arrival of more 'scientific', physiological concerns, was still largely based on much earlier expressive priorities.

The legacy of the eighteenth century meant that a genuinely British treatise of international importance would fail to emerge and that, born out of real demand and/or convenience, British works reflect a pervasive foreign dominance. As with performers, native examples often just filled the gaps left by foreign musicians, although, by the same token, in areas where they were able to excel as performers there was also some scope to contribute valuable teaching texts.

A vibrant tradition of written instruction developed in response to the desire for knowledge and social respectability among increasing numbers of consumers in Victorian society and new opportunities for both individual and institutional consumption. In the absence of state provision for music education and the limited quality and quantity of institutional training for professional instrumentalists, the large amount of written material published for different standards, whether for self-instruction or to complement practical tuition, played an essential role in promoting higher standards of musicianship among the profession and society at large. At a practical level more amateurs across a greater range of instruments, if generally without serious long-term aspirations,

---

[142] The fact that the written sources became more specialized is also illustrated by the growing number of methods specifically for the viola (see Heron-Allen (1894), 338–42). Although these are often based on earlier versions for the violin, they are at least a sign of a growing interest in the instrument.

were equipped to attempt 'professional' repertoire and develop their overall musicianship to a degree previously expected only of and tolerated among professionals. This could only have been a positive step towards a wider appreciation of the value and demands of practical music and, by helping to blur the distinction between the amateur and professional, an improvement in the status of musicians generally.

The Vocal Model

As a brief postscript to this chapter and prior to discussions of instrumental performance this section takes a look at the important link between vocal and instrumental performing conventions. We have already established that vocal practice, through its far more 'respectable' associations and inherent purity, enjoyed a higher status than the instrumental sphere. If these trends focused more on musical literacy and 'rational recreation' than the intricacies of vocal technique, there are still numerous examples which demonstrate that the vocal model was an important consideration for instrumentalists who wished to display 'good taste'.

This situation was of course common to virtually all schools of instrumental practice, but what is of particular interest here is the disparity in status between the two spheres and the desire among native connoisseurs to view vocal or 'singing' qualities as paramount in most forms of tasteful instrumental performance. Correspondingly there were a significant number of substantial English texts on singing, original and in translation, published during the eighteenth and nineteenth centuries.[143] Galliard's translation of Tosi's 1723 treatise has already been mentioned and through the later authoritative works of the Corri family (Domenico in particular) Italian models of vocal delivery became fundamental to expressive singing in Britain and offered a style which native amateurs wished to emulate.[144] Once again native style, based firmly on 'foreign foundations', combined the 'restrained sensibility' of the British with Italian technical principles.[145] Following on from this fertile period in vocal pedagogy and physiology we have the significant contributions of Isaac Nathan, Manuel García and others, including Sir George Smart's promotion of Handelian practice.

During a period of over a century and a half major figures in the

---

[143] Toft (2000) is a particularly valuable secondary source in this respect. See also Potter, ed. (2000), Sands (1943–4) and 'Elements of vocal science' in *QMMR*, 5 (1823).
[144] Toft (2000), xii.
[145] Ibid., 9.

vocal sphere were particularly active, either directly or indirectly, in British music education. Consistent with expressive principles we have already highlighted and which appear in following chapters there is a certain level of conservatism in the theories espoused in addition to the more general impact of vocal 'lyricism' and its associated devices (such as the *messa di voce* and portamento) on instrumental performance. Through the treatises we can observe the strong link between eighteenth and nineteenth centuries in terms of expressive ideals. The rejection of 'mere agility' and 'mechanical' performance is a pervasive element.[146] Galliard's translation of Tosi (1742) presented remarks that were 'of advantage not only to vocal performers but likewise to the instrumental, where taste and manner are required; and show that a little less fiddling with the voice and a little more singing with the instrument would be of great service to both'.[147] Tosi's successors were also keen to promote the judicious and sparing use of expressive devices, although the public's appetite for novelty and extremes also conflicted with 'critical' taste in this sphere.[148]

Advice to imitate the singer and apply vocal models was far from restricted to wind and brass players.[149] Many different types of instrumentalist were praised for the successful imitation of the singer and just as García was able to bridge classical *bel canto* and modern practice,[150] instrumentalists and their writings were sought in nineteenth-century Britain which successfully integrated modern elements into essentially 'classical' performance styles.

---

[146] Toft (2000), xii–xiii and 2.
[147] Haynes (2001), 175.
[148] Toft (2000), 12–13.
[149] See Humphries (2000), 65 and 73; and Lawson (2000), 48, 57 and 65. The issue of the use of vibrato is one where the singer was often implored to imitate instrumental (particularly violin) practice, although the emphasis remained on discretion and taste (see Toft (2000), 30–33).
[150] Potter, ed. (2000), 213.

PART TWO

CHAPTER THREE

The Violin Family

This chapter forms a detailed study of many of the contemporary trends as they impacted on the violin family.[1] The section on the violin is followed by much shorter discussions that examine interesting issues pertinent to the viola, cello and double bass.

Violinists in Britain

> There is nothing in which the power of art is shown so much as in playing on the Fiddle. In all other things we can do something at first: any man will forge a bar of iron if you give him a hammer; not so well as a smith, but tolerably; and make a box, though a clumsy one; but give him a Fiddle and a Fiddle-stick, and he can do nothing.
>
> (Dr Johnson[2])

This famous quotation rings true throughout much of the surviving evidence of violin playing in Britain during our period. In short the combination of great technical difficulty with generally inadequate

---

[1] Much of the following discussion draws heavily on Golby (1999b), which provides more detail with respect to many issues, in particular the teaching and intricacies of violin technique in the English sources. More space is devoted to comparisons between different native texts and between native and foreign examples than is available here. A great deal of the extant violin literature, contemporary and modern, is listed in the bibliography of the present study. However special mention should be made of the uniquely large and important Heron-Allen Collection of material on all aspects of the violin which is now housed in the Royal College of Music. The contents of the collection are outlined in Heron-Allen's own catalogue (1900). These include general treatises and essays on the violin and violin playing, syllabuses and prospectuses, and volumes of miscellanea, including newspaper cuttings, periodical articles, catalogues of literature, letters, autographs, anecdotes and reviews. This collection formed the basis of his books from 1885 and 1890–94, with their invaluable bibliographies and source lists. From his writing we gain an appreciation of the evolution of nineteenth-century attitudes to the violin in this country and insights into the most popular and important pedagogical sources for the instrument at this time. Few of the many works he collected on the violin family and included in his books have been referred to let alone examined since the nineteenth century. There are also important lists of pedagogical sources in Dubourg (1878, *Appendix*, pp.3–5) and Brown (1886).

[2] J. Boswell, *The life of Samuel Johnson* (London, 1835), vol.3, 267.

amounts of ambition and application or support and opportunity naturally produced relatively low levels of proficiency among both amateurs and native professionals. As with many nineteenth-century British musical phenomena, we can trace the origins of this lack of success back to the eighteenth century.

Interest in the violin increased in Britain following the Restoration of Charles II in 1660 and the formation of the King's 'Twenty-Four' violins, although this was not without some resistance from those who remained faithful to the viol.[3] This development in fact set the tone for the whole period, as foreign models and virtuosi were sought by the upper classes and so allowed to dominate from the early history of the violin and violinists in this country.[4] First the French and then the Italian styles influenced violin playing in England, as reflected in the writings of Playford (1658 and 1669) and Lenton (1693) and repertoire such as Purcell's *Sonnata's of III Parts* for two violins and continuo (c.1680, published 1683).[5] As discussed above, the continued prevalence of foreign musicians was ultimately detrimental to the potential proficiency and status of native performers and violinists in particular. From the 1650s when Thomas Baltzar's German technical standards overshadowed Davis Mell, then the best violinist in England,[6] and Nicola Matteis's proficiency provoked astonishment in the 1670s,[7] foreign violinists enjoyed the pick of professional opportunities.

It comes as no surprise that eighteenth-century pedagogical sources generally demonstrate a very limited ambition among the majority of gentleman amateur violinists, and, with the instrument regarded as unsuitable for the often more dedicated female instrumentalists until the latter part of the nineteenth century, the 'fiddle' and the 'fiddler' emerge

---

[3] Including Roger North, who 'identified the violin as a critical force for change, and condemned it outright' (Weber (1992), 85). See also Burney (1776–89), vol.2, 322; Pulver (1920–21), 14–18; Wilson (1959), 222; Grant (1983), 205; and Harvey (1995), 13–14. Harvey's study of violin making in the British Isles, an important and long-overdue contribution, provides many valuable insights into the violin's position in Britain since the time of its introduction.

[4] The contributions of Boyden (1965), Stolba (1968–9), Boyd and Rayson (1982), Walls (1990), Holman (1993) and Cyr (1995), concerned with early musical and pedagogical sources, are particularly important in this area.

[5] See Cyr (1995).

[6] A comparison of the respective abilities of Mell and Baltzar, drawing on evidence in Playford's *The division-violin* (1st edn, 1684), is contained in Dubourg (5th edn, 1878), 328–36.

[7] See Boyden (1965), 142–3; and Walls (1990), 578–9. Matteis's *Ayrs* (London, 1676–85) introduced the Italian style to the English prior to Corelli's Op.5. They also have a pedagogical function and are far more advanced in this respect than the native tutors of Playford and Lenton (see Walls (1990), 581).

as generic derogatory terms and images representing low entertainment and standards, principally among amateurs.[8] Contemporary engravings and paintings, particularly by William Hogarth, commonly depict the afflicted, itinerant solo fiddler.[9] Moreover in keeping with prevalent and persistent attitudes concerning general music education during the period, the 'fiddler' or 'scraper' was considered the antithesis of the 'scholar' or 'theorist'.[10] His association with low society and a perceived lack of artistic refinement naturally hindered attempts to establish a professional middle class of players at this stage. It persisted at the higher levels of society throughout the nineteenth century.[11]

Nineteenth-century attempts to nurture interest in and more positive attitudes towards practical music-making among the burgeoning middle classes spread, eventually, to the violin. George Dubourg's *The violin* (1836, with a 5th edition in 1878) is evidence of the rising interest in its status during the first half of the nineteenth century. Written by the grandson of a pupil of Geminiani, this is an important book that covers most of the significant events and trends in the instrument's history in England and, through its popularity,[12] reflects a widespread and sustained interest in the subject during the period. Dubourg identifies factors such as the pursuit of business and the vestiges of 'the spirit of Puritanism' as leading to a view of musical talent 'rather as a snare to be shunned, than as a resource to be cherished'.[13] The growth of musical appreciation throughout society as the nineteenth century progressed promised greater opportunities and rewards for the future;[14] but, with a cohesive structure to professional music-making and education particularly slow to emerge, the amateur remained, as Dubourg acknowledges, a significant force in violin playing in England during the period. He devotes a whole chapter to the discussion of this group of performers,[15] which Haweis later describes as 'the best possible index to the musical taste of a people'.[16] It is clear that the desire to raise the proficiency of the growing body of amateurs is motivated by a wish to increase the value that is placed on musical performance by society at

---

[8] See McVeigh (1989), 143–4.

[9] See Leppert (1988), which contains much of interest on the sociological implications of Hogarth's engravings and other visual representations involving music.

[10] See Rohr (1983), 28; and Brewer (1997), 533.

[11] Gillett (2000b), 337.

[12] In addition to the number of editions issued, numerous extracts appeared in periodicals, including *MW*, 2 (1836), 86–91, 108–9 and 161.

[13] Dubourg (1878), 193–4.

[14] Ibid., 215 and 229.

[15] Ibid., 234–53.

[16] Haweis (1881), 505.

large, beyond just those with professional interests. Dubourg is also keen to encourage participation among those who are likely to take the study of the instrument more seriously and therefore promote higher standards. He is explicit in his approval of female violinists, stressing their suitability to the instrument.[17]

The potential power and influence of the amateur violinist and dedicated student is gradually realized later in the nineteenth century, most notably through the huge demand for written material.[18] In addition to instructional works, there are also numerous articles and individual periodicals dedicated to the violin and stringed instruments in general.[19] Harvey's recent work (1995) provides fascinating insights into how the burgeoning of interest in all facets of the violin is reflected in the literature of the second half of the nineteenth century, including both periodicals and books.[20] It appears however that English violin playing was not thought worthy of much comment by foreign authors.

With the tastes and consumer power of the aristocracy and upper classes, in marked contrast to France, continuing to influence trends and tastes in English culture, writers on music naturally identified the potential of this group to inspire confidence in and add legitimacy to native art. Any sign of serious interest was therefore seen as a cause for celebration, even for 'fiddlers', apparently the lowest of the monarch's subjects.

> Things are looking up ... Let the Queen and the Prince betray an interest in the progress of a native school of art, and the people will quickly follow in the wake of Majesty. Unhappily, our public, though a good public in its way, and not an indifferent judge as times go, must positively be led by the nose. The press might do it, but will not. Let us hope better of the Queen, the natural protector of her loyal subjects, including the entire body corporate, from statesmen to fiddlers.[21]

As we have seen, opinion formers and musical connoisseurs were able to select, through direct and indirect patronage, essentially conservative and particularly well-refined individuals and performance styles from abroad that native musicians of all levels would seek to emulate. In this cultural climate it is easy to see how figures like Spohr and

---

[17] Dubourg (1878), 255.
[18] See Heron-Allen (1894), xvii.
[19] Heron-Allen (ibid., 233–56 and 382ff.) gives numerous examples, in addition to which there is *The Violin Soloist* (London, 1886–94) and *The Cremona, with which is incorporated 'The Violinist'* (London, 1906–11).
[20] See in particular the chapter 'The power of the pen: Heron-Allen and his legacies' (1995: 265–83).
[21] Anon., 'English music in high places', *MW*, 26 (1851), 162–3.

Mendelssohn, who contradict the negative qualities with which musicians were most often associated, could become the acceptable face of the profession. Such figures would eventually help to raise the status and respectability of music and music-making in England and, in a complete turn-around from the eighteenth century, assist in the quest to establish music as moral and 'improving', even among polite society. Similarly, the works of writers with strong beliefs in the improving qualities of music, particularly the striking example of Revd H. R. Haweis, a gifted violinist himself, and others such as Charles Reade, did a great deal to popularize the instrument and raise its status.[22]

Turning to the promotion of general performance styles and corresponding teaching material, we have already met the two works which were fundamental to the British violin-playing scene: Geminiani's treatise of 1751 and Spohr's of 1832, which became established as a seminal text in English in the 1840s (Chron., 1843). The presence and popularity of Geminiani, whose approach was greatly indebted to Corelli although technically more advanced, assured the prominence of the 'old style' and its ideals in British violin playing during the eighteenth century.[23] His execution on the violin 'had none of the fire and spirit of modern performers; but he possessed an abundance of grace and feeling: nearly all the powers that engage the attention of the hearer, and render it subservient to the will of the artist, were united in him'.[24] This won him many admirers among high-born musical amateurs. In addition to his published pedagogical writings his status as the most respected violin teacher of the time in England and Ireland ensured the promotion of his ideas throughout all levels of native violin playing.[25] His influence led Jousse to remark that 'we are greatly indebted to Geminiani for the improved state of the Violin in England' (Chron., 1811: xiv).

The impact of Corelli and Geminiani on violin playing in England is reflected in many works for the instrument by English composers. A visual representation of this can be found in a portrait of Joseph Gibbs by Thomas Gainsborough from the mid-1750s.[26] There are two volumes of music positioned behind Gibbs bearing the names of the two Italians,

---

[22] See Harvey (1995), 155 and 269.

[23] See Burney (1776–89, ed. 1935), vol.2, 990; and Grant (1983), 210. Other important references to Geminiani's activities in England, in addition to McArtor (1951) and Careri (1993), include 'Memoir', Harmonicon, 3 (1825), 145–7; Hogarth (1838), vol.1, 158–9; Boyden (1965), 350–2; and Kassler (1979), 379–87.

[24] Harmonicon, 3 (1825), 147.

[25] Geminiani's pupils, along with other native violinists, are discussed below.

[26] This portrait, which is now housed in the National Portrait Gallery in London, is reproduced on the front cover of an edition of two violin sonatas by Gibbs (Oxford, 1990) and in Holman (2000), 581.

which were probably selected by the composer to represent the most significant influences on his musical style. Gainsborough himself was a close acquaintance of Felice Giardini and had at least some proficiency on the violin.[27]

The music of another Italian, Tartini, which was well known in London and is well represented in the catalogues of the period,[28] 'shows a knowledge of the violin, both in regard to the bow and the fingerboard, which Corelli had not been able to attain'.[29] Nevertheless the famous *Letter* (1771), translated and published by Burney as soon as he returned from Italy, continues to promote the pedagogical role of Corelli's compositions and recommends their use for practice. Tartini focused his attention on the development of mastery and complete expressive control of the bow, as required in his own writing for the instrument. Tartini's works were criticized for their lack of 'energy, fire, and freedom of bow, which modern symphonies require',[30] but this probably contributed to their continued popularity among English violinists.

Felice Giardini continued the Corellian tradition (via G. B. Somis) in England during the second half of the eighteenth century and also promoted the newer Italian style characteristic of Tartini and Sammartini. He was admired by many, including Burney, as one of the best violinists of the century[31] and was a friend of the nobility and an influential teacher in England. The beauty and elegance of his performance and his 'taste and purity of tone'[32] were often noted. Moreover he 'did not aim to surprise', unlike the 'charlatan' Lolli.[33] The conscious efforts of the eighteenth-century English connoisseur to assert his 'fine taste' invariably placed expression above virtuosity. Consequently, violinists such as Giardini and Cramer were easily able to outshine someone like Lolli, whose tricks were not appreciated by the English and considered a bad example, particularly for amateurs.[34]

---

[27] See McVeigh (1989), 174–6.
[28] See Grant (1983), 208. A memoir of Tartini appears in the *Harmonicon*, 4 (1826), 188–9.
[29] Hogarth (1838), vol.1, 166.
[30] Burney (1776–89, ed. Mercer (1935)), vol.2, 450.
[31] See 'Memoir', *Harmonicon*, 5 (1827), 215–17; Hogarth (1838), vol.1, 167–70; Hart (1885), 375; and McVeigh (1989), in particular pp.195–200.
[32] Heron-Allen (1885), 20.
[33] Parke (1830), vol.1, 154.
[34] See Heron-Allen (1885), 14–15 and 20; Hart (1885), 375; and McVeigh (1989), 118 and 197–8. The extreme virtuosity of the native violinist J. A. Fisher was viewed in much the same light (see McVeigh (1989), 108 and (1993), 126 and 146). His violin concertos are discussed in White (1992: 309–15), along with the much more conservative examples by Thomas Linley jun. and Samuel Wesley.

Prominent German figures also influenced British violin playing, although they published very little teaching material. Salomon had an important role as a teacher (Jousse dedicated his 1811 treatise to him), in addition to his activities as an impresario.[35] The important contributions of Johann Stamitz and the Mannheim school were represented chiefly by the Cramer family. Wilhelm Cramer was, from his arrival in London in 1772 until the early 1790s and the arrival of Viotti, the most eminent violinist in England. Observers particularly appreciated his combination of rapid execution and facility with neatness, precision and tasteful expression in performance.[36] His son Franz became a prominent leader and soloist during the nineteenth century and an important member of the teaching staff of the early RAM.[37] The influence of Franz Eck on Spohr also contributed to the continued presence of the Mannheim tradition in English violin playing.

Those, such as Geminiani, who represented the 'ancient' school were only gradually superseded by the modernists in the nineteenth century. While some viewed compositions in the old style as 'cold and dry in the extreme', it was admitted that 'the labour which has evidently been bestowed on their construction gives them a grand and intellectual air, that seems to ensure continual respect and admiration'.[38] As the father of the French violin school in the nineteenth century, Viotti's innovations signalled a major advancement in technique, but as a continuation of the Corellian tradition (through Pugnani) still remained within the boundaries of good taste and refinement. The French and German schools took the place of the Italian in the nineteenth century as the most significant influences and Viotti was a pivotal figure with connections to all three.[39] He made a huge impact in England from the end of the eighteenth century and his virtues and musical qualities were still admired well into the nineteenth. Hogarth praises Viotti's style (and that of his disciples) and his compositions, presenting them as an ideal model for emulation and raising doubts as to 'the improvement in writing for, and playing on, the violin since his time'.[40] 'Such is their brilliancy and variety of effect', he continues, 'that we really see no occasion (beyond that of making the audience gape and stare) for any degree of execution beyond that which is called forth in their

---

[35] A memoir appeared in the *Harmonicon*, 8 (1830), 45–7.
[36] See McVeigh (1989), 112–13, and (1993), 184.
[37] See *MW*, 11 (1839), 198–9; and Palmer (1997), 128–9.
[38] 'The musical student No.2 (30 September 1819)', *QMMR*, 2 (1820), 60–61.
[39] Viotti's first compositions were published in Germany where he enjoyed much success (see White (1992), 329–31).
[40] *MW*, 2 (1836), 164–5.

performance.' He also recommends the concertos for 'our young performers', such as Henry Blagrove, in order to 'advance in the road towards nature and simplicity (the only real road to improvement in the fine arts)' and discard the 'present heaps of fashionable rubbish'.[41]

Louis Spohr, a disciple of Viotti (via Rode) and therefore a descendant of the Corellian tradition, found favour with the English in the nineteenth century in much the same way that Corelli and his school had enjoyed sustained popularity in the eighteenth. Both figures were able to prosper on account of the personal and musical qualities they represented. In Spohr's character 'simple dignity [was] engagingly blended with gentleness and modesty'[42] and, in combination with his profound musicianship, this brought him many friends and admirers.[43] Spohr's approach to the violin assimilated the clean bowing and expressive execution of the Mannheim school (through Franz Eck) and the elegant and graceful as well as brilliant style of Viotti and Rode. He therefore managed to combine virtuosity tempered by refined and tasteful performance.[44] These qualities allowed him to define the German school of violin playing during the greater part of the nineteenth century and make a considerable impact in England.[45] Hogarth believed that his reputation as 'the first violinist of the age' was justified and noted that he 'was particularly distinguished for his pure and delicate tone, the smoothness and facility of his execution, his expression, and the vocal character of his style'.[46] Other contemporary writers highlight the refinement and beauty in Spohr's performing style and his '*classical* taste ... [N]one as a performer combines so many great qualities'.[47]

It is common for both contemporary and present-day commentators to view Spohr as the antithesis of Paganini, whose approach is characterized by its extreme bravura and virtuosity.[48] Paganini did of

---

[41] See also Hogarth (1838), vol.1, 177. A lengthy biography appeared even later (*MW*, 14 (1840), 196–9), praising Viotti's conduct and personal attributes, while recommending some of his concertos for amateurs and praising his reluctance to pass 'the limit of appreciable sounds' (p.198).

[42] *MW*, 13 (1839), 339.

[43] See Brown (1980 and 1984) for important studies of Spohr's general popularity in England.

[44] It is not surprising that Spohr appreciated the 'somewhat conservative and old-fashioned' style of Franz Clement (Stowell (1998), 6), who also had strong connections with Beethoven and the French violin school. See discussion of repertoire below.

[45] Spohr's direct influence on the set-up of the violin in England is discussed below.

[46] Hogarth (1838), vol.2, 187.

[47] *Harmonicon*, 2 (1824), 215.

[48] Roth is typical of modern writers in his description of Spohr as 'a pillar of respectable musicianship', while focusing on Paganini's technical accomplishments (1997:

course enjoy much popular success in England in the early 1830s, but he was admired for the magical qualities and technical brilliance of his technique[49] rather than respected as an honourable man and a complete artist.[50] His performances were without doubt thrilling experiences, but his style and what it represented was, like Lolli's, considered inappropriate for young native artists to aspire to.[51] As Beedell has suggested, it 'was all very well for the already "respectable" to pick any musical delicacy they fancied from the Continental platter with perfect impunity – but altogether a different one for English musicians to supply them'.[52] This is consistent with Dubourg's view of the Englishman as 'a better recipient of the more intense emotions that lie within the province of the "king of instruments," although its more brilliant characteristics are less within his reach'.[53]

The large amount of material produced by English writers about figures such as Paganini and the extravagant Norwegian virtuoso Ole Bull testifies to their prominence and popular success during the nineteenth century. However, contemporary commentators, particularly in the 1830s, frequently refer to the importance of steering popular taste away from their approach in favour of the qualities exemplified by Viotti and Spohr. The virtuosity of 'pipers and fiddlers' is considered of less value than the desire to appeal to the 'noblest passions and affections of the heart'.[54] Hogarth discusses Paganini's appeal to popular taste through his 'quackery', with 'the perception of the higher beauties of the art' as yet 'confined to the few'[55] and Potter complains that tone on the violin 'is often sacrificed for the sake of surmounting great difficulties, and intricacies of execution'.[56]

---

14). Interestingly, Corelli and Paganini are compared in much the same way in the nineteenth century (see Heron-Allen (1894), 122–3).

[49] See Dubourg (1878), 120 and 128; and Schwarz (1984), 186–7.

[50] Spohr, who met with Paganini a number of times, was himself critical of the frivolous and extreme elements in the Italian's style while revealing some admiration for his technical accomplishments (see Spohr (1865), vol.1, 279–81, and vol.2, 168; and Schwarz (1984), 184).

[51] Heron-Allen's comments on F. J. M. Fayolle, *Paganini et Beriot* (Paris, 1831) are interesting in this respect as they show Fayolle's opinions on the subject to be consistent with his own, more than 60 years later. He states: 'It is an argument to the effect that Paganini was a charlatan, – a virtuoso rather than an artist ... The pamphlet was designed as a warning to young artists, whom the author (rightly) considered to be in danger of being dazzled and led away by the worship that was offered to Paganini' (1894: 44–5). See also ibid., 186 and 194.

[52] Beedell (1992), 113.
[53] Dubourg (1878), 195.
[54] Hodges (1836), 40–41 and 149.
[55] *MW*, 2 (1836), 162–3.
[56] C. Potter, 'Companion to the orghestra [*sic*]; or, hints on instrumentation. – No.I', *MW*, 3 (1836), 99.

Spohr therefore provided the ideal model after Viotti's death. Paul David, whose father Ferdinand was perhaps Spohr's most significant pupil, provides a neat summary and assessment of Spohr's contribution and influence through his 'example' rather than technical innovations, which is borne out by English pedagogical sources and other writings of the nineteenth and early twentieth centuries. He is seen as the preserver of 'the great qualities of the Classical Italian and the Paris Schools', in contrast to Paganini, whose approach and innovations inform the work of some later French writers, including Baillot (Chron., 1884).[57] Spohr's expressive priorities, in keeping with the 'serious spirit'[58] and 'soulful reserve'[59] of the Germans, appealed equally to the English connoisseur who also instinctively rejected frivolity and excess and sought to promote 'solid virtues' and 'sobriety'.[60] Sophisticated listeners and those involved with the serious promotion and cultivation of the art were therefore naturally sympathetic to his style of performance and composition and wished to establish him as a figure for adulation and emulation.[61] It is not without significance that the Philharmonic Society, which usually took sole charge of selecting programmes, broke with convention and allowed Spohr to perform his own 'Gesangsszene' Concerto (No.8, Op.47) at the opening concert in 1820,[62] a work which epitomizes his lyrical treatment of the instrument.

The nature of his style meant that its appeal to popular taste was limited,[63] but this was to his advantage. As discussed previously, specifically non-popular and 'intellectual'[64] qualities appealed to the British (as well as the German) connoisseur's sensibility and could serve to legitimize the art in the eyes of polite society. Spohr's emphasis on technique as the servant of tasteful expression, rather than as a tool used to astonish, could not have been better suited to the increasingly prevalent 'seriousness of taste' affecting the general cultural climate during the 1830s, a by-product of the greater economic and political

---

[57] David (1889), 294–5.
[58] Ibid., 295.
[59] Straeten (1933), vol.2, 200–201.
[60] Beedell (1992), 112–13. Dubourg refers to the 'honest solidity of execution' of the German school and adds that as 'violinists of *display*, therefore, they must be content to rank below the French' (1878: 166). Spohr himself distinguishes between 'Italian virtuosi and dilettanti' who 'direct their whole attention to the acquirement of mechanical skill' while neglecting tasteful performance, and the 'very cultivated style, and much feeling' of 'our German instrumentalists' (1865, vol.1, 302).
[61] See Brown (1980), 21–4.
[62] Ibid., 129–30.
[63] Ibid., 32 and 46.
[64] *The Analyst*, 8 (1839), 483.

power of the middle classes.⁶⁵ He was not alone in believing in the need to 'strive, at all times, after that which is noble in Art, and disdain all kind of charlatanism' and that he 'who seeks only to please the multitude, will sink ever lower and lower'.⁶⁶ These qualities and their appreciation among English audiences and critics are reflected in a review of a performance he gave of his Fourteenth Violin Concerto ('Sonst und Jetzt', Op.110) at the Norwich Festival in 1839, a piece designed to contrast the old and new styles of playing.

> In his playing, Spohr made no use of the resources of the modern school. In his most rapid flights and ascents into the highest regions of the scale, he did not introduce a single harmonic note, but produced every note by stopping the string, and with a perfection of tune, and an etherial purity of sound, which showed that the kind of instrumental *falsetto*, so profusely employed now-a-days, is useless to a performer of Spohr's powers, who can produce greater effects without it. His tone is not so full or so brilliant as that of some other violinists of the day: but in sweetness and equality (an equality produced by the cause we have just indicated) it is unrivalled. It is the most vocal tone, too, that we have ever heard; and his style has been formed on the model of the most exquisite Italian singing. With all this, his command of the bow, and rapidity of finger, are immense.⁶⁷

Also a letter from Ferdinand David to Mendelssohn (London, 31 May 1839) suggests that the appeal of technical trickery among most performers and listeners was short-lived in the capital:

> I was delighted to notice that harmonics and pizzicato no longer are fashionable here. Even the least perceptive listeners realize that they are mere charlatanry. Some performers, however, will have to do without their most effective tricks. It's strange that the Germans always are the last to catch on to such things.⁶⁸

Even in Henry Holmes's 1878 edition of Spohr's treatise the distinction is maintained between 'the brilliant school' and 'the lofty purpose of genius', and Paganini is once again portrayed as a genius but an unsuitable example for emulation.⁶⁹ While admitting 'modern' techniques to supplement Spohr's original, Holmes is careful to associate them with the bravura style, which is contrasted sharply with the compositions of the 'classic school' represented chiefly by Corelli and

---

⁶⁵ Brown (1980), 45–6.
⁶⁶ Spohr (Chron., 1843), 181–3 and 235.
⁶⁷ Anon., 'The Norwich Festival', *MW*, 13 (1839), 340.
⁶⁸ Quoted in Kolneder (1998), 389. Hogarth (*MW*, 2 (1836), 163–4) also refers to the short-lived desire among 'young violinists' to imitate Paganini's 'peculiarities' and 'faults', including the 'over-use' of harmonics.
⁶⁹ Chron., 1878: 193, 217 and 219.

Tartini, which are also recommended for study (Chron., 1878, pp.165, 174 and 193). Locatelli's Caprices,[70] famous for the extent of their technical demands, were seen as exciting 'more surprise than pleasure'[71] even in the nineteenth century. This was still the opinion of Ferdinand David's son over 60 years later.[72]

The 1840s were the high point of Spohr's popularity in England, and by this time his influence as a teacher and composer had spread to many young musicians. He did not perform a great deal in public in England: the London season of 1843 was his first public appearance in London as a violinist for 23 years.[73] If some critics at this time considered his playing more 'polished than exciting',[74] most appreciated and approved of the lack of technical fireworks and viewed him as an ideal role model for young violinists. Even Chorley, who was often critical of Spohr,[75] wrote that for 'purity of taste, and exquisite measurement of time, M. Spohr's performance is still admirable, and should be long remembered by our rising violinists, if such there be'.[76]

The level of technical difficulty in Spohr's works was widely accepted as the benchmark of tasteful performance, but, particularly during the early nineteenth century, this would have proved too demanding for the majority of amateur performers. As referred to earlier, the sustained popularity of Corelli and his followers among this group allowed their technical proficiency to remain independent of and generally inferior to the developments made elsewhere, particularly on the continent and among native female pianists. Although Spohr's approach to the violin was far more conservative than many of his contemporaries, even his music was criticized in reviews during the 1820s and into the 1830s for being too difficult and therefore inaccessible to the dilettante.[77]

However, this issue illustrates a fundamental change in attitude towards standards among native musicians and middle-class amateurs in particular. In contrast to the complacency of the eighteenth century it was increasingly felt during the nineteenth that the deplorably low levels of musical ability among the public needed to be remedied. Therefore in conjunction with a generally more serious approach to music and a steadily increasing number

---

[70] From *L'arte del violino* (Amsterdam, 1733).

[71] *QMMR*, 4 (1822), 58.

[72] David (1889), 292.

[73] It is probable that the Bishop translation of his violin treatise (Chron., 1843) was published to coincide with this resurgence in his public profile as a performer.

[74] Brown (1980), 141–2.

[75] See, for example, his *Thirty years' musical recollections* (London, 1862), vol.2, 183–6.

[76] *Athenaeum*, 16 (1843), 637.

[77] Brown (1980), 89–91. See also 'Review of music', *Harmonicon*, 6 (1828), 18.

of more ambitious amateurs, the difficulty and popularity of Spohr's music highlighted the need to improve proficiency across the board. Significant improvements in standards among amateurs were required if his music was not to become the sole property of professionals. His popularity and the influence of the musical qualities he represented grew to the extent that the more serious and dedicated amateur wished to acquire sufficient technical facility in order to play his music. Although separate from the more direct effects of his activities as a teacher and writer, this influence was fundamental in providing for the first time a real incentive for native violinists to achieve a higher standard. It was the practical realization of a plea made in some 1820s literature for native musicians, not inferior in terms of natural talent, to 'emulate, not envy' foreign artists.[78] The desire to inspire higher amateur standards certainly helped to nurture a more widespread respect for both music and performance.

Spohr continued to be identified with the highest ideals of art in Britain throughout the 1840s. As an icon of good taste and sincerity who was at one with the Victorian ideals of progress and self-improvement, Spohr's popularity exemplified to many an increase in taste and judgement among the public and was a welcome sign of resistance to less refined musical and performance styles. It is easy to see how appealing his approach to the violin would have been (akin to 'Spohr-worship' in some quarters) in this climate, and, following the impact of Paganini, why the technical innovations made and promoted elsewhere were resisted in England.

Given these circumstances it is only natural that the English thought of Mendelssohn, who promoted very similar expressive ideals to Spohr, in much the same light. Referred to by some as Spohr's 'younger brother'[79] he was also held aloft as a beacon of good taste and judgement by the nobility and other figures of influence who wished these qualities to be emulated by the public at large. Both Spohr and Mendelssohn were 'proper' geniuses, epitomizing order, control and refinement without any risk of excess.[80] Even after Spohr's popularity in England had begun to wane (largely in favour of Mendelssohn), his works for violin retained their position and value and formed 'one of the most extensive and valuable bequests that have been made to musicians'.[81] In the words of the violinist John Ella, they were considered 'by a large number of amateurs the *ne plus ultra* of modern art'.[82]

---

[78] Anon., 'Sketch of the state of music in London', *QMMR*, 5 (1823), 275.
[79] *The Spectator*, 20 (1847), 709.
[80] See Schonberg (1970), 443.
[81] *MW*, 19 (1854), 252.
[82] *The Record of the Musical Union*, 8 (1852), 11.

Spohr's posthumous reputation placed him 'second to none as a profound teacher' and viewed him as 'an artist in the purest sense'.[83] He was the chief representative of 'the great German school of playing, the most solid, legitimate, and classically pure, if not the most graceful, impetuous, and brilliant' and 'the rock against which the so-called *virtuosity* of his time could make no head'.[84] Although Mendelssohn caught the English taste in a higher degree during the second half of the nineteenth century, his works were never going to deprive Spohr of his pre-eminent position as far as the violin was concerned. As a composer his 'excess of refinement'[85] became a barrier to the appreciation of a wider musical public, but as a pedagogue and arbiter of tasteful performance his influence lived on. The lack of new effects in his violin style was more easily rectified, such as in later editions of the treatise,[86] than the absence of novelty and variety in his compositions. Therefore towards the end of the nineteenth century he is judged as 'the greatest composer for the Violin that ever lived', from whom 'has grown up a school of Violin-playing of a very distinctive character'.[87] Similarly an influential teacher of music and writer can refer to him representing 'a splendid school of violin playing; and by the charm of his writing for his own instrument' exercising 'a fascinating spell upon violinists'.[88]

It is therefore possible to assert that Spohr's style of violin playing was adopted by the English in the nineteenth century as the basis of a native school. He had nearly two hundred pupils from all over Europe and some from North America,[89] but his influence on English violin pedagogy was particularly strong. In addition to the native pupils of Spohr (discussed below) and the teaching material published by those influenced by him, several foreign disciples held prominent positions and continued the tradition of Spohr's methods in various English institutions. These include Bernhard Molique, Professor at the RAM, and August Wilhelmj, pupil of David and Professor at the Guildhall School of Music, London from 1894 and 'one of the first players' of the time.[90] In addition Joachim, one of those 'over whom the attractions of

---

[83] *MW*, 34 (1859), 712.

[84] Excerpt from *Programme of the Monday Popular Concerts*, quoted in 'Spohr and the violin', *MW*, 38 (1860), 811.

[85] Eaton (1872), 113–14.

[86] The Holmes edition of Spohr's treatise (Chron., 1878) appeared six years after Eaton's comments.

[87] Hart (1885), 393–4.

[88] H. C. Banister, 'The music of the Victorian era', in *Interludes* (London, 1898), 191–2.

[89] See Kolneder (1998), 410.

[90] Hart (1885), 394. See also Chron., 1898 and Heron-Allen (1894), lxi.

Spohr's music had cast a lifelong spell',[91] continued his influence well into the twentieth century.

An overview of the most prominent and influential violinists in England during the period presents a remarkably consistent picture. The foreign figures who achieved cult status display the same personal and musical qualities and represent all that is respectable and sincere in musical performance. The distinction between the 'virtuoso' and the 'artist' characterizes English taste to a large extent.[92] The typically limited and regulated access to instrumental instruction during the period allowed the conservative tastes of opinion formers and the musically literate to be promoted among native musicians of all standards.

Native violinists during our period were, needless to say, not as distinguished as the foreign visitors, but some did achieve prominence as teachers and performers and contributed to the promotion of the styles discussed above. While a few native players went to Italy in search of quality tuition during the early eighteenth century, others studied in England with Geminiani. Besides the contribution that his violin treatise made, his two most eminent pupils, Michael Festing and Matthew Dubourg, occupied leading positions in the musical life of England and Ireland, where their pupils 'fostered not only the general interest in the violin but also the taste of good music'.[93] Festing was the leader of many London orchestras[94] and the teacher of Philpot (see Philpot [1766]), and Dubourg's performance 'appears, from every account of it, to have been remarkable for its delicacy, grace, and expression'.[95]

British players, like most of their instrumentalist colleagues, struggled to compete with the foreign masters. Even relatively prominent violinists were not qualified to stand alongside and compete with, as leaders and soloists, the likes of Giardini, W. Cramer, Barthélemon and Salomon, and later Giornovichi, Yaniewicz, Viotti, F. Cramer and Weichsel. The nineteenth century brought some improvement in the achievements and fortunes of native violinists, following the increasing prevalence of more enlightened attitudes and greater opportunities. Lists of violinists and violists in the Philharmonic Society orchestra from the earlier part of the

---

[91] Brown (1980), 233. See also Heron-Allen (1894), Fourth Supplement, lxxi.

[92] According to Heron-Allen, the Revd H. R. Haweis, son of a prebendary of Chichester, was, at the age of fourteen, 'already a remarkable violinist, a virtuoso, perhaps, rather than an artist, and an amateur, in every sense of the word, above all' (1894: 204).

[93] 'Great Britain: to 1750' in Straeten (1933), vol.1, 399. Straeten also provides an interesting summary of activities in 'Great Britain: to 1850' (ibid., vol.2, 295–6).

[94] See Johnstone (1996), 623–4.

[95] Hogarth (1838), vol.1, 161–2. See also Dubourg (1878), 203–7; and Kolneder (1998), 376.

century consistently contain the names of Blagrove, Challoner, Cobham, Cooke, Dando, Gattie, Loder and Mori alongside F. Cramer, Kiesewetter and Spagnoletti.[96] The most significant of these as performers were Nicolas Mori (1796/7–1839) and Henry Gamble Blagrove (1811–72), who associated with and were both greatly influenced by Spohr and his school. The fact that various other figures, such as Spagnoletti, F. Cramer, Viotti and Barthélemon, were associated with their training as violinists reflects the vibrant and vital (as well as transitory) nature of the English musical environment during the period.

Hogarth admits that 'England has produced few great performers on the violin', but selects Mori as 'our only native violinist, of long established reputation as a concerto-player ... a pupil of Viotti, and one of the preservers of his pure and admirable school'.[97] The son of an Italian wig maker but born in London, Mori had earlier been described as a 'champion of England upon his instrument'[98] and 'one of the finest violin players in Europe'.[99] He was the dedicatee of Howell's 1825 treatise and had a great deal of contact with Spohr, including performances with him in 1820. Also Spohr's Octet Op.32 was given for the first time at Mori's concert on 17 May 1833 and Mori gave the English premiere of the Ninth or Eleventh Violin Concerto at his concert on 15 May 1835.[100] Dubourg remarks that 'few professional men have possessed equal influence in our musical circles'.[101]

Blagrove is the only nineteenth-century English violinist whom Davey mentions by name, describing him as 'perhaps the best' of the 'few of eminence'.[102] Hogarth, after mentioning the 'highly distinguished' orchestral leaders 'Francois Cramer, Weichsell, Mori, Loder of Bath, and T. Cooke', comments on Blagrove's position among 'our younger violinists' and how he 'has acquired great reputation by his talents both as a solo-player and a leader'.[103] Blagrove played a 'Solo' by Viotti at the RAM public concert at the Hanover Square Rooms in 1824, which prompted one commentator to write:

> this boy has a true genius for his art, as well as for his instrument. We were never more pleased with any performance than with his; his tone is delightfully firm and round, yet brilliant; he entered into

---

[96] See Rohr (1983), 263–6; Harvey (1995), 148; and Palmer (1997), 146–50.
[97] Hogarth (1838), vol.2, 265.
[98] 'Messrs. Mori, Spohr, and Kiesewetter', QMMR, 3 (1821), 323–7.
[99] Harmonicon, 2 (1824), 32. See also Duffin (1839); and Heron-Allen (1894), 194–5.
[100] Brown (1980), 37, 63 and 67.
[101] Dubourg (1878), 214.
[102] Davey (1921), 440.
[103] Hogarth (1838), vol.2, 265–6.

all the spirit of the author, and executed the double-stop passages admirably: he promises to be a second Mori.[104]

Towards the end of the century, Blagrove and Dando[105] are seen as 'thoroughly representative English Violinists' who 'have done much to raise the standard of the public taste'.[106] David, who classes Mori as foreign, identifies Blagrove and the Holmes brothers, Henry and Alfred, as the 'most eminent' English players.[107]

The Violin and Bow

It is only to be expected that the picture that emerges of violin making in England during the period is very similar to that of violin performance and pedagogy, bearing in mind the interdependence of aesthetic and organological developments. Hence there is no distinct school of English makers who were able to develop their own models and flourish independently of the continent. Rather, as Harvey has suggested, we see a *'mélange* of influences which were brought to bear in England by the influx of immigrant craftsmen'.[108] Barring a few isolated examples, the absence of a native tradition of violin making, as with violin playing and teaching, resulted in a lack of guidance and inspiration for the multitude. In all areas, therefore, access and success depended largely on the opportunities provided by birth or wealth, with instructional literature often a necessary complement or useful alternative to both.

The primary consumers of the products of British stringed-instrument makers were wealthy and interested amateurs, not professional musicians.[109] We have already seen the power of the eighteenth-century amateur to dictate the market and resist change through his penchant for anachronistic models and styles with which he was familiar and felt

---

[104] *QMMR*, 6 (1824), 80–81. Further discussion of Blagrove and his association with the early RAM can be found in Chapter 5.

[105] Joseph Haydon Bourne Dando (1806–94) was a pupil of Viotti for seven years (1819–26) and achieved his reputation primarily as a chamber musician, with Blagrove, Henry Gattie and John Fawcett Loder (second son of John David Loder). He was a friend of Spohr and Mendelssohn and became music master at Charterhouse School, Godalming in 1875. See Dubourg (1852), 293–302 for further details.

[106] Hart (1885), 387.

[107] David (1889), 298–9. It is well known that the Holmes brothers received guidance from Spohr, who dedicated some duos to them (see for example 'Holmes, Alfred', *Grove* 7 (2001), vol.11, 641). Henry, in addition to publishing an edition of Spohr's treatise (Chron., 1878), became violin professor at the RCM in 1883. Later prominent native violinists, including Carrodus and Sammons, are dealt with below.

[108] Harvey (1995), 66.

[109] See ibid., 121; and Holman (1993), 268.

comfortable. This situation is reflected in violin making in England by a preference for the Stainer model, which persisted during the eighteenth century and well into the nineteenth. The Stradivari-Guarneri patterns, which responded better to the modernization that took place around the turn of the nineteenth century, superseded the Stainer model later in England than elsewhere. Jousse comments that 'the Violins of Cremona are equalled, if not surpassed, by those of Stainer ... whose Instruments are remarkable for a full, and piercing tone'.[110] The new models required the assistance of Viotti and Paganini respectively to achieve prominence and were beyond the financial means of the vast majority of professional musicians.[111] Many English makers made copies of the Stainer model, including the leading figures Richard Duke and William Forster.[112]

Britain and especially England had a significant part to play in the development of the bow.[113] Much has been written on the transition from Baroque to Tourte-model bows and its implications for the technique of the violin.[114] The Tourte design and its new expressive qualities gained acceptance only gradually and pre-Tourte bows were made well into the nineteenth century. Bow management relevant to the new design was not examined in any detail until the treatise of Rode *et al.* (1803, cited under Chron., 1823).[115]

The number of different transitional bows (between the 'Corelli-Tartini' and the Tourte models) makes it extremely difficult to generalize about the kind of equipment that would have been in use during the

---

[110] Jousse (Chron., 1811), xviii. This passage, like some others in Jousse's treatise, is originally attributable to Hawkins (see Senn/Roy, 'Stainer, Jacob' in *Grove 7*, vol.24, 260), and it reappeares in one of the *QMMR* articles dedicated to the violin (1821: 445). Straeten (1911: 274) adds that this 'admiration of Stainer lasted right into the second half of last century, and the author remembers well the time when a Stainer violin or violoncello was looked upon as equal to an Amati, which was almost as much valued as a Stradivarius. It is curious to read Jousse's remarks about the full and piercing tone of the Stainer instruments, as they are now more known for perfect workmanship and sweetness of tone while lacking in power.' See also Harvey (1995), 62–5, 70, 186 and 223–31, and John Bishop's appendix to Hamilton's *Catechism* (Chron., 1835, 15th edn (1883), 88) states that the 'Steiner' [sic] model is still 'greatly esteemed', although it differs 'both in shape and tone, from the Cremonese instruments'.

[111] Like Viotti, Mori, Kiesewetter and Loder played on Stradivari instruments and, in addition to Paganini, Bull, Spohr, Sainton and Carrodus all owned Guarneris which they used as their primary concert instruments (see Hill (1902), 258).

[112] See Dilworth (1994); and Harvey (1995), 118.

[113] See Harvey (1995), 199–214.

[114] The most important contributions in this area include Babitz (1957); Curry (1968); Goldsmith (1979a and b); Boyden (1980); Jacoby (1980); Brown (1988); and Stowell (1984, 1985 and 1991).

[115] See Stowell (1985), 18–23. Further discussion of the interrelationship between bow design and technique can be found below.

period. This is particularly true of Britain. New designs were often associated with prominent virtuosi, and, as we have seen, many of these found favour and settled here. The 'Cramer' bow is a particularly interesting example and was popular in London towards the end of the eighteenth century.[116] Its ability to allow the precise attack characteristic of the Tourte design combined with 'a natural softness of articulation'[117] common to earlier examples, influenced English bow makers and appealed to native performers.

Although Viotti took over from Cramer as the leading and most influential violinist in England and introduced the Tourte design to Britain, the British remained behind the French in terms of the evolution of modern bow construction, despite the work of John (Kew) Dodd. Charles Beare has suggested that the Tourte-design head and metal ferrule, found in France well before 1800, arrived in England much later, perhaps only after the end of the war in 1815.[118] The Dodd bows are also generally shorter and lighter than the Tourte design. The fact that Jousse's comments (Chron., 1811: xviii) quote Hawkins[119] illustrates that the latest innovations in bow design were not a great priority even for French writers on the violin in England during the early nineteenth century, and that the way the bow was portrayed changed little in 35 years.

As with much of the teaching material of the period, evidence for the design of eighteenth- and early nineteenth-century British bows suggests less advanced and refined models compared with the continent, although they share many important qualities and features. Perhaps the continued popularity of the 'ancient' style of music among many wealthy consumers and a general reluctance to accept change delayed the acceptance and widespread use of the latest designs. Later in the century, as the new expressive ideals eventually achieved prominence in England, the Tourte model and its derivatives were able to dominate and acquire a truly 'European celebrity'.[120] The Great Exhibition (1851) and other exhibitions later in the century provided British violin and bow makers with the opportunity to display their goods and allowed the viewing of Italian masterpieces by a wider public.[121] The rapid growth in

---

[116] See Boyden (1980), 206–10; and Harvey (1995), 146 and 201.

[117] Boyden (1980), 207.

[118] 'Dodd' in *Grove 7*, vol.7, 417–18. The evidence provided by Jousse's diagrams (Chron., 1811: 2), reproduced on the title-page of Keith (Chron., 1813), is inconclusive but perhaps supports this view.

[119] Hawkins (1776), vol.2, 782.

[120] Spohr (Chron., 1843), 9. Dubourg (1878), 280, also refers to the prevalence of the Tourte design in this way. See also Spohr (Chron., 1878), 10 (n.).

[121] See Dubourg (1878), 279; and Harvey (1995), 256–61.

interest in all aspects of violin and bow construction is reflected in the large number of sources that were published on related subjects during the period. In addition there were a number of (often curious) ideas for changes to the design of the instrument.[122]

Violin Technique

Having discussed the evolving nature of the pedagogical material for violin, relative to general trends in British instrumental pedagogy (Chapter 2), we can now turn to technical concerns. Violin technique, like singing style (and largely because it was widely viewed as the instrumental equivalent), has a great deal of relevance beyond the instrument itself, a fact recognized by both contemporary and present-day commentators. A consistently popular instrument among leading continental 'schools' of performance style (Italian, German and Franco-Belgian) and increasingly practised in Britain during the nineteenth century, it gave rise to internationally famous exponents and substantial and authoritative pedagogical texts. The proliferation of conservatoires and touring virtuosos and teachers, prior to the birth of recording, assisted with the trend towards homogeneity in musical performance (although it remained generally far more subtle and 'nuanced' than today), not only between schools of performance on a particular instrument but also between instruments. As part of this trend during the age of virtuosity, we find other instrumentalists, including wind players,[123] appropriating string techniques. This section and the following chapter will examine further how the 'melting pot' of British culture and the dominant amateur market dealt with the convergence of styles and techniques, an issue made all the more relevant by the transitional nature of the early nineteenth century.

It would be a mistake, however, to expect to find the whole panorama of technique presented here. The treatment of individual issues reflects the nature and priorities of the works and writers themselves, and so the discussion of some aspects of technique appears limited compared with some mainstream continental examples, whereas other aspects receive a greater, perhaps even disproportionate, amount of attention. Discussion of technique and other performance practice issues (dealing first with the left hand (position and movement), then right hand (position and movement) and finally other aspects) is followed by a section examining how the contents of the teaching material relate to mainstream violin repertoire in Britain.

---

[122] See Heron-Allen (1894), 366–9, and (1885), 110 and 112.
[123] See Lawson (2000), 55.

Violin Hold

Some of the most basic and fundamental information contained in sources of this kind is that concerned with how the violin is positioned in relation to the player. For many of the earliest treatises the frontispiece is the main source of information on the violin and bow holds and posture.[124] The small amount of text in the early tutors generally means that little or no written instruction is given in this area, and where it does exist it is often confusing and ambiguous.[125] Evidence for the violin hold itself is diverse and often contradictory.[126] However unlike instructions for the stance, some written directions are given by eighteenth-century English writers, with the short passage from part V of Prelleur's treatise (1730/31: 2) providing the model for Rutherford (c.1750) and all of the 'Geminiani-attributed' sources examined (c.1770 and Chron., 1790, 1792 and 1800). These examples make no mention of the chin or collarbone positions. The slightly more detailed instructions of Geminiani (1751, text pp.1–2) refer to a position 'just below' the collarbone, which progresses to 'upon' the collarbone with Philpot (1766: 6). Also Philpot does mention the chin and its placement to the right of the tail-piece, which might suggest a position similar to that proposed by Leopold Mozart,[127] even though the chin may not be used to 'grip' the instrument. In addition a passage from Crome (1765: 34), originating as early as the 1740s, is a more detailed version of the comments in Prelleur and introduces the concept of the chin as a means of securing the instrument. It is evident from the available pedagogical material that a variety of different positions were used in eighteenth-century England, displaying different stages of development.

The position of the left hand on the neck of the instrument is another contentious issue, and again the tutors based on Prelleur part V are not very helpful. By far the most important information on the subject of the violin hold contained in a British source is the 'Geminiani grip', which 'shews a Method of acquiring the true Position of the Hand' (1751, text p.1). This method for positioning the left hand is unique in its simplicity and adaptability to the individual hand and ensures that the left elbow is well under the middle of the instrument, allowing the fingers to curve

---

[124] Some facsimile reproductions of frontispieces are contained in Golby (1999b), vol.2.

[125] Generally the posture of the player did not become an issue of discussion until the latter part of the eighteenth century.

[126] See Stowell (1992), 122–4, for a discussion of the main issues and trends in continental sources.

[127] L. Mozart (1756), ch.II, §1–§3, Eng. tr. (1948), 54–7.

naturally and fall perpendicularly onto the strings. The importance of this elbow position for the facility of the left hand is stressed by Philpot (1766: 6), whose directions also inform Jousse (Chron., 1805: 8, and 1811: 3) and related works (see Chapter 2). The importance of the 'Geminiani grip' as a technical device is reflected in its appeal to other writers.[128]

Writers in English from the early nineteenth century who comment on the playing posture and position of the violin generally present an amalgam of eighteenth-century theory and some more modern trends. This is partly attributable to Jousse and his influence on other sources. His initial treatment of this subject (Chron., 1805: 8) is based mainly on Geminiani and Philpot and promotes the collarbone hold without mention of the chin. A few years later (Chron., 1811) Jousse makes use of the 'Geminiani grip' for the correct positioning of the hand (p.5)[129] and provides more specific instructions than any of the other early nineteenth-century English examples for the holding of the instrument (pp.2–3). These include detailed illustrations (p.2)[130] which are comparable in quality and broadly similar in the posture and left-hand technique depicted to examples in the much later publications of Spohr (Chron., 1843, plates 2 and 3) and Baillot (1835).[131] Jousse's directions, although partly informed by much earlier theories, are largely consistent with general trends in violin technique at this time. They demonstrate that the angle of the violin increased towards the horizontal (and so the left elbow moved away from the trunk) and that it was held more directly in front of the player.[132] Both these developments were aided by the firmer support provided by the chin and its position on the left side of the tailpiece,[133] although with echoes of an earlier tradition Jousse prescribes the pressing down of the chin only when changing position; at other times it is to 'lean gently' (p.3).

---

[128] These include Leopold Mozart (1769–70); Campagnoli (?1797, Chron., tr. Bishop (1856), 2); Rode et al. (1803, Eng. tr., Chron., 1823: 5 and 7), Baillot (1835: 15 and 18); and David (Chron., 1874: 5). Spohr's treatise is one of the few not to mention it, and Wessely (1913: 13) considers it 'ingenious' but 'awkward' and 'almost impossible for beginners to achieve'.

[129] This can also be found in Goodban (Chron., 1810: 15) and Keith (Chron., 1813: 13).

[130] Jousse's diagrams (figs 5, 6, 8 and 9) are reproduced on the title-page of Keith (Chron., 1813), who also makes use of many of his written directions.

[131] Baillot's illustrations are reproduced in Stowell (1985), 36 and 51.

[132] Jousse's instruction that 'the head of the Violin should face the middle of the left shoulder' (p.3) is based on Rode et al. (1803, art.1, p.5; English tr. Chron., 1823).

[133] Jousse recommends, as Baillot does much later (1835: 15), that 'lads' with short left arms playing a full-size instrument place their chin on the right side (Chron., 1811: 3, n.2).

In common with other writers[134] he points out that some of the most common bad habits with regard to posture and presentation are 'to move the head and body, [and] to distort the features in playing difficult passages' (p.3).[135]

Howell provides some of the most detailed instructions for a nineteenth-century British treatise, and the section on the 'Relative Position of the Body, Instrument &c.' summarizes many of the points advocated in the treatises of the period as a whole (Chron., 1825: 22). A direction to lower the right side of the instrument a little to facilitate bowing on the lower strings originates in Geminiani (1751, text pp.1–2) and is common to many other native works. Interestingly Howell proposes a central rather than a left-sided chin position. In addition to the frontispiece of the third French edition of Geminiani (?1763), this central position is given credibility by the invention (c.1820) of the chin rest by Spohr, which was designed to be placed over the tailpiece in the centre of the violin (Chron., 1843: 2–3 and plates 1–3).[136] If the chin rest is not used (it is not mentioned by Howell) then Spohr states that the chin should be placed 'partly on the belly to the left of the tailpiece, partly on the tailpiece itself' (p.13).[137] It appears that a different chin rest invented by James Stewart, which was higher and placed to the left of the tailpiece, like most modern examples, became popular and was preferred by many to Spohr's invention.[138] The use of such devices naturally increased the facility of both hands.[139]

The variety of styles, both progressive and anachronistic, that vied for prominence in Britain during the early nineteenth century produced an especially inconsistent and confusing scene with regard to performance practice on the violin. In keeping with this situation, and in contrast to Jousse and Howell, the treatise of Paine recommends a very old-

---

[134] Such as Löhlein (1774: 12–15, arts. 20 and 21) and Baillot (1835: 15–16).

[135] As early as Lenton (1693: 11) English players had been warned against 'unseemly actions'. Thomson (Chron., 1840: 13) stresses that the performer should 'avoid an affected manner or ungraceful negligence'.

[136] See also Stowell (1985), 29–30.

[137] Farmer, whose directions for holding the violin are based on Spohr's method (Chron., 1847: 4), makes no mention of the chin rest and directs the chin to be placed on the left side of the tailpiece.

[138] Good publicity for Stewart's device was provided by letters from 'A player' and 'A looker-on, but no player' recommending its use (MW, 21 (1846), 597 and 609–10), and advertisements including testimonials from Sainton, Blagrove, Farmer and Cooke (ibid., 647 and 663). Its simplicity and usefulness for beginners were highlighted as important innovations (MW, 22 (1847), 25–6).

[139] Also Spohr introduced the shorter tailpiece to English violinists, 'to give a quicker return of the string from the finger-board, and to confer greater facility in execution' (see QMMR, 2 (1820), 385 and Brown (1984), 131).

fashioned hold, with the left elbow close to the body[140] and no chin-braced grip (Chron., 1815, title-page and p.9).

The Left Hand

Naturally the posture of the player and the position of the left hand are closely connected to the movement and freedom of both hands. The ability of the left hand and fingers to change position with ease and perform a variety of techniques, while maintaining accurate intonation, became increasingly important with advances in the technical demands of the repertoire.

In keeping with contemporary keyboard technique, unnecessary finger activity was to be avoided. The idea of 'finger economy' is naturally important for the discipline of the fingers and especially the performance of fast passage-work and smooth, sustained lines, which became an increasingly important consideration during the late eighteenth and nineteenth centuries. This principle is included in a large number of English sources ranging through Geminiani (1751, text p.2), Jousse (Chron., 1811: 6), Paine (Chron., 1815: 21–2), Howell (Chron., 1825: 25), Thomson (Chron., 1840: 12, based on Campagnoli), Loder (Chron., 1841: 46) and Hamilton (Chron., 1835: 32). Howell's later publication for the violin demonstrates how important this principle had become (Chron., 1829: 4, 5, 10 and 22), and also raises the issue of finger pressure and its relevance to tone production (p.4).[141] Also the 'hammer-like' finger action specified by Jousse (Chron., 1811: 3), with the fingers falling perpendicularly on the strings, is consistent with other writers, including Campagnoli (Chron., 1856: 3).

In spite of these examples most of the native treatises, at least from the eighteenth century, contain very little written instruction on the mechanics of the left hand. The information provided, other than fingerings and other technical demands in compositions, is usually confined to scales, exercises and fingering charts. Therefore private instruction would have been essential for an appreciation of anything other than the most basic aspects of technique. The sources related to Prelleur part V certainly provide few such insights, recycling (with few

---

[140] This elbow position is also advocated by Keith (Chron., 1813: 12) and Hack (Chron., 1835: 11), and Hamilton (Chron., 1835, 15th edn (1883), 30) prescribes a position 'quite close to the side'.

[141] Discussion of a detail (albeit an important one) such as left-hand finger pressure was less common in the eighteenth century, and extremely rare in English sources. This makes Philpot's mention of it early in his treatise (with reference to the G major Gamut) all the more significant (1766: 6).

changes) the 'Scale of the GAMUT'. Eighteenth-century sources in English (excluding Geminiani (1751) which refers to seven 'Orders') frequently adopt the phrase 'half shift' for modern second position and 'whole' or 'full shift' for third position. Also sixth position was often called 'double shift' and seventh 'last shift'. The modern system, codified by the violinists at the Paris Conservatoire, was promoted in England by translations of mainstream texts, including those by Rode *et al.* and Campagnoli,[142] but the comments of Howell and others suggest that, in spite of his disapproval, the old terminology was still in use in England well into the nineteenth century (Chron., 1825: 41 and 43). It certainly pervades nineteenth-century examples through to at least the late 1840s.[143]

The role of the fourth finger reflects a growing concern for lyricism and uniformity of tone and an increasing interest in sonority and projection in general. Philpot discusses the importance of the fourth finger with respect to sound-quality (1766: 10) and a similar but more substantial passage is found in Howell (Chron., 1825: 26).[144] The comments in the Geminiani-attributed *Compleat instructions* suggest that the importance of the fourth finger came to be appreciated even at the most elementary level (Chron., 1800: 2); although, crucially, here the concern is primarily intonation and so 'theoretical'. The reference to the fourth finger being more 'equal in tune' than the open string in some circumstances relates to the use of meantone or some other historic temperament in which major thirds and not fifths were pure. Open strings were therefore avoided to preserve both the homogeneity of the sound and avoid Pythagorean fifths—perhaps a curious element in a treatise where so much else is left to the imagination (see further discussion of temperament below). *Compleat instructions* is still technically retrospective compared with Geminiani's treatise from half a century earlier (1751), which utilizes a range of up to a^3 on the E string (or 'three Octaves and a Tone' as specified on the first page of text) and c^2 on the G string.[145] It is also acknowledged that Geminiani demands

---

[142] The translations of these works give precedence to the new terminology but do refer to the old system.

[143] It is therefore remarkable that Crome's tutor (originating *c.*1740) includes directions for modern second and third positions (up to d^3).

[144] L. Mozart (1756, ch.5, §13, Eng. tr. (1948), 101) stresses the need, in the context of a solo, to use the fourth finger instead of open strings in the interests of a 'natural and delicate' sound (as well as importance of playing 'everything, when possible, on one string, in order to produce consistently the same tone quality').

[145] David (1889), 292, notes that the exploitation of this range is exceptional in a violin tutor of the period, although earlier sources do refer to it (see below). The detail and idiosyncratic nature of the Italian's directions for the fingering of the scales and exercises

very advanced left-hand technique, the true extent of which can only be appreciated from the music in the treatise. Less well known is the use of some of the advanced fingering exercises from the 1751 source in some of the later Prelleur-related treatises, although *Compleat instructions* adds some original material.[146]

The treatise of Philpot (1766) owes much to Geminiani and sits somewhere between the most elementary English works and that of the Italian with respect to technical demands. It does not contain lengthy exercises on a single concept but does incorporate separate 'Minuets' and 'Lessons' to introduce technical challenges, and so does not confine its exploitation of the whole range of the instrument to just scales. It marks a definite step forward in terms of pedagogical method in native instrumental treatises.

The subject of harmonics is seldom discussed in eighteenth-century sources,[147] although composers from early in the century exploit natural harmonics.[148] The brief survey in the treatise of L'abbé *le fils* (1761), which did not appear as a separate English publication until nearly 70 years later (Chron., 1828), is perhaps the most important discussion before the contributions of virtuosi such as Paganini.[149] It is therefore significant to find in Gehot's treatises a passage with some technical direction and an exercise, relevant to the viola as well as the violin, which demonstrate an extensive range of natural and artificial harmonics (Chron., 1784: 18–19).[150] Also Jousse discusses harmonics at some length (Chron., 1811: 53–4), including complete two-octave diatonic and chromatic scales and a Tempo di Minuetto (p.54)[151] which make use of both the natural and artificial varieties.[152]

Comments from the early 1830s refer to violin harmonics as 'an extension of the scale of this instrument beyond what may be called its natural boundary', which 'is of no practical utility, and would scarcely

---

have been widely appreciated, in particular his preference for shifts involving larger movements of the hand (such as 123, 123 or 1234, 1234 fingerings). This technique is different from most mainstream writers of the eighteenth century. Stowell (1992), 124–6, provides a useful summary of issues relating to shifting during the eighteenth century.

[146] Wybrow (Chron., 1858) borrows extensively from *Compleat instructions*, which explains the presence (pp.7 and 9) of other material from Prelleur part V (1731: 2) and from Geminiani (1751, text p.2).

[147] They are not included in Geminiani (1751) or even in Rode *et al.* (1803, Eng. tr., Chron., 1823), and Leopold Mozart's comments are mainly concerned with their inferior tone quality (1756, ch.5, §13, Eng. tr. (1948), 100–101).

[148] See Stowell (1985), 211–12.

[149] See Dubourg (1878), 119.

[150] These examples appear to be taken from Gehot (Chron., 1780), 12–13.

[151] This is taken from L'abbé *le fils* (1761: 73; Eng. tr., Chron., 1828).

[152] See also Keith (Chron., 1813: 39).

ever be resorted to, but for the purpose of displaying the dexterity of the performer'.[153] Spohr's thoughts on harmonics are at one with these later attitudes towards their use in England. He accepts natural harmonics, which are not substantially different in sound from 'the natural notes', but rejects the artificial variety outright (Chron., 1843: 96). The British appear to have shared the reluctance of the German writers to accept harmonics as a legitimate aspect of the core technique of the instrument. The significant number of specialist articles and methods on harmonics written in Germany in the first half of the nineteenth century, inspired largely by the antics of Paganini,[154] is echoed in England;[155] but these works, both original and selected from earlier sources, are designed to supplement general violin treatises and so promote the use of harmonics as novel effects rather than as part of the serious study of the instrument. Even Holmes, who incorporates artificial (Chron., 1878: 217) and double (p.218) harmonics into his edition of Spohr's treatise, confines the technique to an appendix and, careful not to dismiss Spohr's views, is equally critical of their incorrect and too frequent use. Hamilton (Chron., 1835, 15th edn, 62–3) does not mention artificial harmonics but does recommend the surveys of L'abbé (Chron., 1828), Campagnoli (Chron., 1830) and Guhr (n.d.).

Naturally the use of harmonics substantially extends the range of the instrument, which is otherwise up to around a^3, the extent of modern seventh position, in most treatises from the period.[156] However the full range is not utilized in the main substance of the sources, beyond just scales and fingerboard charts, until the more advanced works of Barthélemon (Chron., 1790) and some nineteenth-century writers. In fact the prominence and frequency of chromatic scales and fingering charts in British treatises compared with other aspects of technique, including their illustration of the concept of unequal semitones,[157] displays a bias in

---

[153] *The Harmonicon* (1833), 130.

[154] See Stowell (1985), 4.

[155] For example Cobham (Chron., 1819); L'abbé *le fils* (Chron., 1828); Campagnoli, *A compleat treatise* (Chron., 1830); Anon. (Chron., 1831) and Anon. (Chron., 1840).

[156] This is consistent with Leopold Mozart, Campagnoli's writings and general eighteenth-century practice (see Stowell (1992), 124). Some sources (such as Burton, Chron., 1886) suggest that this was considered, in Britain at least, the extent of the 'normal' violin range for a significant period. Hamilton's instructions (Chron., 1835, 15th edn, 54–8) are consistent with this, although, like Campagnoli (?1797, Eng. tr. Hamilton (1834), 1), whose works he recommends, he also includes the 'sur-acute or extreme octave' up to thirteenth position (p.58).

[157] See Boyden (1951); Barbour (1952); Barbieri (1991); and Haynes (1991). Although Boyden's article is the oldest it is especially useful as it concentrates mainly on English examples. The existence of a system in which flats are higher than their equivalent sharps is confirmed in the various chromatic scales and fingerings found in the eighteenth-

favour of a 'scientific', 'intellectual' approach, even at the most elementary practical stage.[158] The mechanics of instrumental technique, such as the process of shifting, necessary for any significant progress to be made, is not deemed worthy of anything like comparable treatment.

The evidence in eighteenth-century British sources points towards the existence of a type of meantone temperament, even if, as Philpot suggests (1766: 13), the distinction between semitones was only required or expected of more advanced players. This further demonstrates the incongruity of the chart's position in the Prelleur-related sources as highlighted in Chapter 2. The eighteenth-century system continued to be promoted in some retrospective British sources well into the next century, although the general trend was towards inflections with sharps higher than corresponding flats, especially leading-notes (as is common in modern practice), and equal temperament. Native nineteenth-century sources generally illustrate this progression, while remaining aware of past theories. Howell's comments (Chron., 1825: 60–61) suggest that the intervals are to sound the same, whether written as sharps or flats, but they are still fingered differently. Potter's discussion of the violin states that 'the enharmonic scale is artificial', adding that

> a practical performer will consider C# higher in the scale (more acute) than D-flat; – a theoretical performer is well aware that the latter is the higher note, from the consideration of its situation in the chromatic scale, and from the division of the monochord; although it must be admitted, from the force of habit, that often the first mode of taking the note is more congenial with our ears.[159]

However he does concede that 'some of the greatest beauties in music arise out of [the] imperfections' of the enharmonic scale (ibid.). Also equal temperament is considered the most appropriate system for 'modern music' and 'the pupil' by the time of Bishop's edition of Spohr's treatise (Chron., 1843: ii–iii, footnote), although mention is made of major and minor semitones. Holmes's edition of Spohr (Chron., 1878: 153) restates the concept of unequal semitones, but, reflecting contemporary thought, sharps are presented as sounding higher than corresponding flats.

---

century sources, including the more detailed and comprehensive examples from Philpot and Geminiani.

[158] Because of the detail of Prelleur's chart and the fact that its full implications are not realized in the rest of the treatise, some have suggested that it was produced by a second party, probably a mathematician, using geometric methods (see Barbour (1952), 232; and Riley (1954), 191).

[159] C. Potter, 'Companion to the orchestra ... No.II', *MW*, 4 (1836), 2.

Howell demonstrates how changing attitudes and new expressive aims changed other aspects of left-hand technique in the nineteenth century. As mentioned above the use of the fourth finger became increasingly important during the period for the production of a more homogeneous tone quality (Chron., 1825: 26) as its role in achieving accurate intonation diminished with changes in temperament. Expanding on some eighteenth-century precedents[160] and in line with continental developments, the use of higher positions and position changes for their own sake acquired significance as means of expression, and not just for soloists.[161] Accordingly advice on the mechanics of shifting and fingering is provided in relative detail in many nineteenth-century native sources. Jousse (1811) refers to factors such as the movement of the thumb (p.3), chin pressure 'on the Violin to prevent its falling' (p.22),[162] finger and bow pressure (and the assistance the teacher can give to intonation by accompanying an octave lower) (p.23), shifting with the second as well as the first finger (p.26), and shifting by finger substitution (p.27).[163] Keith's discussion of shifting (Chron., 1813: 34–6) advocates, contrary to Geminiani, small movements of the hand for upward and downward shifts (12–12 or 21–21). Like Jousse he also gives details of finger substitutions, extensions and 'borrowed' fingerings (which are in effect a reference to modern half position). Paine's treatise, in many ways an anachronism, offers the fretted 'Patent finger-board' to aid intonation (Chron., 1815: 13 and 47)[164] and advice

---

160 In particular L. Mozart (1756, ch.5, §13, Eng. tr. (1948), 101).

161 Jousse (Chron., 1811), 70; Howell (Chron., 1825), 41. The expressive potential of fingering is also discussed in Goodban (Chron., 1810), 38; and Hack (Chron., 1835), 52. Hamilton, in his little *Catechism* (Chron., 1835, 15th edn, 1883), reveals a similar desire to Mozart (Eng. tr. (1948), 101) for 'passages of expression' to be played on the least number of strings as possible (p.56). In a separate section he gives each string a range of about two octaves and illustrates a two-octave G major scale on the G-string using the 12–12 fingering common in the eighteenth century (p.59).

162 Unusually for a nineteenth-century writer Goodban (Chron., 1810: 38) prefers the downward shift to be without the aid of chin pressure, using just the wrist. This is 'the most graceful and proper' method, although the use of the chin is 'the most easy to a Learner'.

163 His discussion of left-hand technique also includes particularly useful and difficult exercises for double stopping ('simple' and 'complex', involving two independent lines) (pp.30–34) and arpeggio figures (pp.38–40).

164 Playford had much earlier recommended that beginners use violins with frets that could later be discarded (see Kolneder (1998), 293). The long tradition in English sources of including charts or other types of intonation aid that can be applied to the fingerboard directly or copied onto it continues well into the nineteenth century. Challoner (Chron., 1825: 7) provides a chart and recommends using small marks made 'with a penknife' to indicate the position of the lines and make their reapplication easier. Hack (Chron., 1835: 5) includes a 'Paper fingerboard' to assist the student without 'the advantage of

on the use of open strings for changing position (p.43).[165]

Spohr, however, is without doubt the most significant nineteenth-century figure with regard to instruction on left-hand technique published in English. He provides rare detail on the mechanics of shifting, including directions for the movement of the left elbow, hand and thumb in higher positions (Chron., 1843: 90). Of particular interest are his theories on portamento.[166] The central issue is the prominence of the device in the nineteenth century. Although used earlier it became, in accordance with vocal practice, much more freely employed and exploited as a means of expression, in non-solo contexts and to a greater extent than vibrato. Spohr, probably inspired by Rode, became a great exponent,[167] while continuing to emphasize its tasteful application, the prime concern of British critics. The 'charlatan' Lolli's exaggerated use of the device[168] no doubt contributed to his lack of success in this country and Dubourg's comments on Kiesewetter are consistent with this.

> These squeaking notes, and marked sliding of the finger up the strings [by Kiesewetter], as it has justly been observed, may show a certain kind of mechanical skill that partakes of the nature of practical wit, but they also betray the weaker part of the instrument, and are apt to be (except when *insured* by the skill of a Paganini) more provoking than pleasing.[169]

Spohr's shifting technique is based on the use of unsounded anticipatory notes, 'the stopped finger sliding forwards (or backwards) in order to be substituted by another finger'.[170] Sliding with the finger which is to stop the second note, resulting in a more conspicuous effect, was a French habit later in the century[171] and is forbidden by Spohr unless it is to a harmonic.[172] Although it is to be distinctly heard on some occasions (Chron., 1843: 196–7), the use of portamento, in imitation of the

---

Professional instruction' and Farmer (Chron., 1847) produces a 'Printed Plate' indicating the placement of the fingers.

[165] L. Mozart, Eng. tr. (1948), 138, and Hamilton (Chron., 1835, 15th edn), 56, offer similar advice.

[166] Brown (1988), 119–28 provides a useful survey of the subject.

[167] See ibid., 123–5.

[168] See ibid., 122–3.

[169] Dubourg (1878), 179. Sainton was also criticized for the over-use of portamento (see Bashford (2000), 109).

[170] Stowell (1992), 126.

[171] Brown (1988), 125.

[172] For example, Chron., 1843: 108–9. Much later Kinsey (1954) also stresses that 'care must always be taken not to slide up with the finger about to be played, otherwise an ugly scoop results' (p.20).

human voice (p.114), should never result in a 'disagreeable whining' (pp.108 and 173).[173]

Spohr's approach to left-hand technique appears to have held sway in Britain for most of the nineteenth century and remained particularly useful for the purposes of instruction. Holmes adds nothing on the subject of portamento in his edition of the treatise (Chron., 1878), and, 70 years after the Bishop translation, Wessely notes the usefulness of Spohr's anticipatory notes for the 'young beginner' and the importance of practising restraint in the interests of good taste.[174]

The Bow

Many writers during the period emphasize the importance of the bow and draw attention to its fundamental role in the playing of the violin and related instruments, in particular its ability to breathe 'life' into a performance.[175] The ability of the bow to add expression and nuance to the music is an essential part of the technique of the instrument and the changes made to its design and construction during the late eighteenth and early nineteenth centuries naturally had a great impact on this.

As with the posture of the player and the placement of the left hand the information on the position of the bow and bow arm in the earliest sources and those related to them is contained mainly in the frontispieces. The information provided by these is generally consistent with mainstream eighteenth-century thought,[176] which recommends a 'natural' position with the arm and bow in the same geometric plane (or slightly lower), leaving the elbow detached from the body but not held too high. It is impossible to discern the precise position of the hand, fingers and thumb on the stick of the bow from the frontispieces, and so additional details are required. Unfortunately neither Prelleur (1730/31) nor Rutherford (c.1750) describe the bow hold, and so Geminiani (1751) is one of the first English sources to contain written instruction on it. The relevant passage[177] describes the typical Italian bow grip of the first part of the eighteenth century, which uses all four fingers and the thumb, inserted between the bow stick and the hair.[178]

---

[173] Hamilton (Chron., 1835, 15th edn, 56) states that the position change 'may not be audible'.

[174] Wessely (1913), 84–5.

[175] Jousse (Chron., 1811), xviii.

[176] Such as found in L'abbé *le fils* (1761: 1; Eng. tr., Chron., 1828) and Campagnoli (Chron., 1856), 1.

[177] Example 1 (B.), text p.2.

[178] Although the Italian grip was introduced to England by Matteis during the 1670s (see Cyr (1995), 56), the French grip, with the thumb on the hair, is the technique described by Lenton (1693: 11).

However, as with the violin hold, there are inconsistencies between the text and the frontispiece from the third French edition, with the original description of a hold 'a small distance from the nut' (or frog) illustrated as a much larger distance. Geminiani's directions therefore appear retrospective compared with Leopold Mozart (1756), who also illustrates a Baroque bow but stipulates in the text and diagrams that it is to be held 'at its lowest extremity, between the thumb and the middle joint of the index-finger, or even a little behind it'.[179] This lower position combined with pressure from the second joint of the index-finger (instead of the first joint, as illustrated in the frontispiece to Geminiani) and the rejection of the Italian's turning of the hair 'inward' in favour of a position 'more straight than sideways on the violin',[180] exemplify a more advanced approach and a desire for a stronger, more robust, or 'honest and virile' tone.[181] I mention this detail because Geminiani's comments on bowing from example 1(B.) are not only reproduced in the 'attributed' sources from the late eighteenth century, but also inform the directions of many others from the nineteenth century. These include Jousse (Chron., 1805: 8 and 1811: 4), Goodban (Chron., 1810: 15), Keith (Chron., 1813: 12–13), Challoner (Chron., 1825: 6), Hack (Chron., 1835: 21) and Wybrow (Chron., 1858: 9). The period of distribution of this material in Britain therefore extends beyond a century.

As previously highlighted, early nineteenth-century British sources are a product of a vibrant and transitional musical environment and consequently in some cases attempt to stand between two contrasting expressive and aesthetic ideals. The instructions on bowing in Jousse's violin method appear, from the evidence in the diagrams (Chron., 1811: 2), to be based on the use of a transitional bow, rather than a fully-fledged Tourte design. These diagrams and portions of the text expand on the approach adopted in his earlier treatise (Chron., 1805: 8) and demonstrate a rather retrospective view of some aspects of technique. The thumb is to be placed 'on the Stick at about an inch from the Nut' (1811: 4), which is similar to Geminiani and Philpot but not Leopold Mozart or L'abbé *le fils*. In other ways Jousse proposes in the text and diagrams similar ideas to the progressive L'abbé, such as advocating that the thumb should 'support the whole weight of the Bow' and be placed opposite the second finger.[182] Like Geminiani he requires that the hair be 'turned inwardly against the outside of the Thumb' (which is therefore bent) and adds that 'the knuckles must be kept rather high above the Stick'.[183] The position of the right arm, with

---

[179] Ch.2, §5, Eng. tr. (1948), 58–9, slightly modified in the 1787 edition.
[180] 1756, ch.2, §6, Eng. tr. (1948), 60.
[181] Ch.2, §5, Eng. tr. (1948), 58.
[182] Chron., 1811: 2 (fig.11) and 4.
[183] Ibid., 2 and 4.

the elbow 'always at a little distance from the body' (p.4), is different from what became the typical nineteenth-century position. Spohr requires a high wrist and the elbow 'low, and as near to the body as possible' (Chron., 1843, plates 2 and 3 and p.13).[184] Paine, for whom bowing is 'the grand master-piece' (Chron., 1815: iii and 13), also illustrates and describes in relative detail a very high hand position on the stick (title-page and p.9), which is to be turned 'a little outwards' (p.9).

In Howell's words it is necessary to have 'command over the Bow, so as to produce a fine round smooth tone from the Instrument' (Chron., 1825: 24). Again the back of the thumb is to be placed against the hair 'close down' to and not at the nut,[185] with the stick held principally between the thumb and second finger and 'the other fingers falling easily into their places near to each other on the stick' (p.22). The stick is to 'incline from [the player]', and, in uncommon detail for a native source, Howell explains how this ensures that the amount of hair in contact with the strings is in proportion to bow pressure, lending 'clearness and delicacy to the tone' (ibid.). In common with most theorists who discuss the matter, including Geminiani (1751: 2), Howell stipulates that the bow is to be drawn straight, 'at a right angle with the strings'.[186] Again he adds extra detail, specifying that the bow is to move 'generally at about an inch distant from the bridge' (ibid.), which is consistent with many British violin treatises during a period of nearly two hundred years, from Lenton (1693: 11) to Hamilton (Chron., 1835, 15th edn (1883), 34).

The gradual fusion of national styles and the standardization of violin and bow construction in the late eighteenth and early nineteenth centuries resulted, as with other aspects of technique, in a growing consensus with respect to the relationship between the player and the bow. But, as is evident from the examples above, important differences and a variety of practices did persist, and British sources, the products of a unique musical environment, exhibit more than most a need and a desire to refer to past traditions and assimilate ideas from elsewhere.

The importance of bowing technique is reflected in the amount of attention it receives, even in the British sources. Relative to other aspects

---

[184] This direction is integrated into some later English sources, including Anon. (Chron., 1846), 30. Significantly Holmes's edition of Spohr's treatise (Chron., 1878) includes a different plate 2 (p.11), in which the player has a lower wrist and flatter, straighter fingers, implying that the elbow is detached further from the body in something closer to a modern position.

[185] Thomson (Chron., 1840: 12) places the hand 'near to' rather than at the nut.

[186] Geminiani's comments on this subject appear to have informed Paine (Chron., 1815: 10), whose 'Bow guide' (pp.13 and 47) draws its inspiration from Löhlein (1774, ch.5, §34, p.21, cited in Stowell (1985), 65–6).

it is covered extensively in the text and musical examples.[187] This detail is exemplified by the two whole pages devoted to bowing technique in Prelleur part V (1730/31: 8–9), which find their way into Rutherford's treatise (c.1750) and, in part with additions, into Crome (c.1740). The rule of playing 'the first Note in every Bar with a down Bow' (ibid., p.46), in keeping with contemporary approaches to metric accent, is ultimately an important objective. Also Crome's sparing use of the lower half of the bow (p.35) creates a typically short, articulated stroke, common to the execution of rapid notes during much of the early to mid-eighteenth century. However the general trend, especially for long notes and/or slower tempos, was towards a freer use of the whole bow and a more thorough investigation into its potential expressive qualities. Leopold Mozart's discussion of the divisions of the bow[188] demonstrates how the effective management and control of the whole bow is fundamental to 'purity of tone'[189] and stresses that 'the longer and more even the stroke can be made, the more you will become master of your bow'.[190] However, five years earlier Geminiani was promoting an equally if not more progressive attitude to the use of the bow in Britain, which influenced sources well into the nineteenth century.

It has been well documented[191] that Geminiani refers to the practice described in the earlier sources discussed above as 'that wretched Rule of drawing the Bow down at the first Note of every Bar' (1751, example VIII, text p.4) and cautions 'the Learner against marking the Time with his Bow' (example XXIV, text p.9). It is true that Geminiani was refuting a long-held principle in his treatise, but his desire to see a greater equality between the execution of the up and down strokes was shared by others.[192] A more flexible approach among experienced violinists, breaking with the universal application of the metric accent when clearly not appropriate, rather than an outright dismissal of the principle, is surely Geminiani's wish. The bow's physical properties are not to dictate

---

[187] Only a general survey of principal issues in native texts is possible in the space available. A detailed examination of the fundamental bow stroke as discussed in continental sources can be found in Stowell (1985: 67–77). The same author then concentrates on individual bow strokes and their execution using both pre-Tourte and Tourte-model bows (ibid., 166–201). Also Brown (1988 and 1994: 143–5) provides very useful surveys of the issues affecting violin bowing in the nineteenth century.

[188] 1756, ch.5, §§4–10, Eng. tr. (1948), 97–100.

[189] Ibid., §10, Eng. tr., 99.

[190] Ibid., §9, Eng. tr., 99.

[191] Including by McArtor (1951), 343; Boyden (1952), viii; Riley (1954), 216–17; Stowell (1985), 303; and Careri (1993), 176–7.

[192] Including Quantz (1752, ch.17, §§10–11, tr. Reilly (1966), 222–3); Reichardt (1776: 28); and Tartini (1771: 56).

the effect of the music and gradual changes to its design returned its role to servant instead of master. Spohr recommends a strict adherence to 'the old rule' for orchestral players in order to achieve the difficult task of 'coinciding exactly with the other Violinists in the division of the bow'.[193] However, for soloists there are numerous exceptions to the rule[194] and it is difficult to see Geminiani objecting to the application of the rule in the manner suggested by Spohr.

Just as interesting (especially in the light of Leopold Mozart's comments referred to above), but less frequently highlighted, are Geminiani's directions for the use of the whole bow and the bowing action itself (1751, text p.2). The 'best Performers' can be distinguished partly by their use of the bow 'from the Point to that Part of it under, and even beyond their Fingers' (ibid.). Also, in unprecedented detail, the Italian describes the 'Motion' of the bow, which, consistent with many later continental sources (such as L'abbé *le fils* (1761; Eng. tr., Chron., 1828), 1), requires the use of wrist and elbow, and the shoulder only for the playing of long notes. The late eighteenth-century account given by Campagnoli, in circulation in Britain for most of the nineteenth century,[195] is generally consistent with Geminiani in its preference for only a 'slight movement' (up and down but not lateral) of the upper part of the arm.[196] The principle that the motion of the bow should generally not 'proceed' from the upper arm or shoulder (although these may 'follow' the motion in some cases) is echoed in many of the comments from the nineteenth century, such as those made by Baillot (1835: 13–14). This naturally requires the wrist to be extremely flexible,[197] and

---

[193] Chron., 1843: 234. Significantly Spohr partly blames the lack of uniformity of bowing in orchestras, outside the conservatoire orchestras of Paris, Prague and Naples, on the lack of consistent and standardized teaching methods (ibid.). A review of the Rudolphus edition of his treatise (1833) refers to the uniformity of bowing in these places and adds that 'though some approaches to it are made at the Philharmonic concert, it is far from enforced in its rigour, and we may now see on what point there is room for improvement' (*MW*, 11 (1839), 198). The contrast between the uniformity and ensemble in the orchestras of Paris and London is also noted elsewhere ('Literary notice', *MW*, 1 (1836), 73–4).

[194] Chron., 1843: 174–5 and 183.

[195] In addition to the translations by Hamilton and Bishop the substance of Campagnoli's directions for the general management of the bow (Chron., 1856: 2, reproduced in Stowell (1985), 68 and 71) can be found in Hamilton (Chron., 1835, 15th edn, pp.34–5).

[196] Chron., 1856: 2. Campagnoli also includes an illustration of how to immobilize the upper arm by tying a cord round the player's elbow and securing it to a button on his clothing.

[197] Hamilton's description of the wrist as 'the spring which governs all the movements of the bow' (Chron., 1835, 15th edn, p.31) is based on Campagnoli (Chron., 1856: 2). Thomson (Chron., 1840: 12) also includes these comments along with other bowing directions based on the Italian's treatise.

Geminiani, probably for the first time in a written tutor, describes its action and how this can facilitate smooth bow changes.[198] The directions given imply the use of the fingers, but explicit mention of these and their 'imperceptible movements' is not made until the treatise of L'abbé *le fils* (1761: 1; Eng. tr., Chron., 1828), whose comments can be found in various later works published in England.[199]

Given the reprinting of the section from Geminiani's example 1(B.) in the sources later attributed to him, and its influence on Philpot's progressive treatise for 'young beginners' (1766) and the numerous nineteenth-century sources referred to in the previous section, many of the Italian's thoughts on bowing remained in almost constant circulation from the 1750s to the 1850s. The important theories of Tartini also remained influential during the late eighteenth and nineteenth centuries in Britain, thanks largely to the continued reprinting of the Burney translation of his 'Letter' (1771).[200] Tartini, like Leopold Mozart, stresses the importance of being able to use every part of the bow and swell upon a note, 'beginning with the most minute softness, increasing the tone to its loudest degree, and diminishing it to the same point of softness with which you began, and all this in the same stroke of the bow'. The first editions of Burney's translation were published by Bremner, a pupil of Geminiani, who mentions and recommends the letter in *Some thoughts* (1777) while discussing the management of the bow.

British sources from the latter part of the eighteenth century add little with respect to written instruction on the use of the bow[201] and consequently do not contain the same comprehensive coverage and explanation of individual bow strokes found in some continental examples. After Geminiani much of the progressive material contained

---

[198] These directions exemplify the gradual adoption of smoother bow strokes during the mid- to late eighteenth century (later aided by the Tourte-model bow), which contrasted with the normal articulated, non-legato stroke of the pre-Tourte bow.

[199] These include Jousse (Chron., 1811: 4), Thomson (Chron., 1840: 12) and Campagnoli (Chron., 1856: 2).

[200] See also Grant (1983), 208.

[201] The treatise of Barthélemon (Chron., 1790) does refer to the different uses of the up and down bows, instructing the player to 'Begin always with a down Bow when the Piece of Music begins the BAR with a NOTE, either Semibreve, Minim, Crotchet, or Quaver, &c. &c ... and begin up bow if the Minim, Crotchet or Quaver, is before the Bar' (p.7). An important distinction between this direction and earlier statements referring to the 'rule of the down bow' is that this later comment (which is consistent with the examples) refers only to the beginning of a piece and not each separate bar, and so is generally consistent with modern practice. Much later Howell also mentions using an up bow when a piece begins 'with less than a bar ... [on] an unaccented part of the measure' (Chron., 1825: 39). He adds that in 'common time each bar should generally begin with a down bow' (ibid.), but goes on to contradict this in the examples.

in these works, including Barthélemon (Chron., 1790), Gehot (Chron., 1784) and Tashanberg (Chron., 1796), appears in the compositions in the treatises.

With the gradual adoption of the Tourte-model bow during the early nineteenth century the execution of smooth changes and the *cantabile* style was made much easier and the variety of possible strokes increased dramatically to include more accented and virtuosic 'thrown' bowings.[202] However Jousse's approach to bowing in 1811, which expands on his earlier Geminiani-influenced 'Directions for playing' (Chron., 1805: 8), is based on what appears to be a transitional bow and reflects the treatise's combination of predominantly eighteenth-century methods.[203] Jousse's instructions for the different styles of bowing (including the staccato and legato) are particularly interesting (Chron., 1811: 20). His discussion of the 'puntato' and the 'Staccato' and 'Legato' is based firmly on the directions of Rode *et al.* (reproduced in Chron., 1823: 12 and Chron., 1828: 12) and includes some of the original exercises. However, unlike Jousse's general approach the original 1803 treatise was conceived with the capabilities of the Tourte-model bow in mind. This once again demonstrates how writers in Britain struggled to reconcile the old and the new in their publications during this crucial transitional period. The directions from Rode *et al.* are very closely related to Campagnoli's treatment of detached bowing and staccato, which received separate exposure through English translations[204] and Hamilton's treatise (Chron., 1835, 15th edn, 38–9).[205] Hamilton also includes a relatively lengthy discussion relating length of stroke to tempo (pp.39–41), which is consistent with Jousse's intention that the different bowing styles are used in accordance with the character of the music. Following Jousse's example Keith (Chron., 1813: 8) includes the slurred staccato and the 'Punta D'Arco', which requires a firm articulation at the point. The 'punta d'arco' of Challoner (Chron., 1825: 15) and Hack

---

[202] See Curry (1968).

[203] In contrast to Geminiani and Jousse, Goodban (Chron., 1810: 18) promotes 'Marking the Time' and sees no need for two succeeding bars to begin with an up bow. Also Keith (Chron., 1813: 16) directs the player to adhere to the rule of the down bow 'as close as possible', but acknowledges that there will be exceptions. Challoner (Chron., 1825: 10), who uses = and v to indicate down and up bows, mentions the rule but believes that it 'cannot always be attended to'.

[204] Including Chron., 1856: 7 and 11, reproduced in Stowell (1985), 168 and 173.

[205] Although the passages are very similar it is possible to differentiate between Jousse's version, based on Rode *et al.* (1803; Eng. tr., Chron., 1823), and that of Hamilton, based on Campagnoli (?1797; Eng. tr., Chron., 1830 and 1856). However the question of which is the original version is, at present, a matter of conjecture, as the dating of Campagnoli's treatise is far from definite. Campagnoli is known to have been in Paris in 1801 and did have contact with Kreutzer.

(Chron., 1835: 33) is also to be played at the point but is given dashes rather than dots.

Paine's treatment of the bow continues his anachronistic approach. In addition to the very high hand position on the stick and his endorsement of the rule of the down bow (Chron., 1815: 24), he also refers to the lifting of the bow when the 'point' (meaning staccato) is used (p.21), which became less common in the nineteenth century.[206] However Paine does expand on some of Geminiani's basic principles (1751: 2) and provides relatively detailed and advanced advice on the use of the fingers and wrist (rather than the shoulder) when bowing (pp.9–10 and 31).

The first treatise of Loder (Chron., 1824) is also an odd synthesis of the old and the new. The 'rule of the down bow' (and not even the 'old' rule as Spohr describes it)[207] remains a fundamental aspect of technique. Theoretically at least an up bow at the beginning of a bar is exceptional (Chron., 1841: 4 and Chron., 1842: 1). This is the case even though Loder's theories are conceived with the Tourte-model (or very similar) bow in mind, as suggested by the use of a 'marcato' bowing style (1841: 31 for example).[208] It is not the appearance of this principle at this time that is surprising, but rather the prominence it is given and its strict application to every bar.[209] Such references to earlier practices and teaching methods appear to be particularly common in nineteenth-century British sources.[210]

There are however some examples of a more sophisticated approach to the technique of the right hand during this period. Loder's own treatise on bowing (Chron., 1842), although preoccupied with the down-bow rule, does provide detailed, progressively more difficult exercises. Also Howell's writings on bowing are particularly detailed and comprehensive for a native source at this time. Both of his sources consulted mention the motion of the bow coming from the action of the

---

[206] Spohr is one figure who retained the use of the lifted stroke (see Stowell (1985), 196–7).

[207] Chron., 1843: 30 and 231.

[208] This type of stroke, indicated with a dash, does not feature in Jousse (Chron., 1811).

[209] Baillot requires the use of the down bow when a phrase begins on a strong beat and on long and final notes, but not at the beginning of every bar (1834: 16).

[210] West (Chron., 1840: 8) and Hamilton (Chron., 1835, 15th edn, 35–6) also require each bar to begin with a down bow, although every other bar is sufficient in triple time. Thomson (Chron., 1840: 12–13) prescribes a down bow for the accented notes 'of the tune' as a general rule, which the 'performer should attend to ... as closely as possible'. However the bowings marked in 'the Tunes' (pp.16–24), 'according to the most approved method', do not require a down bow at the beginning of each bar.

elbow and the wrist[211] and the need to use the whole bow.[212] More importantly they also refer to the need to 'proportion the pressure [applied to the bow] to the Velocity'[213] and consider at length the proportioning of the velocity to the length of the note. Although far from controversial these are new considerations for a native violin treatise and reflect a growing desire for more detailed technical instruction and a willingness to provide it.

Howell is consistent with other British writers in his reluctance to break with earlier principles. The 'down bow' rule is present, but Howell's approach, in keeping with others discussed above, is more advanced and less restrictive than Loder's. Also the advanced and thorough exercises complete with detailed written explanation included in Howell's later source (Chron., 1829) are based on the same principles as *Original instructions* and use the bow divisions employed by Leopold Mozart as a point of departure.[214]

Spohr's theories on right-hand technique are generally consistent with principles promoted in British sources.[215] His bowing exercises (Chron., 1843: 112–14), like Howell (Chron., 1829), owe a debt to Leopold Mozart's divisions. Also Spohr's references to the vertical movement of the upper arm as a consequence of using the whole bow (Chron., 1843: 17) are comparable to Geminiani's comments on the shoulder (1751: 2). In both cases the use of this movement is restricted and Spohr repeatedly stresses the importance of the 'steady back-arm' in other contexts.[216] The raising of the upper arm when playing on the lower two strings is also described by Spohr (pp.15–16), but again this movement is never lateral and should be no more than is required to reach the lower strings.[217] In his edition of the Spohr treatise (Chron., 1878) Holmes includes a sketch illustrating the elevations of the arm (p.16) but adds the direction to 'call but little attention to the raising or depressing of the elbow, mentioned

---

[211] Chron., 1825, p.22 and Chron., 1829, p.1.

[212] 1825: 23 and 1829: 1 and 6. This is a view shared by Geminiani (1751: 2) and Hamilton (Chron., 1835, 15th edn, 35).

[213] 1825: 22; and 1829: 1. See also Spohr (Chron., 1843), 14.

[214] The original purpose of L. Mozart's divisions is retained in their role in many nineteenth-century British sources, including Hamilton (Chron., 1835, 15th edn, 43–4), which was no doubt influenced by Campagnoli and his promotion of the original principle (see Stowell (1985), 292–3).

[215] As with the violin hold many of Spohr's ideas regarding the holding of the bow and its movement (Chron., 1843: 13–17) find their way into Farmer's popular treatise (Chron., 1847: 5), albeit in a far more concise form.

[216] For example Chron., 1843: 14, 17, 124, 185, 187, 192 and 198. Jousse appears to endorse some (probably indirect) movement of the upper arm and shoulder (Chron., 1811: 4).

[217] Campagnoli (Chron., 1856: 2) and Farmer (Chron., 1847: 5) offer similar advice.

in the author's text'. An elbow position further from the body, such as suggested elsewhere by Holmes, would have made Spohr's earlier discussion less relevant.

Holmes also supplements Spohr's collection of on-the-string *détaché*, staccato, *martelé*, and whipped (i.e. thrown) and lifted bowings (Chron., 1843: 112–25), with various springing and 'rebounding' examples (Chron., 1878: 123, 141, 165, 167 and 219). In keeping with his general approach to the instrument Spohr, unlike Baillot (1834), chose not to include these more virtuosic techniques in his original work. He in effect shunned the newer French influences and the approach of Paganini in favour of remaining faithful to his musical roots, as more closely reflected by the treatise of Rode *et al.* (1803).

In terms of what came before and after Spohr a remarkably consistent picture emerges in British violin pedagogy and there is little to contradict his rejection of springing bowings until the Holmes edition of his own treatise. Even this, nearly half a century after Baillot's treatise, chooses to add to the bowing vocabulary of Spohr rather than replace his original instructions.

The increased elasticity of the developing bow facilitated the use of springing bowings and these were exploited at an early stage. Wilhelm Cramer was a notable exponent.[218] However this 'frivolity' is in marked contrast to the aesthetic emerging during the early nineteenth century, as developed by Viotti, codified by Rode *et al.* in 1803 and later promoted by Spohr and his disciples, which emphasized a singing style and broad bowstrokes.[219] Campagnoli's *Metodo*, which appeared in English and in German, does include two strokes similar to the modern 'flying staccato', which perhaps reflect a desire to exploit the new bows.[220] However neither of these nor anything like them feature in Jousse's repertoire (Chron., 1811: 20), which was based on the method of Rode *et al.* (1803, Eng. tr. 1823 and 1828), even though he considers a heavy style of bowing a defect and stresses the need for lightness and 'a true quickness' (p.4). Hamilton (Chron., 1835, 15th edn, 38–9) does not include them either, although he does quote Campagnoli's instructions for the standard early nineteenth-century slurred staccato stroke executed on the string in the upper half, a stroke for which Spohr was famous. There is no mention of Campagnoli's 'springing' bowings in Thomson (Chron., 1840), who quotes other sections of his instructions on bowing technique. Also, according to Challoner (Chron., 1825: 19),

---

[218] See Brown (1988), 99–100, and (1999), 273–8.
[219] See in particular Brown (1984), 213, (1988), 101–4, and (1999), 278, for interesting comments on this subject.
[220] Chron., 1856: 11, reproduced in Stowell (1985), 173–4.

a prominent performer, the slurred staccato was 'much in use'. These springing strokes therefore appear to be short-lived novelties rather than fundamental aspects of technique, and elsewhere even Campagnoli stresses the need to give detached bowings their maximum length.[221]

Through the British versions of writings by Campagnoli, Spohr and Rode *et al.* covering most of the nineteenth century (and the relative rarity of Baillot (1834) and similar works), it is possible to see how this approach to bowing was promoted in Britain as well as in Germany. The treatise of Ferdinand David (Chron., 1874), a Spohr disciple and, like his son, an influential figure in British violin playing, includes two types of 'springing' bowing (p.38). However he appears to have remained faithful to the German school of the early nineteenth century and employed slurred staccato where others would probably have used lifted or bounced separate bows in the lower half.[222] Although the lighter bowings were not completely rejected after Spohr the influence of the broad bowing style continued in Germany through Böhm and Joachim,[223] who influenced violin playing and promoted the German school in Britain into the twentieth century.

The treatment of bowing in the sources is more detailed and consistent than left-hand technique. This is to be expected considering the fundamental role of the bow for all players as the 'Tongue of the Instrument'.[224] It is true that details such as the position of the hand on the stick may vary between the sources, but without the ability to draw the bow across the strings and produce a clear and pleasing sound the left hand becomes almost irrelevant. Of course after this has been achieved the student must go on to develop the subtleties and 'special effects' of the art, and these are demanded in varying degrees in the pieces contained in the tutors and the general repertoire. Because of the importance of the bow it is not surprising to find the more common nuances and subtleties, such as the swell and lifted staccato stroke, already given at least some attention in many of the sources discussed above.[225]

---

[221] Chron., 1856: 7. These comments are echoed by Spohr (Chron., 1843: 118).

[222] See Brown (1994), 141–3. In truth, of the two types of 'springing' stroke referred to by David, only one involves the bow leaving the string entirely, and then 'harshness and dryness of sound' are to be avoided 'by grazing the string for a short distance' (Chron., 1874: 38).

[223] Brown (1988), 107–8.

[224] Crome (*c.*1740), 48.

[225] Heskett's tutor (Chron., 1886), following on from Howell and Loder, epitomizes the more thorough treatment (informed by mainstream continental works) of bowing technique in the later nineteenth century.

Tuning

The British treatises contain valuable information relating to the general approach to the instrument and the application and finer details of the techniques discussed above, providing further insights into general contemporary performing conventions. Many of the issues discussed below are concerned with the often uncertain relationship between description, notation and execution, covering subjects such as ornamentation and varieties of articulation and nuance.

Some of the earliest and also most curious instructions given in treatises for the general maintenance of the violin are for the tuning of the four strings. From the time of Playford English sources instruct the player to tune by initially 'screwing up' the treble (E) string 'to as high a pitch, as it can moderately bear' (Prelleur part V (1731), 2). The player is then to tune by fifths, using octaves or the unison to assist him if necessary. Remarkably this instruction, impractical and unreliable in itself, can also be found in Goodban's generally retrospective treatise (Chron., 1810: 17). Jousse (Chron., 1805: 6) recommends the conventional method of tuning the A-string with a tuning fork and then using fifths to determine the pitch of the other strings, although the 'Pupil who has not the assistance of a Master' is to tune the A with a fork and then measure the position of the fourth finger in order to tune the other strings.[226] By the time of his 1811 method however he suggests just the standard practice of tuning the A-string first with a tuning fork (p.5), which is also recommended by Paine (Chron., 1815: 44), Howell (Chron., 1825: 23) and Hamilton (Chron., 1835, 15th edn, 25). Hack's approach is to use a different tuning fork for each string (Chron., 1835: 12).

Tempo and Articulation

As we have seen, the recycling of old material in later treatises can produce inconsistencies and anachronisms in these sources. The use of metre to determine tempo is a case in point, as for a long time more faith was placed in time signatures than in tempo descriptions. Beyond the Prelleur-derived sources the principle of a metre/tempo relationship is also advocated in Bremner (1756: 6–7); Gehot (Chron., 1784: 2);

---

[226] Similar instructions are included in Challoner (Chron., 1825: 8–9); Thomson (Chron., 1840: 13); Bates (Chron., 1845: 6); Anon. (Chron., 1846: 31); Dean (Chron., 1852: 3); Hancock (Chron., 1853: 6); and Wybrow (Chron., 1858: 10). Keith (Chron., 1813: 13) recommends using the fourth finger to check the tuning after using the conventional method.

Barthélemon (Chron., 1790: 4); and, into the nineteenth century, Bemetzrieder (Chron., 1803: 3). Geminiani's *The art*, being less concerned with such basic theoretical issues, does not discuss this matter in the text, and metre does not appear to be used as a guide to tempo in the musical examples and compositions.

Written directions, usually in the form of Italian terms, often suggest mood, character and style in addition to tempo. An interesting example is *andante*, which 'signifies that all the Notes must be play'd equal and distinctly' in many eighteenth-century sources, including Gehot (Chron., 1780: 14 and Chron., 1784: 44), and so is more concerned with a style of playing, and particularly bowing, than with tempo. From the nineteenth century Jousse's 'Slow and distinct' (Chron., 1805: 38 and Chron., 1811: xxv) is very similar,[227] although tempo is indicated here. Both Jousse and the 'rather slow' of Rode *et al.* (Chron., 1828: 29) are echoed in Howell's 'rather slow and distinct, requiring an exact and expressive performance' (Chron., 1825: 62).

The term staccato consistently refers to a 'plain' and, like *andante*, 'distinct' execution,[228] and, in common with other eighteenth-century instrumental idioms, is consistent with a basic 'non-legato' articulation in many contexts. The slur, the only means of achieving legato with the pre-Tourte bow, therefore appears as an ornament in itself in the early sources. The closest term is *sostenuto*, which is interpreted as 'to hold a note in an equal steady manner' by Gehot.[229] Consistent with the nineteenth-century concern for strength of tone and projection the term legato is included by the time of Jousse (Chron., 1811: xxviii), who requires a 'smooth and connected' execution,[230] and in an Allegro 'the notes must, generally speaking, be played staccato, except where the word legato is marked' (p.44).

Ornamentation

A thorough treatment of the subject of ornamentation, a complex and controversial issue, is not possible here.[231] Comments will therefore be

---

[227] West (Chron., 1840: 24), Bates (Chron., 1845: 28), Dean (Chron., 1852: 37) and Wybrow (Chron., 1858: 12) include the same definition and Anon. (Chron., 1846: 48) is the same but for the addition of 'moderately'.

[228] Gehot (Chron., 1784), 44.

[229] Ibid.

[230] Jousse (Chron., 1811: 20), like Rode *et al.* (Chron., 1823: 12), views the legato as a means of imitating the singing style of the human voice.

[231] Much of the difficulty surrounding this subject is attributable to its very nature. The purpose of ornamentation is to provide variety and so with the personal interpretation of the performer such a significant factor there are few permanent solutions. Such inherent

restricted to some main issues arising from the native sources. The discussion is concerned primarily with specific ornaments, as opposed to free embellishment and improvisation. With a few exceptions[232] sources in English do not have the performance conventions of the soloist in mind and are of insufficient scope to address the treacherous area of extemporization.

Perhaps the most frequent comments made on ornamentation in contemporary treatises of all nationalities are those warning against the common practice of over-using embellishments and the lack of 'good taste' often applied in their employment. Discrete application in keeping with the intentions of the composer is the key, with the soloist enjoying greater freedom than the orchestral player. These principles unite the influential theories of Geminiani and Spohr and their disciples, encompassing well over a century of British writings on the subject. Geminiani's pupil Robert Bremner (possibly with errant amateurs in mind) wishes to quiet 'the restless finger' (1777: iv) and asks the gentleman to 'lay aside the graces of the finger, for some time, even when playing alone, and attend to the plain sound'. He observes that 'those who feed upon the graces of the finger, seldom pay any attention to the bow; in the judicious management of which, all power, taste, and expression, chiefly consist' (ibid.).

Turning briefly to the ornaments themselves, the descriptions and illustrations of 'the usual Graces' in the early British sources display certain similarities, through Prelleur, Crome and Rutherford; but Geminiani provides the first comprehensive treatment of the subject in a violin treatise, demonstrating the vital role played by the correct use of ornaments in 'tasteful', expressive performance. His table of ornaments, originating in the *Treatise of good taste* (1749) and reproduced in *The art* (1751), finds its way into the later 'attributed' sources, resulting in a wide and constant circulation of this material during the late eighteenth and early nineteenth centuries in Britain. Unfortunately the descriptions of the individual ornaments in *The art* do not survive the transfer, and so the details of the expressive capabilities of each example are lost although the general variety and diverse nature of the embellishments (copied with varying degrees of accuracy) remain intact. Of the 'attributed' sources examined the last (*c.*1800) is the only one to include an introduction to the 'Graces'. This draws its inspiration from Crome

---

freedom makes the provision of simple, succinct instructions in treatises impossible and something that many British examples are reluctant even to attempt.

[232] Such as the written-out cadenzas and quasi-improvisatory passages contained in Barthélemon's 'Capricios' (Chron., 1790: 21–36); Tashanberg (Chron., 1796); and Jousse's instructions (Chron., 1811: 51–2) for embellishing cadences and passages.

(c.1765: 62), a treatise written up to 60 years earlier than *Compleat instructions* (Chron., 1800: 9-10) and, like Prelleur part V, conceived with a totally different idiom in mind. Perhaps the publisher Thomas Dodd decided that such an introduction (albeit brief and unoriginal) was necessary after the table had previously been used repeatedly without explanation.[233]

The difficulty of presenting and teaching the subject of embellishment in a treatise is acknowledged by some writers, some of whom choose to avoid discussion of the intricacies of individual ornaments, leaving it to practical instruction. Bemetzrieder states that 'ornamental steps, bindings, vibrations, and shakes ... are better explained by the voice or fingers of a master, than by an article of a book' (Chron., 1803: 15). Later in the nineteenth century, at a time when written-out embellishments in the music itself were becoming a more satisfactory way of bridging the increasing gap between composers and performers, the increased flexiblity demanded in the application of ornaments became a dilemma for writers attempting to codify the practice. Howell's description of the appoggiatura could be applied to any of the main groups of ornament: 'the manner of performing appogiaturas [sic] in a great measure depends on the style of the composition, and the taste and feeling of the performer, as they are not always written so as to form a correct representation of the intended effect' (Chron., 1825: 46).

Of the more specific variations on standard ornaments, the accelerating trill is an interesting example and receives special treatment in many native sources. Barthélemon's illustrations of the 'Shake', 'turned Shake' and 'prepared and turned Shake' clearly show the use of this technique (Chron., 1790: iii).[234] Gehot applies the same principle to the 'Shake' (not the 'Turned shake') (Chron., 1784: 4), and Philpot suggests the technique as a means of practising both the 'Shake' and the 'Beat' to 'arrive at some Degree of Quickness' (1766: 9). The general application of this ornament during the period would appear to be for the practice of the plain shake and for trills on longer notes.[235] Jousse

---

[233] It is not surprising to find Geminiani's ornaments also recommended by Philpot, although different, often more detailed descriptions are provided in the later source, including helpful suggestions for practising the examples (1766: 3 and 9-10).

[234] Unfortunately the examples use only minims as the main note for the trills, and so it is impossible to judge how this practice relates to the trills on shorter note-values, which are required elsewhere in the treatise.

[235] Tartini's 'Letter' (1770), which is probably the origin of many of these subsequent instructions, recommends a gradually accelerating trill, allied to a swell, for practice purposes. Leopold Mozart's directions for its limited use, 'mostly in cadenzas' with a gradual crescendo (1756, ch.10, §7, Eng. tr. (1948), 189), are perhaps closer to actual practice than the more general use implied by some of the British sources.

(Chron., 1811) also refers to the accelerating shake for practice (p.46)[236] and the playing of the ornament 'quicker at the end than at the beginning, especially when on the penultimate note of a movement, or a piece' (with a *crescendo*) (p.47). Paine is another advocate of this ornament (Chron., 1815: 36) and Spohr advocates its use in 'an *Adagio*' and 'in shakes serving to embellish a melody ... united either with a *crescendo* or a *decrescendo*' (Chron., 1843: 144 and 185).

Reflecting the continued importance of embellishment in the nineteenth century Jousse devotes seven pages to the subject (Chron., 1811: 46–52). He includes the 'Double' and 'Accompanied' shakes, the latter illustrated by an excerpt from Tartini's 'Devil's Trill' Sonata (p.48); the 'Beat' (although it is 'seldom used in Modern Music') (p.49); the turn; and the appoggiatura; and freer examples for the variation of cadences, the 'reprise' and melodies generally (pp.51–2). Jousse continues the tradition of stressing the importance of embellishment in determining the 'taste' of the performer and considers Corelli's Solos embellished by Geminiani as 'excellent models on this subject' (p.52). Straeten, writing exactly a century later, makes significant observations on the practice of embellishment during the nineteenth century with reference to these examples:

> [T]he latter two Cadences [intermediate and reprise] are now obsolete ... They may be of interest to violinists, as very few works give any explanation of these embellishments, and yet they are distinctly indicated in compositions of that period by the pause signs. To use a simple shake or a full cadenza in their place would be distinctly contrary to the intention of the composer.[237]

Straeten also refers to Jousse's 'Observations' (p.52) as providing excellent 'guidance to those who wish to acquaint themselves with the use of these ornamentations in olden times'.[238] Similarly conceived with eighteenth-century principles in mind, Paine's treatise (Chron., 1815) stresses the importance of embellishments, which prevent many passages from becoming 'insipid', although they are not 'to interfere with the regular time' (p.36).

Spohr's method recommends Leopold Mozart's treatise for 'the Graces of former times' which are to be included in 'the performance of compositions written at the period when they were in vogue' (Chron.,

---

[236] Howell (Chron., 1825: 47), Thomson (Chron., 1840: 6) and Hamilton (Chron., 1835, 15th edn, 52) also recommend gradually increasing its velocity when practising. Hamilton also enters into relatively detailed discussion of the appoggiatura, turn and shake (including double shake) (ibid., 45–53).
[237] Straeten (1911), 279.
[238] Ibid., 281.

1843: 142).[239] Although Mozart's treatise may not have been as readily available in England as in Germany at the time of Spohr's writing,[240] this comment does promote a sympathetic attitude towards the stylistic performance of earlier repertoire which has perhaps not been fully appreciated by modern commentators.

An important issue as far as violin performance in Britain is concerned is the subject of vibrato. The secondary literature has discussed Geminiani's controversial comments on the subject (1751, text p.8) at length[241] and the extent of the application of the 'close shake'.[242] An examination of the popularity and dissemination of his idea of a continuous, 'as often as possible' vibrato in the second half of the eighteenth century and beyond is particularly interesting and relevant to other sources published in Britain in English.

In addition to the explicit rejection of the pervasive 'close shake' by Bremner in 1777 (pp.i–ii)[243] and deletions from subsequent editions of *The art* attributed to him,[244] the 'attributed' sources also describe the technique but not its application beyond that of any other ornament (for example, c.1770: 13).[245] Geminiani therefore appears isolated in the eighteenth century, with even Philpot limiting the 'close Shake or Swell' to 'long Notes in an Adagio' (1766: 9).[246] But does this mean that the

---

[239] Spohr's own directions for graces and embellishments are outlined in Stowell (1985), in particular pp.387–90.

[240] Some graces are included in the heavily abridged English translation of the Mozart treatise (Chron., 1812: 16–18).

[241] Investigations into the development of the violin vibrato necessarily refer to Geminiani's contribution. Important surveys and discussions include McArtor (1951), 269–72; Boyden (1965), 386–90; Stowell (1985), 203–11; Standage (1989), 369; Careri (1993), 168–9 and 178–9; and Johnson (1994). More general articles which extend beyond the violin include Donington (1988); Neumann (1991); and sections of Brown (1999).

[242] The term 'Close Shake' is used at least as early as Playford (2nd edn, 1658) for a type of vibrato using two fingers which is in fact half trill and half vibrato (see Riley (1954), 187 and 372–5).

[243] Zaslaw (1979), n. 3 (pp.48–9) provides a useful summary of other contemporary evidence that appears to contradict Geminiani. It should be noted however that Bremner highlights and laments the fondness among 'gentlemen players' for the device. Also his comments are perhaps only applicable to the orchestral player, as later directions provide the solo-player with the freedom to apply 'all the different graces of the bow and finger ... when and where he pleases' (Bremner (1777), p.ii).

[244] See Hickman (1983).

[245] As well as omitting the direction 'as often as possible' the passage also does not refer to the condition 'when it is long continued' in connection with the use of the swell. Remarkably Bates's treatise (Chron., 1845) reproduces this section (p.14), and other parts of the hybrid model, almost verbatim.

[246] It is consistent with long-standing practices and prevailing trends that Philpot considers the term 'Swell' to be synonymous with the 'close Shake'. The two effects

Italian's expressive language and tone quality were unique among the violinists of the eighteenth century? As McArtor proposes, 'if a frequent [let alone continuous] vibrato was a characteristic peculiar to Geminiani's tone, it would seem logical that Hawkins or Burney would have commented to that effect'.[247] In fact, far from pointing to any undesirable idiosyncrasies, Hawkins praises Geminiani's tone production.[248]

The range of sources which contain discussion of the 'close shake' demonstrate that it was widely used and, theoretically at least, not just an 'advanced' technique. However, it does seem likely that its more frequent, if not continuous, use would have been more acceptable in the context of a solo performance, and the manner of its execution would have produced a generally smaller oscillation with consequently less pitch fluctuation.[249] Also the often-cited criticisms of the over-use and abuse of the 'close shake'[250] testify to the common application of the vibrato beyond that of the occasional ornament. Even though these are very critical statements, it is difficult to believe that Geminiani's well-considered concept of what was in 'good taste' would have been at odds with that of the Mozarts. Both Leopold Mozart and Bremner (1777) consider the vibrato to be detrimental to good intonation and W. A. Mozart warns against overstepping the 'proper limit' of what is beautiful and producing something 'contrary to nature'. Geminiani would surely have identified with their sentiments. But problems of intonation and the creation of a 'united effect' are, as stated by Bremner, less of an issue for the soloist, whose experience and good ear should also ensure sound judgement and a 'tasteful' performance. It should be remembered that soloists performing in public would at this

---

continued to be used in combination in violin playing well into the nineteenth century (see Brown (1988), 118–19). Much earlier Roger North had described Matteis's *messa di voce* combined with some vibrato (Cyr (1995), 64). Philpot applies the *messa di voce* effect to long notes, which, similar to Geminiani's directions, is allied to a vibrato that increases in intensity. Leopold Mozart also discusses a variety of vibrato with an 'increasing oscillation' (1756, ch.11, §4, Eng. tr. (1948), 204) and implies its use with his 'first division' (*ibid.*, ch.5, §5, Eng. tr., 98). It is not clear however if Philpot's accelerating vibrato is reserved only for the practice of the ornament (as with the Shake and the Beat), or if it is to be applied generally in performance. Nevertheless it is evident, as in other sources, that the technique can only be assimilated through observation and imitation of those already proficient in the art.

[247] McArtor (1951), 272.
[248] Hawkins (1776), vol.2, 904.
[249] See Zaslaw (1980); and Gable (1992).
[250] Especially Leopold Mozart (1756, ch.11, Eng. tr. (1948), 203–5) and W. A. Mozart's letter to his father, 12 June 1778 (tr. E. Anderson, *The letters of Mozart and his family* (London, 1966), 552).

time have been almost exclusively professional musicians, as it was not possible (or generally desirable) for amateurs with access to music to achieve anything like the standard required. Therefore Geminiani is happy to trust the well-developed taste of the advanced player to regulate the use of the close shake as an ornament and decide when it is *not* 'possible'.

I mention this here because nineteenth-century British sources are similar to many of the eighteenth-century examples in their treatment of vibrato.[251] In keeping with his treatment of other ornaments Jousse (Chron., 1805: 15) bases his treatment of the 'close shake' on Geminiani's text (1751, text p.8), quoting the first half of his first paragraph and adding that the device is 'marked ∿∿∿'. Around six years later Jousse (Chron., 1811: 48) considers the ornament 'obsolete' and dismisses it for similar reasons to those discussed above. His comments replace Geminiani with other eighteenth-century models and include a substantial section plagiarized from Bremner (1777: i). Jousse implies the use of the swell in combination with the device and refers to its over-use as the equivalent of a singer with the 'Palsy'.[252] The references to its detrimental effect on intonation in harmony (again derived from Bremner) suggest that in practice the ornament was often executed with more rapid and wider oscillations than was considered in 'good taste'. However, he does, like Bremner and Philpot, admit its use on some long notes for the sake of 'variety'. It is therefore uncertain how 'obsolete' the device could have been in 1811, although Jousse's use of Bremner's rather than Geminiani's directions (whom he quotes elsewhere) suggests that its frequent use, at least among students, is less desirable than Geminiani had proposed for more advanced players 60 years earlier.[253] Keith's comments on the 'tremolo (trembling) shake'

---

[251] See Brown (1988: 110–19) for a very useful survey of the main continental treatises from the nineteenth and early twentieth century and their approach to the device.

[252] This is obviously based on L. Mozart's comment (1756, Eng. tr. (1948), 203). Bremner, drawing on the same model, refers to 'the voice of one who is paralytic'.

[253] Nothing is described as 'obsolete' in Bremner. However the term 'Close Shake', which is technically a different device to the 'Tremolo', had been in use for over a century and a half by 1811, and Jousse notes that it has been used 'improperly' by 'Geminiani and others' to indicate the distinct vibrato effect. Indeed the 'close shake' was already considered 'old' in the early 1770s by Burney, who refers to the Beat associated with Giardini and his 'school' as an alternative (1959, vol.1, 299). This technique involves 'the rapid depression and release of a consonant note on a neighbouring string', producing 'an ethereal effect not unlike vibrato' (McVeigh (1989), 202). It is impossible to gauge the popularity of this device in England outside Giardini's circle, but it is referred to by Spohr (Chron., 1843: 168) who warns against its over-use, although he accepts its value on some natural harmonics as 'these cannot be animated by any *tremolo*'. The term 'close shake' was still in use in the 1840s (for example in Anon. (Chron., 1846), 27), although it refers

(Chron., 1813: 10) are based on Geminiani and Jousse. He goes some way towards offering a middle path, omitting any reference to the device as 'obsolete' but stating that it 'should only be introduced on long notes'.

Many British sources, even the more substantial examples, make no reference to vibrato. No mention is made of it in the treatises of Loder, including the 1911 edition of his first publication. Howell discusses its occasional use only as an ornament (Chron., 1825: 48), which is consistent with Spohr's comments on the *tremolo* (Chron., 1843: 163–4). The illustrations in the third part of Spohr's treatise demonstrate the varied (there are four variations of tempo) but sparing use of the device, making use of only a small movement and with the degree of emphasis given to certain notes dependent on their context.[254] Interestingly Holmes chooses not to add to the content of this discussion in his edition (Chron., 1878: 157), in contrast to his treatment of some other aspects of technique. Also Wessely's method, dedicated to Fritz Kreisler,[255] warns against 'excessive *vibrato*' (1913: 85) and its use becoming a 'mannerism' (p.89).[256] 'Moderation' is the 'invariable rule' (p.90).

The general use among advanced players of a small vibrato, limited by the parameters of 'good taste', appears to have been the most widely endorsed and prevalent practice for the whole period. Native sources are generally consistent with a basic 'non-vibrato' sound, with the bow remaining the most significant factor in the variation of tone quality.

Expression and Style

Geminiani's frequent references to the expressive power of music admirably illustrate that the aspects of technique and performance discussed above were merely the tools required by the performer to 'move' the listener. The nineteenth century witnessed the expansion of this quite strictly prescribed expressive language as performance sought to keep pace with the changing qualities and priorities of new music.[257]

---

not to vibrato but to a trill between notes a semitone apart (as opposed to the open shake where the interval is a tone).

[254] F. David also warns against over-use (Chron., 1874: 43), as does Bériot (1858: 242), who, like Spohr, uses wavy lines to indicate the ornament, and Joachim and Moser (1902–5, vol.2, 96a), who quote Spohr verbatim. Auer, a pupil of Joachim, also classes vibrato as an ornament (1921: 22–4).

[255] Kreisler is often associated with the introduction of the continuous vibrato into modern violin playing (see Stowell (1992), 131 and Philip (1992)).

[256] Quoting H. C. Deacon, 'Vibrato' in *Grove 1*, vol.4, 260.

[257] See Stowell (1992), 140–41.

However there was a growing awareness that not all music should be played the same way, and reference was to be made to older traditions when appropriate. The translation of a greater number of continental sources, such as Rode *et al.* (1803; Eng. tr., Chron., 1823, 1828 and 1880), promoted this new approach among the British, who had always closely identified with the 'doctrine of the affections' and had repeatedly shunned virtuosity for its own sake. The resulting developments in violin technique also gradually filtered down into the greater number of more substantial native treatises.

The 'style in which each piece must be played' is of vital importance to a writer such as Jousse, whose principles are based firmly on the theories of the second half of the eighteenth century (Chron., 1811: 45). Technique is the servant of expression, and its application to that end is consequently discussed in detail (pp.44–5). Spohr's priorities are similar, at a time when some of those around him viewed technique as an end in itself. To Spohr the cultivation of the *'fine style'*, after achieving the *'correct style'*, involves the application of 'all the technical expedients' but with the ability to convey the character of a piece through tasteful and refined performance. Therefore 'the highest mechanical perfection' must be united with 'an expressive delivery', rather than the desire to merely 'astonish' (Chron., 1843: 181–3). These principles are admirably illustrated in the text and examples of repertoire provided in the third part of the treatise,[258] and remain a fundamental concern of later writers such as Wessely (1913: 115).

The technical content of the native sources is generally consistent with the principles and priorities of those foreign figures the British connoisseur most admired. The writings of Geminiani and Spohr and their disciples, and to a lesser extent Tartini, Leopold Mozart, Campagnoli and Rode *et al.*, therefore dominate the scene of British violin pedagogy for the period 1750 to 1850 and beyond.

This is in keeping with an essentially conservative and retrospective approach, although, in a delayed reaction to continental trends, the British sources do, as discussed in Chapter 2, become a great deal more sophisticated as pedagogical works. Many eighteenth-century examples, almost completely derived from other sources, tend to focus on and devote a disproportionate amount of space to certain issues, such as beating time and chromatic scales, while neglecting the fundamentals of technique. Some eighteenth- and most nineteenth-century specimens are closer to treatises in the true sense of the word and make some attempt to treat the subject more systematically and often more comprehensively.

---

[258] Rode's Seventh Concerto, Op.9 and Spohr's Ninth Concerto, Op.55, both arranged for two violins.

This is particularly true of right-hand technique, reflecting its fundamental role in violin playing and the increasing demands made on its technique as the period progressed and the vocabulary of musical expression expanded.

Repertoire

Some of the most popular violin repertoire in Britain during the period, separate from the treatises, was produced by many of the same prominent figures. It therefore displays an affinity with the technical and expressive principles promoted in the sources and plays its part in a largely consistent approach to the cultivation of the instrument among native violinists during the period and a gradual but definite improvement in standards.

Independent repertoire naturally has an important role to play in the teaching of an instrument. The most obvious examples are duos, which serve a pedagogical as well as a purely musical purpose, even if they are not contained in a treatise (as they often are) or this is not specified on the title-page (as it often is). Duos conceived in this way do not exploit the extremes of technique, although they do generally incorporate more advanced practices than the early treatises. For example looking at Barbella's duos, published by Bremner, it is evident that double stops and chords are used to thicken the texture and produce greater sonority, but it is unnecessary for either player to move out of first position. The *Sei duetti a due violini* Op.2 (c.1763) of Giardini, also published in London, contain demanding double stops and figuration in both parts, but have only e^3 as the extent of their range. Similarly Barthélemon's Op.8 demands the same proficiency of both players but the technical demands are below those of his treatise, the range rising on only one occasion to a^3 in the first violin part.

In the nineteenth century the duo was still popular for teaching or simple entertainment. Like Barthélemon, Howell and Loder both published works that make technical demands that are lower than those of their treatises, although they are impressive and innovative in their attention to detail and in particular to the directions added for expression.[259] It was for foreign composers such as Viotti, Rode, Spohr

---

[259] Howell's *Six quartetts for two violins* (Bristol, ?1826) were written as 'a sequel to the Author's "Original Instructions for the Violin"'. The range extends only to e^3 (and then often with a harmonic). This is the same for Loder's *First set of three duets for two violins, dedicated to his pupils for their instruction* (London, 1837). A *Second progressive set of duets* was advertised but has not been located. Other interesting native examples include Sanderson's *Six duets* (Chron., 1825) and the *Six duetts* of T. A. Hughes

and de Bériot to cultivate the increasingly popular and technically demanding genre of the 'duo concertant'. Viotti's duos and trios receive a prominent and comprehensive listing in Dubourg of 'Standard classical works for violin, &c.' (5th edn, 1878, *Appendix* p.6), and Hogarth highlights the value and popularity of Viotti's duets for two violins among players of all standards:

> [T]hough worthy to exercise the talents of the finest professional players, they are within the reach of accomplished amateurs. By musicians of this description they are still prized, and we hope they will long be so; for we know of no violin music so well calculated to nourish a pure and elevated taste, and to impart elegance and freedom to the style of the performer.[260]

The duos and trios also receive special mention and recommendation in Hamilton's hugely popular *Catechism* (Chron., 1835). Along with the works of Mozart, Beethoven and Pleyel, 'perhaps no publications whatever are so desirable to amateurs in general' (15th edn, 1883: 69). In addition to the sustained popularity of the musical qualities represented by Viotti these comments also suggest a significant improvement in the standard and aspirations of amateurs during the early nineteenth century, which is consistent with the general developments in instrumental pedagogy and music education discussed above. In light of this it is not surprising to discover the popularity of Spohr's works in this genre. As mentioned previously Spohr's music during the 1820s was significant in highlighting the poor standard of native amateur musicians, many of whom were attracted to it but criticized its difficulty. Its appeal was such that standards of performance improved during the 1830s in order to meet its technical demands. For the violin, in addition to the concertos, his unaccompanied duos (in particular Op.13 for violin and viola) became very popular during the 1840s and were valued not merely as concert pieces but as useful tools for the development of technique.[261]

An improvement in standards is also evident in the demand for solo repertoire during the period, which naturally tended to be more

---

(?1827–9), published by R. Hack and advertised in his treatise (Chron., 1835), for the 'improvement of practitioners, and the use of teachers'. It is noted on the title-page that Hughes's duets were published at the same time as his *Twenty four favourite pieces as duetts for two violins, selected from the best composers, for beginners*. Howell's *Twelve very easy duets* (price 5s.) are recommended for the early stages by Hamilton, along with his *Twelve select airs for violin and piano* (price 2s.) (Chron., 1835, 15th edn, pp.65 and 67).

[260] MW, 2 (1836), 164.

[261] See *The Athenaeum*, 25 (1852), 707; Hamilton (Chron., 1835, 15th edn, 69); and Straeten (1933), vol.2, 203.

innovative in terms of technique. The concerto and eighteenth-century solo continuo sonata (a very popular genre among musical societies) were ideal vehicles for the composer to explore the potential of the instrument and expand its capabilities; but, without a great desire to improve their proficiency, amateurs continued to make use of the works of Corelli, long after they were considered old-fashioned and professionals had moved on to new challenges. Their relatively modest technical demands and unquestionable refinement gave them an important pedagogical function for many generations of British amateurs, although their value as models for composition and performance was appreciated among a wider circle for a significant period.[262] Paul David, son of the chief disciple of Spohr, still refers to Corelli as the 'norm and model of violin-playing' and the source of all of value that succeeded him (1889: 291).

The particular importance and role of Corelli's Violin Sonatas Op.5 as teaching material in eighteenth-century England has been studied fairly recently.[263] As a supplement to this it is useful to highlight the special attention they receive in nineteenth-century literature. According to Jousse (Chron., 1811: xii), the 'excellence' of Corelli's works 'is well known, and they need no commendation'. Also their value 'for forming the hand of a young practitioner' (p.xx) is repeated and developed by Hogarth (1838, vol.1, 155). There are numerous advertisements in various journals for new editions of Corelli's trios (revised by J. Bishop) and solos (including MW, 18 (1843), 89 and 97) and Hamilton (Chron., 1835, 15th edn, 68) recommends his '12 Grand Solos' (ed. Czerny, price 10s. 6d.). Holmes (Chron., 1878: 174 and 193) contrasts the 'classic school' of Corelli with the 'modern "brilliant" style', and recommends that Op.5 is played, with embellishments, in keeping with the composer's original intentions. The sonatas also have a prominent position in the works listed by Dubourg (5th edn, 1878, *Appendix* p.6), alongside Viotti's duos and trios. The 'immortal solos of Corelli' are recommended, in addition to scales, 'for the acquisition of *tone* and *steadiness*', although they are 'not a sufficient authority as to the varieties and subtleties of *bowing*' by this time (ibid., pp.245–7). The works of Tartini are greatly influenced by Corelli but also display a more advanced approach to bowing. Tartini's contributions to violin pedagogy were enormously popular among British violinists, particularly in the nineteenth century.[264]

---

[262] They continued to be performed in England by prominent violinists, including Salomon and Barthélemon.

[263] There are a number of interesting articles in *EM*, 24 (1996) that deal specifically with the Op.5 sonatas.

[264] English editions of the complete 50-variation *L'arte del arco* in the British Library,

The success of the solo violin repertoire of Corelli and Tartini in Britain and its contribution to violin pedagogy suggests a more serious, albeit conservative approach to the learning of the instrument among some amateurs than is evident in the majority of the treatises. Other examples of solo violin music available in England during the eighteenth century, such as repertoire by Gibbs and Barbella, further illustrate the inadequacy of Prelleur part V and related sources as teaching tools, while promoting a higher level of proficiency among some non-professionals. This is still in marked contrast to what is found in the solo works of Viotti, who introduced the latest in continental repertoire and technique to England. The change from expressive ideals based on the use of Baroque and transitional bows to those exploiting the Tourte model are demonstrated much earlier in the imported repertoire than in the native repertoire or treatises. The versatility of the Tourte design and its potential for expression are later illustrated by the variety of bowings (and dynamics) found in Howell's *Six quartetts for two violins* (?1826) referred to above, which require the use of accented, lifted, sustained varieties of bowing and *messa di voce* and *flautando* effects. By 1840 Viotti's 'concertos in G, in A minor, in D, and in E minor', as well as his other works, were being recommended 'to the amateurs of instrumental music' (*MW*, 14 (1840), 198).

It appears that this solo repertoire provided a useful if not essential supplement to written methods for the ambitious student. As more serious aspirations became more commonplace during the nineteenth century, teaching material sought to regain lost ground and assimilate more of the technical developments made elsewhere. However the core violin repertoire (in particular Corelli and Tartini) continued to be consumed alongside the new examples. This is consistent with earlier discussions which have shown that the general principles behind these earlier models often inspire and mould the new material.

Earlier chapters have demonstrated that the majority of eighteenth-century elementary native sources were conceived with the primary aim of issuing new, simple repertoire, with minimal textual explanation. However the increasingly demanding repertoire and greater seriousness of purpose among learners demanded a new approach and in many nineteenth- (and some eighteenth-) century examples this independent repertoire is either excluded completely or used more effectively to complement the progressive presentation of text and musical examples. This trend created an opportunity and an

---

all published in London, are dated ?1805, ?1815, *c.*1825, 1881, and 1950. Tartini's works are recommended by Jousse (Chron., 1811: xii and xx), Holmes (Chron., 1878: 193) and David (1889), 291.

expanding market for the publication of separate collections of elementary pieces for the beginner and some more ambitious examples for the later stages, forming part of a more systematic and integrated approach. Prominent native figures often issued collections of this kind to complement their own treatises, which could be used to advertise any new works. For example Paine recommends his own *Amateur selection of marches, waltzes ... purposely for a young beginner* in his treatise (Chron., 1815: 45 and 48) and Hack (Chron., 1835, title-page) advertises duos (with fingering and bowing) to complement his instructions. Henry Farmer, author of some extremely successful pedagogical works, also contributed a large number of evidently popular arrangements for the amateur.[265] There are numerous other examples spanning most of the nineteenth century.[266]

Generally the more substantial foreign methods are pedagogically and technically more advanced and deal with the demands of contemporary repertoire in a different way. After all their authors are often the pioneers responsible for these developments. Therefore Spohr (1832) and Baillot (1834) are able to incorporate their own and other compositions from the core repertoire into their instrumental treatises to illustrate technical and expressive principles. The translations of Spohr's treatise presented this concept to the British, who were in no position to emulate it. Followers rather than leaders, they relied largely on foreign sources for models of advanced instruction and their priority was to provide original musical examples and studies that would complement

---

[265] These include *The amateur violinist. A selection of the most favorite airs from the standard foreign operas*, with second violin, cello and pianoforte accompaniment, published in various editions (London, 1846–52 (24 sets) and 1894, and 1906 and 1920, both revised and edited by G. Papini). There is also a *Sacred series of the amateur violinist* (London, 1853 and 1872) and *Operatic gems for the violin, being a continuation of the amateur violinist* (1856–8 and 1872).

[266] Such as the periodical *The musical gem ... containing a choice selection of the most popular and favourite airs, easily and carefully arranged for the violin and various other instruments*, which was published in London and appeared between 1829 and 1860. Various figures were involved including Mori. There was also the anonymous *The violinist, or, violin player's companion* (London, 1845) and *A selection of one hundred and fifty easy tunes progressively arranged for beginners on the violin* (Glasgow, [1850]). A review of *One hundred exercises, studies, and extracts, for the violin – from the works of the great masters* (Boosey & Sons) states that they 'would make anyone an accomplished fiddler who contrived to master them all. They form one of the most carefully made and comprehensive collections of the kind we have seen, and do infinite credit to Mr. George Case, their compiler' (*MW*, 37 (1859), 99). A. R. Reinagle wrote *Twelve studies for the violin* (London, 1851); *The violinist's portfolio. A selection of airs with variations ... for the use of amateurs* (London, [1852–4]); and *For violin students, a selection of popular airs varied, to which are added a few exercises* (London, 1859).

the theory presented more successfully than unrelated anthologies of simple tunes.[267]

Spohr's use of examples to illustrate his text, principally Rode's Seventh and his own Ninth concertos arranged for two violins, naturally enabled more violinists, amateur and professional, to attempt and appreciate mainstream repertoire in keeping with the prevailing musical tastes of the British. As far as the concerto is concerned the popularity and longevity of Viotti's examples has already been mentioned. Considering his particularly strong influence on the concertos of Beethoven and Spohr, and Mendelssohn's debt to Spohr's school, it is natural that these works should have enjoyed enormous and continued popularity in this country when their appeal elsewhere was often limited by a lack of gratuitous virtuosity.

The Beethoven concerto, imbued with the qualities of the early French violin school, had suffered from its lack of technical fireworks and seriousness and sobriety until a performance in England at the Hanover Square Rooms on 27 May 1844, when its permanent place in the violin repertoire was firmly established.[268] The situation was in fact ideal for the successful presentation of the work. The approach to the violin epitomized by Viotti, Rode and Spohr was widely cultivated in Britain by the 1840s and was naturally sympathetic to a work that emphasizes the lyrical and makes relatively modest technical demands.[269] The young Joachim was the ideal soloist: his style was formed by the school of Rode and Spohr and he was the natural heir to Spohr's pre-eminent position in native violin playing. He became the most respectable and respectful of virtuosos who appreciated and championed works that now form the canon of violin repertoire. A comparable figure is Sainton who performed the work at the Philharmonic six years later. A reviewer writes of the concerto: 'a work of more difficulty, one more ungrateful to the player who looks to mechanical facility for the means of producing effect, was never written' (*MW*, 25 (1850), 255). This is consistent with the belief among

---

[267] Holmes suggests works, including some of his own, to supplement his edition of Spohr's treatise and develop certain aspects of technique (Chron., 1878: 40 and 78).

[268] Stowell (1998) provides invaluable background to the composition of this piece and its performance history.

[269] The playing of Franz Clement, the work's dedicatee, was ideally suited to this style, and he was a prominent violinist in England for some time (see Stowell (1998), 20–21). Spohr, an admirer of Clement's musicianship, was, perhaps out of professional jealousy, not the work's greatest admirer, although he championed other works of Beethoven. However his pupil Eichler appears to have promoted it in Leipzig from 1833 (see Stowell (1998), 33–4).

the British that manual dexterity was not the gauge of true musicianship.[270]

It is not surprising that the Mendelssohn concerto Op.64 became very popular in England. In fact it is hard to imagine how such a work could fail, uniting both a composer and a style of violin playing which always placed refinement and sobriety above mere *bravura* and technical exuberance and so perfectly encapsulated the expressive ideals of the time. In addition to a number of different editions and arrangements,[271] the piece received sympathetic performances in England by prominent violinists, including Ernst, pupil of Böhm (*The Spectator*, 23 (1850), 132), and Joachim (*MW*, 30 (1852), 355). Mendelssohn's much earlier D minor violin concerto (1822) also has some relevance to British violin playing. It was published in England by Mori, who was taught by Viotti and influenced by Spohr, in 1837.[272] A fine work in its own right, requiring accurate intonation and precise and controlled bowing, it was probably used by the maturing violinist wishing to develop a style of performance akin to that of Spohr.

Despite the popularity of the Mendelssohn concerto the British connoisseur and amateur alike upheld Spohr's position as the greatest composer for the violin. His Eighth Concerto in A minor Op.47 ('Gesangszena'), published in Leipzig in 1820, enjoyed enormous popularity and was considered 'a truly splendid and unique composition' (*MW*, 13 (1840), 358). It received far more performances than any other of Spohr's concertos, although the Ninth Concerto in D minor Op.55 (Offenbach, 1823) came to be thought of as superior, no doubt partially as a result of its prominence in the violin treatise.[273] Sainton appears to have been a champion of Spohr as well as Beethoven and his acclaimed performance of the Ninth Concerto at the Philharmonic in 1845 further increased its profile and contributed greatly to the promotion of Spohr's other works.[274] Following its

---

[270] The concerto also made regular appearances at the Crystal Palace under Manns (Musgrave (2000), 188).

[271] It appeared in an edition with piano accompaniment in London in 1845 and the solo part was edited by Wilhelmj, a pupil of David, for an 1895 edition. Also the second and third movements were transcribed for the piano (by H. Baumer) in 1881, and during the later nineteenth century there were numerous separate editions of the second movement, including arrangements for the piano.

[272] E. Heron-Allen, 'Mori, Nicolas', *DNB*, vol.13, 940.

[273] Brown's list of 'Performances of Spohr's music in England 1820–58' (1980: 331–59) includes the Eighth Concerto 21 times (not counting the numerous instances when the number of the concerto is not specified) and the Seventh and Ninth, the next most popular, only four times each. Violinists associated with the performances of Spohr's works, as cited in the list, include Blagrove, H. C. Cooper, Dando, Joachim, Molique, and Mori.

[274] *MW*, 20 (1845), 157. Haweis (1898: 24) refers to the performance of Spohr's violin duets by Sainton and Cooper.

performance by Joachim at the Philharmonic Jubilee Concert, it was described as 'the most admired' of all Spohr's extended compositions among 'the majority of professors and advanced amateurs' (*MW*, 40 (1862), 552).

The Violin: Stigma and Solace

The violin has been presented as a case-study at the heart of this more general look at instrumental teaching in Britain in order to allow an appreciation of the impact of general trends on a specific area. Firstly we can observe a quite striking consistency of (generally conservative) taste governing the principles espoused in violin pedagogy during the period c.1750 to c.1900. Secondly it is possible to trace an evolution of pedagogical method, placing greater emphasis on practical instruction (to the benefit of pupil and master) and a more progressive and coherent approach to the application of that instruction. In both cases and as a consequence of the all-powerful consumer demand, the most influential protagonists, as consumer and provider respectively, are the native amateur and the foreign professional musician, with the native professional a distant third. However there is an important, additional development to observe towards the end of the nineteenth century and into the twentieth with respect to the violin, as its use spread to the vital and relatively ambitious lower-class and female markets. This section continues the discussion of these three main trends.

The advanced methods of Geminiani and Spohr provided the models for violin playing in Britain in their respective periods. Their treatment of the violin, promoted in general literature as well as teaching material, informed a wide range of works by pupils and others. To a large extent they came to represent the technical and expressive ideals specific to British violin playing, their compositions and technical priorities epitomizing the moderation and tempering of passions and emotions, the sobriety 'regulating even our warmest feelings' that is the 'national disposition' (*QMMR*, 5 (1823), 442).

The treatises themselves and the principles they represent emerge as a constant and unifying thread in a musical environment characterized by variety and vibrancy. Their influence went beyond the whims of fashion and remained relevant long after their ideas had been superseded elsewhere. Geminiani's work is the unique example of an advanced text of international standing originally in English, and Spohr's method, which dominated British violin pedagogy from the 1830s to the end of the century, presents in many ways the nineteenth-century equivalent of the Corellian school. They share very similar expressive aims, although they are conceived with different equipment and technical demands in mind. Ferdinand David's son Paul refers to Corelli's 'artistic purity and simplicity' (1889: 291) and Spohr's 'purity of style' (p.295), and his articles on Geminiani (1879 and 1906) provide a direct link between the Italian master of the eighteenth century and the adopted father of British violinists in the nineteenth.

Further evidence of a continuous tradition of expressive priorities, independent of Spohr, is provided by extracts quoted in Hogarth (1838, vol.2, 279) from Charles Avison's *An essay on musical expression* (London, 1752). Avison's 'immutable principles of taste', formed as a pupil of Geminiani, are recommended by Hogarth and judged to have 'lost none of their value and interest by the lapse of nearly a century'. Without wishing to stretch the point too far, Spohr's amalgamation of both the Corellian (through Viotti and the early French violin school) and Mannheim traditions (through his teacher Eck) in his own unique blend, brought together the most potent influences on violin playing in eighteenth- and early nineteenth-century Britain in a style that remained prominent in Britain throughout the nineteenth century.

Native and foreign violinists who achieved prominence in Britain during the second half of the nineteenth century generally demonstrate an approach to the instrument that is consistent with the first. Spohr's violin-playing style remained influential up to and beyond the turn of the twentieth century and his pupils and the figures influenced by him, native and foreign, held key positions in British educational institutions throughout the nineteenth century. Although the limitations of his style in terms of modern technique were identified, its value continued to be appreciated.[275]

The greater virtuosity incorporated into Holmes's edition of Spohr's treatise (Chron., 1878) discussed in earlier chapters is part of an increasingly homogeneous approach to violin playing during the second half of the nineteenth century. However it is significant that Holmes, an important teacher and violinist in his own right, chose to issue a revised and to a large extent updated edition of the method by his old master rather than a work in his own name based on the principles of Spohr. Also Carrodus, a similarly important and influential individual (see below), produced works based on Spohr's model (Chron., 1896), even though the 1890s witnessed his relegation to the second rank as a composer in England.[276] The revisions made by prominent contemporary players, such as Holmes, Carrodus and Wessely, ensured the contemporary validity of works by Spohr and Loder into the twentieth

---

[275] See Cobbett (1910), 330.
[276] See Brown (1980), 217–18.

century. Their longevity is a testament to the respect and authority associated with their authors as instrumentalists and pedagogues.

The most important figures in British violin playing during the second half of the nineteenth and early twentieth centuries share strong connections with Spohr and his style. They include Joachim, Sainton, Carrodus and Sammons. Joseph Joachim (1831–1907), whose qualities have been touched on previously, was Spohr's natural heir, and his success reflects the longevity of the refined 'classical' approach to the violin in Britain (see Courvoisier (Chron., 1899) and Joachim and Moser (Eng. tr., ?1907). The French violinist Prosper Sainton (1813–90), trained by Habeneck (Baillot's pupil) in Paris, was professor of the violin at the RAM from 1845 until his death. A very active performer in London and the provinces, he was a close friend of Mendelssohn, often shared duties with Henry Blagrove, and promoted Spohr's works. He was a prolific teacher and was able to boast that 'at the last Birmingham Festival that he played at every single violinist in the orchestra had either been a pupil or a pupil of a pupil of his'.[277] He was succeeded at the RAM in 1890 by the 'brilliant' Emil Sauret (1852–1920), who 'left a very broad mark on the Academy, especially during his first years', when 'there was a perfect craze for learning the fiddle – a craze which lasted about ten years'.[278]

John Tiplady Carrodus (1836–95), from Yorkshire, was a pupil of Bernhard Molique (1802–69), a Spohr 'disciple' who lived and taught in London between 1849 and 1866. Carrodus himself became a 'follower of Spohr',[279] who expressed his admiration for the Englishman's playing. In addition to editions of the treatises of Loder (Chron., 1884) and Spohr (Chron., 1896), Carrodus published his own *Chats to violin students on how to study the violin* (Chron., 1895) and taught at the National Training School (established in 1876), the Croydon Conservatoire of Music (established in 1883) and at the Guildhall School of Music and Trinity College, London. He was also the first president of the College of Violinists. A powerful and skilful soloist, particularly in the concertos of Beethoven, Spohr and Molique, he contributed a great deal to the improvement of string playing in Victorian England. A concert he gave at St James's Hall on 20 Jan 1881, including works by Molique and Spohr, is widely recognized as the first public violin recital. This type of performance no doubt appealed to the increasing numbers who owned pianos and were engaged in solo and ensemble domestic music-making.

---

[277] Corder (1922a), 84. See also *MW*, 20 (1845), 80 and 157; *MT*, 31 (1890), 665; and Dubourg (1878), 157–9.
[278] Corder (1922a), 84.
[279] David (1889), 298.

Carrodus was one of the first British virtuosos on any instrument. His example helped to inspire the increasing number of important native violinists who were emerging from the various colleges.[280] Following his achievements Albert Sammons (1886–1957) helped further to raise the status of the British performer and violinist in particular during the early twentieth century. He received his first tuition on the violin from his father, a good amateur musician, but besides a few isolated lessons from John Saunders and Frederick Weist-Hill (a pupil of Ysaÿe) he was, like Paganini and Ole Bull before him, self-taught. In addition to his professorship at the College of Violinists, Sammons became a professor at the RCM (1939–56) and wrote a violin treatise (1916), a copy of which is in the RAM. The performing style of Sammons in the twentieth century, as revealed in his recordings, with its discreet use of portamento and a quite fast continuous vibrato, contrasts with what was prescribed in many nineteenth-century methods, including those of Spohr and his followers.[281] However Sammons 'was never a showman',[282] and his qualities as a violinist have much in common with those long admired by the British connoisseur and emulated by the student that can be found in the performance styles and writings of figures such as Geminiani and Spohr. When Ysaÿe heard him play for the first time, he exclaimed 'At last, England has found herself a great violinist!';[283] but, as his foreign predecessors had done, he shunned the pyrotechnical feats of other more virtuosic violinists who sought more 'popular' acclaim.[284] Typically Sammons saw perfect intonation and artistic interpretation as marking the difference between the great violinist and the mediocre.[285]

Despite the progress that had been made, the prevailing attitudes of the last two centuries ensured that the arrival of a native virtuoso of Sammons's ability was greeted with suspicion and resistance in some quarters. Even Henry Wood found difficulty in trying to promote him.[286] Nevertheless he appears to have transcended the prejudice and furthered the cause of British violinists. After his first performance of the Elgar concerto on 23 November 1914 at the Queen's Hall, with Vassily Safonov conducting the London Symphony Orchestra, the critic of *The Star* commented: 'His performance of the difficult solo part put him in

---

[280] See Straeten (1933), vol.2, 295–6 and a portrait facing 321. See also MW, 31 (1853), 460; MW, 32 (1854), 109; Heron-Allen (1894), lxii; Colles (1933), 3; and Harvey (1995), 154–5.
[281] See Brown (1988), 110–28; and Philip (1992).
[282] Wetherell (1998), 55 and 115.
[283] Quoted in Brook (1948), 148.
[284] See Wetherell (1998), 55.
[285] Brook (1948), 155.
[286] Ehrlich (1985), 187.

the front rank of violinists, and the public cheered him with as much enthusiasm as if he had had a foreign name.'[287] The predilection of some for talent from overseas is still worthy of comment, but the sarcastic tone suggests that attitudes were changing.

The Russian violinist Adolf Brodsky thrived in Manchester as a teacher and performer. Although not a direct descendant of Spohr's school, it is significant that his reputation as an artist was based largely on his performances of Mendelssohn, Beethoven and Elgar.[288]

Turning to the evolution of the sources as teaching material, it should be remembered that British texts emerged from a totally different environment to most continental examples, such as the official texts of the Paris Conservatoire. The absence of an identifiable native tradition forced writers and publishers to rely on the assimilation of mainstream foreign texts when constructing their own 'primers', drawing on their pedagogical method as well as technical content. Along with general principles, material sometimes appeared in quotation, most often without acknowledgement. Naturally Geminiani and Spohr fed into the pedagogical literature and consequently gave some authority and homogeneity to works that were conceived as a private enterprise by writers, publishers and teachers rather than prominent performers. Native sources from the transitional period of the early nineteenth century, including those by Jousse, Goodban, Paine, Loder, Challoner and Howell, also had the difficult task of meeting demand while falling in between these two seminal works. They had to remain faithful to old-fashioned but deeply ingrained principles and also cater for a greater range of ability as the market for instruction increased. Consequently, drawing on a range of earlier sources with prominence given to the contents of Geminiani, they perpetuate conservative tendencies.

As demand increased, the inadequacies of both the Geminiani and Spohr methods in dealing with the early stages of instruction left an increasingly large gap in the market that many native writers were able to fill. Numerous works of an elementary or intermediate level appeared in the nineteenth century. Many of these later in the century were designed to complement Spohr and compensate for his failings. The moralist and violinist Haweis remarked that 'SPOHR's violin school is likely to hold its place as a comprehensive class book, though I am told that modern professors have a perfect mania for introducing shorter manuals of their own invention' (1898: 337).

The loyalty of the consumer to certain models, be it in their demand

---

[287] Quoted in Campbell (1980), 146.

[288] See Zaltsberg (2002), 526–9. It is interesting to note that a pupil of Brodsky, Naoum Blinder, later became Isaac Stern's teacher.

for music, instruments and bows or pedagogical publications, continued the promotion of the 'ancient' school and their ideals of taste, while admitting only some of the more modern elements that were achieving prominence elsewhere. Therefore the conservative nature of the content of the sources is preserved even though their presentation becomes more sophisticated. In addition the arrival of foreign texts in English many years after their original publication added to the amount of retrospective material.[289] As a result, native works display little concern for the latest technical devices and tend to avoid anything controversial. For example material from Geminiani's treatise can be found in British sources from the 1750s through to the 1850s, but the innovative aspects of his theories, such as his views on the 'close shake', rule of the down bow, chromatic fingerings, and large leaps when shifting are seldom mentioned. Rather most of what he has to say on the bow hold and right-hand technique is retained and promoted.

The continued use of early nineteenth-century sources well into the twentieth, such as the treatises of Spohr and Loder, is in some ways reminiscent of the eighteenth century. However it has now progressed beyond mere convenience and demonstrates a real concern for pedagogical method and contemporary practice. Also in addition to the continued importance of the Viotti/Spohr/Joachim tradition there appears the significant presence of Sauret and Ševčík, who were involved with the RAM and Guildhall respectively.[290] Therefore some of the most progressive pedagogues of the time and their new 'scientific' principles took violin playing in Britain into the twentieth century, alongside those who kept the most important traditions of the nineteenth alive. Hans Wessely's retrospective and critical view of violin pedagogy during the late eighteenth and nineteenth centuries (1913), drawing on models from Geminiani to Ševčík, is consistent with this now familiar combination of the old and the new. He reflects the demand for and the proliferation of serious and comprehensive tools for learning and teaching among both amateurs and professionals and the more positive attitudes and proactive approach of the early twentieth century.

So, in terms of standards, trends in the pedagogical material and elsewhere suggest that the aspirations and achievements of native amateurs were a great deal higher at the end of our period than at the beginning. Advanced texts, including Spohr's treatise, were increasingly

---

[289] A notable exception among works for the violin, Spohr's treatise, translated a year after its original publication, was, as discussed above, inherently retrospective, even allowing for the general nature of such works.

[290] Articles on Ševčík, his teaching methods and legacy, can be found in *The Strad* (September 1998), 942–9, and Kolneder (1998) provides valuable insights.

accessible to and used by amateurs as well as budding professionals. The general appeal of the lyrical violin style, continually promoted in performance and practical instruction as well as written material, helped to inspire this improvement in standards. A performance of the Beethoven Concerto by a 'Mr Brand' with the Amateur Musical Society prompted one reviewer to observe 'what vast strides music is making in England when an amateur is able to enter upon so very arduous an undertaking' (MW, 32 (1854), 311).

Native professionals had benefited both as students and teachers from the improvements in the materials for instrumental teaching, as only a fortunate few could take advantage of the Royal Academy of Music when it finally arrived. However, the most significant change came with higher standards of participation and appreciation among amateurs, which encouraged and promoted improved perceptions of the musician's skills and worth. It is interesting to compare the considerable achievements of the chemist and accomplished amateur violinist, Dr T. Lamb Phipson,[291] and the Duke of Edinburgh, self-taught violinist and supporter of musical institutions, but of 'notoriously poor musicianship'.[292] Not for the first time we have the greater application and musical achievement displayed by those amateurs otherwise regularly employed, making the most of the limited time available to them for music, compared to the often fickle, arrogant leisured classes, prominent beyond their abilities and continuing to promote the refined amateur and boorish professional dichotomy.[293]

It is significant that the discussion has so far centred on male activity and the literate, 'art' tradition of music, as for much of our period violin-playing amateurs were primarily from polite male society. Nevertheless there had long been the potential for large-scale and more proficient participation among female and lower-class society, who had managed to outshine male achievements in other areas of musical activity. Both social and practical factors had prevented the realization of this huge potential, but when the market and opportunity had diversified further the results were all the more rapid and far-reaching. Although, as we have seen, the expansion of the music industry and the raising of standards had begun much earlier, new developments in the later nineteenth century were essential catalysts.

A particularly striking and significant trend in British violin playing in the later nineteenth century is the increased involvement of women

---

[291] Gillett (2000b), 328–9.
[292] Ibid., 335.
[293] See ibid., 337.

and young ladies,[294] and especially the huge increase in their numbers at the various music colleges at the end of the century. Their suitability for the instrument and the potential for raising standards had been recognized for a significant period and there had been renowned female soloists,[295] but their participation on a such a large scale had not been socially acceptable earlier in the century.[296] Music apprenticeships for women had been rare, and the instruments they were taught at the RAM in 1823 were restricted to the piano and harp and singing (the first woman violin student appeared in 1872). The Royal Society of Musicians had not admitted women until 1866, and, other than a few harpists, they were not employed in the established orchestras.[297]

The rise of the violin in feminine circles and the trends behind it have been discussed in detail elsewhere,[298] but it is important to consider one or two general issues here. Of great importance are the long-standing associations of the instrument itself with sin, death, and Satan (as the leading instrument of the dance) and also its ascribed female gender, in voice and shape, but 'male-defined mode of performance'.[299] Up to the third quarter of the nineteenth century these associations, absent from the piano, guitar and harp, had given the idea and reality of the female violinist a 'disreputable aura'.[300]

Although these associations did not disappear, the appeal of the violin, musically and socially, among the huge numbers of middle-class girls and young women overrode most objections. Considering the ubiquity of the piano in middle-class households and its growing

---

[294] The recent contributions of Paula Gillett (2000a and b) are very welcome and important additions to the literature on this subject, particularly in their discussion of how changes in society affected perceptions of female musicians (especially violinists) and the existence of amateur/professional tensions.

[295] See 'Female performers on the violin', MW, 12 (1839), 34–7, and Dubourg (5th edn (1878), 254–63) devotes a whole chapter to female violinists and their suitability.

[296] Parke's comments on a performance by Mme Gautherot suggest that a female violinist, despite evident proficiency, was considered an unwelcome curiosity in male society during the early nineteenth century. See Beedell (1992), 126–8.

[297] Henry Wood's hiring of six female string players, on violin and viola, in 1913 was exceptional. However women did have their own amateur string orchestras, performing on the full range of instruments during the 1880s, including the famous example founded by Lady Radnor in 1881. Professional ladies' orchestras appeared around the turn of the century (see Ehrlich (1985), 159).

[298] See in particular Gillett (2000a), chapters 4 and 5. Other references to the popularity of the violin among young women include Spohr (Chron., 1878), Editor's preface, iv; Heron-Allen (1894), xvi; David (1889), 298; Cobbett (1910), 328; Wessely (1913), 2; Ehrlich (1985), 112 and 156ff.; Harvey (1995), 160–61; Fuller (1998), 63–4 and 70–71; and Hyde (1998), 40.

[299] Gillett (2000a), 87.

[300] Ibid., 81.

popularity even among the lower classes, the violin allowed the young lady to set herself apart from the throng and attract attention, as well as offering many more possibilities for domestic music-making. A trickle in the face of objection soon became an irresistible tide and the rapid adoption of the violin by girls produced the intense 'violin fad' of the 1880s and 1890s.[301]

We should not overlook the impact of a growing number of role models among the numerous 'star' violinists, combining artistry and virtuosity, of the late nineteenth century and early 1900s, who helped to dispel prejudice as well as increase aspirations. These include, most notably, Wilma Norman-Neruda (Lady Hallé from 1888) and Marie Hall (a pupil of Ševčík). There is also the 'allure' of the woman violinist to consider, especially among men most often confronted by the image of the seated pianist.[302] There is no escaping the 'sexual dimension of female musical performance', particularly with respect to bowed stringed and wind instruments, which had only recently entered the woman's domain.[303]

This element of male voyeurism highlights the fact that, although women were able to enjoy greater emancipation through music than had been allowed earlier,[304] the level and extent of their activity (particularly in performance) remained limited and determined by the conventions and tastes of male society. As mentioned previously women were still educated primarily for marriage and motherhood, and so there remained a definite ceiling on the potential of women instrumentalists throughout society. We return therefore to the now familiar cycle of poor instruction standards and stifled ambitions. Teacher proficiency was not helped by the level of diploma 'mania' found at the time and the financial concerns of the growing numbers of music colleges.[305] Women amateur violinists, although probably a definite improvement on most male amateurs,[306] were therefore not fully able to realize their potential for raising performance standards at this stage, and instead inflicted cheaper competition on the established male professionals.

---

[301] Ibid., 108. Naturally a large number of publications appeared in response to the requirements of this significant group of consumers (see Heron-Allen (1894), 246–7, 250, 255 and 261).

[302] Gillett (2000a), 113.

[303] See ibid., 109–11.

[304] See Leppert (1988), 147.

[305] Most violin students at British conservatoires were women by the end of the nineteenth century.

[306] Shaw (1932, vol.1, 153–4, and vol.3, 92) offers some indication of the achievements of a significant number of female violinists in the context of a general improvement in amateur standards. See also Ehrlich (1985), 157.

Discussion of other areas of musical activity in this study highlights how the spread of opportunity to the lower orders tapped into a seemingly limitless reservoir of enthusiasm and application, often with corresponding levels of achievement. Free of the stringent and long-standing codes of behaviour that shackled polite society (at least in public) the working classes sought to take musical performance, in whatever form, to the highest level possible. In the case of the violin, the 'fiddle', in name and practice, did not have the same stigma attached to it as in elite culture, and its negative connotations did not have the same prohibitive effect. The instrument was made use of in both formal (church) and informal (domestic) contexts,[307] and practised by prominent individuals such as the 'rhyming peasant' John Clare.[308]

The spread of the instrument among the lower classes was not limited by appetite but by opportunity, as the middle classes sought to preserve the 'genteel' areas of instrumental practice (outside the brass band) for themselves. While sufficient in the eyes of most in positions of power, this situation stifled the potential of the lower classes in many areas of instrumental music. The brass band thrived in its morally and financially supportive environment, which allowed men to exploit the playability and tonal qualities of their instruments, having perhaps gained some musical skills while at school. An early start to tuition was (and is) of more relevance to an instrument such as the violin and the provision of instruction for children on a formal basis was a crucial obstacle. Financial hurdles stood in the way of any desire to introduce instrumental teaching into state elementary schools. Fortunately private enterprise, ever keen to exploit latent demand, came to the rescue and classes in violin playing were widely introduced into elementary schools in the early years of the twentieth century. We should not be surprised that, within a few years (1910), a massed 'orchestra' of several thousand elementary school children playing violins was performing to great acclaim at the Crystal Palace.

With perhaps more ground to recover than most instruments the violin enjoyed a remarkable reversal in its fortunes from the middle of the eighteenth century to the end of the nineteenth: from the devil's own instrument, associated with all that was considered inferior, musically and morally and commonly neglected by men and considered unsuitable for women, it came to fit perfectly into the moral climate of the time and was promoted from the later nineteenth century as a symbol of civilized recreation and self-improvement. The promotion of higher standards and the active participation of a greater cross-section of society helped

---

[307] See Russell (1997), 180 and 187.
[308] McCalman (1999), 217.

to narrow the harmful gap, in terms of proficiency and status, between the well-to-do amateur and struggling professional player. This was an important step forward, not only towards negating the derogatory connotations of the amateur 'fiddler', but also with respect to the public estimation and perception of music and musicians generally.[309]

The Viola, Double Bass and Violoncello

This section, a necessarily brief postscript to the above discussion, highlights certain issues of special relevance to other members of the violin family. Like the violin, though perhaps not to the same extent, their popularity among society as a whole increased dramatically with the proliferation of women string players and ladies' string orchestras during the last quarter of the nineteenth century.

The viola (or tenor) has long been perceived as the poor relation of the violin family[310] and the violist continues to struggle in some circles against the notion of being a 'failed' violinist with limited technical dexterity. As far as our period is concerned the gradual realization of the importance of real proficiency on the instrument came with the increasingly popularity, in public and in private, of the core chamber music repertoire. Although in most cases proficiency would have been another string to the bow of first-study violinists and would have been based on the application of violin technique to the viola, written sources published in English, in line with increasingly specialized pedagogical material in general, demonstrate a growing concern for the nurturing of violists.[311] There is a significant gap in time between the anonymous example based on the generic 'Complete instructions' format (Chron., 1795) and the next crop; but, alongside examples derived from earlier versions for the violin, we find a few translations of mainstream continental methods.[312] Also in keeping with the propensity for British musicians to shine in certain 'minority' areas not dominated by foreign instrumentalists, there is the example set by the leading viola specialist Henry Hill. His prominence and professional stature, particularly in the increasingly important chamber music circles, are demonstrated by his participation in the esteemed Beethoven Quartett Society concerts and Ella's Musical Union, where the bias was very much in favour of

---

[309] See Hogarth (1838), vol.2, 271–2.
[310] See Quantz (1752), Eng. tr. (1965), 237.
[311] See Brown (1886), 636; Heron-Allen (1894), 338–42; and Kruse (1986).
[312] Saint Jacome (Chron., 1879); Firket (Chron., 1884); Langey (Chron., 1885); Althaus (Chron., 1890); and Bruni (Chron., 1895).

eminent foreign players.³¹³ Hill's influence continued through his teaching activities at the RAM, where he taught Richard Manning Blagrove, brother of Henry Gamble Blagrove and later a prominent performer and teacher on the viola.³¹⁴ Another important native violist and former student at the RAM, Lionel Tertis, became a teacher at the Guildhall School of Music during the early twentieth century.

The status of the double bass, also a vital if minority instrument, was greatly enhanced in nineteenth-century Britain by the presence of Domenico Dragonetti.³¹⁵ Although performers on the instrument had long been active in the church and theatre and London became an important centre for bass makers in the early nineteenth century,³¹⁶ Dragonetti's arrival and achievements set new technical standards in performance. Despite the fact that contemporary native double-bass methods³¹⁷ appear reluctant to acknowledge fully these (particularly left-hand) advancements,³¹⁸ the Dragonetti underhand, outcurved bow-pattern retained its popularity in England into the twentieth century.³¹⁹ In addition the Italian's general approach to technique lived on in Britain through his performing activities and private pupils. As in the case of Spohr, Dragonetti naturally sought the wealthiest pupils (including the Duke of Leinster) and the RAM was unable to secure his services. However, again like Spohr, his influence spread to RAM students through a proxy, in his case the professor James Howell, a pupil of Anfossi who taught Dragonetti's methods.³²⁰ Like the German he appears to have inspired a native 'school' characterized by precision and strength of tone.³²¹ As well as the native 'digests' of double-bass

---

³¹³ See Bashford (2000), 109.

³¹⁴ See Atlas (1996), 54. Blagrove, also an influential concertinist, is discussed further in the following chapter.

³¹⁵ Palmer (1997) contains a mass of invaluable information on this colourful character and musician.

³¹⁶ The recent article of Martin and Lawrence ('Founding Father', *The Strad* (Sept. 2000), 988–93) is interesting in this respect and for its discussion of the bass-making tradition that emerged in the north-west of England with the birth of orchestras around the middle of the century. It is clear that a variety of influences persisted, with the northern school of William Tarr remaining faithful to the Bavarian model while the London school of Lott, Fendt and Kennedy referred mainly to the Brescian Italians. Individual instruments also varied between the common three-string, viol-shaped, three-quarter-sized model and the four-stringed, violin-shaped, full-size pattern. See Langey (Chron., 1885) and also Harvey (1995), 34–6.

³¹⁷ Including the 'composite' methods of D'Almaine and Co. (Chron., 1843) and Hamilton (Chron., 1833).

³¹⁸ See Palmer (1997), 65–6.

³¹⁹ Ibid., 66 and 78ff. See also Brun (2000).

³²⁰ Palmer (1997), 86–8.

³²¹ Ibid., 86.

technique already mentioned from the first half of the nineteenth century, we also find several original methods in English[322] and translations of seminal continental methods.[323] Bottesini (using the French overhand bow pattern) was no doubt a significant influence later in the century.

The famous (if often exaggerated) professional partnership of Dragonetti and Robert Lindley, both prominent performers at the top of the profession, was an important positive influence on British string playing. However the distinction between the revered Italian and the home-grown virtuoso points to the fact that the cello was a special case as far as practical music among the male social elite was concerned, achieving a status beyond other instruments (especially the violin) during the crucial transitional period. Besides its common appearance in church and village bands, the cello was the instrument of the male aristocracy, replacing the viol as the instrument of the gentleman.[324]

With a higher status and level of endorsement came the higher standards culminating in the achievements of Lindley. His appearance was not a 'fluke' to the same extent as Albert Sammons's later arrival. The presence of distinguished foreign (mainly Italian) cellists ranging from Bononcini, Giacobbe Cervetto, Caporale, Francis Pasquali (also prominent on the double bass), Cirri and the Duport brothers to James Cervetto had created a tradition of high standards, particularly in England and Scotland. However, owing to the lower level of competition than in the case of the violin, native players, often taught by the eminent visitors, were still able to carve out a niche for themselves. These included the Scot John Gunn and John Crosdill, who even toured abroad and became a chamber musician to Queen Charlotte and cello teacher to George Frederick, Prince of Wales (later George IV).[325] Teaching at this level was an honour most often reserved for foreign virtuosos. His legacy continued through his pupils, including Lindley. It is significant that names such as the Reinagle brothers, Cudmore and Crouch retain a familiarity far beyond contemporary British violinists. Lindley, initially instructed by his amateur musician father, changed from the violin to the cello at an early age and went on to study with James Cervetto. Besides a highly successful solo, orchestral and chamber

---

[322] Rowland (Chron., 1876) and Langey (Chron., 1885).

[323] Fröhlich (Chron., 1840) and Bottesini (Chron., 1880).

[324] Harvey (1995), Walden (1998) and Stowell (1999) provide important surveys of the history, organology, technique and literature of the cello.

[325] Frederick Lewis, Prince of Wales (son of George II) had also been a keen amateur cellist. The famous 'Royal George' cello was made by Forster for George IV (see Harvey (1995), 140–2).

music career (promoting the works of Corelli with Dragonetti), Lindley became the first cello professor at the RAM, teaching the future principal Charles Lucas. It was an unusual appointment for someone in his enviable position, but it was also unusual for a native musician to achieve so much. His successor in the hearts of the British public was the Italian Alfredo Piatti, appearing as soloist and chamber musician with the likes of Joachim and Neruda (Hallé). He also became professor at the RAM but taught mainly privately. As to be expected, the combination of technical brilliance with 'good taste' made him a true artist in the eyes of the British public.

The pedagogical material issued was in keeping with the relatively high status and level of male amateur cultivation the instrument enjoyed, particularly during the first half of the nineteenth century. In comparison to the violin and flute (and with no part of Prelleur (1730/31) to plagiarize) there are a greater number of more substantial pedagogical works at an earlier stage (see Chronology), although a name such as Cervetto was still a valuable asset to publishers (see Chron., 1800). From Crome's example (c.1765), noteworthy for its discussion of a forerunner of the endpin for use by beginners,[326] through to Broadley, there are tutors by key native proponents as well as translations of important continental works, including various versions of the official Paris Conservatoire text.[327] Once again we see the need to assimilate and select from a variety of influences as a common thread in British instrumental pedagogy.

The fortunes of the cello in Britain had perhaps peaked early compared to other instruments, which increased their popularity as the market diversified. Although the cello benefited from the new trend of women playing other instruments in preference to the piano, guitar or harp,[328] native players comparable to the likes of Lindley did not appear until the twentieth century.

---

[326] Walden (1998), 97–8.

[327] See also Heron-Allen (1894), 343; Walden (1998), particularly 26–33 and 300–301; and Stowell (1999), 224–5.

[328] See Ehrlich (1985), 161 and Gillett (2000a), 101 and 190–91.

PART THREE

CHAPTER FOUR

Other Instruments

Constraints of time and space preclude comprehensive coverage of instruments outside the violin family and the following short surveys are intended to draw together key issues pertinent to the general trends, cultural and social, highlighted elsewhere in the study. There is much work to be done in this area particularly with respect to pedagogical issues concerning individual instruments and families of instruments.

Keyboard

Keyboard performance is one of a few rare success stories in British instrumental practice during the period. We find advancements in the areas of teaching practices and material, organology and repertoire occurring at an earlier stage and in greater numbers than in the case of other instrumental families. To what do we owe this success? We cannot ignore the sustained position of the keyboard as a domestic status symbol in a consumer age, particularly as the piano came to be seen as an improvement on the harpsichord, or its use to both men and women, offering the former a means by which they could impose restrictions on the latter. Nevertheless it did offer women a certain level of emancipation, both in terms of their ability to fulfil social 'requirements' such as marriage and find an outlet for some self-expression, which grew in time as opportunity spread.[1] However the keyboard's close association with the general education and gentility of young ladies restricted their personal musical achievements. This was a utilitarian art and humdrum mediocrity was the order of the day.[2] It is

---

[1] Miss Graham's keyboard tutor (Chron., 1829) is interesting and fairly unusual in its explicit intention to enhance the pupil's 'mental treasures' as well as 'mechanical dexterity' (see Kassler (1979), 407–8).

[2] Burgan's 1989 article, which concentrates on the depiction of music in Victorian fiction, including Dickens and Eliot, is particularly illuminating on the issue of music in female genteel education and the importance of the piano as an often satirized symbol of female respectability and emancipation (it is also interesting to note its presence in modern historical novels such as Duncan Sprott's *The Clopton Hercules* (London, 1991)). Once again music and the images associated with it are most significant in terms of their extra-musical meaning. Ehrlich (1976, 2/1990) is of course a seminal work in the area of

true that great dexterity and technical accomplishment raised suspicion and censure although repertoire such as the 'accompanied' sonata demanded far more of the keyboardist than it did of the male instrumentalist and sonatas such as Clementi's Op.2 required some proficiency.

Although in the vast majority of cases the reality was of 'forced labour' despite a lack of talent or unfulfilled potential where ability was evident,[3] keyboard instruments and the (mostly male) professionals associated with them benefited greatly from high levels of consumer interest and their established role in the lives of the middle and upper classes. Also, particularly in the form of the piano (often duet) transcription, they were important in promoting an understanding and appreciation of increasingly complex musical structures and as a complement to the attendance of live performance. As discussed above (see Chapter 1) the keyboard's intrinsic role in the creation as well as performance of music afforded it rare intellectual credibility in the instrumental sphere.

Turning to specific examples which demonstrate an unusually advanced and sophisticated interest in keyboard practice, it is interesting to compare the influential and prolific Antonius Bemetzrieder's harpsichord treatise (Chron., 1785, available in an English translation from 1778–9), a comprehensive work of more than 250 pages,[4] with the staple fare of regurgitated 'Prelleur-format', 'New and compleat' examples, covering a variety of instruments and published throughout the late eighteenth century. We have already encountered Pasquali's extremely popular and relatively progressive thorough-bass tutor (Chron., 1810),[5] but it is also important to highlight the fact that he and other prominent and accomplished figures, including Giardini, were very active as keyboard teachers. Practical instruction was offered to wealthy ladies and, as in the case of Giardini's morning 'academia' established at his house, there were even opportunities for students to perform. Despite being most accomplished as violinists, individuals such as Pasquali and Giardini reserved their most concentrated and serious pedagogical efforts for the teaching of women keyboardists (and singers). This provides some indication of the market, as do the significant number of keyboard tutors dedicated to wealthy ladies,

---

keyboard development and its social and economic context. See also Ferguson (1975), Pollens (1995), Komlos (1995) and Rowland (1998 and 2001) for important surveys of contemporary keyboard technique, practice and organology.

[3] Burgan (1989), 51. See also Rainbow (1989a), 36.
[4] See Kassler (1979), 67–72.
[5] See Rowland (2001), 123.

including Queen Charlotte. The ladies of polite society therefore provided a role model for keyboard practice sadly lacking in the case of most other (male-dominated) instruments, and consequently the demand for clear, progressive pedagogical sources, addressed to young pupils, teachers and parents, came to the fore at a relatively early stage.

We do not have to look too far to discover the signs of an emerging piano culture based on consumerism and social emulation. A market evolved which could prompt a large amount of pedagogical and other literature (including London's *Piano-forte magazine*, published in 16 volumes between 1797 and 1802) and make the piano a leading British export. It also symbolizes the descent of opportunity in music through the various strata of society, as the piano, an 'orchestra' for the home, became within the reach of the lower-middle and then, during the later nineteenth century, the lower classes and as a result loosened the monopoly of female consumers.[6] Of course it was still possible to differentiate between the classes by the type of instrument they could afford, be it a square (later upright) or grand piano, new or second hand, purchased or hired. The transition from harpsichord to piano performance and ownership was, particularly in the domestic setting, a fairly drawn-out process, as the work of the German émigré makers such as Zumpe in the 1760s transferred to Americus Backers and the squares and grands of the likes of Broadwood and Stodart. Casting a glance over the title-pages of repertoire and teaching material one can observe, from the 1770s onwards, a change of emphasis from 'for harpsichord or piano forte (or organ)' to 'piano forte or harpsichord (or organ)' to, around the turn of the century (as in Clementi's treatise), 'for piano forte'.[7] The harpsichord remained popular for longer in the provinces, where conspicuous consumerism was not such a potent force.[8]

If we turn to the major nineteenth-century protagonists it is evident that Britain, and more specifically London, was, uniquely, at the cutting edge of mainstream developments and that an impressive lineage of teacher–pupil relationships was allowed to form, much of it emanating from the famous virtuosos of the 'London Pianoforte School'. It is worth noting that Beethoven was influenced by the London-based pianists to

---

[6] Burgan (1989), 45. See also Russell (1997), 5, 177 and 180. As raised in the previous chapter the affordability of pianos among the lower orders did not please everyone, and the middle classes began to look elsewhere (especially to the violin) in search of exclusivity. It is clear that Lord Salisbury was unconvinced of the usefulness of this trend (see Chapter 1).

[7] See Pollens (1995), 225–8; and Schott (1985).

[8] See Kassler (1985), 143–4.

the same extent that he was influenced by the Paris-based violinists. As an example of this lineage we can trace the influence of the 'classical' Clementi through J. B. Cramer to Sir George Smart. It is also well known that John Field benefited from an unusually fruitful apprenticeship to Clementi and influenced pianistic styles and genres in his own right. Some women keyboardists achieved prominence, including Jane Mary Guest, Fanny Davies (a pupil of Clara Schumann) and 'Mrs Anderson' (who taught Princess (later Queen) Victoria at the recommendation of Sir George Smart), although the norm was far less impressive as 'semi-professionalism' spread rapidly during the second half of the nineteenth century and diploma-hungry young ladies sought to make some profit out of their pianos.[9]

As far as institutional training is concerned, keyboard instruments (and with them composition) fared much better than other areas although conditions were still far from ideal. Cipriani Potter, Moscheles (co-author with Fétis, Chron., 1841), Mrs Anderson, Ernst and later Otto Goldschmidt at the RAM, and Franklin Taylor (Chron., 1877 and 1897) and Oscar Beringer at the RCM were among the influential affiliated teachers. There are of course also the examples of keyboard teaching, for an additional charge, in schools for young ladies (and even among the boys at Harrow)[10] and the 'mass-production'[11] of the private piano 'academies' raised earlier involving Logier and others. The influence of Logier on piano teaching, though criticized fervently in some quarters, was international and his methods encompassed harmony and form as well as manual dexterity.

Significantly, the expertise of these influential figures was often transferred directly, in person, to other serious musicians rather than principally to wealthy dilettanti and through teaching material, as in the case of the violin and Geminiani and Spohr. However, textual instruction was also of great importance and many of the period's biggest names also developed systems of instruction suitable for the improvement of amateur standards, and translations of earlier mainstream texts, including Türk's treatise (Chron., 1804), were relatively quick to arrive.[12] We find large numbers of new, carefully constructed and targeted teaching material intended to provide a firm technical foundation and an introduction to a variety of musical demands. From the late eighteenth century there are examples by Hook

---

[9] Gillett (2000a: 212–14) raises the interesting issue of young girls being trained as piano-tuners.
[10] See Rainbow (1989a), 34 and Rainbow (1981), 43.
[11] Ehrlich (1995), 8.
[12] See Komlós (1995), 122–32.

(Chron., 1785), Broderip (Chron., 1788), Camidge (Chron., 1795), Dussek (Chron., 1796), who was closely connected with the Corri family and the development of the Broadwood piano, and Danby (Chron., 1790). From the turn of the century there is Clementi (Chron., 1801), complete with 'fifty fingered lessons, in the major and minor keys mostly in use, by composers of the first rank ancient and modern' (title-page) and a large appendix of complementary pieces. Not wishing to rest on his laurels, in the 11th edition (1826) the author is careful to point out that there is no 'intention of superseding the indispensable aid of a Master', but rather the treatise is offered 'as an assistant to the labours of both Master and Pupil' (p.2). Also 'many lessons are substituted for those, which were found too difficult in the former editions' (ibid.). Hammond (Chron., 1802) set out to be 'more elaborate and explicit in the elementary part, than the generallity [sic] of his predecessors' and was concerned with rendering the lessons 'at once easy and agreeable, for the purpose of blending instruction with delight, and therefore more effectually [sic] promoting the improvement of the pupil' (p.3).

Other popular examples from around this time, as 'the general notion of keyboard playing gave way to the specific technique of *pianoforte* playing',[13] include those by Challoner and P. A. Corri (Chron., 1810), Stevens (Chron., 1811), Goodban (Chron., 1814) and the works of Jousse, Keith and Howell mentioned previously. There are also the various inventions designed to assist the teacher and pupil such as Logier's 'chiroplast' and Hawker's 'hand-moulds'. Hummel (Chron., 1829), a swift translation of the original, follows a little later and, as a pupil of Mozart, promotes his 'cleanness and clarity' and lends intellectual credibility to the 'mechanical' art.[14] Also noteworthy is Fétis and Moscheles (Chron., 1841) and the extraordinary popularity of Hamilton's 'Modern instructions' (Chron., 1849), which reached an incredible 1135th edition, although it did require the use of contributions by Czerny, Beethoven's pupil and teacher of Liszt, in order to sustain market appeal following the author's death.

As far as style and expressive priorities are concerned it is well known that the English pianos offered a fuller and thicker tone compared to the 'perfectly damped, light sound' of the 'Viennese' fortepiano.[15] They were ideally suited to the new levels of virtuosity being forged by the London School and Dussek in particular. The fact that the environment was conducive to these advancements highlights a marked contrast in

---

[13] Komlós (1995), 124.
[14] Ibid., 141. See Kassler (1979), 558–60.
[15] Komlós (1995), 53.

fortunes and circumstances between the piano and other instruments. The issues of legato touch, developed through C. P. E. Bach and Türk, and the use of damper pedals as part of the new aesthetic of a new era placed English theory at odds with German/Viennese conservatism. Clementi, Cramer and Dussek all promoted the new 'legato' approach, although Clementi and Cramer (and later Hummel, Moscheles and Sterndale Bennett) retained a 'classical', retrospective restraint in their playing, in contrast to Dussek's 'grand style',[16] and were all the more successful as a result.[17] It is evident that the popularity of the piano allowed much greater scope for experimentation and innovation on British soil, but that the essential qualities of refinement and 'good taste' were still prerequisites in most cases if amateur emulation, particularly among women, was to have the desired outcomes.

In closing this section it is important to make some comment on the organ in Britain.[18] Earlier discussion highlighted the fact that the organist, as a result of his education, acknowledged 'usefulness' in a variety of respectable institutional contexts (naturally church, university and, later, schools), and guaranteed performance and teaching opportunities and consequently local prominence, enjoyed a relatively secure, structured and high-status existence. It was even possible for complacency to ensue, although opportunities did not necessarily result in an easy life.[19] S. S. Wesley and Henry T. Smart are just two organists who were in receipt of those allusive privileges for the native musician: respectability and social standing.

During the nineteenth century opportunities increased as the church bands were replaced by mechanically improved organs, organists were sought as music teachers, performers and choir trainers in independent secondary schools and universities (professors of music were often organists),[20] and large organs were installed in concert halls as a sign of civic pride and for public performance.[21] There were even a few openings for women organists and choir trainers[22] and small organs, such as the

---

[16] Ibid., 139–40.

[17] It is possible to view the contribution of Hummel, 'Europe's master of pianistic refinement' (Ringer, ed. (1990), 219) as equivalent to that of Spohr for the violin. Their success was not necessarily in the form of popular acclaim but both had a highly durable influence as suitable models for emulation and published important pedagogical texts which were highly influential in their respective English translations.

[18] See Bicknell (1996); Thistlethwaite (1990); Thistlethwaite and Webber, eds (1998); and Hopkins and Rimbault (1855).

[19] See Ehrlich (1985), 95; and Beedell (1992), 54–5.

[20] See Rainbow (1989a), 38; and *idem.* (1981), 29.

[21] See Scholes (1947), 587.

[22] Gillett (2000a), 214.

harmonium, became popular as drawing-room and church instruments. Accordingly we find an increasing number of pedagogical works for a variety of organ types as the period progresses (the name Hamilton again features quite prominently, see Chron., 1842 and 1889).[23] Also a dedicated institution in the form of the College of Organists opened in 1864, although it appears to have been largely an examining rather than teaching body for a significant period.[24]

Wind

The huge expansion in the provision and consumption of instrumental performance in nineteenth-century Britain naturally affected wind and brass instruments. However the trends in this area were somewhat different from those experienced elsewhere in that the involvement of the well-to-do amateur was, with exceptions, limited to a greater extent by the exertion required by the instruments themselves and their limited repertoire and scope for domestic, recreational use. Tuition and teaching material were consumed by (predominantly male) amateurs, but there was a greater professional, public performance bias which, with a lower concentration of foreign competition, placed native wind and brass players in an unusually strong position. Home-grown talent, nurtured through family connections, apprenticeships and learning by practical experience, was able to thrive in some cases and a lineage of expertise developed. For instance the expertise of J. C. Fischer on the oboe provided a talented player like John Parke with an incentive to improve and achieve success in his own right rather than pale into insignificance (Sammartini had a similar influence on Thomas Vincent). However, as mentioned in Chapter 2, it is Fischer's (like Geminiani's) name which appears on the teaching material in the place of a native instrumentalist. The lack of teaching opportunities on such instruments, prior to the scope for specialization offered by increased demand, did deprive many of a valuable source of regular income.

The most momentous changes came as a result of the growth of the popular music movement and associated amateur bands as well as the increase in the number of military and other ensembles. They had a functional, ceremonial role to play as well as a place in more private, insular music-making. Practice and proficiency increased, particularly in

---

[23] See Scholes (1947), 601.
[24] See Rainbow (1981), 39; and Scholes (1947), 609–11. Scholes's chapter XVI, 'Organ building and organ playing' (ibid., 569–614) contains much information of interest.

the provinces, with men, not concerned with notions of gentility, keen to devote time and energy to the learning of these instruments, which in themselves improved with changes in design to facilitate ease of use, projection and homogeneity of sound. The cooperative, uplifting nature of much of this activity fostered an enduring, 'useful' place for music in lower-class communities and military contexts.

Eighteenth-century gentleman wind players had in most cases limited themselves to the German (transverse) flute and various types of flageolet,[25] which, like the violin, they appear to have approached with a great deal of nonchalance. As with the violin, the flute sources of the period demonstrate that most consumers had very basic requirements and were generally content with self-instruction. There were relatively few teachers, success stories like J. Wragg being exceptions.[26] This situation remained largely consistent among the middle classes of the nineteenth century although the oboe (or 'hautboy'), clarinet and bassoon did increase in popularity as opportunities for group performance increased.[27] As with string and keyboard sources the teaching material did improve in comprehensiveness and sophistication. Wind tutors, like those for the violin, finally moved on from the numerous generic 'Prelleur'-, rudiments/airs-format methods of the previous century which repeated inadequate instruction in order to sell easy pieces.[28] Also in a similar vein to the violin there were a few more ambitious early examples, including Wragg (Chron., 1792) and Gunn (Chron, 1793),[29] offering instruction perhaps equivalent to Philpot's approach to the violin. The anonymous *Clarinet instructor* (Chron., 1780) broke with tradition and offered advice on holding the instrument: instructions which 'continued to appear in most other English-language publications as late as 1840'.[30] However, as with the

---

[25] See Waterhouse (1999). On the recorder in England see Lasocki (1982).

[26] Kassler (1985), 143.

[27] Haynes (2001) is an important recent contribution on the early history of the oboe, following on from the much earlier studies of Bate and Baines. He includes important sections on England, tracing the arrival of the new French hautboy (and its players) alongside the traditional shawm, and interesting discussions of pedagogical material from Banister's *The sprightly companion* (1695) onwards, including versions of the section in Prelleur (see pp.177–9).

[28] See Warner (1967), Riley (1958) and the Chronology below. It is interesting to note that as *Nolens volens* (1695) formed the basis of Prelleur's and its derivatives' violin instructions, the part dedicated to the flute, also widely republished, draws on Hotteterre's *Principes ...* (1707, tr. *c*.1729/R1968), the first tutor to include the transverse flute. See Powell, ed. (1996), 5–9, which discusses anonymous as well as 'named' sources from the late eighteenth century.

[29] See Powell, ed. (1996), 8–9.

[30] Lawson (2000), 42.

violin, the market was not at this stage sufficient to demand and support translations of the seminal continental texts of the last half century, such as those by Quantz and Tromlitz. A short extract from Quantz (Chron., 1790), like that from Leopold Mozart (Chron., 1812), was of general rather than specialist interest.

Meanwhile there was, at least until the mid-nineteenth century, a great deal of skilful and enthusiastic activity taking place throughout the country in bands connected to the Anglican church, most commonly made up of strings (violins and cellos) with woodwind (flutes and clarinets) and occasionally brass instruments, as well as various other village and dance bands.[31] The precedents set by these and militia and volunteer bands provided a firm basis for a coherent, ambitious amateur band movement and the successful reform of military music during the second half of the century.[32] The military band provided the model for numerous bands formed in Britain and elsewhere and, through a new-found public-entertainment role, provided a great number of opportunities for both wind and brass instrumentalists.[33] The clarinet, used by Arne as early as 1760, featured prominently in military bands prior to the expansion of the brass family in the 1830s and the transition from reeds to brass, greatly assisted in Britain by the Distin family and successful mechanical innovations (see below). Even so reed instruments continued to be used in (even 'brass') bands, if in reduced numbers, and proficient wind players were in great demand among amateur orchestral societies.[34]

If demand was less extensive where it did exist, even among amateurs, it tended to be at a relatively ambitious level. We find therefore fewer written works than in the case of either the violin or piano but the examples we do have from the nineteenth century are generally of a more definitive nature, often written by major figures of national or even international repute who were active as teachers and performers. However it is significant that, after the innovations of the keyboard, we return to conservatism in terms of the promotion of the instruments themselves and broader expressive priorities and, as mentioned above, the recycling of elementary material.

Taking the clarinet as an example the Albert- (simple-) system instruments, a variant of the 13-keyed design, remained popular in

---

[31] See Russell (1997), 187–8 and Herbert, ed. (2000a), 16–17, 141 and 174. The industrialist Samuel Greg encouraged group performance on wind (and other) instruments among his workforce (Russell (1997), 27).

[32] See Herbert, ed. (2000a), 144–8.

[33] See Ess (1981), 135ff.

[34] Russell (1997), 219 and 242.

Britain 'until the inter-war era' and formed an important part of the teaching of Willman (Chron., 1826) and Lazarus (Chron., 1881).[35] This is in spite of the Boehm system, devised by Klosé and in popular use today, being exhibited in 1843. The Boehm supplanted the Albert only when composers' demands made it essential.[36] Lazarus covers both systems in his treatise (1881), although 'he did not himself change to the Boehm'.[37]

Henry Lazarus is an especially important native figure for us to consider, as he achieved great success as a teacher (professor at Kneller Hall, National Training School of Music (later RCM) and RAM), performer (principal clarinet at Covent Garden) and writer. His approach to the clarinet is in keeping with what we know of British tradition in his striving for 'purity' of sound, in contrast to the rich, vibrato-laden tone of Richard Mühlfield (who inspired Brahms) for example.[38] The treatise itself, part of Lafleur & Son's successful 'Alliance Musicale' series, is an assimilation of earlier methods combined with some of the author's own contributions. In particular he draws on Müller's *Méthode ...* (Paris, *c*.1821), whose improvements to the clarinet had apparently received support from George IV (Chron., 1881: 1). Lazarus stresses the role of the teacher and the need to 'hear the lessons to form some conception of the correct meaning of the text' (p.v). The work's 350 pages are devised as an effective and easy-to-use guide for both teacher and pupil, with progressive practical exercises and a definite emphasis on the practical (p.1). His contribution brings coherence, consistency and comprehensiveness in its approach to technique.

---

[35] Lawson (2000), 7 and 17. There are many valuable insights concerning sources of various kinds and technique in this work and its parent volume, Lawson, ed. (1995). See also Charlton (1988); Halfpenny (1954, 1965 and 1977); Lyle (1977); Rendall (1941–2 and 1954); and Rice (1984).

[36] Lawson (2000), 26. Lawson also reveals that 'bandsmen and amateurs' ensured the longevity of the five- (and six-) keyed clarinet, represented in numerous instruction books, and that English clarinets retained their 'lighter timbre' much longer than elsewhere (p.23), which is reminiscent of the faithfulness of the English to the Stainer-model violin. It is interesting to note that although Klosé's 1843 method dealt with what is now known as the Boehm-system clarinet it did receive English translations (see Chron., 1857, 1874 and 1885), possibly because he was consistent with British critical thinking in believing that 'taste', rather than virtuosity, 'revealed the true artist' (Lawson (2000), 62).

[37] Ibid., 26. Langey, prolific during the late nineteenth and early twentieth centuries, also covers a variety of systems in his wind (and brass and string) tutors ('Tutors' become 'Practical' tutors in their early twentieth-century editions). The comprehensive nature of these works ensured their popularity well into the twentieth century and their use by prominent players such as Michael Collins.

[38] Lawson (2000), 94.

The growth in the number of wind players, through both amateur and military music, was complemented by and benefited from relatively high standards of practical instruction. Traditionally minority-interest instruments received a real boost from the huge expansion in banding of various kinds during the nineteenth century, prompting publications such as Cocks & Co's series of 'Modern tutors' for wind instruments (?1840–?1860). Improved amateur standards were rewarded with professional opportunities. Mann's band at the Crystal Palace featured acclaimed wind players[39] and the millwright William Millington played bassoon in the Hallé Orchestra over a long period,[40] not to mention the achievements of Archie Camden during the early years of the twentieth century and beyond.[41]

Despite the vast majority of music college students being women, only a small number of female flautists and clarinettists emerged, including a few at the RAM during the 1890s. Acceptance beyond the piano, violin and harp was easier to achieve through groups such as Salvation army bands, which provided a fertile (if unwilling) training ground for the secular movement.[42] The unusual male student bias was perhaps partly responsible for the greater (and equally unusual) vocational emphasis in some college wind (and organ) departments.[43]

Brass

The expansion and greater organization of the various band movements discussed above naturally brought about an increasing proliferation of brass instrumentalists and achievement among both amateur and professional players.[44] Considering the origins of much of this activity it is not surprising that, perhaps to an even greater extent than with wind instruments, for brass players tuition and training were a means to an end rather than an end in themselves. The focus was therefore on achieving a high standard of performance and gaining expertise in the

---

[39] See Bashford and Langley, eds (2000), 181 and Humphries (2000), 44.
[40] Russell (1997), 280.
[41] Ehrlich (1985), 47 and 102.
[42] See Gillett (2000a), 29, 193 and 200; Bashford and Langley, eds (2000), 309; Ehrlich (1985), 160–61; and Russell (1997), 212.
[43] Ehrlich (1985), 111.
[44] Herbert and Wallace, eds (1997); Herbert, ed. (2000a); Humphries (2000); Bevan (2000); and Russell (1997) are important recent contributions in this area. See also Baines (1976); and Mackerness (1964). See in particular A. Myers in Herbert, ed. (2000a), 155–86 for an illuminating discussion of the development, qualities and performing techniques of individual brass instruments.

shortest possible time. It was a practical, functional endeavour and, despite the apparent popularity of Arban's cornet treatise (1864),[45] it was founded, like professional instruction, on practical, aural and oral instruction and experience, 'learning by osmosis' through the family and group practice,[46] rather than on a time-consuming literary and largely insular tradition of instruction. Leisurely one-to-one practical instruction and paper qualifications were of limited value to working men and male professional performers.

Given this participatory, public performance bias instrumentalists in bands were often receptive to emerging new technologies, including significant modifications and new instruments, which offered much greater ease of use in terms of their chromaticism, fingering and, later, notation.[47] As with new keyboard technology in the industrial age the innovations extended the range of the instruments and brought ease of performance and maintenance as well as enabling mass production. New developments often enabled greater accessibility and where this mattered, particularly in burgeoning areas of lower-class music-making and middle-class consumerism where music was not the only demand on time, these were eagerly taken up.

In simple terms, during our period we can observe a progression from 'natural', to keyed, to valved instruments: new technology which led to the modification of existing instruments and prompted the creation of new ones. The range of instruments available therefore extended beyond the trombone, trumpet and horn, although cost was inevitably a factor in their purchase and use, particularly for small, provincial bands without the support of an employer or patron. The multiplicity of possibilities ensured that the standardization of the brass band did not occur until the mid-1870s.[48]

The highly significant piston valve system had been in development since the late eighteenth century, but in Britain the use of 'keyed' technology, such as that patented by Joseph Halliday in 1810, continued for a significant period. The keyed bugle (and ophicleide) survived longer in Britain than German-speaking countries, where the valved bugle quickly took hold. Valves were applied in the form of the new *cornet-à-pistons* or 'cornopean' in Britain only from the late 1830s. The cornet signalled the demise of the keyed bugle after 1840 and even more

---

[45] It was presumably the musical content and Arban's approach to the *air varié* rather than textual content which was of the greatest interest to band players (see Herbert and Wallace, eds (1997), 242, and Ehrlich (1985), 83).

[46] Herbert and Wallace, eds (1997), 199; and Russell (1997), 221.

[47] See Carew in Samson, ed. (2002), 257; and Russell (1997), 220.

[48] Russell (1997), 217.

momentous changes came as a result of the widespread adoption of the new saxhorn family of brass instruments ('improved bugles') in the 1850s, following their endorsement by the Distin family from the mid-1840s.[49] Although keyed and valve instruments coexisted in bands for a time (established players were after all keyed instrument players) valve skills quickly supplanted keyed or slide techniques among many of the 'best British brass players'[50] when they eventually became widely available.[51]

Bands therefore took advantage of the new technology when they could. However in areas where accessibility was not such an issue, as demand was limited and/or there was a desire to maintain some level of exclusivity among practitioner or consumer, a persistent faith in the old often remained. This familiar trait resulted in a reluctance to embrace or commit to organological innovation, such as that represented by the valve technology that was so appealing to brass band players. The trumpet and French horn, which were eventually replaced in the bands as the new technology and instruments such as the clavicors and saxhorns established themselves,[52] remained prominent in more 'elite' (even eminent) areas and clung on to old performing traditions.

As with wind instruments there are examples of native figures achieving relative success in the absence of market saturation and foreign dominance, and these individuals did not compromise their best interests by swimming against the tide of 'genteel' conservatism. The English slide trumpet had been promoted (and perhaps invented) by John Hyde in the late eighteenth century. It continued to be used and taught extensively through the nineteenth by the Harpers, father (b. 1786) and son (d. 1898).[53] The Harpers' influence on delaying the acceptance of the valved trumpet in favour of the old 'slide' variety is a particularly interesting example of resisting change in the face of developments elsewhere. Both managed to establish themselves as players of some standing, including both holding the prestigious office

---

[49] Ibid., 217–18. The tours of the Distins and Jullien highlight the importance of these and other travelling bands in bringing music and skills (their musicians often taught local teachers, band leaders and students) to a wide audience. They were an invaluable source of inspiration and model for emulation (see ibid., 229 and Herbert, ed. (2000a), 23–4 and 168ff.). The Distin firm was bought out by Boosey in 1868.

[50] Herbert, ed. (2000a), 27.

[51] However the designs of the valves themselves, perhaps again because of cost implications, did remain fairly retrospective (see Herbert, ed. (2000a), 165–8).

[52] Herbert, ed. (2000a), 157 and 283.

[53] Ibid., 26; and Herbert and Wallace, eds (1997), 95-6. See also Sorensen and Webb (1986).

of 'Sergeant Trumpeter' (trumpeter to the monarch),[54] and their steadfast adherence to the old certainly did not hinder their position.

The situation regarding the French horn is also interesting as the arrival of valves raised the issue of whether they should be adopted by horn players or 'natural' instruments retained with the use of hand stopping. Broadly speaking the Germans took them on board with relish and the French rejected them. The British, ever ambivalent even without divergent opinions on the continent to deal with, saw the merits of both approaches and so were reluctant to commit to the new technology. The 'entire use of valves' was objected to by many well into the twentieth century and the two-valved instrument was preferred for many years.[55] Significantly, it was the military band which was most sympathetic to the horn with valves and made the most of its greater ease of use.[56]

There were a number of prominent foreign horn players who arrived in England during the later nineteenth century, including the Germans Borsdorf and Paersch, who promoted the three-valved instrument. The developments they brought with them did not receive universal approval, as Tom Busby's comments on Borsdorf's new-style ('choked-bore') mouthpiece illustrate. As with the use of valves the gains in terms of ease of use were not seen to compensate for the perceived adverse changes in sound quality.[57]

Native performers on the horn, such as Henry Platt (RAM professor), do appear to have suffered more than other brass instrumentalists from foreign competition and a consequent lack of teaching and performing opportunities.[58] Amateur avenues dried up as new instruments were introduced in the brass band and so proficient players were faced with either the military route or a difficult freelance existence, without the esteem and security offered (albeit very few) trumpeters.

It is apparent that new instruments were eagerly consumed in areas of new practical activity whereas developments affecting existing instruments in familiar contexts, where a choice had to be made, were most often either rejected in favour of the 'tried and tested' or forged a 'middle path', a compromise of some kind. It is important to remember that the traditional instrumental groups had established certain roles in 'genteel' areas and had come to represent widely accepted qualities

---

[54] Herbert, ed. (2000a), 14 and 22.
[55] Humphries (2000), 3, 22, 33–4, 39 and 49.
[56] Ibid., 22.
[57] Ibid., 44 and 49. The result of these trends is still in evidence as 'English players have arrived at a compromise with a tone which is lighter than the German and less strident than the French' (ibid., 69).
[58] Ibid., 22–4.

which audiences (and players) were reluctant to forsake. Given the nature of the pedagogical material during the period already discussed, it was not difficult for these 'qualities' to be reinforced among both professionals and the literate classes.

For the reasons explained above, brass instruments did not inspire a great deal of published teaching material in Britain, far fewer examples than for string or keyboard instruments.[59] Also, in keeping with even lower levels of 'genteel' (particularly female) amateur demand and low expectations among authors, there appear to be fewer than for wind instruments, although there is a similar reliance on a few choice examples rather than a plethora of sources at all levels. In this climate it is natural that study material for euphonium and tuba should be 'a bass clef version of method books for other instruments'.[60] Naturally, written instruction was of most interest to those who stood outside the working-class 'popular' banding movement, principally male amateurs and professionals, and so the texts, like the instruments themselves, are generally conservative and retrospective: old methods certainly die hard.

From the eighteenth century there is a tutor for French horn attributed to Winch (c.1746), who like Geminiani and Fischer offered some kudos through his association with Handel's operas and oratorios.[61] There is little help with the specifics of technique, despite one or two 'pragmatic' comments,[62] and the horn is portrayed primarily in its original context as an outdoor instrument. The familiar rudiments/airs format is in evidence and appeared in other derived publications from the 1750s (horn duos were particularly popular in these and other collections).[63] A closely related work, the anonymous *New instructions* (Chron., 1780), is critical of Punto's promotion of the technique of hand stopping in England during the preceding decade. Burney was in agreement but this is another case of conservatism in print intended for a specific audience while others in the musical world (such as Hawkins) were eager to embrace the new.[64]

A treatise on the slide trumpet and bugle horn by Hyde appeared later in the century (Chron., 1798). The longevity of the key-based technology, prior to the arrival of the saxhorns, is illustrated by Charles Tully's tutor for keyed bugle (Chron., 1831, part of the R. Cock's & Co's

---

[59] See Herbert, ed. (2000a), 299–300.
[60] Herbert and Wallace, eds (1997), 195.
[61] See Humphries (2000), 51ff, for insightful discussions of individual tutors and their contents, including the far more comprehensive continental (particularly French) examples.
[62] Humphries (2000), 64.
[63] See ibid., 14.
[64] Ibid., 12–13.

Series referred to above) and works such as *The cornopean companion of scales* (1836).

The Harpers' (principally slide) trumpet tutors (Chron., 1835 and 1875), the Cocks & Co Series, numerous examples by Kappey and Langey and several other tutors for cornet and bugle are among the most important examples from the 1800s. The sixty-eight pages of Harper senior's tutor have an authoritative quality, not least because of the author's teaching position at the RAM (he was himself a pupil of Eley) and performances as first trumpet at the King's Theatre and Philharmonic concerts, for example. Harper and his son were able to achieve eminence in a small market and benefited as trumpeters from a regulatory system of licensing, which operated as a rare system of quality control in the instrumental sphere.[65] Like the clarinettist Henry Lazarus they enjoyed respect and acclaim among performers and middle-class audiences.

Tully's horn tutor (Chron., 1840) is perhaps a unique native example and it is significant that he continues to endorse the late eighteenth-century 'master crook and coupler system' for the hand horn.[66] The *Grand method for the French horn, by Meifred, Gallay and Dauprat* (Chron., 1880, published by Lafleur), a compendium of seminal foreign methods in translation, brings together exponents of both hand and valve technique but, typically, emerges as 'hostile to valves'.[67]

Considering the strong critical consensus governing the selection of British pedagogical material in general and even the common origin of much it, we should not be surprised that the language of musical style is largely consistent in these sources with what we have found elsewhere. From the combination of the *messa di voce* with vibrato, to the 'restrained' use of ornamentation, to the accelerating trill, to the rejection of tapping the feet while playing, 'good taste' is always the arbiter.[68]

Instrumentalists trained in the brass-band tradition offered 'reservoirs' of skill and technique.[69] The flexible but coherent systems of training, created with high standards in mind, allowed for the introduction of expertise from outside, especially in the form of trainers for top contesting and even beginners' bands.[70] Increasingly prominence could also be achieved by the band members themselves as soloists and

---

[65] Herbert, ed. (2000a), 14.
[66] Humphries (2000), 28.
[67] Ibid., 22 and 39.
[68] Ibid., 71–6.
[69] Russell (1997), 221.
[70] See Russell (1997), 222–3.

trainers. Some entered (and continue to enter) first-class orchestras and teaching institutions, where their unique range of skills, honed through the demands of the 'test' piece and competition movement in general, was increasingly demanded by the new repertoire. One of the first areas to display this trend was, unsurprisingly, Manchester, where the Hallé Orchestra and RMCM provided opportunities for bandsmen.[71] Far removed from the parental ambivalence or even the hostility we have seen in some other areas, there was enormous (even 'excessive') parental interest in banding circles.[72] Effective and authoritative instruction was also offered by the likes of the Harpers at the RAM and the ophicleidist Samuel Hughes at Kneller Hall and the Guildhall.

It is of course no accident that the achievements of native brass instrumentalists during the nineteenth century outshine any others in terms of their unification of quantity and quality. They were able to take advantage of a captive and receptive audience in industrial areas. Also the virtual absence, through both practical and social constraints, of a role for brass instruments in 'genteel' amusement (allowing for middle-class endorsement and enforced conservatism on behalf of their social inferiors), allowed an effective, separate tradition to emerge, free of most (if not all) of the preoccupations and prejudices which held the others back. The majority of brass instrumentalists gained a great deal from their distance from the conventions of polite society and the increased scope for men within working-class communities to raise their status and improve their quality of life through music.

Plucked Strings and Miscellaneous

New markets opened up as the depth and breadth of the musically active population increased, providing opportunities for minority and even new instruments. Some, such as the harp and guitar, had an established position in the education of the young lady,[73] requiring, like the keyboard, a passive, seated position; others, such as the concertina, reflected closely the demands, technology and entrepreneurial spirit of the time.

As the lute declined in popularity in England following the Restoration there was a rise in interest in the guitar. The respected position of the plucked string instrument among high society remained

---

[71] See Bashford and Langley, eds (2000), 241.
[72] Ibid.
[73] It appears that importance of the guitar and harp in 'cultured' circles was not confined to Britain during this period (see Ringer, ed. (1990), 241).

intact and the 'English guitar' (a form of cittern with six courses of double metal strings and the bottom two single) enjoyed enormous popularity during the second half of the eighteenth century in England, prompting a sizeable market for written tutors and instruction (see Chronology).[74] There are a fair number of anonymous rudiments/airs-format works from the late eighteenth century as well as a few more ambitious examples, although most of these from the early nineteenth century (and particularly from the 1820s onwards) concern themselves with the increasingly popular six-string Spanish guitar and a range of (principally amateur) demands.[75] It is apparent, if Dora in Dickens's *David Copperfield* is anything to go by, that the greater accessibility of the guitar compared to the piano encouraged a great deal of superficial activity and led it to be associated with images of ineptitude.[76]

The harp, long a potent symbol of Celtic traditions, was also a useful musical outlet for women, offering respectability and even some professional opportunities without the worries of great male or imported competition.[77] The Frenchman Nicholas C. Bochsa was the notable exception in both respects: an eminent professor of harp at the RAM but of dubious character to say the least.[78] Standards of harp playing must have been relatively high at the RAM given Bochsa's close involvement. There were also a number of important treatises published, including examples by Bochsa himself (Chron., 1817) and an important work by the famous maker Erard (Chron., 1821). Turning to Dickens once more, Rosa Dartle in *David Copperfield* was able to use performing on the harp as a rare means of self-expression.[79]

Towards the end of the nineteenth century, although the market for solo harp and guitar music remained buoyant, the popularity of plucked strings in general (including also the mandolin, zither and banjo) declined in line with the rise of their bowed relatives. Mechanical and technical advancements made the harp less accessible to the amateur. It demanded greater expense and dedication than most practitioners were willing to commit to.[80]

Another important instrument in nineteenth-century Britain was the concertina.[81] It is particularly deserving of comment here as its appeal

---

[74] Spring (2001), 414–16. See also Tyler (1980) and Turnbull (1974).
[75] These include Bennett's 'pasticcio' method (Chron., 1828), Pelzer (Chron., 1830) and Bruni (Chron., 1834).
[76] See Burgan (1989), 54.
[77] See Fiske and Johnstone, eds (1990), 6–7.
[78] Ehrlich (1985), 82; and Bashford and Langley, eds (2000), 66ff.
[79] Burgan (1989), 56–7.
[80] Gillett (2000a), 3–4 and 206–7.
[81] Atlas (1996 and 1999) provides a great deal of information on the concertina, its

was across a broad range of society, although naturally division persisted and can be seen through the different types of instrument which appealed to the different classes. From the mid-1830s to the 1870s the 'English' concertina achieved great popularity among the social elite who attended concerts and small-scale recitals featuring virtuosos such as Giulio Regondi and Richard Blagrove (also a successful violist and brother of the violinist Henry Gamble Blagrove) and the performance of 'art' music such as Molique's two concertos. These well-to-do audiences also took it up themselves as a drawing-room instrument.[82] In addition there were concertina bands and a 'duet' concertina for the musically ambitious. Later in the century the English concertina, like the piano, 'joined its fellow concertinas in more "popular" milieux'.[83] The concertina had an important role to play in 'underground' vernacular music-making, particularly so as the brass band had had little choice but to take the middle-class agenda on board.[84] Prior to the 'descent' of the English concertina the Anglo (Anglo-German) version had been the preserve of 'ear-players'.[85]

Percussion instruments had a primarily functional role as part of band (although not competitive) and orchestral performance, therefore making use of professional and band training methods and generating little published material for the amateur. Their use therefore is most often covered in guides to the military band and similar works such as Potter (Chron., 1817 and 1886), in which the concentration is on the bass drum, side drum and cymbal, the most prominent instruments in these contexts.[86] Other dedicated works did appear later in the century, offering instruction on the drum in particular. The increasing use of and demands on percussion in orchestral repertoire necessitated mechanical innovations including rival designs for quickly retunable timpani.[87]

Regarding the limited amateur and recreational usage of percussion instruments it is interesting to note the popularity of the tambourine among ladies towards the end of the eighteenth century and into the nineteenth,[88] resulting in a number of tutors (including Dale, Chron.,

---

development, practice, repertoire and reception, including valuable insights into the purchasers of the different types of instrument and Wheatstone's important role. See also Russell (1997), 178, 180, 186 and 239.

[82] Atlas (1999), 241–2 and 251. Some sophisticated teaching material was published in accordance with this demand (see Chronology).

[83] Ibid., 242.

[84] See Herbert, ed. (2000a), 149–50.

[85] Ibid.

[86] Ibid., 172 and 184.

[87] Ringer, ed. (1990), 229.

[88] Kidd (1968), 39.

1800 and Anon., Chron., 1813). Some pianos associated with the Cori and Dussek firm even came with an in-built tambourine and/or triangle.[89]

There are a huge number of musical instruments, including some weird and wonderful inventions, which constitute the musical fabric of a consumer-led, entrepreneurial industrial Britain during the nineteenth century. There is not space here to discuss the melodeon, mouth organ, musical glasses, handbells, ocarina or curiosities such as the Aeolina (a form of harmonica), or Symphonion (a form of flute or flageolet). However, mention should be made before closing this section of the group of written works touched on above concerned with instrumentation, orchestration and arranging, which can offer valuable insights into musical practices beyond individual instruments as well as useful information on percussion and the less mainstream examples. A number of nineteenth-century writers built on the eighteenth-century legacy of Prelleur, Tansur, Gehot, Bertini and others who published works in English which covered a range of instruments with varying degrees of comprehensiveness. In addition to various series of articles in periodical publications, including those by Potter in the *Musical World*, we find increasing numbers of examples by respected native figures such as Hamilton (Chron., 1844), Prout (Chron., 1878 and 1898) and Corder (Chron., 1896), as well as translations of important texts by Berlioz (Chron., 1856) and Widor (1906).

---

[89] P. W. Jones, R. E. Cowgill *et al.*, 'Corri', *Grove 7*, vol.6, 501.

CHAPTER FIVE

Institutions

Reference has been made to the institutional training of musicians throughout this study; here the intention is to pull some of those strands together.[1] The appeal of organizing musical instruction under the auspices of an 'umbrella' body of some kind, itself an endorsement and promotion of the subject, is evident in a number of (often unsuccessful) initiatives from the second half of the eighteenth century onwards.[2] Significantly these increased during the second half of the nineteenth century and received support from more than a few forward-thinking and opportunistic individuals as the value of music, to the individual and society, was more widely recognized. As a result many more initiatives were put in place, although their success and contribution to the good of British music naturally remained dependent on the aspirations of the consumer and expectations of the provider. The circumstances surrounding the various forms of institutional training on offer are fundamental to the different levels of success we have observed among various groups of amateurs and professionals.

Whether or not native attempts to emulate evidently effective foreign methods of instruction achieved their aims depended to a large extent on the priorities and incentives behind their actions. The existence of successful institutional training is an intrinsic part of encouraging, through high professional standards and well-informed amateur appreciation, a widespread belief in the inherent worth of a subject. Inevitably moral and social considerations provided the main impetus behind many plans, but naturally little could be achieved in musical terms unless the musical skills themselves were viewed as sufficiently important to warrant effective and relevant instruction methods. Unsurprisingly success came where the identification and nurturing of

---

[1] There is no intention of reiterating the contents of generally accessible and reliable secondary material on this subject although naturally these will be referred to during the course of this chapter. The propensity of individual institutions to write their own histories or of individuals to research distinct collections of archive material has resulted in this area of British music education being covered to a greater extent than most. However, many stones remain unturned.

[2] For our purposes institutional training refers to organized instruction given to many by an individual or organization. It does not necessarily involve a specific location or building, although this is obviously true in some, perhaps more 'official', cases.

genuine potential, rather than leaving it to chance or ability to pay, and the promotion of positive attitudes, among students and the public, were high on the agenda. Unfortunately this was an unlikely prospect in many parts of a consumer-led, status-conscious British society. In addition the precarious circumstances of the musician were often not conducive to the nurturing of high levels of musicianship in traditional areas of professional activity. Given a general lack of ambition or incentive among the profession for much of the period, superficiality in the music-making of the middle and upper classes, complemented by higher levels of appreciation, offered for many the best prospect of short-term rewards. The 'lack of judicious cultivation of professional musicians by regular courses of discipline and study' had severe long-term ramifications.[3]

Prior to *c.*1850

The long-standing involvement of the church in music education diminished further after the Restoration with the decline in church music careers, although it naturally maintained an interest in the training of singers and organists. Through the late eighteenth and early nineteenth centuries attempts were made to move organized musical instruction into the secular sphere, in specialist music schools and elsewhere, but these were slow to gain acceptance and support in the face of continued ambivalence and the fears and disunity of the profession.

Conservatoires

As we have seen, the rich and powerful had little concern for the musical ability of their countrymen when they could 'buy in' the best foreign musicians for their own entertainment. The fierce competition for English musical patronage between musicians from Italy, Germany, France and other European countries left the large number of native musicians at the bottom of the pile with no means or incentive to compete.[4] The foreign visitors were in the vast majority of cases better skilled and better educated generally as a result of being much more highly trained and the products of the more supportive European courts and established successful pedagogical traditions, often created in

---

[3] See details of G. F. Graham's proposal to establish a music school in Edinburgh in Kassler (1979), 402–4.

[4] See Rohr (1983), 25 and 62.

emulation of the Italian *conservatorio* found in Naples and elsewhere.[5] They were able to move to the elite levels of the secular branch of the profession with greater ease than native musicians and so enjoy much greater support from aristocratic patrons. Consequently the numerous (unsuccessful) plans for an English conservatoire during the period and various other attempts at reform by musicians themselves were, in the interests of survival, motivated by a desire to infiltrate this market and reduce the prominence of foreign musicians.[6] In this context the development of professional standards of musical ability came second to other (albeit important and relevant) concerns, particularly the need for a liberal education to eradicate the perception of the native musician as the ignorant 'mere fiddler' with next to no general education.[7] Given that their interests were not considered by many outside of the profession, the failure of musicians to focus on and establish strategies that would ensure higher standards of training in purely musical skills was ultimately disastrous. This emphasis on non-musical instruction continued even with the establishment of the RAM.

There is not space here to go into the various unsuccessful plans for specialist institutions for the training of musicians in Britain prior to the RAM; besides, these are covered in varying degrees of detail by Kassler, Ehrlich, Ringer and Rainbow among others.[8] The essential point to be made is that they could not get off the ground and all came to nothing, through a general lack of public support, moral and financial, and lack of professional clout or inclination. Only when this climate had changed to a great extent could significant changes be made. The RAM was in many ways a false dawn in its time. Its amateur, aristocratic patronage turned out to be a heavy price to pay. Significantly it had succeeded over the 'professional' plans associated with the Philharmonic Society which had looked to the training and qualification standards created by the successful Royal Academy of Art and been supported by Bacon and the *QMMR*. The social and cultural climate of the time had ensured a victory for amateurism and a constitution which looked more closely at the marketing of native success than at the means of achieving it. This did not serve the profession or British music well.[9] Despite signs that

---

[5] See Arnold (1965), 77.

[6] See McVeigh (1989a), 179–80, and (1993), 183; and Rohr (1983), 163.

[7] See Rohr (1983), 166–7 and 373.

[8] In particular Kassler (1972) and entries under Bacon, Bentham, Ayrton, Burney, Defoe, G. F. Graham, Horncastle, Kemp, Livius, Potter, Relfe and Walmisley in *idem* (1979). See also Rainbow (1981), 35; Ehrlich (1985), 9–11 and 238; and Ringer, ed. (1990), 33, 175 and 213.

[9] Langley in Bashford and Langley, eds (2000) offers important new insights into the origins of the RAM.

attitudes in Britain towards music education were beginning to change (see Chapter 1), the legacy of the upper classes, their nonchalance and preference for foreign musicians, would, even after their influence diminished, take well over a century to reverse. Corder's references to the RAM's 'honest battering against the stone wall of indifference'[10] and its continued struggle to gain widespread support exemplify the long-term difficulties experienced by native musicians.

The situation in France was very different. In the wake of the Revolution in 1789 the role of the Paris Conservatoire in music education became fundamental. As Gessele has stated, the 'Conservatoire's enduring legacy was the centralization of musical training in Paris and the standardization of teaching methods in France', with the emphasis 'on its pedagogical programme, rather than on a national programme of music education'.[11] The creation of the Conservatoire was largely inspired by the feeling that a musical nationalism needed to be enforced, and as a result foreign musicians actively discouraged. The French government supported its belief in the value of music, including its ceremonial and political uses, with a significant financial commitment. The Conservatoire was founded on the basis of providing free (or almost free) tuition in music for *all* gifted pupils, regardless of rank or social position. Many eminent professors from the former Ecole Royale de Chant (founded in 1784) joined the staff, and the student to teacher ratio at the opening in 1796 was a remarkable 3 to 1 (351 to 115).[12]

In keeping with nationalistic feeling and the desire to standardize, the teaching was based firmly on texts across a wide range of instruments written by distinguished professors employed by the institution and published and edited by the Conservatoire's own publishing firm. These became seminal works across Europe (including in Britain in cases where demand was sufficiently advanced) for much of the nineteenth century. In the case of the violin we have the *Méthode* of Baillot, Rode and Kreutzer (1803), and later Baillot's *L'art* (1835), both of which played an important part in reaffirming the dominant position of the French violin school on the continent and in codifying its technical innovations during the period. In addition the études and caprices by Rode and Kreutzer became part of the course of study at the Conservatoire, and only Viotti's concertos were used in the violin competitions.[13]

---

[10] Corder (1922a), 101.
[11] Gessele (1992), 191.
[12] Humphries (2000), 18.
[13] This was the case 'until 1853 (with one exception in 1845)' (Stowell (1998), 12).

The provision in France of an organized and centralized system of public instruction,[14] and more specifically a 'systematic method for the technical training of violinists',[15] is in marked contrast to the British approach to instrumental pedagogy. It is undoubtedly a significant factor in the disparity in achievement between the two countries. Jousse observes that the establishment of the Paris Conservatoire brought the violin in France 'to a degree of perfection unknown before' (Chron., 1811: xiii), and the value and success of the French system became widely acknowledged.[16] Its influence and the need for state intervention in education is reflected in the thinking of some native intellectuals of the period, including Adam Smith, Thomas Paine and, as mentioned earlier, William Wordsworth.[17] Unfortunately a comprehensive and integrated system was not to be provided by government until towards the end of the nineteenth century, enforced by the education acts of Forster (1870) and Balfour (1902). Nevertheless the need for a central teaching institution for music in England had long been acknowledged and the RAM was founded in 1822 and opened in 1823 with 'the object of promoting the cultivation of music among the natives of this country'.[18]

Unfortunately the basis for its foundation was in complete contrast to the highly successful Parisian model, which had been widely emulated as a result of Napoleon's conquests. The directors of the institution (including its founder, the amateur violinist and composer Lord Burghersh, later Eleventh Earl of Westmorland) formed an aristocratic oligarchy, which planned, funded and initially managed the institution. In complete control of the RAM, the aristocrats (and the controversial Bochsa, the sole professional musician) endeavoured to use it to form their model of a musician. As referred to above, the common contemporary view of the musician was symbolized by the ignorant 'fiddler' with very little non-musical education. Accordingly the provision of a liberal education became a priority, to the detriment of professional training and in complete contrast to Paris.[19] The

---

[14] Barnard (1969) provides valuable insights into the formation and nature of the French system, including the prominent position of music and the Paris Conservatoire (in particular pp.162–3 and 207).

[15] David (1889), 295.

[16] See review of Rode *et al.* in *QMMR*, 6 (1824), 527–31.

[17] See Barnard (1969), 230–37.

[18] Hogarth (1838), vol.2, 269.

[19] The 'Original rules and regulations' of the RAM state that the 'first object in the education of the students will consist in a strict attention to their religious and moral instruction', followed by 'the study of their own and the Italian language, writing, and arithmetic', and then 'their general instruction in the various branches of music,

preoccupation with social rather than professional aspirations among (and on behalf of) potential musicians during this period hindered the construction of a self-regulating professional hierarchy, which was necessary to ensure a widespread and sustained improvement in standards. The desire to enable native musicians 'to enter into competition with, and rival the natives of other countries' had been the main 'Object of the Institution',[20] but this emphasis on securing employment and publicity for native over foreign musicians was over-ambitious in the absence of an effective professional framework to regulate individual advancement. Also there was an understandable reluctance to get involved in such an institution among existing professional musicians, who had market control in mind rather than the encouragement of competition. For them the Philharmonic Society was a more appealing cause.

The RAM's financial circumstances were extremely precarious and the first principal, Crotch, offered genial but undynamic leadership.[21] The importance of such an institution for musicians and the country as a whole is noted in some contemporary writings,[22] but, as continually stressed by Cazalet and in contrast to the Academy of Arts,[23] government support was lacking. Also further private funding (in the form of subscriptions and donations) failed to emerge. The years of neglect and consequent low standards among native instrumentalists were, despite signs of improvement, deeply ingrained in the minds of the public at large at this stage, and there was reluctance to support such a project both financially and morally.[24]

The original good intentions, to provide greater accessibility to affordable instruction for as many native musicians as possible, were inevitably at the mercy of financial considerations, and a lack of funds dominated the early history of the RAM. Attendance fees were raised and consequently entry was denied to some of the most deserving from

---

particularly in the art of singing, and in the study of the pianoforte and organ, of harmony, and of composition' (Cazalet (1854), 336).

[20] Ibid., 329.

[21] It says a great deal about the state of music education in Britain at the time, and to what end most of it was directed, that the self-taught Crotch acquired the Chair of music at Oxford at 21 and became the first principal of the RAM. Although no doubt an extremely able and precocious individual, the contrast with the affiliation of Cherubini at Paris and Mendelssohn at Leipzig are all too revealing. The relative status of the individuals concerned says much about the importance of the institutions themselves within the cultural community of the respective cities and countries.

[22] For example Anon., 'Sketch of the state of music in London', *QMMR*, 5 (1823), 266.

[23] Cazalet (1854), 167 and 174.

[24] See ibid., 119–20.

families of poor to moderate income.²⁵ Also more advanced pupils were admitted for free, in return for donating any profits from engagements to the Academy.²⁶ In fact, in contradiction of the original intentions, the high fees were justified as a means of attracting the most deserving students,²⁷ although the committee of management no doubt also had the potential social and professional contacts in mind rather than raw talent. As highlighted by Fétis, the inability of the Academy to provide free or even cheap tuition stifled its potential effectiveness and allowed the general neglect of the music profession in England to continue.²⁸ Even by 1874 the sums allocated by government for professional training were only £500 to the RAM and £250 to the Irish Academy.²⁹

It is not surprising, considering the importance given to non-musical education and the lack of funding, that musical training at the Academy was extremely limited.³⁰ In contrast to Paris there was relatively little time for instrumental lessons, students often practised in the same room simultaneously and each professor instructed 'according to his own system'.³¹ There is little information on the actual teaching methods employed at the RAM during the nineteenth century.³² What does exist suggests a very meagre provision for the violin in particular, which was taught only to boys at this stage.³³ The difficult circumstances seldom

---

25 Ibid., 119–20 and 232.
26 Ibid., 170. Significantly the 'Original rules and regulations' specify that 'the children of professors in music, when properly certified to be so by the subscriber proposing them, shall be admitted at half the first subscription' (ibid., 338–9).
27 Ibid., 181.
28 Ibid., 239.
29 Ehrlich (1985), 70. See also Rink in Samson, ed. (2002), 82–4, on the RAM's financial difficulties compared to Paris and Leipzig.
30 Ehrlich (1985: 79ff.) provides a useful discussion of the inadequacies of the RAM as a teaching institution. Rohr (1983: 167–76), who perhaps looks upon the early years of the institution more favourably than other commentators have done, provides important details of the course structure.
31 Cazalet (1854), 91 and 342.
32 Save for the histories of Cazalet (1854) and Corder (1922), the only other records of teaching practices are RAM prospectuses and syllabuses (which reveal details of professorial staff and other teaching appointments, scholarships and internal and external examinations), and the treatises contained in the Academy library. Unfortunately, as is so often the case in this area, it is impossible to say with any certainty what material was used when and by whom. However it is possible to construct a picture through the sources present in the library and the background of and the influences on the main figures connected with the institution.
33 Cazalet (1854), 56. Although he doubts its accuracy Corder (1922) reproduces a weekly (Mon.–Sat.) timetable for the boys, which in total includes five one-hour slots and two half-hour slots for violin tuition (pp.10–12).

attracted the best teaching staff,[34] and the system of 'mutual instruction', in which senior and advanced students were appointed as teachers or 'sub-professors', provided a convenient and cheap but inevitably inferior alternative. This system became increasingly prevalent as the financial difficulties continued.[35] In 1855 the professors 'were mostly paid 3s. 6d. per hour, but a few stood out for 5s and got it', whereas the 'sub-professors, who did much spade-work, were not paid at all'.[36]

The lack of a coherent, professional approach to teaching at the RAM and in the country as a whole prompted Fétis in 1829 to note that 'musical science in England ... is still in its infancy'. This comment is part of an important letter to his son.[37] Extracts are reprinted by Cazalet (1854: 230–39), and these (along with the sections from the original not included) reveal some of the shortcomings of British (and specifically) English music education in relation to the continent.[38] Allowing for the Belgian's allegiances to the Paris Conservatoire the less than flattering picture of the new institution that he paints is significant and in keeping with the views of some outspoken native figures such as Bacon.[39] He appears to regret that the opportunity was not being taken to rectify a situation that had been allowed to exist for far too long, leaving much native talent unfulfilled and untapped. The plight of the violin is highlighted in this regard. Fétis, in a section omitted from the Cazalet transcription, is particularly damning of the technically inferior RAM violin professors (Mori, Spagnoletti, Oury and F. Cramer), although Oury is praised for his appreciation of foreign styles.

Although Spohr was not on the staff of the RAM, he was, as a prominent disciple of the acclaimed French school, ideally suited to fill this void and influence violin playing in Britain to an extent that Viotti never managed. Given that the professors at the RAM decided their own

---

[34] Cazalet (1854), 97. Large numbers of 'professors' did not necessarily equate with high levels of instruction and dedication (see Ehrlich (1985), 92). A notable exception in the case of the violin is the Frenchman Prosper Sainton (see Chapter 3). Some of the other relatively high-status areas of study, such as the keyboard, harp and composition, appear to have fared a little better in terms of the teaching staff available. See Ehrlich (1985), 35 and 82–3.

[35] Cazalet (1854), 148 and 152.

[36] Corder (1922a), 63.

[37] Dated 21 May 1829, the letter later appeared in the *Revue Musicale*, 5 (1829), 409–17.

[38] The extracts in Cazalet and the omitted sections are quoted in Golby (1999b), vol.2, 219–20. Corder also refers to the letter and Fétis's views, which 'when afterwards published, caused much indignation amongst English musicians, who characterised them as superficial, illiberal, and even untruthful'. 'From this', he adds, 'we may guess that the learned writer told some unpleasant truths' (1922: 38).

[39] See the discussion of Bacon's various 'Vetus', *QMMR* articles in Kassler (1979).

system for teaching, it is significant that the library of the RAM contains more copies of Louis Spohr's violin treatise in its various editions than any other example from the nineteenth century. The details of this work and its importance in Britain have been discussed elsewhere in this study, but its strong association with the RAM, the only institution devoted specifically to the training of instrumentalists at this time, is of obvious importance. The management committee of the RAM, under the presidency of Lord Burghersh, became patrons of the Bishop edition (Chron., 1843) when it was published, and placed a copy in the library of the Academy. A letter to this effect from the secretary of the RAM to the publishers is reproduced in Dubourg (1878, *Appendix* pp.3–4). In addition to the Bishop edition, there are three copies of the version edited and revised by Henry Holmes (Chron., 1878) in the library.[40] It is likely that Henry Blagrove would have adopted Spohr's method and used it to teach at the RAM, and Henry Holmes probably used his own version as violin professor at the newly founded RCM from 1883. Also regarding Spohr's continued influence on standards of native violin performance, the whole of his Seventh, Eighth and Eleventh Violin Concertos featured in the syllabuses for the Metropolitan Examinations (for the LRAM diploma) between December 1894 and January 1901.

In light of the problems discussed above, it is not surprising that the RAM did not succeed in enabling native musicians to replace foreign talent, and the frequently superior foreigners continued to visit or emigrate to London throughout the 1830s and 1840s.[41] However along with the Society of British Musicians (established in 1834),[42] it did promote higher standards and provide professional opportunities for some native musicians. Compared with private lessons or apprenticeships, students had much greater contact with their peers and professional musicians and benefited from the status, respectability and patronage connections associated with the College. Consequently the best RAM graduates enjoyed relatively rapid success and became prominent in various areas of British musical life. They were therefore able to appear alongside, if not enjoy equal status with, prominent foreign figures.

The Academy provided opportunities for native teachers, and the London-born Nicholas Mori, taught by Barthélemon and Viotti and influenced by Spohr, was appointed the first violin professor there.

---

[40] The library also contains another copy of the Bishop edition and one of the version by Rudolphus (Chron., 1833).

[41] Moser (1966–7, vol.2, 154) observes the continued importance of foreign violinists after the founding of the RAM.

[42] See Hogarth (1838), vol.2, 270–1.

J. D. Loder, the first Englishman to lead the orchestra at the Philharmonic Society of London (from 1817), became a professor in 1840.[43] As far as students are concerned Henry Blagrove, in Ehrlich's words 'one of the few nineteenth-century British violinists to achieve more than a modest competence',[44] was one of the first to be admitted to the RAM in 1823. He was taught by F. Cramer, having already received tuition from Spagnoletti. Blagrove acted as a 'sub-professor' at the Academy after he had 'been given up by Mr. Cramer as an advanced pupil'[45] and then became a professor in 1831, writing studies and other teaching material[46] and performing widely as a leader and chamber musician.

As reflected by the relatively lengthy autobiography included in Cazalet (1854: 285–6) Blagrove is one of the few violinists 'among the trophies of the Academy'.[47] However the influences he received from outside the RAM were no doubt equally (if not more) significant and instrumental in his success. His father (R. M. Blagrove) had been a prominent violin teacher and writer on the instrument in Nottingham (see Chron., 1827) and his uncle also contributed to the literature of the instrument (Chron., 1850). Moreover following his 'noviciate at the Academy' Blagrove studied with Spohr in Germany and subsequently 'exhibited delightful traces' of the 'purity and refinement' of his style.[48] With reference to the tuition Blagrove received John Bishop comments: 'Here, again, we have an admission that the renowned Spohr was *the* master of another clever Royal Academy student.'[49] This observation reveals a great deal about the extent of Spohr's influence among native violinists as well as the ineffectiveness of the violin teaching at the RAM. In a similar vein Dubourg also highlights the case of Mawkes (of whom little is known), 'a performer of very great promise, who had the benefit of aid from the master-hand of Spohr' before disappearing from the public eye.[50] In addition to the direct influence of Spohr's teaching and his violin treatise, his musical qualities were generally appreciated by students at the Academy. They were, according to Brown (1980: 37),

---

[43] Two copies (one hardback and one paperback) of Carrodus's edition of Loder's treatise (Chron., 1884) are still housed in the RAM library.
[44] Ehrlich (1985), 85.
[45] Cazalet (1854), 286.
[46] This includes *Viola, violin and violoncello class music* Book 1 (London, [1853]).
[47] Dubourg (1878), 231.
[48] Ibid.
[49] Ibid. This edition of Dubourg is edited by Bishop.
[50] Ibid., 230. Dubourg also refers to C. A. Seymour (p.231), another relatively successful violinist from the RAM whose biography is contained in Cazalet (1854: 315–16).

exposed to his works within two years of its foundation and also performed them in public.[51]

Dubourg's general comments on the conservatoire system view it as a means of achieving uniformity of style and consistency of standard, as achieved in Paris.[52] With students of the RAM such as Blagrove becoming professors at the same institution there appears a tradition of native musicians and a line of descent that suggests the formation of a local English 'school'. For all its failings and limitations the RAM facilitated this advancement, even though the skills of many of the most prominent and successful students appear to have been formed by figures from outside the institution.

During the first half of the nineteenth century the RAM was generally unable to provide the stable and supportive teaching environment and systematic approach to pedagogy that was essential if standards were to improve on a large scale, and RAM-trained natives were indeed going to displace foreign musicians.[53] In this sense the existence of the institution at this stage was more symbolic than revolutionary for instrumental teaching and 'the imperfect means of education' which Britain had 'furnished to musical students'[54] persisted. The influence of the aristocracy was evident well into the second half of the nineteenth century and the RAM continued to suffer from the non-professional bias in its constitution and administration.

In the absence of a cohesive approach general musical education throughout the country for most of the nineteenth century remained, as Beedell has discussed, 'limited to small pockets of activity' and dependent on 'individual enthusiasts', who focused on 'music as a form of social work rather than for its own sake'.[55] In this environment the RAM was able to become a 'preserve of mediocrity', a teachers' training school, with the 'habits of self-satisfaction' taking the place 'of that ardour which is so necessary to excellence'.[56] Its management, products

---

51 Seymour and Blagrove performed Spohr's Concertante Op.48 for two violins at the RAM concert, Hanover Square on 30 June 1825. Mori had performed the same piece, with the composer, on 14 April 1820.

52 See Dubourg (1878), 231–2.

53 See 'The Royal Academy of Music', *QMMR* 6 (1824), 77–86; and Rohr (1983), 167–76. Despite its failings, some writers did their best to promote the RAM, often through criticism of the French system (for example, see 'French encouragement of young musicians', *MW*, 3 (1836), 103–5).

54 Hogarth (1838), vol.2, 264.

55 Beedell (1992), 116. The 'enthusiasts' referred to include Robert Owen, who introduced music into his factory schools (see below), and the sight-singing pioneer Sarah Glover.

56 'The State of Music in England during the year 1830', *Harmonicon*, 9 (1831), 2.

of the age, was more concerned with the promotion than the education and training of native musicians and so did not provide the systematic and professional training that was needed and was in Britain often only accessible to 'useful' church and military musicians from a variety of backgrounds.

However, it was a start and on balance probably better than the void it replaced. Its existence symbolized the all-important and much-needed recognition of the need for reform that paved the way for the widespread change in attitudes to the role of music later in the century. The lessons learned from the Academy and the involvement of prominent native and foreign instrumentalists prompted a more professional and enlightened pedagogical approach in institutions founded after the RAM. However the demands of the amateur or semi-professional still needed to take precedence over those of the career professional in the interests of solvency and rapidly expanding amateur markets were too tempting for many to resist.

Schools

School education like any other form of formal instruction during the period formed part of a system based on the reinforcement of the status quo: the individual's predetermined station in life as defined by their class and/or wealth. Such a system, again consumer- rather than state-led, particularly in England and Wales, gave rise to a wide variety of schools with no coherent purpose or overriding pedagogical strategy.[57] Different priorities applied across the range of institutions as the different classes and sexes received (if any) different forms of formal schooling at different stages in their lives. The place of music varied greatly depending on the institution and its clientele. In fact an examination of the place, status and cultivation of music in schools allows us to view society's broader attitudes to the art in microcosm.

For the lower orders there was paltry government support for what was, up to the 1870 Act, essentially a voluntary elementary sector (the elementary school leaving age was ten in 1880). In this system (vocal) music came to play a prominent, sanctioned role as something of 'use' to both consumers and social reformers. As such it established itself within the classroom to be taught by ordinary class teachers rather than

---

[57] See Chapter 1 for general comment and background on the often unhelpful role of the state (and church) in education and, with respect to the spread of 'popular' music education and singing classes, the contributions of Kay, Hullah and others. Regarding music in schools there are particularly valuable contributions from Rainbow, Leppert, Russell and Scholes.

specialists. Instrumental music had to wait until the turn of the next century in this sector.

For those higher up the social scale there was independent, exclusive, fee-paying secondary education, which often followed home tuition from the early years. As a result of their concerns for their children's later prospects this was a massive growth area among middle-class families during the nineteenth century, encouraging a proliferation of institutions, especially private boarding schools for girls. In this sector the acceptance of music was more conditional and patchy as a consequence of opinion formers looking to the education of their own sort. As with the position of music in British society in general, the more 'elite' the social status of the consumer the more its acceptance was limited and subject to strict social convention.

For British boys and young men, particularly as far as practical instrumental performance was concerned, a passing acquaintance was sufficient. There were however notable exceptions later in the century in the new boarding schools. Initiatives from enlightened senior staff (and even students) and a belief in student involvement in the school chapel and choral worship (such as at Radley College) created opportunities for specialist music masters (mainly organists). Instrumental music, including orchestras, had an increasingly important role to play among these older and wealthier students even if it did not involve formal class teaching.

Significantly the ancient, more expensive 'public' schools for the sons of the gentry were most steadfast in their adherence to Chesterfield's indelible influence (see Chapter 1) and a belief in the need for students to be directed away from the supposed detrimental effects of practical music-making. Professional chapel choirs were the order of the day in this context, such as at Eton and Winchester, as musical performance of any kind was not a good use of the gentleman's time.[58] However there were some pioneering exceptions even here as the century progressed (see below).

As we have seen for young girls and women, music as a practical accomplishment had an acknowledged purpose for most of their formative years but its cultivation, in keeping with the male agenda, remained limited to 'modest' skill among young women in polite society. It was to the detriment of standards that throughout the nineteenth century music's role among this section of society was almost compulsory regardless of talent.

---

[58] In addition to the constraints on the violin playing of the 'too well-born' E. H. Fellowes (see Ehrlich 1985), 71–2 and Chapter 1), it is interesting to note how W. A. Fearon, later Headmaster of Winchester, was given 'no time for fiddling' when first a student there in 1852 (see Matthews (1984), 217).

The 'lethargy' which characterized the practice of music in most British schools following the Reformation, in contrast to the continent,[59] allowed poor standards and conditions to exacerbate its already low status. This is particularly true of those numerous girls' boarding schools which provided private instruction of sorts (usually in playing the piano or harp for an extra fee) and a 'desultory' (if relatively stable) form of employment for the sometimes eminent teacher.[60] Despite the efforts of certain individuals improvements were slow to arrive in this area as demands and aspirations remained largely static (serious students would have little option but to pursue their studies outside school on a private basis and probably withstand parental opposition).

It hardly needs reiterating that serious innovation and progress were at this stage reserved for the more readily accessible and evidently beneficial and 'moral' vocal sphere, particularly the potential offered by the increasing urbanization of the lower orders and the young children in elementary education. This area was the 'testing ground' for music's reintroduction into the mainstream school curriculum.[61] It was here that the formal, integrated music lesson, taught by a non-specialist teacher perhaps following the system of Hullah or Mainzer, had a role to play.[62] There was even a move away from rote-learning methods, the norm in school teaching, with Sarah Glover's practical method.[63] In contrast to most recipients of secondary education there was a belief in the desirability of continuing the serious study of music beyond the classroom. In this sense these pupils, like their wealthier equivalents, were being equipped for what was perceived in each case as a 'useful' future.

Although these developments had a huge impact on the musicality of the nation in general and no doubt filtered through to enhance later instrumental skills in many cases, it is difficult to avoid the fact that instrumental teaching in schools did not progress a great deal during the first half of the nineteenth century.

---

[59] Kassler (1979), 979.

[60] See Chapter 1. On the inadequacies of music education in female boarding schools see also Leppert (1985), 136–8 and entries under Callender, E. Darwin, Dibdin, Goodban, Hook, Miller, Moxley, Tipper, Türk and Williams in Kassler (1979). See also Chapter 2 for comment on the publication of teaching material and the devising of methods to assist the overworked music master in schools.

[61] Rainbow (1989a), 32.

[62] Ibid., 20.

[63] Ibid., 29–30. The assimilation process so common in British music pedagogy is apparent in Curwen's 'synthesis' of Pestalozzi and Glover.

Other

Looking beyond dedicated institutions and the place of music in schools, there are examples, the number of which also increases as the century progresses, of musical instruction being organized and delivered through the auspices of an identifiable 'body' of some kind. Universities are one example, although, as in the ancient public schools with which they (Oxford and Cambridge) to a large extent shared their clientele and Anglican affiliations, the position of music as a participatory activity was far from elevated. There was of course a functional, ceremonial and devotional role for both choirs and organists but the cultivation of instrumental performance beyond the organ was most often on a superficial level and primarily as a complement to other concerns.[64] This is not to deny that it took place but it would be surprising if the application it inspired at university differed from that engendered in private, at school or when a professional life had been embarked upon.[65] The study of music at university was at this stage naturally derived from its original position within the *quadrivium* of the liberal arts. In practical terms this resulted in the awarding of degrees based solely on (generally conservative) composition exercises and a lack of esteem (and salary) for the professors of music, themselves most often organists. Crotch and Ouseley at Oxford and Walmisley at Cambridge set about making improvements through musical activity and examinations,[66] but theirs was an uphill task in the academic climate of the times. The foundation of new universities and (albeit limited) reforms at Oxbridge brought an increase of acceptance and musical activity, particularly through music societies, and as a result greater (if far from complete) academic credibility. Nevertheless instrumentalists with serious aspirations, other than organists, were seldom university students and the priorities of a university education did not allow music to interfere to the detriment of other studies. Again any latent talent or palpable enthusiasm was effectively stifled. Universities were not concerned with practical skills, with examinations in the subject based on 'paper work' which was mostly prepared for in private and externally.[67]

At the other end of the social spectrum (and somewhere in between) we do encounter aspirant instrumentalists receiving instruction via an institution as part of their day-to-day working lives. Factory schools,

---

[64] See Fiske and Johnstone, eds (1990), 316.
[65] See entries under 'Vetus', Berkenhout and Birkbeck in Kassler (1979). See also Wollenberg (2001).
[66] Rainbow (1981), 30–31. See Ehrlich (1985), 37.
[67] See Ehrlich (1985), 42–3 and 137.

mechanical institutes and colliery bands all offered training to often eager and receptive students. The names of Owen and Strutt (see Chapter 1) each promoted the potential improving qualities of music, vocal and instrumental, among their workforce.[68] Employers were quick to identify and utilize the 'passifying' qualities of music in close-knit working environments. A belief in the value of music was therefore complemented by practical concerns.

Music also formed an important part of the curriculum of the burgeoning mechanics' institute movement which played a significant part in the education of the lower-middle-class artisans and skilled labourers. The first opened in London in 1824 and there were more than 700 across the country by mid-century. Naturally there was the familiar angle in popular education of the financial and intellectual control being held by middle-class patrons, but valuable instruction in general, practical and factual subjects did come together in these institutions and vocal and instrumental music classes and lectures featured (at least by 1830) at most of the larger examples.[69] Activity cultivated there as instruction and entertainment then spread into the local community.

Additional examples of institutional instruction in music include Kay's involvement with the singing classes for practising teachers at Exeter Hall (see Chapter 1), which helped to deliver singing to tens of thousands of children of the working classes by the 1840s. There are also the numerous piano 'academies', often inspired by Logier's (sometimes controversial) methods, which were complemented by various study aids and tapped into a uniquely large and relatively ambitious amateur market (see Chapter 2).[70] Other success stories along the lines of simultaneous music instruction in classes include Goodban's provision for rudiments (c.1820), an adjunct to the monitorial system, and Kemp's various written contributions and his work at the Exeter Musical College from 1814 which forwarded the cause of music theory and practice.

c.1850–c.1900

Moving into the second half of the nineteenth century institutional training, like private and more ad hoc, *in situ* instruction, benefited from

---

[68] Mackerness (1964), 131.

[69] See ibid., 147–51. See also Elbourne (1980), 64; Russell (1997), 172; and Scott (2001).

[70] See also Kassler (1979), 709–11, for insights into Logier's methods including reception, terms for lessons and a comparison of private lessons and classes.

the growing acceptance of the moral benefits and 'usefulness' of music, even extending beyond provision for the lower orders and the later role of music in nationalistic concerns. We find, as touched on above, an enhanced role for instrumental music in new and even traditional secondary education and, at the end of our period, also in the elementary sector. Music colleges were also very much part of this expansion, although their necessarily amateur bias reduced their usefulness and effectiveness in many cases.

Improvements in status and standards often came following the instigation of the new as a result of the increasing appetite for music. The reform of the old, whether specific institutions or methods of delivery, was, although appealing to many, generally less successful in musical terms.

Conservatoires

The limited success of the RAM provided valuable lessons for later institutions. Its aristocratic 'amateurism', in particular the placing of social above purely musical considerations, had limited its success. This order of priorities needed to be reversed if genuine progress was to be made at the highest level and talent was to be exploited effectively. The final demise of the Ancient Concerts in 1848 signalled a rejection of social exclusivity among audiences and a widespread concern for higher, professional standards, although 'professionalism', in terms of the implementation of a cohesive strategy, was a much-needed and much-delayed addition to the cultivation of music in Britain.

The consumer power of the individual middle-class amateur had created a market for musical training centred primarily on private enterprise, which, although important for the appreciation and status of the musician, had left institutional training limited and the aspiring career musician dependent on the traditional local and family networks. But with a much greater demand for more proficient musicians came an incentive to provide recognized and codified standards of training and performance. The new, professionally managed institutions (see Appendix 1) provided opportunities to access this more systematic musical training, both for their own students and through the hugely popular local examinations for external students and teachers.[71] The

---

[71] See Corder (1922a), 79–80. See also Ehrlich (1985), 105–20, 190ff. and 238, for a discussion of some of these issues and a list of colleges founded during the period. More research is required, beyond the existing histories, into the appearance of individual teaching institutions towards the end of the nineteenth century in order to shed more light on the nature of their teaching as it was practised day to day.

explosion of interest, symptomatic of the general broadening of opportunity and more conspicuous activity, was such that the market was unable to support all of those who wished to take advantage of these new opportunities. Out of an overcrowded profession emerged organizations such as the Incorporated Society of Musicians, which sought to promote high standards and respectability through its restricted membership.[72]

The new music colleges, although not without their teething problems and fundamental flaws, were generally in a better position to make instrumental teaching a much higher priority than the early RAM had done. The role of the RCM, for instance, 'was no longer to induce a careless world to take an interest in the art of music, but to direct into profitable channels an exuberant but uninstructed popular enthusiasm'.[73] For the violin the appointment of Ysaÿe and Joachim as examiners and Fernandez Arbos, a pupil of Vieuxtemps and Joachim, as a violin professor is symptomatic of this new, more professional approach. Similarly Wilhelmj (pupil of Ferdinand David), T. H. Weist-Hill and Viotti Collins were connected with the Guildhall School of Music, founded in 1880. The RAM itself improved its standards during the second half of the nineteenth century, principally through the influence of Sainton and Sauret, and Wessely, who produced his own pedagogical works and editions of Spohr and Campagnoli (1913 and Chron., 1830).

It is true to say that new specialist institutions such as the RCM had a more practical and 'professional' bias than the RAM (which had refused to 'merge' with the new college) and laudable intentions. Both the National Training School (1876) and its later larger incarnation as the RCM (1883) offered a substantial number of free scholarships, but a large degree of exclusivity was maintained and the RCM accepted fee-paying students (of not less than nine years old) from the outset.[74] Circumstances had not kept pace with intentions, and aims such as training performers and instrumentalists and selecting talent from all social classes were inevitably subject to financial pressures. The relatively early success of Trinity College (from 1875) was no doubt aided by its initial 'ecclesiastical', choral angle, worldwide examination centres and female bias,[75] and the Guildhall School of Music was

---

[72] See Ehrlich (1985), 126–36.
[73] Colles (1933), 46. See also Caldwell (1999), 550.
[74] See Rainbow (1981), 38ff. By the end of the first ten years there had been 310 pupils, of whom 61 were scholars and 249 paying students. As at the early RAM there was a strong tendency for scholars to join the teaching staff and so 'earn their keep' (see Colles and Cruft (1982), 9).
[75] Mackerness (1964), 196. See also Ehrlich (1985), 116–19.

progressive and successful in so far as it sought to satisfy the demands of amateur/semi-professional middle-class girls rather than holding higher pretensions.[76] The London College of Music had similar aims. The proliferation of such institutions replaced the lean period following the struggles of the RAM. Levels of musical activity had never been higher but the (largely superficial) training of musicians in large numbers despite a lack of professional performing opportunities was never going to be sustainable or beneficial to standards.

The continued lack of financial assistance from the state (the death of Prince Albert robbed the cause of an ardent supporter) prevented British colleges from acquiring the necessary high-mindedness to ensure standards took precedence over the need for substantial and continuous income.[77] Also the nature of the market itself meant that a constant flow of primarily female amateurs or aspirant 'semi-professionals', with limited or short-term ambitions and prospects but with the ability to pay, was readily available and exploited by the 'uniquely British enterprise' of examining external students.[78] The institutions themselves did not have the financial freedom (or perhaps competence) to differentiate between the demands of amateurs, semi-professionals and career professionals.[79] Inevitably the focus was on the amateur and external teacher/diploma revenue rather than on the effective nurturing of native talent within the institution itself. As a consequence vigorous professional standards were sadly lacking. The Society of Arts report (1865), initially stimulated by the Prince Consort, had, in the context of a failing RAM, highlighted the fundamental and on-going problem of balancing artistic ideals with survival.[80]

In marked contrast to the professional bias of continental examples quantity was easily able to win over quality, at a time when precisely the reverse was required. With more than a hint of myopia the bias was (and to some extent still is) very much in favour of training teachers rather than performers, which not only reflected but also perpetuated a predominantly female amateur market. It therefore would be a distortion of the true situation to see conservatoires as the breeding grounds for professional performers at this time. Naturally college principals such as Grove, not a practical musician, often struggled to

---

[76] Ehrlich (1985), 114–15.
[77] The RCM received £500 from the government in 1892 while the Paris Conservatoire received the equivalent of £10,000 in the same year (Hughes and Stradling (2001), 33).
[78] Ehrlich (1985), 116.
[79] Ibid., 99.
[80] See ibid., 88ff. Improvements to the management and curriculum of the RAM came about with the appointment of Mackenzie as principal in 1888.

recruit eminent figures onto the teaching staff as a result. Notable exceptions included the wind departments and highly respected performers and teachers such as the clarinettist Henry Lazarus.

It appears that institutions founded beyond the remarkable concentration of (generally unambitious) consumption and provision in London enjoyed higher levels of professional success and status. The 'dilettante' element was naturally still in evidence but perhaps had less of a suffocating influence within different market dynamics. The Manchester College of Music, founded in 1893, certainly benefited from the presence and vision of Hallé and his orchestra and the potential for students at the College, including those nurtured through the band movement, to achieve a great deal within the profession. Brodsky, professor of the violin while leader of the Hallé orchestra (and later Hallé's successor as director of the college), was among the high-calibre teaching staff, which also included Carl Fuchs. Diploma examinations, for performers and teachers, were more exacting than elsewhere and women did not outnumber men to the same extent.[81] Dublin's Royal Irish Academy also appears to have been able to focus more on 'talent alone' than the financial clout of amateurs in this 'innately musical country'.[82]

There were even better prospects for new examples working in areas widely acknowledged as 'useful' and which could therefore offer greater specialization with a self-evidently valuable purpose. As with lower-class music-making and activities beyond British shores musical success came where instruction was a means to a practical end, something relatively rare in a society where demand was so skewed towards the amateur. In this category we find the relatively early arrival of the College of Organists (1865) and, even earlier, the (Royal) Military School of Music at Kneller Hall (1857).

Much of the undoubted success of Kneller Hall can be attributed to the extent to which it differed from the majority of the institutions discussed above, particularly its teaching methods as dictated by a tendency towards centralization, specialization, standardization and professionalism.[83] At the time of its foundation foreign influence was prevalent (even dominant) among bands as elsewhere, but this initiative succeeded where the RAM failed in promoting native musicianship by purposeful and heart-felt initiatives to convince the central authorities of

---

[81] Ibid., 115–16.
[82] Pine and Acton, eds (1998), 8 and Appendix 2: 'Teaching and administrative staff'.
[83] Turner and Turner (1996) is an enjoyable and informative study of the history of the military school at Kneller Hall. See also Ehrlich (1985), 96–7 and 112; Ess (1981), 137; and Herbert, ed. (2000a), 63.

the significance of bands in the armed forces. In truth their case was much easier to put than that on behalf of downtrodden civilian musicians as there was a far more potent utilitarian element and also a genuine belief in the abilities of native musicians in this area to fulfil the aims of those behind the initiative. It was not just wishful thinking: civilian bands and bandmasters and their beneficial role within society already had a proven track record.[84] The call for a central institution and consequently some 'unity of style' had teeth in light of the French Gymnase de Musique Militaire founded in 1836. The result was gradual but nevertheless real acceptance of the idea and by 1865 only fifteen regiments were not supporting the initiative. Civilians and foreign musicians were sidelined and in 1867 the government took over the running of Kneller Hall. Direct funding, grants to band funds and (eventually) warrant officer rank and pay for bandmasters followed.[85] In 1890 Samuel Griffiths (see Chron., 1896) became the first soldier to hold the post of Director of Music of the School and with it was promoted to 2nd Lieutenant. He was appointed following a 'competitive examination' of the seven applicants.[86] The Directors of Music at Kneller Hall proved to be 'a distinguished and accomplished line of musicians'.[87]

The methods employed reflected the seriousness of the intentions and the focus on a valued end product. Needless to say the military musician's career was a great deal more secure and in many ways predetermined than his civilian counterpart, although an elite group did enter the top orchestras. The normal day included 'more than eight hours' work' and the emphasis was on public performance, participation and appreciation (through access to concerts and Covent Garden for example), from the beginning.[88] The all-round education of the military musician was also catered for, an initiative sadly missing and lamented elsewhere. Belief in the value of Kneller Hall as a centre for advanced, 'in-house' study increased and, in marked contrast to the RAM, it was possible to reduce the annual subscription (paid by each regiment) in 1865. Among an impressive line-up of professors was Thomas Sullivan (clarinet, lower brass and violin), father of Sir Arthur Sullivan, who later visited the school, Carl Mandel (theory, see Chron., 1859), Carl Zeiss (formerly of the Brussels Conservatoire, cornet and trumpet), Sam Hughes (ophicleide) and, from 1858, the previously mentioned Henry Lazarus, who helped to ensure an unusually elevated

---

[84] Turner and Turner (1996), 16.
[85] Ibid., 32.
[86] Ibid., 41.
[87] Ibid., 59.
[88] Ibid., 24–5.

position for British clarinettists.[89] The presence of such respected and authoritative figures encouraged the publication of 'set texts' in much the same way that had occurred at the Paris Conservatoire many years earlier.

Interestingly the role of string instruments within military circles had long been a contentious issue. Many acknowledged the 'valuable social and public roles' of string bands but others 'in the army hierarchy' saw them as a 'frivolous diversion from the true function of soldier-musicians'.[90] Attitudes towards certain instruments naturally crossed contextual boundaries when those in positions of influence were of a similar class, particularly when issues of 'usefulness' and 'masculinity' were at stake. Nevertheless the 1891 timetable and Arthur Stretton, Director of Music from 1896, strengthened the role of the string orchestra and non-'martial music'.[91]

Given the infrastructure and support in place at Kneller Hall it is not surprising that it produced many fine wind players and percussionists, some of whom could stand shoulder to shoulder with the finest exponents from the rest of Europe. This legacy of British-trained excellence, particularly among bandmasters, naturally impacted on regimental and a range of other bands up and down the country. Perhaps uniquely, native models could be held aloft as a beacon for emulation in the amateur sphere and there was sufficient enthusiasm and incentive within the appropriate amateur community to take full advantage of them. Another testament to the success of Kneller Hall was the opening of a Royal Navy School of Music at Eastney in 1903.

Schools

Work-based and institutional training and eventually greater state intervention in education changed the emphasis of musical instruction. Talent and enthusiasm were encouraged and tapped, to varying degrees, rather than left solely to the initiative of the individual. The place of vocal music in mainstream elementary education (60 per cent of children by 1891 and the establishment of tonic sol-fa)[92] and instrumental music in secondary education for girls (albeit often as an adjunct to the main

---

[89] Ibid., 35–8. The School also attracted students from Britain's colonies and dependencies from the mid-1870s. See ibid., 152–4 for lists of professors at Kneller Hall (1857–1995).

[90] Ibid., 45.

[91] A copy of this timetable is reproduced ibid., between pp. 45 and 46. Its comprehensiveness, covering both musical and 'general' subjects, is immediately apparent, as is the diversity and frequency of classes and rehearsals.

[92] Russell (1997), 54.

curriculum) were well established by the middle of the nineteenth century.[93] Significant signs of progress came during the second half of the century and independent of the 1870 Act as boys' secondary education and elementary schools in general incorporated instrumental teaching to a much greater extent.

The fact that in public schools music had a much greater role to play in the education of girls than boys[94] makes the activities of an individual such as Paul David (the son of the Spohr pupil Ferdinand and also a product of Leipzig) all the more significant. In addition to his influential articles on the violin and violinists in various editions of *Grove's Dictionary* David was music master (from 1864) at the ancient Uppingham School for boys for 40 years (he is the only non-headmaster whose portrait hangs in the Hall). He was able to nurture 'the very poorest plant' with the support of an unusually enlightened (if unmusical) headmaster in the form of Edward Thring, who had appointed him under the recommendation of Sir William Sterndale Bennett.[95] Together they established a strong musical tradition in the school where it was cultivated as 'a refining and elevating influence' as well as impacting on the development of music in other public schools.[96] It is worth quoting Thring's own words at this point:

---

[93] The 1868 Schools Inquiry Commission highlighted the fact that 'Music (which appears not always to be taught in the cheapest schools) is equally demanded of all girls, however little taste they may have for it'. It went on to point out that 'one of the considerations which mainly influence parents of the middle class in selecting a school for their daughters is that instrumental music is to be the leading subject of instruction for women except in the lower ranks of life. It is said to be seldom more than the acquisition of manual skill, to be taught without intelligence, and too much confined to instrumental music to the neglect of singing' (quoted in Mackerness (1964), 173). New girls' schools such as Cheltenham Ladies' College preserved earlier traditions of private instruction for piano, harp and voice but also promoted 'concerted music' in order to improve appreciation of the works of 'the great masters' (Rainbow (1989a), 36). Singing lessons and instrumental teaching were also a prominent feature of the schools which operated under the auspices of the Girls' Public Day School Trust. Private and school teaching remained by far the most common professional outlet in music for women. Unfortunately the profusion of college diplomas had created a surfeit of school music mistresses and so their market value was low (see Gillett (2000a), 210–11).

[94] See Ehrlich (1985), 72.

[95] Matthews (1984), 136 and 218. Though himself unmusical Thring had benefited from the fact that his wife's family were of middle-class German descent and so had experienced music as 'a daily part of their life' (ibid., 217). This is a very valuable volume on Uppingham, including a chapter devoted to 'Music – a genial solvent' (217–25), a title which quotes Thring's own words. I am also grateful to James Peschek (Director of Music 1969–78) for his assistance.

[96] Ibid., 217. See also Barnard (1961), 152–3; Woodward (1962), 486–7; and Rainbow (1989a), 34.

> Music supplies the want, a common object, a social object, room for self-respect for young and old, a boon to the ignorant, a refinement to the intellectual, the little boy's hope, the elder's pleasure, a family tie including ladies, an all-pervading influence which takes little heed of differences of age or knowledge.[97]

David began the succession of inspirational figures which not only ensured the reputation of Uppingham for music but also created an opening for instrumental rather than just vocal practice. The musical activities of boys were not just directed towards the daily chapel services, house-singing and choral society. Instrumental activity was naturally suited to independent secondary boarding schools where there was money to purchase instruments and the leaving age was normally eighteen.[98] He and Joachim were both pupils of his father and David led by example as an instrumental teacher and set high standards, which his assistant music staff helped to maintain. Joachim often played at the school, even sitting at the back of the violins in the string orchestra, an important move towards communal music-making among the higher orders. Programmes consisted of 'the best classical music', including, unsurprisingly given the Leipzig connection, Mendelssohn oratorios.[99] An orchestra was formed in 1890 after David had been impressed by high standards at Marlborough College, although the instruments the boys played were (until the 1930s) limited mainly to the violin and cello.

David's legacy was certainly a significant advancement in terms of the cultivation of music in public schools and secondary education in general. However, despite his pioneering achievements, the position of music and the music master remained somewhat separate to the mainstream curriculum and certain levels of ambivalence were still in evidence.[100] Moves were made during Sir William Sterndale Bennett's grandson Robert's tenure (under Headmaster Owen) to integrate the music lessons into the normal teaching timetable, rather than giving optional lessons out of normal school periods (and receiving lower pay than their 'academic' colleagues).[101]

---

[97] Quoted in Matthews (1984), 218.

[98] Rainbow (1989a), 37–9.

[99] Matthews (1984), 219.

[100] Robert Singleton encouraged Radley's musical tradition on the grounds that 'the devil hated industry' and considered that playing instruments was desirable 'provided it did not interfere with cricket and other manly and muscular diversions' (see Graham (1996), 39, which includes a photograph of the Radley College orchestra in 1878). This attitude is typical of the upper and upper-middle classes' view of the cultivation of music among young men during the period. It was tolerated, even sanctioned eventually, but only to a certain level. The harbouring of musical ambition was still inappropriate.

[101] Matthews (1984), 220.

INSTITUTIONS 263

The serious study of the violin was encouraged by figures such as John Farmer, uncle of Henry (see Chron., 1847) and also a Leipzig student, and music master as well as violin teacher at Harrow School from 1862, A. H. Raikes, who was a school teacher and published material on the instrument (Chron., 1891), and Joseph Dando, music master at Charterhouse School, Godalming from 1875 (see Chapter 3).

In addition, as instrumental teaching became better established in schools at the end of the nineteenth century and beginning of the twentieth, the violin established itself as the main instrument in elementary as well as boys' secondary schools. It benefited from its size and the commercial skills and opportunism of a few pioneers who combined a cheap hire-purchase scheme with the presence of private teachers in urban schools throughout the country.[102] As a result school orchestras often consisted of little else.[103] The mass production and importation of cheap violins[104] and sources for ensemble teaching complemented this development which also aided the development of the amateur orchestral society. The piano was far less elitist than it had been a century earlier but it was still too expensive to be taught in state-funded elementary schools. Significantly aural training and sight-singing, the means of gaining a 'sound musical training', became increasingly common in secondary schools.[105]

Music, vocal and then instrumental, naturally had a more integral role when it arrived in the elementary school curriculum, beyond the mere accomplishment 'ceiling' of most provision in girls' home tuition and girls' and eventually boys' secondary schools. However the progress in various forms of school music, instrumental as well as vocal, during the period (boys' grammar schools excepted), affecting the vast majority of children in some way or other, represented in many ways progress in national music, whether through heightened appreciation, participation or both.

---

[102] Rainbow (1989a), 40.

[103] For a discussion of this trend and the role and importance of the 'Maidstone System' in introducing violins and violin tuition into schools, see Russell (1997: 54), who provides an excellent survey of the expansion of state and private music education in England. Harvey (1995: 156–9, 162 and 255–6) also discusses the gradual proliferation of instrumental and general music tuition in English schools, private and state, and other institutions during the latter part of the nineteenth century. In addition Scholes (1947) offers numerous insights into trends in violin playing and teaching (including violin 'classes') during the second half of the nineteenth century and beyond (pp.339–69), and valuable material on music education in schools and elsewhere (vol.2).

[104] See Ehrlich (1985), 101, and Harvey (1995), 128–9 and 162. A marked increase in the value of old instruments as collectors' items is evident in keeping with the general rise in the status of the instrument. See Heron-Allen (1885), 12–13; *idem* (1890–94), 362; and Harvey (1995).

[105] Rainbow (1989a), 40.

Other

The demand which was catered for and to a certain extent directed through the proliferation of music colleges and the greater role for music in different types of school also led to greater provision in other institutional forms. Naturally qualifications 'fever' played its part, with the Society of Arts organizing local examinations, mainly through mechanics' institutes and working men's clubs, from 1866 and the ABRSM beginning business in 1890.[106] Some old and new universities improved provision in favour of more practical musicianship but the 'narrow, arid, and doctrinaire' content and 'organ-loft' mentality, which had produced 'neither scholars nor skilled musicians', persisted well into the twentieth century.[107]

Perhaps the most significant developments outside of the music colleges and schools came as part of the progressive trend towards specialization, as earlier demonstrated by the College of Organists and the RMSM. In keeping with these precedents initiatives such as the College of Violinists (1889), where Albert Sammons later became a professor, were less biased in favour of the amateur. Instruments and lessons were provided for a fee of 3s. and 1s. a week, which no doubt further widened the appeal and accessibility of the violin.[108] B. Althaus, a prolific writer of teaching material for stringed instruments during the late nineteenth century, appears to have provided a prototype for the College of Violinists with his Tavistock Violin Academy.[109] Althaus in fact was one of a number of figures to produce material to complement the study of the instrument at the College (see Chron., 1889 and 1892).

---

[106] Ehrlich (1985), 116.

[107] Ibid., 140, 192 and 230–31. See also Rainbow (1981), 32–3.

[108] Ehrlich (1985), 106 and 173. Syllabuses and prospectuses for the College of Violinists can be found in the Heron-Allen Collection, Royal College of Music, London, and *The gazette of the College of Violinists ltd*, afterwards *The violinists' gazette*, nos 1–52 (London, 1914–39) is located in the Bodleian Library, Oxford. Further discussion of violin and other 'classes' in a variety of institutions can be found in Russell (1997), 43, 56 and plate 8.

[109] See Heron-Allen (1890–94), 403.

CHAPTER SIX

Conclusion: Realized Potential and Stifled Ambition

The principal arguments of this study do not require lengthy repetition here; but, to sum up, where music itself was truly valued, by providers and consumers of instrumental teaching, real achievement was at least possible and often occurred. The fundamental problem that music faced in nineteenth-century British society (and the remnants are still with us today) is that so many other issues and considerations, moral, utilitarian and financial, came between the instrumentalist and significant achievement. In contrast to other European centres of acknowledged excellence and innovation a true passion for and belief in the value of the art were often tempered by other, social concerns, and an undercurrent of ambivalence is evident with respect to music throughout the period. Positive and negative attitudes, some with widespread repercussions, were often heightened by the strength of feeling that a contentious subject such as music could inspire. Opinion-formers in a consumption- and status-obsessed society seldom had the inclination or courage to put a convincing case for music and lead by example, as often happened elsewhere. It was hardly a priority comparable to vocations such as the law or medicine. Complacency was born out of affluence and more than a hint of island mentality. A palpable shift in favour of music came about as the consumer balance shifted away from those with wholly entrenched opinions and prejudices and towards the populace who were more naturally disposed towards and receptive of music's inherent qualities and other benefits as a means of improving themselves.

In a society divided by class and gender it was inevitable that the fortunes of instrumental practice would depend on its context, in relation to these factors, and consequently on the value placed on it by providers and consumers and the potential for success. When the achievements of native musicians, amateur and professional (and the various grey areas in between) are assessed with the benefit of hindsight, the general story is of flashes of brilliance arising out of the general haze of mediocrity. High expectations (and consequently aspirations) are fundamental to success in education; here, with notable exceptions, they are generally very low and/or short-term with social stigma attached.

The ceiling on ambition did rise with the burgeoning of middle-class consumerism and concern for self-improvement, but it was still very much in evidence, among men and women, at the end of the nineteenth century. In such a commercially mature (and artist-unfriendly) environment, provision is a reliable indicator of demand. While attempts to lead taste during the period are significant in themselves, naturally the greatest success was achieved by those who were astute to subtle shifts in market demands and sought to give the consumer what they wanted in a palatable form. Market creation and manipulation needed to come from above and therefore were generally associated with broader social concerns rather than individual commercial or cultural interests.

Despite being the 'Cinderella' subject within the 'Cinderella' art, instrumental performance eventually thrived in pockets of activity, particularly where the traditionally higher-status theoretical study was of little concern or it could complement or represent a development out of widely accepted and valued vocal training. However with the upper- and then middle-class male agenda firmly in place there was little chance of shrugging off strong conservative tendencies. These were the result of long-term ambivalence and a consequent distrust of novelty in the face of unrivalled public access and a vast array of visitors, and a willingness to follow and assimilate rather than lead and innovate.

A strong connection between standards, aspirations and social status is in evidence and as patterns of consumption changed with a descent and broadening of opportunity there was a chance for a shift in emphasis and greater levels of achievement. New areas emerged where practical music-making could work in partnership with, rather than contrary to, fundamental social issues. Philanthropists, industrialists and social reformers sought to harness the increasingly acknowledged 'pacifying' and 'civilizing' qualities of music within increasingly centralized working-class communities with designated leisure time in order to maintain the status quo in a revolutionary climate and improve productivity. This granting of freedom and opportunity in order to exercise overall control, a familiar trend in British society and domestic circumstances at the time, was eagerly exploited by the lower orders as a means of improving their quality of life rather than as an outlet for superficial recreation. In fact if these initiatives had not improved the conditions and motivation of the workforce then, they would have failed in their purpose. The control of other social groups, including women, did not necessarily have their contentment in mind to the same degree.

It was indeed rare for provision and consumption to be mutually beneficial and dependent to the same extent in the cultural environment of the period and for active participation and appreciation to come from within the same peer group. Of course it was possible for musical activity to be at one with and blossom within its environment in this context precisely because it was a product of that same environment and of a common identity. There was a genuine desire to create from within rather than purchase from outside. As a result the expansion of communal, instrumental practice among working-class men, inspired and facilitated by industrialization, offered great potential. Alongside church and military music it was also possible for this area to gain credibility through its 'usefulness' to society at large and moralizing influence on both the individual and wider community. For once the extra-musical preoccupations of opinion-formers, long a fundamental concern, would facilitate positive musical consequences.

There is no escaping the presence of harmful class and gender divisions in British society at this time. In music these gave rise to further divisions in status between the amateur and professional, audience and artist, the practical and theoretical, vocal and instrumental, teacher and performer, conservative and innovative. Despite the protestations of some, the fervency with which these divisions were retained as a result of society's preoccupations made the music profession in Britain ineffective and certainly something less than the sum of its disparate parts. Real progress required the blurring or in some cases sweeping away of these divisions as part of a movement towards 'music for music's sake', devoid of social stigma and engineering, and musical success during our period was relative to the ability to break down these barriers. Vocal music, particularly in the form of the choral society and oratorio, was able to bring genders and classes together with social, moral and musical benefits across the country. The work of many musical pioneers of the nineteenth century was dedicated to improvements in the provision of vocal training at an amateur level, through the home, school and church. For instrumental music progress was slower and more difficult and there were very few opportunities for classes and genders to mix in group performance. Each initiative required justification on moral and social grounds, but success was therefore all the more significant when it came. Amid increasing diversity amateurs of different types had very different stories to tell, while the isolated native professional remained under threat, financially and socially, from prejudice, competition and lack of status.

Following the intellectualization of music during the early eighteenth century the practice and priorities of the social elite remained largely unchanged and continued to be promoted through the ancient universities and grammar schools. As opportunity spread they sought to preserve social differentials through the conspicuous consumption of 'celebrity' for private amusement. Practical music, especially 'unscholarly' instrumental performance in an increasingly secular society, was regarded as superficial and even damaging among polite society and those concerned with the emulation of their social superiors. The growth of the middle classes brought significant new markets and scope for higher levels of participation and appreciation, including among children, a positive development, and young ladies and gentlemen, although much activity was literary based and, for men at least, there remained little incentive to cross the amateur/professional divide. Professional musicians, as performers, teachers and writers, and critics were able to benefit from this trend as market opportunity did finally outweigh fear of competition and practical concerns took precedence. More importantly music came to be seen as 'useful' among significant sections of the population, although, naturally, the extent and nature of its value to the consumer depended to a large extent on the familiar issues of class and gender.

The all-important am/pro division was blurred by the growing army of semi-professional female teachers, who had some unique but temporary earning and expressive power through music prior to (in most cases) the relative security offered by marriage and motherhood. Here too provision and consumption came together within the peer group, but their influence on the profession and new music colleges was significant but unhelpful, creating a culture of self-perpetuating mediocrity and a devaluation of skills. In a consumer age it was far easier to achieve quantity than quality of music-making. However, not all 'popular' music movements, 'boom' areas within the multi-faceted British amateur music scene, had the same priorities and were limited to appealing to the lowest common denominator.

Far more beneficial was the removal of the division by lower-class activity: essentially professional (or better) standards among amateurs with the communal, public performance of music the priority and a reward in itself. This was in contrast to earning power and genteel accomplishment, through generally individual, private activity, being the initial impetus and desired end.[1] Unsurprisingly the nature of activity in the wider communities in many ways mirrored provision, and the balance between leading and following demand, in different types of school. Crucially the perception of music, performed for the most part on a different, largely new range of instruments, changed in this working-class environment among those both supporting and participating in the activity. It had no stigma, in fact quite the opposite,

---

[1] Where women were able to work together and as performers, such as in organizations that brought music to the people, music could be a source of esteem and significant achievement as well as public exposure (see Gillett (2000a), 40 and 162).

and genteel appreciation from a safe distance and private 'dabblings' were of little interest or relevance from an early age. There was more to gain than to lose, from both sides, and a pride in an amateur status did not in this instance equate with low standards. Musical achievement was a far higher priority than earning power (these were already working men), although, as among music-mistresses, the two did come together on rare occasions. There was regular public, informed scrutiny through performance and the 'central element' of formal competition,[2] which related to widely recognized and codified standards of excellence. As in choral societies amateur and professional interests were reconciled and expansion and diversification in this new area created new professional opportunities, for insiders and outsiders, rather than threats to old ones. Dedication and the desire for high standards, all in keeping with middle-class values and tastes, formed efficient, often non-literate training methods, which shared the practicalities of professional traditions, but a far more supportive environment encouraged experimentation and a freer exchange of expertise. We find functional instruction for functional music rather than the 'genteel' equivalent.

Here circumstances were conducive to the realization of potential, to the benefit of British music as a whole. Conspicuous success here could be reconciled with the agenda of the ruling classes far more easily than in many other areas involving their own sort. Men from the lower classes, supported by their families and local communities, therefore became the real achievers of instrumental music in nineteenth-century Britain. Inevitably new and alternative forms of entertainment and recreation emerged around the turn of the twentieth century, particularly sport, but the established role and 'usefulness' of music within working-class communities, where it formed 'a central feature of people's existence' and native role-models could emerge,[3] had engendered a sincere love of the art and ensured its survival.

To judge music by professional achievements, as is perhaps the most natural and frequently adopted angle, is to portray British music at this time in a dismal light in comparison to other countries. Trends in music education, formal and informal, had no small part to play in this, but if we broaden the perspective, as has been the intention throughout this study, the picture is more favourable. As the most progressive and outspoken advocates were aware during the period, amateur musicians hold the key to the 'musicality' of a nation, and where their achievements were significant during this period, as facilitated by more effective systems of training and greater potential for success and self-

---

[2] Russell (1997), 15, 267 and 287.
[3] Ibid., 284–5.

improvement, we find much to be celebrated and a much healthier environment for the improvement of professional standards. The 'roots' and 'topmost branches' of amateur activity all played their part and the majority of children, in theory at least, had access to musical instruction of some kind through either state or private initiatives.[4] Vocal and instrumental music had a role to play in both elementary and secondary schools by the beginning of the twentieth century, although instrumental studies remained somewhat separate to the mainstream curriculum.

Towards the end of our period we find an environment in which to a far greater extent than before music is valued and even accepted on its own terms: in effect a 'national' music (before music became viewed more widely as a vehicle for nationalism) and the origins of a long overdue 'British Musical Renaissance'. Music remained (and probably will always remain) a relatively insecure existence for most. The rather 'patchy' success of instrumental practice in nineteenth-century Britain is at least in part attributable to the isolation of different pockets of activity, with their different aims and priorities, in contrast to the unifying qualities of vocal music on a much broader social scale. Significant achievement was possible, but for instrumentalists this seldom accommodated more than one class or gender.

It must be greatly regretted if, after the advancements of the late nineteenth and twentieth centuries, the twenty-first signals a return to the priorities and prejudices of two centuries earlier. It is far too easy for a 'non-essential' subject such as music to suffer from high levels of ambivalence, particularly when funding issues come to the fore, and achieve 'luxury' status. It should be remembered that the concept of elitism is self-perpetuating and that the divisions it creates can, as the past has shown, only work to the detriment of British culture and society in general.

---

[4] See 'Amateur music', *Cornhill Magazine*, 8 (1863), 93–8, quoted by Rainbow (1989a), 35.

APPENDIX ONE

A Chronology of Nineteenth-Century British Music Education

Parentheses are used for music education developments outside Britain and some British events of general cultural or political significance.

1795 (Paris Conservatoire established, opening the following year)
1797 William Crotch elected professor of music at Oxford
1801 Crotch publishes his *Specimens of various styles of music* in three volumes; R. J. S. Stevens elected to the Gresham professorship of music; Clementi's *Introduction to the art of playing on the pianoforte*
1810 Chappell's firm established in London; Haliday's 'keyed bugle' patent
1811 Novello's publishing firm founded; (Prague Conservatoire established)
1812 A. F. C. Kollmann's *Quarterly Musical Register*
1813 Philharmonic Society founded
1814 Joseph Kemp opens his Musical College at Exeter, employing his system of 'simultaneous teaching in classes'; Foundation of Stalybridge Old Band, Lancashire; Logier patents his 'chiroplast'; (Stölzel's valves in Berlin)
1816 Boosey & Co established in London
1817 Johann Bernhard Logier opens his Music Academy at 20 Bedford Place, Russell Square, London; (Vienna Conservatoire founded)
1818 *QMMR*, ed. Richard Bacon, first published (–1828)
1819 Building of the London Institution at Moorfields, promoting public lectures and adult education in general; Thomas Busby's *General history of music*
1820 Spohr leader of Philharmonic Society orchestra
1822 RAM founded in London; (Cherubini director of Paris Conservatoire)
1823 Opening of the RAM on 24 March, under Dr William Crotch; *Harmonicon* first

published, ed. William Ayrton (−1833); Robert Cocks & Co publishing firm established in London; Wessel & Stodart publishing firm established

1824 London Mechanics' Institute launched in February; Sainsbury's *Dictionary of Musicians*; Cramer, Addison, and Beale publishing firm founded in London

1825 (London première of Beethoven's Ninth Symphony)

1829 English translation of Hummel's piano treatise

1830 William C. Stafford's *History of Music*

1831 Crotch publishes *The substance of several courses of lectures on music read at the university of Oxford, and in the metropolis*; (Paganini's London debut)

1832 Cipriani Potter succeeds Crotch as principal of RAM; Foundation of London's Sacred Harmonic Society; (conical-bore Boehm flute in Munich); (British parliamentary Reform Act)

1833 J. Turner's *Manual of instruction in vocal music, chiefly with a view to Psalmody*; Rudolphus's edition of Spohr's violin treatise; (first state grant (£20,000) for education approved by Parliament and Committee of Council on Education appointed, with James Kay (later Sir James Kay-Shuttleworth) as its secretary)

1834 *The monthly supplement to the musical library*, ed. William Ayrton, first published (−1837); foundation of the Society of British Musicians, dedicated to the advancement of native talent (−1865)

1835 Sarah Ann Glover's *Scheme to render psalmody congregational*; George Hogarth's *Musical history, biography, and criticism*; (Handel Commemoration); (Baillot's *L'art du violon* published in Paris)

1836 Thomas Attwood Walmisley made professor of music at Cambridge; W. E. Hickson, *The singing master*; *The Musical World* first published, edited by J. W. Davison (−1891)

1837 Edward Taylor succeeds Stevens in the Gresham Professorship; Wornum's 'tape-check' piano action; (Queen Victoria's accession)

1838 Founding of the Promenade Concerts in London

1839 Appointment of school inspectors; Henry Chorley

	appointed to review musical events in the *Athenaeum*
1840	Hullah engaged by James Kay, secretary of the Committee of Council on Education, and new teacher-training institution, founded by Kay, opens at Battersea; E. F. Rimbault's *Musical Journal*; Liverpool Philharmonic Orchestra
1841	Hullah begins classes for the teaching of singing by schoolmasters at Exeter Hall in London and publishes his edition of *Wilhem's method of teaching singing*; English translation of Cherubini's *Cours de counterpoint et de fugue* (1835); Louis Jullien's Concerts d'Hiver at the Lyceum-English Opera House; first Reid Concert at Edinburgh University given by first music professor John Thompson; Mainzer arrives in London, publishing his *National Singing-Class Circular* and *Singing for the million*
1842	Course for schoolmistresses at Exeter Hall; *Mainzer's Musical Times and Singing Circular* (–1844) (*MT* from 1844); Sterndale Bennett's Classical Chamber Concerts, London (–1856)
1843	Publication of John Curwen's *Grammar of vocal music*; Bishop edition of Spohr violin treatise and endorsement by the RAM committee; (Foundation of the Leipzig Conservatoire by Mendelssohn)
1844	*The Musical Times* first published, by Novello
1845	Adolphe Sax's 'saxhorns' first marketed by Henry Distin in London; John Donaldson appointed professor at the University of Edinburgh; beginning of the brass-band contest movement; John Ella's Musical Union chamber concerts; A. Day's *A treatise on harmony*
1846	J. Turle and E. Taylor, *The singing book*
1847	(The Ten-Hour Act, offering workers guaranteed leisure time); (Boehm's 'improved' flute design)
1848	Mainzer's *Music and education*; demise of Concert of Ancient Music, London
1849	Philharmonic Hall, Liverpool; London Bach Society
1851	Great Exhibition at the Crystal Palace in London's Hyde Park; Musical Institute of London founded (–1853), with John Hullah as president; John Cassell's *Popular educator*

1852 New Philharmonic Society, London
1853 Edward Thring appointed headmaster of Uppingham School; Belle Vue brass band competition, Manchester
1855 *Tonic sol-fa reporter*; Chappell's *Popular music of olden time*; August Mann's Saturday Concerts at the Crystal Palace (Sydenham); Frederick Ouseley made Oxford professor; (Manuel García's laryngoscope)
1856 William Sterndale Bennett elected to the professorial chair at Cambridge; Free Trade Hall, Manchester
1857 Foundation of the Military School of Music at Kneller Hall; first 'trial' Handel Festival at the Crystal Palace; Charles Hallè's Manchester concerts begin
1858 Musical Society of London (–1867); Monday Popular Concerts begin (–1898) at the new St James's Hall, London; Hallé Orchestra, Manchester; Leeds Music Festival
1859 Charles Lucas becomes principal of RAM, following the retirement of Potter and death of Burghersh (Earl of Westmorland); *Champion brass band journal*
1860 Beginning of brass-band competitions (later National Brass Band Festival) at the Crystal Palace
1861 Robert Prescott Stewart made professor of music at Trinity College, Dublin; London Academy of Music; *Hymns ancient and modern*; (Death of Prince Albert)
1862 J. P. Hullah's *The history of modern music, a course of lectures delivered at the institute of Great Britain*; John Farmer 'invited' to teach the piano by the boys at Harrow; *The Musical Standard* (–1933)
1863 *The Choir and Musical Record* (–1878)
1864 National College of Music; College of Organists (granted Royal Charter in 1893); RAM receives its first ever government grant of £500 a year; Paul David arrives as Director of Music at Uppingham School
1865 An independent committee of the Society for the Encouragement of Arts, Manufactures and Commerce reports on the state of musical education at home and abroad; London Organ School; Sir Herbert S. Oakley made professor at Edinburgh (–1891)
1866 W. Sterndale Bennett becomes principal of RAM; Society of Arts local examinations

APPENDIX ONE

- 1867 Government takes over running of Kneller Hall
- 1869 Tonic Sol-fa College founded by Curwen; London Philharmonic Society's concerts at St James's Hall; (Matthew Arnold's *Culture and Anarchy* published)
- 1870 Forster's Elementary Education Act, introducing compulsory elementary education and Board Schools
- 1871 Royal Albert Hall, London; Leeds Philharmonic Society
- 1872 Appointment of Hullah as Chief Inspector for School Music (–1881); British Orchestral Association founded; Church Choral Society of London and College of Choral Music (later Trinity College of Music); first woman violin student at RAM
- 1873 Royal Normal College and Academy of Music for the Blind
- 1874 (Royal) Musical Association founded with Reverend Professor Sir Frederick Gore Ouseley, Bart., as president, and *Proceedings of the Musical Association* first published
- 1875 Macfarren succeeds Bennett as principal of RAM, and refuses to relinquish the Academy's charter and merge with the National Training School; Trinity College of Music, London
- 1876 National Training School for Music (later RCM); music degrees established at London University
- 1877 Publication of Hullah's *Music in the house*
- 1878 People's Concert Society, London; Trinity College's piano and singing examinations introduced
- 1879 Grove's *Dictionary* (1st edn, –1890)
- 1880 Hullah's report on *Musical instruction in elementary schools on the continent*; Guildhall School of Music, London
- 1881 *Brass band news*
- 1882 Teaching diplomas introduced at Trinity College; (London première of Wagner's *Ring*)
- 1883 Royal College of Music (successor to the National Training School) opens with Grove as director; Croydon Conservatoire of Music
- 1884 *A song book for schools* (later the *National song book* (1906))
- 1886 Birmingham music college; ARCM examinations begin (open to outsiders)
- 1887 Charles Stanford made Cambridge professor; London College of Music; *British Bandsman*
- 1888 Alexander Mackenzie elected principal of RAM (holds post until 1924)

1889	*Musical Herald*; Mackenzie and Grove establish the Associated Board of the Royal Schools of Music; College of Violinists	1895	Henry Wood's Promenade Concerts, Royal Albert Hall, London
1890	Glasgow music college; ABRSM exams begin at 46 local centres in Britain	1897	Chair in music established at Durham University
		1898	'Maidstone' system of violin teaching
1891	Music faculty and residential degree instituted at Manchester University	1901	Arthur Somervell becomes Chief Music Inspector; Publication of the *Oxford history of music*
1892	*School music review*; Manchester School of Music, with Hallè as principal	1902	Lectureship in music created at Queen's College, Belfast
		1905	Elgar becomes first professor of music at Birmingham University
1893	*Cornet*; Royal Society of Organists granted charter; the Union of Graduates in Music; (Royal) Manchester College of Music; Queen's Hall, London	1908	Music Teachers' Association formed; M. A. Langdale's articles on *A plea for broader treatment of music in our schools*, in *The Crucible*

APPENDIX TWO

A Chronology of Principal British Instrumental Treatises, 1780–1900

In cases where there are a number of editions or English translations of a single source these are listed under the first, unless they are by different publishers or differ substantially, in which case they receive separate entries. If the original edition falls outside the 1780–1900 period then the first edition within that period is entered with any details of subsequent versions, and earlier versions are listed in the Bibliography.

1780

Anon., *Compleat instructions for the bassoon or fagotto* (London, c.1780, c.1790, ?1800).
—— *Compleat instructions for the common flute* (London, c.1780).
—— *Compleat instructions, for the fife* (London, c.1780, ?1808).
—— *Compleat instructions for the German flute* (London, c.1780).
—— *Compleat instructions for the guitar* (London, ?1780, c.1790).
—— *The clarinet instructor, by which playing on that instrument is rendered easy* (London, c.1780).
—— [Mr Fischer] *New and complete instruction for the oboe or hoboy* (London, c.1780, c.1810).
—— [Mr Winch] *New instructions for the French-horn* (London, c.1780, c.1790)
—— *Playing the harpsichord, spinnet or piano forte* (London, 1780 and c.1785).
Flack, J. C, *The art of playing the harpsichord* (London, ?1780).
Gehot, J., *Complete instructions for every musical instrument ... the scale or gamut for thirty five different instruments* (London, c.1780).
Schetky, J. C. G., *Twelve duetts ... some observations & rules for playing on that instrument* (London, [c.1780]).
Thompson, C., *New instructions for the violoncello* (London, c.1780).

1782

Heck, J. C., *The art of fingering ... harpsichord ... gradation of fine lessons* (London, 1782).
Miller, E., *Institutes of music, or easy instructions for the harpsichord ... young beginners* (London, ?1782).

1783

Anon., *New instructions for the German flute* (London, 1783, c.1790 and c.1802).
Bemetzrieder, A., *New lessons for the harpsichord ... to which is added an introduction by means of which every one may study this work without the help of a master, & improve rapidly both in practice & theory of music* (2nd edn, London, 1783).

1784

Baumgarten, C. F. W., *The ladies companion, or a complete tutor for the forte, piano forte, or harpsichord* (London, c.1784).
Corri, D., *The beginning and practice*

of fingering the harpsichord ... progressively arranged and adapted (Edinburgh, c.1784), as Art of fingering (Dublin, c.1795).

Gehot, J., A treatise on the theory & practice of music in three parts ... practical music in general ... thorough bass ... counterpoint or composition ... scales of every musical instrument & the art of fingering on keyed, and bowing on stringed instruments, explained in various examples (London, c.1784).

1785

Adams, J. B., A familiar introduction ... progressive examples & instructions for the use of beginners on the harpsichord, piano forte or organ (London, ?1785).

Anon., Compleat instructions for the clarinet (London, ?1785).

—— A new and complete tutor for the violoncello (London., c.1785).

—— The harpsichord preceptor (London, c.1785, c.1787).

Bemetzrieder, A. Music made easy to every capacity ... practical lessons for the harpsichord (2nd edn, London, 1785).

Brewster, H., A set of lessons for the harpsichord or piano forte (London, ?1785).

Crome, R., The fiddle new model'd ... familiar dialogues (London, c.1740, c.1750, c.1760, c.1765, c.1785).

Gunn, A., née Young, The elements of music & of fingering the harpsichord or piano-forte (Edinburgh, c.1785).

Hardy, H., The violoncello preceptor (Oxford, [c.1785]).

Hook, J., Guida di musica ... instructions for beginners on the harpsichord or piano forte ... to save a great deal of time & trouble both to master & scholar (London, c.1785, 2nd pt, London, c.1794).

Leoni, P., A complete introduction to the art of playing the mandoline (London, c.1785, 1896)

1786

Frick, P. J., A treatise on thorough bass (London, ?1786).

Jones, G., The complete instructor for the harpsichord or piano forte (London, c.1786).

1787

Anon., New and complete instructions for the violoncello (London, c.1787, c.1805)

—— Pocket companion for the piano forte (London, c.1787).

Arnold, S., Dr Arnold's new instructions for the German flute (London, 1787).

Corri, D., A complete musical grammar ... the art of fingering; the rules of thorough-bass (Edinburgh, c.1787, 1795).

Miller, E., Elements of thorough bass & composition (London, ?1787).

1788

Bemetzrieder, A., The gamut ... for the harpsichord (London, ?1788).

Broderip, R., Plain and easy instructions for young performers on the piano forte or harpsichord (London, c.1788).

Jones, W., Reeves, J., and Blakemore, T., Clavis campanologia, or a key to the art of ringing (London, 1788, rev. c.1788 and 1796).

1789

Anon., New instructions for playing the harpsichord, piano forte or spinnet ... thorough bass (London, c.1789 and 1790).

Broderip, R., A short introduction to the art of playing the harpsichord ... progressive lessons ... young beginners (London, c.1789).

Parsons, J., The elements of music ...

harpsichord or piano forte (Edinburgh, ?1789).

1790

Anon., *A new assistant for the piano forte, or harpsichord* (London, c.1790).
—— *New and complete instructions for the common flute* (London, c.1790).
—— *The compleat tutor for the hautboy* (London, c.1790).
Auge, P., *New and compleat instructions for the small harp* (London, c.1790).
Barthélemon, F. H., *A new tutor for the violin ... progressive examples and six capricios, from the most easy to the most difficult passages ... for the improvement of the lovers of that instrument* (London, c.1790).
—— New tutor for the harpsichord or piano forte (London, c.1790).
Clagget, C., *A variety of periodical lessons ... teliochordanized pianoforte* (London, ?1790).
Danby, J., *La guida della musica instrumentale, or the rudiments of the forte piano & harpsichord* (London, c.1790).
Gehot, J., *A complete instructor for every instrument* (London, 1790).
Gehot, J., *The art of bowing on the violin, calculated for the practice and improvement of juvenile performers* (London, c.1790, ed. R. Stowell, Early violin series 4, London, 1988).
Geminiani, F. (supposititious work), *The compleat tutor for the violin ... with some useful directions, lessons, graces, &c. by Geminiani ... collection of airs, marches, minuets, song tunes, & duetts* (London, c.1790).
—— (supposititious work), *New and compleat instructions for the violin* (London, c.1775, c.1790, c.1799, c.1806).

Lefevre, J., *A concise method to attain the art of playing on the cistre* (London, c.1790).
Malme, G., *A sett of practical essays for the harpsichord or piano forte ... convenience of master & scholar* (London, c.1790).
Quantz, J. J., *Versuch* (Berlin, 1752), abridged tr. as *Easy & fundamental instructions* (London, ?1790).

1792

Anon., *The elements of music and of fingering the harpsichord, arranged and adapted for the use of beginners* (Edinburgh, c.1792 and c.1800).
Geminiani, F. (supposititious work), *The entire new and compleat tutor for the violin* (London, c.1792, c.1800, c.1800, ?1813)
Kollmann, A. F. C., *An introduction ... for the harpsichord* (London, c.1792).
Wragg, J., *The flute preceptor* (London, ?1792, 2nd edn, c.1793, 15th edn, with additions, 1796, 18th edn, 1799).
—— *The oboe preceptor* (London, 1792, 4th edn, 1799).

1793

Dothel, N., *The art of playing the german-flute ... copious examples in an elegant stile* (London, 1793).
Gunn, J., *The art of playing the German flute* (London, 1793).
—— *The theory and practice of fingering the violoncello* (London, 1793, 2nd edn, c.1794, 1815).
Heck, J. C., *The art of playing thorough bass with correctness* (London, 1793).

1794

Light, E., *A 1st book, or master & scholars assistant ... art of playing on the harpsichord or pianoforte ...*

practical lessons in progressive order (London, c.1794).

Parsons, J., *The elements of music with progressive practical lessons for the harpsichord or piano forte dedicated to ... Lady Charlotte Campbell* (London, [1794]).

1795

Anon., *Complete instructions for the tenor* (London, ?1795).

—— *New instructions for the violoncello* (London, ?1795).

—— *The preceptor for piano-forte, the organ or harpsichord* (London, c.1795)

Barthélemon, F. H., *Tutor for the harp* (London, c.1795).

Blake, B., *9 divertimentos, for the piano forte ... many general rules ... in the absence of their master* (London, c.1795).

Blewitt, J., *A compleat treatise on the organ ... the purpose of rendering theory and practice subservient to mutual elucidation* (London, c.1795).

Camidge, M., *Instructions for the piano forte or harpsichord ... young practitioners ...* (London, c.1795).

Chabran, C. F., *Compleat instructions for the Spanish guitar* (London, c.1795).

Eley, Chr. Fr., *A new tutor for the clarinet* (London, c.1795).

Gunn, J., *An essay... towards a more ... scientific method of ... the study of the pianoforte* (London, c.1795, c.1812).

—— *The school of the German flute* (London, c.1795).

Huellmandel, N. J., *Principles of music, chiefly calculated for the piano forte or harpsichord with progressive lessons* (London, c.1795).

Jackson, G. K., *A treatise on practical thorough bass* (London, c.1795).

Kollmann, A. F. C., *The first beginning on the piano forte ... an improved method of teaching beginners* (London and Edinburgh, c.1795).

Light, E. *The art of playing the guittar* (London, 1795).

Mazzinghi, J., *Tiro musicus ... piano forte* (London, c.1795, c.1797, 2nd book, c.1798).

Tillière, J. B., *Méthode ...* (Paris, 1764, 1879), tr. as *New & compleat instructions for the violoncello* (London, c.1795, 1822).

1796

Anon., *Entire new and compleat instructions for the fife* (London, c.1796, c.1815).

—— *New and compleat instructions for the harpsichord, piano-forte, or organ* (London, ?1796).

Dussek, J. L., *Instructions on the art of playing the piano forte or Harpsichord* (London and Edinburgh, c.1796, ed. Hamilton, 1869, 1886).

Nicholson, J., *A concise treatise on thorough bass with practical lessons* (London, c.1796).

Moller, J. C., *A compleat book of instructions for the piano forte, harpsichord or organ* (London, c.1796).

Ross, J., *Ross's instructions for the piano forte* (London, c.1796).

Tashanberg, J., *The compleat school or the art of playing the violin with seventy-one variations, cadences, preludes and capricios* (London, ?1796).

1797

Anon., *The compleat tutor for the German flute* (London, c.1797, Dublin, c.1810).

Coblenz, A., *A new & easy method for tuning the grand & small pianoforte, & harpsichord; with proper instructions, & descriptions of the rules to be observed in performing the same* (London, 1797).

Preston, J., *Preston's pocket companion for the German flute* (London, 1797).
Sharp, F., *New guida di musica ... beginners on the piano forte* (London, 1797).
Smethergell, W., *Rules for thorough bass ... 3 sonatas ... with an accompaniment for the violin ...* (London, c.1797).

1798

Anon., *Music made easy ... beginners on the piano-forte or harpsichord* (London, 1798).
—— *New and compleat instructions for the clarionet* (London, ?1798).
—— *New instructions for playing the harpsichord, piano forte, or organ* (London, c.1798).
—— *The fashionable preceptor for the piano-forte & harpsichord* (London, c.1798).
Bemetzrieder, A., *1st lessons for the piano-forte or harpsichord* (London, c.1798).
Chinnery, W., *Music made easy ... beginners on the piano-forte or harpsichord* (London, 1798).
Furtado, J., *An essay on fingering the piano-forte* (London, 1798).
—— *An essay on the theory & advancement of thorough bass* (London, 1798).
—— *New elements of thorough bass* (London, c.1798).
Hyde, F., *A new and compleat preceptor for the trumpet and bugle horn* (London, c.1798, c.1800).

1799

Miller, E., *The new flute instructor* (London, c.1799).

1800

Anon., *An easy introduction to playing the piano forte* (London, c.1800).
—— *A new and compleat tutor for the German flute* (London, c.1800).
—— *Modern instructions for the German flute* (London, c.1800).
—— *New & complete pocket preceptor for the English & French flageolets* (London, c.1800).
—— *The hoboy preceptor ... without the assistance of a master ... Mr Fischer* (London, c.1800).
—— *The pocket preceptor for the German flute* (London, c.1800).
Broderip and Wilkinson, *Complete treatise for the violoncello ... Mr Cervetto* (London, c.1800).
—— *New and complete instructions for the lute* (London, c.1800).
Dale, J., *Instructions for the tambourine* (London, 1800).
Geminiani, F. (supposititious work), *Compleat instructions for the violin ... with several excellent pieces for two violins* (London, c.1800).
King, M. P., *A general treatise ... harmony & through bass & its application in composition* (London, c.1800).
McKerrell, J., *A familiar ... beginners on the harpsichord or piano-forte* (London, c.1800).
Mayer, J. B., *Complete instructions for the harp* (London, 1800).
Merelle, Mademoiselle, *New and complete instructions for the pedal harp in two books* (London, 1800).
Perry, J., *New and improved tutor for the violin, comprising the rudiments of music and method of tuning* (London, c.1800).
Reinagle, J., *A concise introduction to the art of playing the violoncello including a short and easy treatise on music, to which is added thirty progressive lessons* (London, [1800], 3rd edn, 1811, 4th edn, c.1815, 5th (enlarged) edn, c.1835, ?6th edn, 1887).
Thompson, [publishers], *Thompson's new instructions for the German flute* (London, c.1800).

Weippert, J. E., *The pedal harp rotula* (London, c.1800).

1801

Anon., *The clarinet preceptor* (London, c.1801, c.1803, c.1808).
Clementi, M., *Introduction to the art of playing on the pianoforte* (London, 1801, 11th edn, 1826).
Dale, J., *Introduction to the piano forte, harpsichord or organ in 4 books* (London, 1796–1801, c.1821).
Kollmann, A. F. C., *A practical guide to thorough-bass* (London, 1801).
Monzani, T. *Instructions for the German flute ... an easy pleasing stile* (London, [1801]).
Reeve, W., *The juvenile preceptor ... piano-forte, with 24 lessons & 4 easy duets* (London, ?1801).

1802

Anon., *New and compleat instruction book for the English and harp guitars* (London, ?1802).
Barthélemon, F. H., *1st. part the principles of thorough bass* (London, c.1802).
Gunn, J., *An essay ... on the application of the principles of harmony, thorough bass and modulation to the violoncello* (London, 1802).
Hammond, J., *A proper guide to music, being a complete book of instructions for beginners on the piano forte* (London, 1802)
Webbe, S., *Harmony ... figured basses ... accompaniment* (London, c.1802/R1830).

1803

Anon., *Thoroughbass at 1 view* (London, ?1803).
Bemetzrieder, A., *A complete treatise on music. The precepts and examples in two separate books* (London, 1800–1803).
MacDonald, J., *A compleat theory of the Scots highland bagpipe* (Edinburgh, 1803).
Mahon, J., *The new & complete preceptor for the clarinet* (London, 1803).

1804

Butler, T. H., *Musical games ... an encouragement for all classes of young persons learning the piano forte* (Edinburgh, 1804).
Türk, D. G., *Klavierschule* (Leipzig & Halle, 1789, 2nd edn, 1802), abridged tr. as *Treatise ... pianoforte* (London, c.1804).
Wragg, J., *Wragg's improved flute preceptor: or the whole art of playing the German Flute etc.* (London, 1st edn, 1804, 16th edn, 1818).

1805

Anon., *Complete instructions for the bassoon* (London, c.1805, c.1806).
—— *Instructions for playing the bagpipe* (London, ?1805).
Attwood, T., *A short introduction to the pianoforte* (London, ?1805, ?1830).
Bainbridge, W. & Wood, *Flageolet tutor ... without the assistance of a master* (London, c.1805).
Cheese, G. J., *Practical rules, for playing & teaching, the piano forte & organ ... teachers & pupils born blind* (London, Dublin and Glasgow, c.1805).
Corfe, J., *Thorough bass simplified ... Geminiani* (London, ?1805, c.1817).
Jousse, J., *The modern violin preceptor ... the art of bowing ... examples and exercises to which is added a selection of favorite songs marches rondos & duetts* (London, [?1805]).
L., F., *Through bass made easy* (London, c.1805).

Marsh, J., *The rudiments of through bass ... use of ladies & amateur performers upon the piano forte or organ* (Chichester, London and Dublin, c.1805, c.1820).

1806

Anon., *Preceptor for the improved octave flageolet* (London, c.1806, c.1811).
Cheese, G. J., *Practical rules for playing and teaching the piano forte and organ ... teachers and pupils born blind* (London, ?1806).

1807

Green, J., *Complete preceptor for flageolets* (London, c.1807).
Gunn, J., *An historical enquiry respecting the performance on the harp in the highlands of Scotland* (Edinburgh, 1807).
Kollmann, A. F. C., *A 2d practical guide to thorough bass* (London, 1807).
Marsh, J., *A catechism for the use of learners of thorough-bass ... convenience of the learner ... reference* (Chichester, 1807).

1808

Anon., *The English and French flageolet preceptor, or the whole art of playing the flageolet* (London, c.1808).
Jousse, J., *Guida armonica ... thorough bass ... musical composition* (London, c.1808).

1809

Gawler, W., *Scale & instructions for the piano forte* (London, c.1809).
Hodges, J., *Short instructions for tuning a piano-forte* (London, 1809).

1810

Anon., *A complete preceptor or the whole art of playing the improved octave flageolet* (London, [c.1810]).
—— *The compleat tutor for the English and French flageolet* (London, c.1810).
—— *New and modern preceptor for the flute* (London, c.1810).
—— *Thompson's new instructions for the German flute* (London, c.1810).
Bainbridge, W., *The preceptor for Bainbridge's new patent double flute and double Flageolet ... by which any lady or gentleman ... without learning music* (London, c.1810).
—— & Wood, *The preceptor, or a key to the double flageolet* (London, c.1810)
Bohlius, J. F., *Short & easy introduction to playing the piano forte* (London, c.1810).
Bréval, J.-B. S., *Traité ...* (Paris, [1804]) tr. as *New instruction for the violoncello* (London, 1810).
Challoner, N. B., *New guida di musica ... beginners ... piano forte ...* (London, c.1810, new edn, London, [1812]).
Corri, P. A., *L'anima di musica ... piano forte playing ... progressive lessons ... progressive preludes* (London, 1810, 1822).
Farrell, O., *Collection of national Irish music for the union pipes* (London, c.1810).
Goodban, T., *A new and complete guide to the art of playing on the violin ... with particular instructions on bowing, fingering & shifting, exemplified by appropriate examples, and illustrated by lessons, airs and duetts, progressively arranged ... to enable the learner to proceed with pleasure in his study thereof* (London, 1810).
Klose, F. J., *Instructions for the piano forte* (London, ?1810).
Monro, J., *The art of playing the*

flageolet ... to supersede the necessity of any assistance from a master (London, c.1810).

Pasquali, N., Thorough-bass made easy (Edinburgh, London & Dublin, 1757/R1974, ed. Jousse, 1810).

Williams, G. E., An introduction to the art of playing on the piano forte ... being a progressive series of lessons for beginners (London, c.1810, 2nd edn, c.1817).

1811

Hale, S., The pupil's friend, or instructions for the piano-forte (London, c.1811).

Jousse, J., The theory and practice of the violin, clearly explained in a series of instructions and examples, particularly calculated to facilitate the progress of learners in the art of bowing with propriety and elegance (London, 1811).

King, M. P., Thorough bass, made clear to every capacity (London, ?1811).

Macdonald, J., Treatise explanatory of the principles constituting the practice and theory of the violoncello (London, 1811).

Parkinson, W., A new book of instructions for beginners on the piano forte or Harpsichord ... progressive lessons, composed & fingered (London and Dublin, c.1811).

Schetky, J. C. G., Practical and progressive lessons for the violoncello (London, 1811).

Stevens, W. S., A treatise on pianoforte expression ... fine playing ... (London, 1811).

1812

Briggs, J., Introduction to the art of playing on the patent double flageolet (London, c.1812).

Corri, P. A., Original system of preluding ... extracted from a treatise on piano forte playing by the above author (London, c.1812, 1817, 1822).

Cramer, J. B., Instructions for the piano forte (London, 1812, 3rd edn, c.1820, 7th edn, c.1840, c.1867).

Crotch, W., Elements of musical composition; comprehending the rules of thorough bass, & the theory of tuning (Oxford and London, 1812).

Light, E., New and compleat instructions for playing on the harp-lute (London, [1812]).

Loeschman, D., Description & use of the patent enharmonic pianoforte (London, c.1812).

Mozart, L., Versuch ... , abridged tr. as Mozart's violin school on the art of bowing ... never before published (London, [1812]).

Panormo, F., Elements of music for the piano forte (London, c.1812).

1813

Anon., Goulding & Co[']s German flute tutor, on a new & familiar plan ... without the aid of a master (London and Dublin, c.1813).

—— Instructions for the tambourine (London, ?1813).

—— New and complete instructions for the German flute (London, c.1813).

Goulding & Co, German flute tutor (London and Dublin, [1813]).

Keith, R. W., A violin preceptor on an entirely new principle ... calculated to lay a regular and stable foundation for young practitioners and to facilitate their early progress ... appropriate exercises & a selection of the most favourite airs arranged as duetts (London, 1813, 3rd edn, c.1825).

Kelly, J., Elements of music in verse ... pianoforte ... juvenile study ... progressive lessons (London, c.1813).

Steibelt, D. G., *Méthode* (Leipzig, [1809]), tr. as *Steibelt's art of playing the pianoforte* (London, c.1813).

1814

Davis, J., *A new & complete system of music, or general instructions for the piano forte, organ, pedal harp &c* (London, c.1814).
Goodban, T., *Complete instructions ... for the use of schools* ... (London, 2nd edn, c.1814, 'new and complete' edn, 1840).
Logier, J. B., *An explanation & description of the royal patent chiroplast or hand-director ... piano forte* (London, c.1814).

1815

Anon., *Instructions for playing the harmonicon* (Manchester, c.1815).
—— *The piano-forte pocket companion ... science & practice of music ... youngest pupils ... scientific professors* (London, 1815).
Beale, J., *A complete guide to the art of playing the German flute ... progressively arranged* (London and Dublin, c.1815).
Coggins, J., *The governess's musical assistant, containing all that is truly useful to the theory & practice of the piano forte* (London, c.1815; 2nd edn, 1822; 3rd edn, 1824).
Keith, R. W., *A new & complete preceptor for the German flute ... a regular & stable foundation for young practitioners* (London, c.1815).
—— *Instructions for the pianoforte* (London, c.1815).
Logier, J. B., *A companion ... piano forte ...* (London, c.1815).
Paine, J., *A treatise on the violin ... true degree of time ... a tune attached to each degree* (London, c.1815, 3rd edn, ?1820).

Shield, W., *Rudiments of thorough bass, for young harmonists ...* (London, c.1815).

1816

Barbieri, C. F., *A new treatise on the theori-practical, fundamental & thorough bass* (2nd edn, Edinburgh, ?1816).
Howell, T., *Practical instructions for the piano forte* (London & Bristol, c.1816).
—— *Lessons ... piano forte* (London & Bristol, c.1816).
—— *Preludes ... piano forte* (London & Bristol, c.1816).
—— *Auxiliary lessons for the piano forte* (Bristol, c.1816).
Logier, J. B., *A syllabus of the 2d examination ... piano forte* (Dublin, 1816).
Maelzel, J. N., *The metronomic tutor ... lessons for the piano-forte* (2 vols, London, c.1816).
Nicholson, C., *Complete preceptor for the German flute ... calculated to afford great facility in the pupils practice* (London, c.1816; 2nd edn, c.1840).
Saffrey, O., *An introduction to music ... progressive lessons, songs & preludes ... beginners: on the piano forte* (London and Canterbury, c.1816).
Warren, M. A., *Piano monitor, or assistant for the wrist* (Glasgow, c.1816).

1817

Anon., *New instructions, for the violin ... collection of minuets, marches, song tunes, duetts* (London, [1817]).
Bochsa, R. N. C., *Nouvelle méthode ...* (Paris, [?1815]), tr. as *A new and improved method of instruction for the harp* (London, 1817, [?1828]).
Bremner, R., *Rudiments of thorough bass* (London, c.1817).

Callender, W. R., *The pianoforte precepteur ... taste & elegance* (London, c.1817).
Hawkins, J. S., *An inquiry ... thorough bass* (London, 1817).
King, M. P., *1st instructions for the piano-forte ... 6 original progressive sonatinas ... to assist the master & to advance the pupil* (London, c.1817).
Potter, S., *The art of beating the drum, with the camp, garrison & street duty by note* (London, 1817).
—— *The art of playing the fife, with the camp, garrison & street duty* (London, 1817).

1818

Hawker, Col. P., *Advice ... piano forte ...* (London, c.1818).
Jousse, J., *Lectures on thorough bass ... to facilitate the theory & practice of that branch of the musical science* (London, c.1818).

1819

Burrowes, J. F., *The thorough-base primer* (London, 1819).
Cobham, C., *Harmonic system for the violin. A treatise on single and double harmonics* (London, [1819]).
Colclough, S. T., *New and complete instructions for the union pipes* (Dublin, c.1819).
Kilner, D., *The child's introduction to thorough bass* (London, 1819).
Monro, J., *New & complete introduction to the art of playing on the piano forte ... observations on musical expression* (London, c.1819).
Paddon, J., *A musical catechism as far as relates to thorough bass ...* (London, c.1819).
Sola, C. M. A., *Instructions for the Spanish guitar* (London, 1819).
Williams, G. E., *Exercises for the piano forte ... school classes* (London, c.1819).

1820

Albrechtsberger, J. G., *Generalbass-Schule* (Leipzig, ?1820), tr. J. Jousse as *Principles of accompaniment or thorough bass* (London, 1820).
Danneley, J. F., *An introduction to the elementary principles of thorough bass, & classical music* (Ipswich & London, 1820).
Gourdez, J., *A treatise on thorough bass, for beginners* (London, c.1820).
Hawker, Col. P., *Instructions to young performers ... patent hand-moulds ... pianoforte* (London, c.1820, 3rd edn, 1840).
Heather, W. E., *A treatise on pianoforte study* (London, c.1820).
Jousse, J., *The piano forte, made easy to every capacity ...* (London & Dublin, 5th edn, c.1820, 10th edn, 1827, 12th edn, 1830).
Kuffner, F., *Complete preceptor for the German flute* (London, c.1820).
Woakes, W. H., *A catechism of thorough bass ... the musical science ... the learner or amateur* (Hereford and London, 1820).

1821

Alexander, J., *Complete preceptor for the flute ... Ashe, Nicholson & Weidner* (2nd edn, London, c.1821).
Anon., *A new preceptor for the German flute* (London, c.1821).
Burrowes, J. F., *The piano-forte primer ... private tuition, or teaching in classes* (3rd edn, London, 1821).
Erard, P., *The harp in its present improved state* (London, 1821).
Nicholson, C., *Preceptive lessons for the flute* (London, 1821, 'Appendix', [1825]).
Relfe, J., *Lucidos ordo ... thorough bass designation ...* (London, 1821).
Weiss, C. N., *A new methodical instruction book for the flute ... a progressive & pleasing course of*

instruction, to the highest pitch of excellence, in a very short time (London, c.1821).

1822

Crotch, W., *Preludes for the piano forte ... the rudiments* (London, c.1822).
Hempel, C. W., *Introduction to the piano-forte ... progressive order* (London, c.1822).
Klose, F. J., *Practical hints for acquiring thorough bass* (London, 1822).
Macdonald, J., *A treatise on the harmonic system ... particularly to the practice of the violin, tenor, violoncello, and double-bass* (London, 1822).
Moxley, A. S., *Elementary instructions for the piano forte* (London, 1822).

1823

Anon., *A correct & easy method of tuning the grand square piano-forte* (London, c.1823).
Baillot, P. M. F. De S., Rode, P., and Kreutzer, R., *Méthode* (Paris, 1803/R1974) [commonly referred to as Rode et al.], abridged tr. as *Rode, Baillot & Kreutzer's method of instruction for the violin: adopted by the conservatory of Paris* (London, 1823).
Ferrari, G. G., *Studio di musica teorica pratica ... rules of thorough bass & composition* (London and Edinburgh, ?1823).
MacPherson, D., *A catechism of music ... learners on the piano forte ... examples & lessons* (Edinburgh, c.1823).
Rode et al. – see Baillot entry above.
Tomlins, T., *Instructions for the piano-forte* (?Shrewsbury, ?1823).

1824

Crouch, F. W. N., *A compleat treatise on the violoncello written ... selected and composed* (London, [1824]).
—— *Supplement to Crouch's treatise on the violoncello composed and selected from the celebrated work adopted by the Conservatoire at Paris* (London, [1824]).
Gutteridge, W., *Introduction to the art of playing on Gutteridge's new patent clarinet* (London, 1824).
Loder, J. D., *A general and comprehensive instruction book for the violin* (London, 1824, 2nd edn, 1826, 3rd edn, 1837, 5th edn, 1841, ed. T. Westrop, 1880, 'Marlborough' edn, ed. J. T. Carrodus, 1884, ed. W. Henley, 1910, 'Hawkes-Loder' edn, ed. R. Fels, 1911).
Mott, I. H. R., *Advice & instructions, for playing the piano forte, with Expression, & brilliant execution* (London, c.1824).
Rimbault, S. F., *1st rudiments to the art of playing on the piano forte* (London, c.1824, 2nd edn, 1830).
Sheppard, W., *A new piano forte preceptor ...* (London, c.1824).

1825

Anon., *Complete instructions for the improved patent double flageolet* (London, ?1825).
Bennett, A. W., *Instructions for the piano forte* (London, 1825, 3rd edn, [?1850]).
Bown, G. W., *The flauto instructive compendium, or preceptor for the flute ... progressive duetts ... particularly eligible to officers or gentlemen going abroad & others who have not access to a master* (London, c.1825).
Challoner, N. B., *Instructions for the violin ... progressively arranged ... with the view of facilitating the progress of the pupil and preventing unnecessary trouble to the master ... original compositions ... favourite airs arranged as duos, for pupil and master or in schools &c for two*

pupils to practise together (London, 1825, 1877).

Eberhardt, H., *For the use of His Majesty's army instructions for the Pandiran reeds* (London, c.1825).

Green, J., *Hints on the Spanish guitar* (London, 1825).

Horsley, W., *An explanation of musical intervals ... exercises for the piano forte* (London, c.1825).

Howell, T., *Original instructions for the violin, illustrated by precepts and examples, composed expressly for this work ... dedicated to Nicholas Mori* (Bristol, 1825).

Jackson, G. K., *Instruction book to the piano forte* (London, 1825).

Nielson, L. C., *Piano-forte tutor* (London, ?1825).

Sanderson, J., *A celebrated study for the bow and fingerboard of the violin ... the modern school for the practice & improvement of amateurs & young professors* (London, 2nd edn, c.1825).

Wood, G., *Complete instructions for the alto fagotto* (London, c.1825).

1826

Crotch, W., *Practical thorough bass ... organ or piano forte* (London, c.1826).

Griesbach, J. H., *Piano-forte-students' companion ... dedicated to his pupils* (2nd edn, London, c.1826)

Huerta, A. T., *A complete book of instructions for the Spanish guitar ... Guiliani* [sic] (London, [?1826]).

James, W. N., *A word or two on the flute* (Edinburgh, 1826).

Lillycrop, S., *Theoretical & practical thorough bass* (London and Edinburgh, c.1826).

Major, J., *The little harmonist; or a mother's introduction to the piano-forte* (London, c.1826).

Malt, T. F., *Piano-forte tutor* (London, c.1826).

Valentine, T., *Instructions for the piano-forte ...* (London, c.1826).

Willman, T. L. A., *A complete instruction book for the clarinet* (London, 1826).

1827

Berbiguier, B.-T., *Nouvelle méthode* (Paris, c.1818), abridged tr. as *A complete system of articulation for the flute* (London, c.1827) and as *Berbiguier's method of instruction for the flute*, ed. W. N. James (London, c.1827).

Blagrove, R. M., *A new and improved system to the art of playing the violin* (London, [1827]).

Dizi, F. J., *École de harpe, a complete treatise on the harp* (London, [1827]).

Dressler, R., *New & complete instructions for the flute*, Op.68 (London, c.1827).

Duvernay, F., *A complete instruction book for the guitar* (London, 1827).

Egan, C., *The royal harp director* (London, [1827]).

Fryer, J., *A practical treatise for the piano forte ... dedicated to J. B. Cramer* (London, c.1827).

Jauralde, N., *A complete preceptor for the Spanish guitar* (London, ?1827).

Latour, J. T., *New & improved method of instruction for the piano forte* (London, c.1827).

Logier, J. B., *A system of the science of music & practical composition; incidentally comprising what is usually understood by the term thorough bass* (London, 1827).

Macfarlane, G., *The complete reader: a course of exercises for the cornopean* (London, 1827).

1828

Anon., *New and complete instructions for the guitar by an eminent master* (London, ?1828).

Baillot, P. M. F. de S., Rode, P., and Kreutzer, R., [*Méthode* (Paris, 1803)], tr. as *R. Cocks & Co's improved and enlarged edition. Of the celebrated method...by J. A. Hamilton, professor of music* (London, [1828]).

Bennett, A. W., *Instructions for the Spanish guitar ... Carulli, Giuliani ... Moretti ...* (London, 1828).

Carulli, F., *Méthode complette ...* (Paris, c.1815), tr. as *A complete method, for the Spanish guitar or lyre ... Bertioli* (3rd edn, London, 1828, [?1840]).

Kollmann, A. F. C., *Ladies' thorough bass* (London, c.1828).

L'abbé le fils [Joseph-Barnabé Saint-Sevin], *Principes du violon* (Paris, 1761/R1961, 2nd edn, 1772), abridged tr. as *An easy method of producing on the violin, the harmonic sounds in all the major and minor keys* (London, 2nd edn, [1828]).

Latour, J. T., *Sequel to ... instructions for the piano forte* (London, c.1828).

Logier, J. B., *A manual, chiefly for the use of preceptors, parents, governesses ... piano-forte* (London, 1828).

McMurdie, J., *Juvenile preceptor for the pianoforte* (London, c.1828).

Tipper, J. E., *Tipper's music primer ... chiefly for the piano forte ... applicable to any other instrument ...* (London, ?1828).

1829

Busby, T., *Catechism of music ... preliminary instructions for the piano-forte* (London, c.1829).

Challoner, N. B., *A new preceptor for the harp* (London, ?1829).

Egan, C., *The harp primer* (London, [1829]).

[Graham, Mary J.], *A letter to a young piano forte player* (London, c.1829).

Howell, T., *Practical elementary examples for the violin ... systematic progression of original lessons ... an effective and elegant method of bowing ... an auxiliary work to the author's Original instructions* (London & Bristol, 1829).

Hummel, J. N., *Ausführliche ...* (1828), tr. as *A complete theoretical & practical course of instructions ... pianoforte* (London, c.1829).

James, W. N., *The flutist's catechism* (London, 1829).

Simpson, J., *Complete preceptor for the improved patent single and double flageolet* (London, c.1829).

Tansur, W., *A new musical grammar* (London, 1746, 7th edn, 1829, 8th edn, 1830).

1830

Alexander, J., *Improved preceptor for the flute ... progressive lessons* (London, c.1830).

Anon., *The German Aeolian tutor* (London, 1830).

—— *Metzler's & son's clarinet preceptor* (London, c.1830).

—— *Metzler & Son's complete tutor for the German flute, (with or without additional keys)* (London, c.1830).

—— *Royal keyed bugle tutor* (London, [?1830]).

Bertini, (B.) A., *New system for learning and acquiring extraordinary facility on all music instruments, particularly the piano forte, harp and violin, as well as singing; with a new and easy mode of marking the fingering of all wind instruments ... That will enable the pupil to make great progress, even in the absence of a master, & without an instrument* (London, 1830, 2nd edn, 1837, 3rd edn, 1849, 4th edn, 1855).

Campagnoli, B., *Metodo* (?Milan, ?1797/R1945, 2nd edn, 1803, ?3rd edn, c.1828; Fr. & Ger. tr., Leipzig, 1824), tr. by J. A. Hamilton as *A new mechanical & progressive course of instruction on the art of*

playing the violin ... composed & dedicated to his Royal Highness the duke of Cambridge (London, c.1830, 2nd edn, 1834).
—— *A complete treatise on harmonics for the violin Op. posth.* (London, 183–?).
Clarke, J., *Instructions for the piano forte* (London, [1830]).
—— *A catechism ... assistance of teachers of the pianoforte* (London, 1830, new edn, London, [1884]).
Clementi, M., *Gradus ad parnassum, or the art of playing the pianoforte* (London, c.1830).
Coggins, J., *New and complete instructions for the flute according to Drouet's celebrated system* (London, 1830).
Drouet, L., Méthode (c.1827), tr. as *Method of flute playing* (London, c.1830).
Eavestaff, W., *Instructions for the piano forte ... & a selection of popular airs* (London, c.1830).
Eley, C., *Improved method of instruction for the violoncello* (London, 1830).
Goss, J., *The piano-forte student's catechism ... designed for the use of schools* (London, 1830).
Hodson, G. A., *Instructions for the pianoforte with progressive lessons* (Dublin, c.1830).
James, W., *A new and compleat tutor for the violin ... with a selection of favourite airs* (London, c.1830).
Jousse, J., *Jousse's fashionable preceptor, or complete tutor for the piano forte* (London, 4th edn, c.1830).
Lindsay, T., *The elements of flute-playing, according to the most approved principles* (2 pts, London, 1828–30).
May, G. T., *Instructions for the Spanish guitar* (London, ?1830).
Metzler & Co, *Clarinet preceptor* (London, ?1830).
—— *Complete tutor for the German flute* (London, c.1830).

Parke, G. W., *A new & complete tutor for the German flute* (London, c.1830).
Pelzer, F., *Instructions for the Spanish guitar* (London, ?1830).
Präger, H. A., *Elementary and practical school for the violin, in three parts* (London, c.1830)
Rodwell, G. H., *The first rudiments of harmony ... a short account of all instruments employed in an orchestra* (London, 1830).
Shade, G., *New & complete tutor, for the German flute* (London, c.1830, 6th edn, 1835).
Voigt, A., *A short & efficient treatise on the art of scoring ... every instrument in the orchestra ...* (London, c.1830).
Wrede, H., *Improved instructions for the flageolet ... progressive lessons* (London, c.1830).

1831

Anon., *Practical rules for producing harmonic notes on the violin* (Bury St Edmunds and London, 1831).
Tully, C., *Tutor for keyed bugle* (R. Cocks & Co's series) (London, 1831).

1832

Baillot et al., Méthode ... (Paris, [1805]), tr. A. Merrick as *Method for the violoncello by Baillot, Levasseur, Catel & Baudiot, adopted by the Paris Conservatory* (London, ?1832, 2nd edn, c.1850, c.1855).
—— *Exercises* [supplement], tr. Merrick (London, 1832).

1833

Goss, J., *An introduction to harmony and thorough bass* (London, c.1833).
Green, J., *Concise instructions ... Royal Seraphine and organ* (London, 1833).

Hamilton, J. A., *Method for the double bass according to the English system of tuning and fingering, compiled from the treatises of Miné, Fröhlich &c.* (London, [1833], c.1845).
Spohr, L., *Violinschule* (Vienna, [1832]/R1960; Fr. tr., Heller, Paris, c.1870; It. tr., Chiasso, c.1840), tr. by C. Rudolphus as *Louis Spohr's grand violin school* (London, 1833, 2nd rev. edn, 1836, 6th edn, 1843, 10th edn, c.1865).

1834

Bruni, M., *Treatise on the guitar* (London, [1834]).

1835

Corri, M. P., *A complete course of instructions on ... arranging music in score ... orchestras, military bands, brass bands* (London, ?1835).
—— *A new and improved pianoforte tutor* (London, ?1835).
Hack, R., *New and original instructions for the violin ... a great variety of rules, examples & preludes in the different keys, with a series of popular airs adapted & progressively arranged as lessons so as to render the students [sic] progress on that masterly & effective instrument both easy & agreeable* (London, [c.1835]).
Hamilton, J. A., *Catechism for the violin* (London, [c.1835], 2nd edn, 1836, 5th edn, 1848, 15th edn, 1883, 19th edn, 1889).
—— *A catechism for the violoncello* (London, [?1835], 2nd edn, rev. and enlarged John Bishop, n.d.).
Harper, T., sen., *Instructions for the trumpet, with the use of the chromatic slide, also the Russian valve trumpet, the cornet à pistons or small stop trumpet, and the keyed bugle* (London, 1835, 2nd edn, ?1836/R1988).

Kalkbrenner, F., *Méthode* (London, 1831), tr. as *Complete course of instruction for the piano forte* (London, [c.1835]).
Meyer, F. C., *A new treatise on the art of playing upon the double movement harp* (London, ?1835).
Wright, T. H., *New preceptor for the harp* (London, [?1835]).

1836

Woodward, E., *The amateur's guide for the violin ... selections from the best works on shifting and double stopping* ([?London], 1836).

1837

Loder, J. D., *A third edition (considerably enlarged & improved) of A general and comprehensive instruction book for the violin ... hundred progressive exercises in the different major and minor keys ... proper bowing & fingering marked* (London, 1837).
Macfarlane, G., *Cornopean instructor* (London, 1837).

1838

Foraboschi, G., *A new and complete instruction book for the cornopean* (London, 1838).
—— *A new and complete instruction book for the three trombones* (London, 1838).
—— *A new and complete instruction book for the trumpet* (London, 1838).
Herz, H., *Méthode* (Mainz & Anvers, 1838), tr. as *A new and complete pianoforte school* (London, c.1838).

1839

Czerny, C., *Vollständige ... , Op.500* (3 vols, Vienna, 1838–39), tr. as *Complete theoretical and practical pianoforte school, Op.500* (3 vols, London, 1838–39, 1846).

Rimbault, E. F., *A child's first instruction book for the piano forte* (London, 1839).
Roy & Mueller, *Tutor for the keyed and valve trumpet, with airs and duets* ('R. Cocks & Co's series of modern tutors for wind instruments' (London, 1839).

1840

Anon., *Paganini's method of producing the harmonic double stops* (London, [1840]).
Bates, T. C., *Complete preceptor for the accordion or flutina* (London, ?1840).
—— *Complete preceptor for the flageolet* (London, ?1840).
Clarke, J., *Exercise in harmony ... thorough bass* (London, c.1840).
Glover, C. W., *An elementary treatise on the violin* (London, c.1840).
Frölich, F. J., *Kontrabass-Schule* (Würzburg, 1829; Eng. tr., ?1840).
Hamilton, J. A., *A complete and popular course of instructions for the violin* (London, c.1840).
—— *Complete preceptor for the violoncello* (London, 1840).
Herz, H., *A standard modern preceptor for the pianoforte* (London, c.1840).
Hus-Desforges, P. L., *Méthode ...* (Paris, c.1829), tr. as *Method for the violoncello* (London, 1840).
Mackintosh, G., *New and improved bassoon tutor* (London, ?1840).
Romberg, B. H., *Violoncell Schule ...* (Berlin, [1840]), tr. as *A complete theoretical and practical school for the violoncello* (London, [1840]).
Thomson, A., *New and improved violin instructor ... catechism ... approved method of bowing ... collection of popular tunes in an easy style, with the bowing marked for beginners* (London, [1840]).
Tully, C., *Tutor for the French horn* (London, 1840).
West, W. H., *The art of playing the violin, on a new principle by which the progress of the learner is greatly facilitated ... selection of popular airs* (London, 12th edn, [1840]).

1841

Fétis, F.-J. & Moscheles, I., *Méthode* (Paris, c.1840/R1973), tr. as *Complete system of instruction for the piano forte* (London, [1841]).
Loder, J. D., *A fifth edition considerably enlarged & improved ... A general and comprehensive instruction book ... a selection of popular melodies, with an accompaniment ... fingering & bowing* (London, 1841).
Reinagle, A. R., *First lessons for beginners on the violoncello* (London, 1841).

1842

Coule, C., *New and complete instructions for playing the French accordion* (London, 1842).
Hamilton, J. A., *A standard tutor, for the organ* (London, [1842], ed. W. Dickinson, [1884]).
Loder, J. D., *For the violin the whole of the modern art of bowing* (London, 1842).
Pelzer, F., *A practical guide to modern piano forte playing* (London, 1842).
Warren, J., *Hamilton's catechism of the organ* (2nd edn, London, 1842).

1843

Anon., *The handbook of the violin, its theory and practice* (London, 1843).
D'Almaine and Co, *Standard tutor for the double-bass translated from the celebrated treatises of Adolph Miné and Herr [F. J.] Fröhlich and adapted to the system of tuning and fingering used in England* (London, [1843]).
Luigi, G., *New instruction book for the guitar* (London, 1844).

Spohr, L., *Louis Spohr's celebrated violin school, translated ... by John Bishop* (London, 1843).

1844

Hamilton, J. A., *Catechism on the art of writing for an orchestra, and on playing from score* (London, 1844, 2nd edn, 1846).
Richardson, J., *A set of studies for the flute* (London, 1844).
Rinck, J. C. H., *Praktische Orgelschule* (Bonn & Cöln, 1819–21), tr. J. A. Hamilton as *Rinck's complete practical organ school* (London, 1844, rev. J. Hiles, 1873); tr. S. Wesley as *Celebrated practical school for the organ* (10th edn, rev. J. Bishop, London, *c*.1850).
Wade, James A., *The hand-book to the piano forte* (London, 1844).

1845

Anon., *Handbook of the violin* (London, 1845).
—— *Instructions for the violoncello* ('Addison & Hodson's standard modern tutors') (London, [?1845]).
Bates, T. C., *Bates' complete preceptor for the violin ... six preludes in the most useful keys, and a selection of popular airs, quadrilles, &c.* (London, [?1845]).
Bertini, H. J., *Complete method for the pianoforte*, tr. J. Clarke (London, 1845).
Blight, S., *Improved preceptor for the cornopean* (London, *c*.1845).
Hancock, C., *Improved accordion preceptor* (London, 1845, rev. 1852).

1846

Anon., *The violin preceptor; or, pocket guide ... a complete course of lessons on music, with instructions, scales, and a selection of favourite airs, arranged in an easy and progressive style* (Glasgow, 1846, 1882).
Clinton, J., *A school; or practical instruction book for the Boehm flute* (London, 1846).
Hancock, C., *Improved flute preceptor* (London, 1846, rev. 1853).
Phillips, W. L., *New and complete instruction for the violoncello* (London, 1846).

1847

Carte, R., *Complete course of instructions for the Boehm fingering flute* (London, 1847).
Czerny, C., *Supplement ...* (Vienna, 1846–7), tr. as *Supplement to ... Pianoforte school* (London, 1846–7).
Farmer, H., *New violin school ... progressively arranged ... selection of favourite airs* (London, 1847, 1857, 1876, 1877, 1903).
Siccama, A., *Theory of the new patent diatonic flute* (London, 1847, 1851).

1848

Rimbault, E. F., *The first book of the pianoforte* (London, 1848).

1849

Camus, P. H., *New and improved method for the Boehm flute* (London, 1849).
Hamilton, J. A., *Modern instructions for the pianoforte* (London, 13th edn, 1849, 14th edn, arranged and fingered by Charles Czerny, ?1849, 34th edn, 1853, 50th edn, [1854], 1135th edn, [1877], ed. J. B. Zerbini, London, [1884], ed. J. Robinson, London, [1885]).
—— *Multum in parvo, or a complete instructor, for the piano forte, with a variety of popular airs ... new edition* (London, [?1849]).

1850

Anon., *The flute preceptor or pocket guide to the art of playing the flute* (Glasgow, c.1850).

Banister, H. J., *One hundred & fifty lessons for the violoncello* (London, ?1850).

Barret, A. M. R., *A complete method for the oboe* (London, 1850, 2nd edn, c.1880).

Blagrove, W. M., *New and complete system of playing the violin, with easy and progressive exercises* (London, [c.1850]).

Clinton, J., *A code of instructions for the fingering of the equisonant flute* (London, c.1850).

—— *Practical instruction book for the Boehm flute* (London, 1850).

Hamilton, J. A., *The universal violin tutor principally selected from the larger work of J. A. Hamilton* (London, [c.1850]).

Kummer, F. A., *Violoncell-Schule* (Leipzig, 1839), tr. as *Violoncello school* (London, ?1850, Leipzig, 1874, rev. A. Piatti, Leipzig, 1877).

Nicholson, C., *Flute preceptor* (London, c.1850).

Waud, W. W., *Instruction book for the violin* (London, c.1850).

1852

Coule, C., *New and complete method (or self instructor) for playing the German concertinas* (London, 1852).

Dean, J., *Dean's violin tutor, a complete & easy guide ... The whole selected, compiled & arranged in a progressive manner* (London, [1852]).

Haskins, J. F., *Tegg's concertina preceptor* (London, 1852).

Rimbault, E. F., *Method for the harmonium* (London, 1852).

Travis, E., *Instructions for the organ and harmonium* (London, 1852, rev. J. Hiles, 1875).

1853

Cruickshank, J. A., *Accordion and flutina teacher* (Aberdeen, 1853).

Duport, J.-L., *Essai ...* (Paris, [1806]) tr. J. Bishop as *Essay on fingering the violoncello, on the conduct of the bow* (London, 1853, ?1878).

Hancock, C., *Improved violin preceptor, on a new and simple principle, by which the art of playing the violin is rendered perfectly easy without the aid of a master* (London, ?2nd edn, 1853).

Haskins, J. F., *Tegg's improved pianoforte preceptor* (London, 1853).

Schiltz, H., *Tutor for the ophicleide (bass and alto)* ('R. Cocks & Co's Modern tutors for wind instruments' 12) (London, 1853).

1854

Anon., *Instructions for the deep toned pipe* (London, [1854]).

—— *The concertina preceptor, or pocket guide to the art of playing the concertina* (Glasgow, [1855], [1883]).

Haskins, J. F., *Tegg's modern cornopean preceptor* (London, 1854).

Kirkmann, J., *A piano instructor for the million* (London, 1854).

Montgomery, W. H., *A standard modern and fashionable pianoforte preceptor* (London, 1854).

Sedgwick, A. B., *Complete system of instruction for the concertina* (London, 1854).

Sloper, L., *Pianoforte instructions* (London, 1854).

1855

Albrechtsberger, J. G., *Collected writings on thorough-bass ...*, ed. I. Von Seyfried, tr. S. Novello (London, 1855, 2nd edn, 1860).

Anon., *Instructions for performing on the French accordion* (London, 1855).

Clinton, J., *The universal instruction book for the flute* (London, 1855).
Lindley, R., *Lindley's handbook for the violoncello* (London, [1855]).
Mandel, C., Memoria technica for the transposing instruments (London, [?1855]).
Neate, C., *An essay on fingering ... general observations on pianoforte playing* (London, 1855).
Reinagle, C., *A few words on pianoforte playing with rules for fingering passages of frequent occurrence* (London, 1855).
Warren, J., *Complete instructions for the concertina* (London, 1855).
—— *Instructions for the double concertina* (London, 1855).
—— *Instructions for the harmonium* (London, 1855).

1856

Anon., *Instructions for performing on Wheatstone's patent duett concertina* (London, 1856).
Berlioz, L. H., *Grand traité d'instrumentation* (Paris, [1843]), tr. M. C. Clarke, *A treatise upon modern instrumentation ...* (London, 1856, 2nd edn, 1858, ed. J. Bennett, 1904, tr. and ed. H. Macdonald, Cambridge, 2002).
Campagnoli, B., *Metodo ... Op.21* (?Milan, ?1797), tr. J. Bishop as *A new and progressive method on the mechanism of violin playing* (London, [1856]).
Coule, G., *Complete self instructor for playing Coule's German concertina* (London, 1856).
Pratten, R. S., *Complete instruction for the concertina* (London, 1856).
—— *Tutor for the flute* (London, 1856, ed. Kappey, London, 1883).

1857

Boosey & Co., *Universal clarinet tutor ... the principal exercises and studies from Klosé's celebrated clarinet school*, ed. J. Williams (London, 1857).
Case, G. T, *The baritone concertina, a new method* (London, 1857).
Engel, C., *Complete instructions for the harmonium* (London, 1857).
—— *A concise treatise on the harmonium* (London, 1857).
Regondi, G., *New method for the concertina* (Dublin, 1857).
Rimbault, E. F., *The harmonium; its uses and capabilities for the drawing-room as well as the church* (London, 1857).
Tamplini, G., *The bandsman, a course of instruction for military musical instruments* (London, 1857).

1858

Anon., *Popular instruction book for the clarionet* (Chappell's 'Popular instruction book' series, 7) (London, c.1858).
Engel, C., *Method for Alexandre's new patent drawing room harmonium ... intended as a sequel to the harmonium tutor* (London, 1858).
Hicks, C., *The tutor for the banjo* (London, 1858).
Purdy, G., *A few words on the violin ... the result of thirty years' experience as a teacher of that instrument* (London, 1858).
Rimbault, E. F., *Directions for playing the drawing-room model harmonium* (London, 1858).
Wybrow, S. H., *New violin tutor, compiled from the works of Campagnoli, Rode, Baillot, Kreutzer, Spohr, &c. containing the newest and most popular airs, from La Traviata, Il Trovatore, &c.* (London, [1858]).

1859

Mandel, C., *A treatise in the instrumentation of military bands* (London, 1859).
Moirato, J. D., *Tutor for the cornet à*

pistons and sax horns (London, 1859).
Neukomm, S., *An elementary method for the organ in general* (London, 1859).

1860

Anon., *The drum tutor, with ... tunes and pieces arranged for the fife and drum* (London, [?1860]).
Brod, H., *Grande méthode* (Paris, ?1830), tr. as *Brod and Muller's tutor* [oboe] (Cock's & Co's 'modern tutors for wind instruments' series, 10) (London, c.1860).
Cameron, G., *New and improved concertina tutor* (Glasgow, 1860).
—— *New and improved flute tutor* (Glasgow, c.1860).
Collinet, A., *Handbook for the flageolet* (London, ?1860).
Cooper, G., *Introduction to the organ, for the use of students* (London, c.1860, rev. 1890).
Kerbusch, L., *Hints to performers on musical instruments played by the touch of the hand: for the use of teachers and students of music* (London, [c.1860]).
Leutgen, H., *First lessons for the violoncello* (London, 1860).
Moirato, J. D., *Handbook for the cornet-à-piston ... selection of popular airs* (London, 1860).

1861

Pratten, C. J. [Madame Robert Sidney], *Instructions for the guitar* (3rd edn, London, 1861, 10th edn, 1882).
Thalberg, S., *Art of singing, applied to the pianoforte* (London, 1861).

1862

Kalkbrenner, F., *Méthode* (Leipzig, 1842), tr. S. Novello as *Method of learning the pianoforte* ('Novello's library for the diffusion of music knowledge', 53) (London, 1862).
Rimbault, E. F., *A guide to the use of the new Alexandre church harmonium* (London, 1862).
Williams, W. L., *A modern tutor for the pianoforte* (London, [1862]).

1863

Rockstro, R. S., *School for the flute* (London, 1863).

1864

Aguilar, E., *Steps to pianoforte playing* (London, 1862–4).
Blagrove, R. M., *Instruction book for ... the concertina* (London, 1864).
Henning, C. [or K.] W., [*Praktische Violin-Schule*] *Practical instructions for the violin on scientific principles, with German and English text* (Boston, [1864]).
Minasi, C., *Instruction book for the German concertina* (London, 1864).
Wade, W. J., *Complete instructions for the cornopean and sax-horn* (London, 1864).

1865

Harper, T., jun., *School for the cornet-à-pistons* (London, 1865).
Luigi, G., *Chappell's popular instruction book for the guitar* (London, c.1865).

1866

Wright, T. H., *Instructions for the harp. New edition* (London, 1866).

1867

Carte, R. *Complete course of instructions for the flute on Boehm and Carte's systems combined* (London, post 1867).

1868

Mullen, A. F., *Easy and complete instructions for the pianoforte* (London, 1868).

1869

Best, W. T., *The art of organ playing* (London, 1869).

1870

Anon., *The harmonium tutor* (Glasgow, c.1870, 1883).
Boosey & Co., *Shilling harmonium tutor*, ed. R. Nordmann (London, c.1870).
Wirth, A., *Practical directions for various brass instruments* (Eng. and Ger., Offenbach a. M., ?1870).

1871

Distin, T., the elder, *Tutor for the ballad horn* (London, 1871).
Hiles, J., *A catechism for the pianoforte student* (London, 1871, 18th edn, 1882).
Mackay, W., *The tutor for the highland bagpipe* (6th edn, Edinburgh, 1871).

1872

Rimbault, E. F., *A new tutor for the American organ* (London, 1872).
Westbrook, W. J., *Practical organ tutor* (London, 1872).

1873

Rimbault, E. F., *Brief instructions for learning the use of Chappell's small organs* (London, 1873).
Wade, James A., *London pianoforte tutor* (London, 1873).

1874

David, F., *Violinschule ... Violinschool* (Leipzig and London, [1874]).
Hall, C. K., *A school for the harmonium* (London, 1874).
Klosé, H. E., *Méthode* (Paris, 1843), tr. F. Clayton as *Complete method for the clarinet ... ordinary clarinet ... Albert and Boehm principles* (Paris and London, 1874).
Tours, B., *The violin* (Novello, Ewer & Co's Music Primers, ed. J. Stainer, No.17) (London, [1874], 1880, rev. and ed., W. H. Reed, London, 1934).

1875

Archer, F., *The organ, a theoretical and practical treatise* (London, 1875).
D'Este, J., *The violin in class. Complete graduated guide to the art of playing* (London, [c.1875]).
Engel, C., *Metzler & Co's harmonium tutor* (6th edn, London, c.1875).
Harper, T., jun., *School for the [slide] trumpet & 100 progressive exercises* (London, c.1875).
Hiles, J., *A progressive introduction to playing on the organ* (London, 1875).
Nicholson., C., *A school for the flute, being a new practical instruction book for the flute* (New York, 1836; London, c.1875).
Rimbault, E. F., *First instructions for the pianoforte* (London, 1875).

1876

Benedict, J., *Exercises for the pianoforte* (London, 1876).
Brewer & Co, *Shilling tutor for the pianoforte* (London, 1876).
Hallé, C., *Practical pianoforte school* (London and Manchester, 1876).
Ries, H., *Violinschule* (Leipzig, [1870]), tr. as *Violin school. First part: Elementary instruction etc. Second part: containing 100 studies* (Leipzig, 1876).
Rowland, A. C., *Method for the*

English orchestral double bass (London, 1876, pt 2, 1881).

1877

Brewer and Co., *Shilling tutor for the harmonium* (London, 1877).
Burch, C., *Metzler & Co's tutor for the banjo enlarged by G. Luigi* (London, [1877]).
Chapman, H., *New and complete modern tutor for the flute* ('Alliance Musicale' series) (London, 1877).
Clark, F. S., *First steps, being a course of elementary instruction for the pianoforte* (London, 1877).
—— *First steps in harmonium playing* ('Augener & Co's tutors', 5) (London, 1877).
Czerny, A., *Method of instruction for the pianoforte* (London, 1877).
Sloper, L., *Technical guide to touch, fingering, and execution on the pianoforte* (London, 1877).
Taylor, F., *Primer of pianoforte playing* (London, 1877).

1878

Anon., *Metzler & Co's tutor for the flute-flageolet* (London, 1878).
Brewer and Co, *Shilling tutor for the cornet-à-piston* (London, 1878).
Cary, A., *Howard & Co's shilling pianoforte tutor* (London, 1878).
Howard and Co, *Flute tutor* (London, 1878).
Junod, L., *New and concise method for the violoncello* (London, 1878).
Metzler and Co, *Tutor for the flute-flageolet* (London, 1878).
Nicholson, H., *New instructions for the flute* (London, 1878).
Prout, E., *Instrumentation* (London, 1878).
Spark, W., *Handy-book for the organ* (London, 1878).
Spohr, L., *Spohr's violin school, revised and edited, with additional text, by Henry Holmes ... translation ... Florence A. Marshall ... illustrations by Henry Holiday* (London and New York, [1878]).

1879

Anon., *Instructions for the new perfected ocarina with tuning slide* (Sydenham, [1879]).
—— *Metzler & Co's tutor for the American organ* (London, 1879).
Howell, E., *First book for the violoncello, adapted from Romberg's school* (London, [1879]).
Marque, A., *Grand method for the violin, the most complete and comprehensive work published in England, suitable to beginners or masters: revised with important additions by Saint-Jacome ... translation by G. Pulleyne and F. Clayton. In three parts* ('Alliance Musicale' series) (London, [1879]).
Rimbault, E. F., *Chappell & Co's instruction book for the Clough and Warren American organ* (London, 1879).
Saint Jacome, L. A., *New & modern grand method for the cornet-à-pistons* (London, [1879]).
—— *The viola tutor* (London, [1879]).
Taylor, F., *Pianoforte tutor* (London, 1879).

1880

Anon., *The art of playing the violin without a master ... selection of popular airs* (Glasgow, [c.1880]).
Arnim, A. L., *A complete course of wrist and finger gymnastics, for performers on the pianoforte, violin and other instruments* (London, [1880]).
Baillot, P. M. F. de S., ed., *Rode, Baillot, & Kreutzer's method of instruction for the violin ... Revised and improved edition* (London, [c.1880]).
Bottesini, G., *Grande méthode complète de contrebasse* (Paris, [1869]), tr. F. Clayton as *Complete method* (Paris, [?1880]).

Brewer & Co., *Shilling tutor for the flute* (London, 1880).
—— *Shilling tutor for the organ* (London, 1880).
Carnaud [the younger] & Saint Jacome, L. A., *Tutor for the musette* ('Alliance Musicale' series) (London, 1880).
Courvoisier, K., *The technics of violin-playing. Edited and translated by H. E. Krehbiel, of the Cincinnati College* (London, [1880], 7th edn, [1894]).
[Honeyman, W. C.], *The violin: how to master it. By a professional player* (Edinburgh and London, [1880]; 18th edn, [1889]; 33rd edn, Edinburgh, [1894]; 58th edn, Newport, 1951).
Jackson, G., *New instructions for the violin, revised by Saint Jacome* (London, [1880]).
—— *New instructor for the violoncello* (London, [1880]).
Jancourt, L. M. E. & Willent Bordogni, J. B. J., *Grand method for the bassoon* ('Alliance Musicale') (London, 1880).
Meifred, J. E., *Grand method for the French horn, by Meifred, Gallay and Dauprat* ('Alliance Musicale' series) (London, 1880).
Peiniger, O., *Violin method embodying the rudiments of music in a graduated form* (London, [c.1880]).
Rawson, T., *Band primo for all instruments contained in reed, brass or flute bands* (Manchester, ?1880).
Rimbault, E. F., *New and complete ... instructions on the art of playing the pianoforte ...* rev. Hiles (London, 1880).
Schiltz and Dauverné, F. G. A., *Grand method for the ... trumpet* ('Alliance Musicale' series) (London, 1880).
Vobaron, F., *Complete trombone tutor ... Vobaron, Berr, and Dieppo* (London, 1880).

1881

Glen, D., *Highland bagpipe tutor* (Edinburgh, 1881, 1899).
Goddard, J., *The new graduated method for the pianoforte* (London, 1881).
Lazarus, H., *New and modern method for the Albert and Boehm system clarinet ... Berr, Muller and Neerman* ('Alliance Musicale') (London, 1881).
Pauer, E., *Training school for the pianoforte* (London, 1881, 1887).
Pratten, C. J. [Madame Robert Sidney], *Guitar tutor* (London, 1881).
—— *Learning the guitar simplified* (London, 1881, 10th edn, 1893).
Smallwood, W., *Tutor for the pianoforte* (London, 1881).
Smith, A. H., *The coach horn tutor* (London, ?1881).

1882

Lee, S., *Méthode ...* (Mainz, [1842]), rev. and tr. as *Method for the violoncello* (Mainz, [1882]).
Mitchell, C. H., *How to hold a violin and bow. With instructions in bowing* (London, 2nd edn, 1882).
Tamplini, G., *Instruction book for the concert or vocal horn* (London, 1882).
Wolff, W., *Celebrated violin-tutor with extracts and exercises from the most famous violin composers, for the self-instruction of students* (London, [c.1882]).

1883

Anon., *How to play the violin: or hints to beginners, by an amateur* (London, 1883).
Bériot, C. A. de, *Méthode de violon* (3 vols, Paris, 1858), tr. J. L. Phipson [part 3 by W. J. Westbrook] as *Violin-School* Op.102, in 3 parts (Mayence, [1877–83], newly revised

and augmented by H. Heermann, 3 parts, London, 1899, 1907).
Case, G. T., *Tutor for the violin* ('Boosey's Musical Instructors' series) (London, [1883]).
Henning, C. [or K.] W., *Henning's first book for the violin ... edited and translated by J. A. Kappey* ('Boosey's Musical Instructors' series) (London, 1883).
Kappey, J. A., *Clarionet tutor* (London, 1883).
Marr, J. S., *New and improved accordion & flutina tutor* (Glasgow, 1883).
—— *New and improved flute tutor* (Glasgow, 1883).
—— *Pianoforte tutor* (Glasgow, 1883).
Mason, ?, *Violin tutor. An easy and simple method for learning this popular instrument* (London, [1883]).
Paige, K., *Daily exercises for the pianoforte* (London, 1883).
Papini, G., *Le mécanisme du jeune violoniste. A complete and progressive course of instruction for the Violin, in four parts* (London, [1883]).
Saint Jacome, L. A., *Rules to transpose with the B-flat or A cornet or clarinet or violin vice versa* (London, [1883]).
Spark, W., *A practical school for the organ* (London, 1883).
Stainer, J., *Tutor for the American organ* (London, 1883).
Turpin, E. H., *Some observations on the manipulations of modern wind instruments* (London, 1883).

1884

Baillot, P. M. F. de Sales, *L'art du violon* (Paris, 1835; Ger. tr., Berlin, 1835; Eng. tr., L. Goldberg, Illinois, 1991), abridged tr. as *Daily exercises of the Paris conservatoire extracted from L'art du violon, by Baillot. Translated ... Westbrook* (Mayence, [1884]).

Dancla, J. P. C., *Méthode ... Op.52* (Paris, [c.1850]), tr. W. J. Westbrook in 2 pts (Mayence, [1882–84], 5th edn, revised and corrected, 1892).
Firket, L., *Méthode pratique pour alto* (Paris, [1873]), tr. F. Corder as *Practical method for the viola* (Paris, [1884]).
Hamilton, J. A., *Catechism of harmony and thorough-bass*, ed. W. Dickinson (London, [1884]).
Howard & Co., *German concertina tutor* (London, 1884, rev. 1885).
Langey, O., *Tutor for the violin* (London, [1884], revised and enlarged edn, London, 1903).
—— *Tutor for the violoncello* (London, [1884]).
Loder, J. D., *Celebrated instruction book for the violin edited by J. T. Carrodus. The Marlborough Edition* (London, 1884).
Minasi, C., *Willey & Co's English concertina tutor without a master* (London, 1884).
Schön, M., *Praktischer Lehrgang* (Leipzig, [c.1850]), Eng. and Fr. tr. as *Practical course of instruction for the violin. Cours d'instruction pratique du violon* (London, [1884]).

1885

[Honeyman, W. C.], *Hints to violin-players* (Edinburgh and London, [1885], 5th edn, 1889 [from which time it appears with a different title], 11th edn, Edinburgh, [1894], 23rd edn, Newport, Dundee, 1938).
—— *The young violinist's tutor and duet book ... full directions for parents, pupil, and teacher ... for the use of beginners by a professional player* (Edinburgh and London, 3rd edn, [c.1885], 54th edn, c.1900).
Klosé, H. E., *Clarinet tutor* (London, c.1885).
Langey, O., *Tutor for the bassoon* (London, [1885], [?1900]).

—— *Tutor for the bombardon in E-flat* (London, [1885], 1911, 1921).
—— *Tutor for the clarinette* (London, [1885], [1908]).
—— *Tutor for the cornet* (London, [1885], [1911], [1937]).
—— *Tutor for the flute* (London, [1885], 1909, 1934).
—— *Tutor for the four string double bass* (London, [1885], new edn, [1908]).
—— *Tutor for the oboe* (London, [1885], 1911).
—— *Tutor for the piccolo* (London, [1885]).
—— *Tutor for the tenor or viola* (London, [1885]).
—— *Tutor for the tenor slide trombone* (London, [1885]).
—— *Tutor for the three string double bass* (London, [1885], new edn [1908]).
Mazas, J. F., *Petite méthode [de] violon* Op.34 (Paris, 1830), tr. by W. J. Westbrook, *Nouvelle édition* (Mayence, [1885]).

1886

Burton, J., *Burton's copyright diagrams illustrating and fingering the seven different positions on the violin* (London, [1886]).
Gresswell, H. W. and Gresswell, G., *How to play the fiddle; or, hints to beginners on the violin* (London, [1886], revised and corrected 2nd edn, London, 1887, 3rd edn, 1888).
Heskett, A. J., *Heskett's theoretical and technical violin course containing instructions for mechanical fingering, technical execution and bowing ... bowings in more than 30 different ways* (London, 1886).
Higgs, H. M., *Metzler & Co's tutor for the bassoon* (London, ?1886).
—— *Metzler & Co's tutor for side drum, bass drum, kettle drums ...* (London, 1886).
Minasi, C., *Willey & Co's instruction book for the flute without a master* (London, 1886).
Potter, S., *Drum, flute and bugle duty tutor*, rev. and enlarged by J. J. Renwick (London, 1886).

1887

Anon., *The violin self-taught, by means of the gamut* (London, 1887).
Fleming, J. M., *Violin school, practical, for home students ... for the use of amateurs, self-learners, teachers, and others ... a supplement on 'Easy legato studies for the violin.'* (London, ?1887).
Forman, E., *Roylance's flute and piccolo tutor* (London, 1887).
Kappey, J. A. *Boosey & Co's complete tutor for the French horn* (London, 1887).
—— *Complete tutor for the althorn in E-flat & baritone in B-flat* (London, 1887).
—— *Complete tutor for bombardons & contrabasses* (London, 1887).
—— *Complete tutor for the euphonion* (London, 1887).
—— *Complete tutor for tenor trombone ... bass trombone, slide and valve* (London, 1887).

1888

Anon., *Violin instruction book* (Salisbury, [1888]).
Hall, C. K., *Estey [sic] organ tutor* (London, 1888).
Riemann, H., *Catechism of musical instruments* (Leipzig, 1888; Eng. tr., London, 1888).

1889

Anon., *The national cornet tutor* (London, [1889]).
Althaus, B., *A standard violin tutor* ('Philharmonic Edition') (2 pts, London, [1889], rev. and enlarged edn, London, [1894]).

Cary, A., *Pianoforte primer* (London, 1889).
Forman, E., *The national banjo tutor* (London, 1889).
—— *The national guitar tutor* (London, 1889).
Hamilton, J. A., *Instructions for the American organ and harmonium* (London, 1889).
Henniker, H. F., *A complete manual for the violin* (London, [1889]).
Polonaski, E. and Roth, F., *Violin primer, first lessons for young violinists* (London, 1889).
Schroeder, C., *Katechismus des Violin-Spiels*, tr. as *Catechism of violin playing* (Leipzig, 1889).
Wright, T., and Round, H., *Wright and Round's amateur band teacher's guide and bandsman's adviser* (Liverpool, 1889).

1890

Anon., *New instruction for the Mezzetti's ocarina* (?London, c.1890).
Althaus, B., *A standard viola tutor* ('Philharmonic Edition') (2 pts, London, [1890]).
De Swert, J., *Gradus ad Parnassum* (Leipzig, [c.1888]), tr. as *The violoncello* (London, c.1890).
Langey, O., *Tutor for the flageolet* (London, [1890]).
Luigi, G., *Chappell's popular instruction book for the mandoline* (London, 1890).
Nicholson, C., *Nicholson's school for the flute with additional scales for the Boehm, Carte and Boehm and Radcliffe flutes*, ed. J. Harrington Young (London, c.1890).
Rockstro, R. S., *A treatise on the construction, the history, and the practice of the flute* (London, 1890, rev. 1928).

1891

André, P. F. J., *Complete organ-pedal-tutor*, tr. and rev. J. Hiles (London, 1891).
Anon., *Pictorial tutor for the pianoforte* (London, 1891).
Cocks & Co, *Shilling pianoforte tutor* (London, 1891).
La Tarche, A., *The violin positions: a concise treatise on shifting* (London, 1891).
—— *The violin student's manual* (London, [1891], 2nd edn, 1892).
Raikes, A. H., *Violin chat for beginners* (London, 1891).
Salvation Army, *Clarionet tutor* (London, 1891).

1892

Althaus, B., *The A.B.C. elementary violin school, being an easy introduction to all violin tutors* (London, [1892]).
Beazley, J. C., *Aids to the violinist ... bowing ... Commended ... Joachim* (London, 1892).

1893

Henniker, H. F., *Addenda to the complete manual for the violin* (London, 1893).
Henry, J. H. and Barber, E. M., *The violin, a few facts for the use of students preparing for the examinations of the College of Violinists* (Derby, 1893).
Hofmann, R., *Practical instrumentation*, tr. R. H. Legge (London, 1893).
Jong, E de, *The national flute tutor* (London, 1893).
Mitchell, C. H., *Violin prosody, or how to play a violin solo; with hints on choosing a violin* (Sunderland, 1893).
Wickins, F., *Rapid method for the pianoforte* (London, 1892).

1894

Glen, A., *How to accompany* (London, 1894).

Radcliffe, J., *School for the flute, a practical instruction book by Charles Nicholson with the original appendix to his preceptive lessons by J. Radcliffe* (London, 1894).

Wood, R., *Tone and expression in violin playing; or, the art of singing on the violin* (Sheffield, [1894]).

1895

Bruni, B., *Méthode pour l'alto-viola* (Paris, c.1820), ed. E. Kreuz, *Tenor method* (London, [1895]).

Carrodus, J. T., *Chats to violin students on how to study the violin. Preface & annotations by H. Saint-George* (Strad Library II) (London, 1895).

Ellis, H. J., *Dallas's modern school for the banjo* (London and Leipzig, c.1895).

Haddock, E., *Practical violin school* (London and Manchester, [1895]).

Howard & Co., *Mandoline tutor* (London, 1895).

La Tarche, A., *Practical violin playing* (London, 1895).

Rockstro, R. S., *School for the 'Boehm'-flute, adapted also for the Rockstro-model* (3rd edn, London, 1895).

1896

Corder, F., *The orchestra and how to write for it. A practical guide* (London, [1896]).

Griffiths, Lt S. C., *The military band: how to form, train and arrange for reed and brass bands* (London, [1896]).

La Tarche, A., *First weeks in violin playing. A ... method for beginners* (London, 1896).

Shand, E., *Barnes & Mullins's improved method for the guitar Op.100* (Bournemouth, 1896).

Sor, F., *Méthode* (Paris, c.1845), tr. A Merrick as *Method for the guitar*, ed. F. M. Harrison (London, 1896).

Spohr, L., *Spohr's celebrated tutor for the violin, edited and revised by J. T. Carrodus* ('The Academic Edition', 59) (London, [1896]).

1897

Cary, A., *The ideal pianoforte school* (London, 1897).

Taylor, F., *Technique and expression in pianoforte playing* (London, 1897).

White, B., *Easy cornet tutor* ('Wickins' sunbeam music books', 9) (London, 1897).

—— *Easy flute tutor* ('Wickins' sunbeam music books', 8) (London, 1897).

1898

Anon., *Mandoline tutor* (London, 1898).

—— *The violin in the first position* (Hawkes & Son's 'Simplicity Instruction Books' series) (London, 1898).

Dunn, J., *Violin playing* (Strad Library VI) (London, 1898).

Ellis, H. J., *Ellis's practical school for the guitar* (London, 1898).

—— *Ellis's thorough school for the five stringed banjo* (London, 1898, rev. edn, 1910).

—— *Ellis's thorough school for the guitar* (London, 1898).

—— *Ellis's thorough school for the mandoline* (London, 1898).

—— *Ellis's thorough school for the six or seven-stringed banjo* (London, 1898).

—— *Turner's mandoline tutor* (London, 1898).

Hill, H. A., *Turner's complete flute or piccolo tutor* (London, 1898).

—— *Turner's instruction book for the ocarina* (London, 1898).

—— *Turner's instruction book for the whistle, flageolet or fife without keys* (London, 1898).

Le Thiere, C., *Turner's complete tutor for the coach horn, post or tandem*

horn, bugle and cavalry trumpet (London, 1898).
Prout, E., *The orchestra* (2 vols, London, 1898–9).
Van der Straeten, E., *The technics of violoncello playing* (Strad Library 5) (London, 1898).
Wilhelmj, A., and Brown, J., *Modern school for the violin* (London, 1898).

1899

Broadley, A., *Chats to 'cello students* (Strad Library 7) (London, 1899).
Courvoisier, K., *The technics of violin playing on Joachim's method* (London, 1899).
Riley, E., *Introductory violin school ... Elementar Violin Schule ... Méthode de violon élémentaire* (Barnsley, 1899).

1900

Baillot, P. M. F. de S., [*L'art du violon* (1835)] *Daily exercises of the Paris conservatoire ... Translated ... Westbrook ... Book 2 ... Revised by A. Pollitzer* (London, [1900]).
Berr, F., *Méthode* (Paris, ?1845), tr. E. Salabert as *Complete method for the clarinet* (London, 1900).
Henderson, P., *The bagpipe tutor* (Glasgow, 1900).
Hohmann, C. E., *Praktische Violinschule* (Nuremberg, c.1840, Köln, [c.1900]), tr. by C. Erben as *Practical violin-school* (London, [1900]).

APPENDIX THREE

Treatises in the Chronology

Strings (violin; viola; cello; double bass; other)
Wind and brass
Keyboard
Percussion & miscellaneous
Combinations of instruments, orchestration, military & other bands

In some cases the author/year reference can include more than a single source.

STRINGS

Violin

Althaus (1889)
—— (1892)
Anon., (1817)
—— (1831)
—— (1840)
—— (1843)
—— (1845)
—— (1846)
—— (1880)
—— (1883)
—— (1887)
—— (1888)
—— (1898)
Arnim (1880)
Baillot (1884)
—— (1900)
Barthélemon (1790)
Bates (1845)
Beazley (1892)
Bemetzrieder (1803)
Bériot (1883)
Bertini (1830)
Blagrove, R. M. (1827)
Blagrove, W. M. (1850)
Burton (1886)
Campagnoli (1830)
—— (1856)
Carrodus (1895)
Case (1883)
Challoner (1825)
Cobham (1819)
Courvoisier (1880)
—— (1899)
Dancla (1884)
David (1874)
Dean (1852)
D'Este (1875)
Dunn (1898)
Farmer (1847)
Fleming (1887)
Gehot (1780)
—— (1784)
—— (1790)
Geminiani (1792)
—— (1800)
Glover (1840)
Goodban (1810)
Gresswell (1886)
Guillemin (1877)
Hack (1835)
Haddock (1895)
Hamilton (1835)
—— (1840)
—— (1850)
Hancock (1853)
Henniker (1889)
—— (1893)
Henning (1864)
—— (1883)
Henry (1893)
Heskett (1886)
Hohmann (1900)
[Honeyman, W. C.] (1880)
—— (1885)
Howell (1825)
—— (1829)
Jackson (1880)
James (1830)
Jousse (1805)
—— (1811)

Keith (1813)
Kerbusch (1860)
L'abbé *le fils* [Joseph-Barnabé Saint-Sevin] (1828)
Langey (1884)
La Tarche (1891)
—— (1895)
—— (1896)
Loder (1824)
—— (1837)
—— (1841)
—— (1842)
—— (1884)
Macdonald (1822)
Marque (1879)
Mason (1883)
Mazas (1885)
Mitchell (1882)
—— (1893)
Mozart (1812)
Paine (1815)
Papini (1883)
Peiniger (1880)
Perry (1800)
Polonaski (1889)
Präger (1830)
Purdy (1858)
Raikes (1891)
Ries (1876)
Riley (1899)
Ritchie (1916)
Rode, P., et al (1823)
—— (1828)
—— (1880)
Sanderson (1825)
Schön (1884)
Schroeder (1889)
Spohr (1833)
—— (1843)
—— (1878)
—— (1896)
Tashanberg (1796)
Thomson (1840)
Tours (1874)
Waud (1850)
West (1840)
Wilhelmj (1898)
Wolff (1882)
Wood (1894)
Woodward (1836)
Wybrow (1858)

Viola

Althaus (1890)
Anon. (1795)
Bruni (1895)
Firket (1884)
Langey (1885)
Saint Jacome (1879)

Cello

Anon. (1785)
—— (1787)
—— (1795)
—— (1845)
Baillot *et al.* (1832)
Banister (1850)
Bréval (1810)
Broadley (1899)
Broderip (1800)
Crouch (1824)
De Swert (1890)
Duport (1853)
Eley (1830)
Gunn (1793)
—— (1802)
Hamilton (1835)
—— (1840)
Hardy (1785)
Howell (1879)
Hus-Desforges (1840)
Jackson (1880)
Junod (1878)
Kummer (1850)
Langey (1884)
Lee (1882)
Leutgen (1860)
Lindley (1855)
Macdonald (1811)
Phillips (1846)
Reinagle, A. R. (1841)
Reinagle, J. (1800)
Romberg (1840)
Schetky (1780)
—— (1811)
Thompson (1780)
Tillière (1795)
Van der Straeten (1898)

Double Bass

Bottesini (1880)
D'Almaine & Co (1843)
Frölich (1840)
Hamilton (1833)
Langey (1885)
Rowland (1876)

Other

Anon. (1780)
—— (1802)
—— (1828)
—— (1830)
—— (1898)
Auge (1790)
Barthélemon (1795)
Bennett (1828)
Bochsa (1817)
Broderip (1800)
Bruni (1834)
Burch (1877)
Carulli (1828)
Chabran (1795)
Challoner (1829)
Dizi (1827)
Duvernay (1827)
Egan (1827)
—— (1829)
Ellis (1895)
—— (1898)
Erard (1821)
Forman (1889)
Green (1825)
Gunn (1807)
Hicks (1858)
Howard (1895)
Huerta (1826)
Jauralde (1827)
Lefevre (1790)
Leoni (1785)
Light (1795)
—— (1812)
Luigi (1844)
—— (1865)
—— (1890)
May (1830)
Mayer (1800)
Merelle (1800)
Meyer (1835)
Pelzer (1830)
Pratten (1861)

—— (1881)
Shand (1896)
Sola (1819)
Sor (1896)
Weippert (1800)
Wright (1835)
—— (1866)

WIND AND BRASS

Alexander (1821)
—— (1830)
Anon. (1780)
—— (1783)
—— (1785)
—— (1790)
—— (1796)
—— (1797)
—— (1798)
—— (1800)
—— (1801)
—— (1805)
—— (1806)
—— (1808)
—— (1810)
—— (1813)
—— (1821)
—— (1825)
—— (1830)
—— (1850)
—— (1854)
—— (1858)
—— (1878)
—— (1879)
—— (1880)
—— (1889)
—— (1890)
Arnold (1787)
Bainbridge (1805)
—— (1810)
Barret (1850)
Bates (1840)
Beale (1815)
Berbiguier (1827)
Berr (1900)
Blight (1845)
Boosey (1857)
Bown (1825)
Brewer (1878)
—— (1880)
Briggs (1812)

Brod (1860)
Cameron (1860)
Camus (1849)
Carnaud [the younger] and Saint Jacome (1880)
Carte (1847)
—— (1867)
Chapman (1877)
Clinton (1846)
—— (1850)
—— (1855)
Coggins (1830)
Colclough (1819)
Collinet (1860)
Distin (1871)
Dothel (1793)
Dressler (1827)
Drouet (1830)
Eberhardt (1825)
Eley (1795)
Farrell (1810)
Foraboschi (1838)
Forman (1887)
Glen (1881)
Goulding (1813)
Green (1807)
Gunn (1793)
—— (1795)
Gutteridge (1824)
Hancock (1846)
Harper, T., sen. (1835)
Harper, T., jun. (1865)
—— (1875)
Haskins (1854)
Henderson (1900)
Higgs (1886)
Hill (1898)
Howard (1878)
Hyde (1798)
James (1826)
—— (1829)
Jancourt (1880)
Jong (1893)
Kappey (1883)
—— (1887)
Keith (1815)
Klosé (1874)
—— (1885)
Kuffner (1820)
Langey (1885)
—— (1890)

Lazarus (1881)
Le Thiere (1898)
Lindsay (1830)
MacDonald (1803)
Macfarlane (1827)
—— (1837)
Mackay (1871)
Mackintosh (1840)
Mahon (1803)
Marr (1883)
Meifred (1880)
Metzler (1830)
—— (1878)
Miller (1799)
Minasi (1886)
Moirato (1859)
—— (1860)
Monro (1810)
Monzani (1801)
Nicholson, C. (1816)
—— (1821)
—— (1850)
—— (1875)
—— (1890)
Nicholson, H. (1878)
Parke (1830)
Potter (1817)
Pratten (1856)
Preston (1797)
Quantz (1790)
Radcliffe (1894)
Richardson (1844)
Rockstro (1863)
—— (1890)
—— (1895)
Roy and Mueller (1839)
Saint Jacome (1879)
Salvation Army (1891)
Schiltz (1853)
—— and Dauverné (1880)
Shade (1830)
Siccama (1847)
Simpson (1829)
Smith (1881)
Tamplini (1882)
Thompson (1800)
Tully (1831)
—— (1840)
Turpin (1883)
Vobaron (1880)
Wade (1864)

Weiss (1821)
White (1897)
Willman (1826)
Wood (1825)
Wragg (1792)
—— (1804)
Wrede (1830)

KEYBOARD
(including accordion, concertina etc)

Adams (1785)
Aguilar (1864)
Albrechtsberger (1820)
—— (1855)
André (1891)
Anon. (1780)
—— (1785)
—— (1787)
—— (1789)
—— (1790)
—— (1792)
—— (1795)
—— (1796)
—— (1798)
—— (1800)
—— (1803)
—— (1815)
—— (1823)
—— (1855)
—— (1856)
—— (1870)
—— (1879)
—— (1891)
Archer (1875)
Attwood (1805)
Barbieri (1816)
Barthélemon (1790)
—— (1802)
Bates (1840)
Baumgarten (1784)
Bemetzrieder (1783)
—— (1785)
—— (1788)
—— (1798)
Benedict (1876)
Bennett (1825)
Bertini (1845)
Best (1869)
Blagrove (1864)
Blake (1795)

Blewitt (1795)
Bohlius (1810)
Boosey (1870)
Bremner (1817)
Brewer (1876)
—— (1877)
—— (1880)
Brewster (1785)
Broderip (1788)
—— (1789)
Burrowes (1819)
—— (1821)
Busby (1829)
Butler (1804)
Callender (1817)
Cameron (1860)
Camidge (1795)
Cary (1878)
—— (1889)
—— (1897)
Case (1857)
Challoner (1810)
Cheese (1805)
—— (1806)
Chinnery (1798)
Clagget (1790)
Clark (1877)
Clarke (1830)
—— (1840)
Clementi (1801)
—— (1830)
Coblenz (1797)
Cocks (1891)
Coggins (1815)
Cooper (1860)
Corfe (1805)
Corri, D. (1784)
—— (1787)
Corri, M. P. (1835)
Corri, P. A. (1810)
—— (1812)
Coule (1842)
—— (1852)
—— (1856)
Cramer (1812)
Crotch (1812)
—— (1822)
—— (1826)
Cruickshank (1853)
Czerny, A. (1877)
Czerny, C. (1839)

—— (1847)
Dale (1801)
Danby (1790)
Danneley (1820)
Dussek (1796)
Eavestaff (1830)
Engel (1857)
—— (1858)
—— (1875)
Ferrari (1823)
Fétis and Moscheles (1841)
Flack (1780)
Frick (1786)
Fryer (1827)
Furtado (1798)
Gawler (1809)
Glen (1894)
Goddard (1881)
Goodban (1814)
Goss (1830)
—— (1833)
Gourdez (1820)
Graham (1829)
Green (1833)
Griesbach (1826)
Gunn (1795)
Gunn (née Young) (1785)
Hale (1811)
Hall (1874)
—— (1888)
Hallé (1876)
Hamilton (1842)
—— (1849)
—— (1884)
—— (1889)
Hammond (1802)
Hancock (1845)
Haskins (1852)
—— (1853)
Hawker (1818)
—— (1820)
Hawkins (1817)
Heather (1820)
Heck (1782)
—— (1793)
Hempel (1822)
Herz (1838)
—— (1840)
Hiles (1871)
—— (1875)
Hodges (1809)

Hodson (1830)
Hook (1785)
Horsley (1825)
Howard (1884)
Howell (1816)
Huellmandel (1795)
Hummel (1829)
Jackson (1795)
—— (1825)
Jones (1786)
Jousse (1808)
—— (1818)
—— (1820)
—— (1830)
Kalkbrenner (1835)
—— (1862)
Keith (1815)
Kelly (1813)
Kilner (1819)
King (1800)
—— (1811)
—— (1817)
Kirkmann (1854)
Klose (1810)
—— (1822)
Kollmann (1792)
—— (1795)
—— (1801)
—— (1807)
—— (1828)
L., F. (1805)
Latour (1827)
—— (1828)
Light (1794)
Lillycrop (1826)
Loeschman (1812)
Logier (1814)
—— (1815)
—— (1816)
—— (1827)
—— (1828)
McMurdie (1828)
MacPherson (1823)
Maelzel (1816)
Major (1826)
Malme (1790)
Malt (1826)
Marr (1883)
Marsh (1805)
—— (1807)
Mazzinghi (1795)

McKerrell (1800)
Miller (1782)
—— (1787)
Minasi (1864)
—— (1884)
Moller (1796)
Monro (1819)
Montgomery (1854)
Mott (1824)
Moxley (1822)
Mullen (1868)
Neate (1855)
Neukomm (1859)
Nicholson (1796)
Nielson (1825)
Paddon (1819)
Paige (1883)
Panormo (1812)
Parkinson (1811)
Parsons (1789)
—— (1794)
Pasquali (1810)
Pauer (1881)
Pelzer (1842)
Pratten (1856)
Reeve (1801)
Regondi (1857)
Reinagle (1855)
Relfe (1821)
Rimbault, E. F. (1839)
—— (1848)
—— (1852)
—— (1857)
—— (1858)
—— (1862)
—— (1872)
—— (1873)
—— (1875)
—— (1879)
—— (1880)
Rimbault, S. F. (1824)
Rinck (1844)
Ross (1796)
Saffrey (1816)
Sedgwick (1854)
Sharp (1797)
Sheppard (1824)
Shield (1815)
Sloper (1854)
—— (1877)
Smallwood (1881)

Smethergell (1797)
Spark (1878)
—— (1883)
Stainer (1883)
Steibelt (1813)
Stevens (1811)
Taylor (1877)
—— (1879)
—— (1897)
Thalberg (1861)
Tipper (1828)
Tomlins (1823)
Travis (1852)
Türk (1804)
Valentine (1826)
Wade (1844)
—— (1873)
Warren (1816)
—— (1842)
Warren (1855)
Webbe (1802)
Westbrook (1872)
Wickins (1892)
Williams, G. E. (1810)
—— (1819)
Williams, W. L. (1862)
Woakes (1820)

PERCUSSION & Miscellaneous

Anon. (1813)
—— (1815)
—— (1860)
Dale (1800)
Higgs (1886)
Jones (1788)
Potter (1817)
—— (1886)

COMBINATIONS OF INSTRUMENTS, ORCHESTRATION, MILITARY AND OTHER BANDS

Arnim (1880)
Berlioz (1856)
Bertini (1830)
Corder (1896)
Corri (1835)
Davis (1814)
Gehot (1780)

—— (1784)
Griffiths (1896)
Hamilton (1844)
Hofmann (1893)
Kerbusch (1860)
Mandel (1855)
—— (1859)
Potter (1886)
Prout (1878)

—— (1898)
Rawson (1880)
Riemann (1888)
Rodwell (1830)
Saint Jacome (1883)
Tamplini (1857)
Voigt (1830)
Wirth (1870)
Wright (1889)

Bibliography

Primary Sources

Abt, F. W. (1871), *Appendix to Hamilton's modern instructions for singing* (London).
Adam, J. L. (1805; R1974), *Méthode de piano du conservatoire* (Paris).
Agricola, J. F. (1995), *Introduction to the art of singing*, tr. J. C. Baird (Cambridge).
Alard, (J.-) D. (1844), *Ecole de violon: méthode complète et progressive* (Paris).
Alison, A. (1790), *Essays on the nature & principles of taste* (Edinburgh & London).
Allen, C. (1760), *The polite lady: or a course of female education* (London).
Anfossi, M. (c.1840), *Tratto ... A theoretical and practical treatise on the art of singing* (London).
Anon. (1695a), *Nolens volens or you shall learn to play on the violin whether you will or no ... for the instructing of young practitioners ... ayrs compos'd by the most ingenious masters of ye age* (London, 8th Book, 1716), afterwards published as *The compleat tutor to the violin* (London, 1717, 13th Book, 1730).
—— (1695b) *The self-instructor on the violin ... improv'd & made easy to ye meanest capacity by plain rules and directions* (London, 2nd Book, 1697, 3rd Book, 1699; collection of all three books, London, 1700).
—— (1724) *A short explication of such foreign words, as are made use of in musick books. An account of printed musick, for violins, hautboys, flutes, and other instruments, by several masters* (London, 1724).
—— (c.1730) *The newest method for learners on the German flute with a collection of the finest minuets, rigadoons and open airs* (London, c.1730).
—— (?1746) *The compleat tutor for the violin ... the best and easiest instructions ... Italian, English and Scotch tunes, with several choice pieces for 2 violins* (London, ?1746, ?1750, c.1760, c.1765, c.1770).
—— (1754) *The Muses' delight...with instructions for the voice, violin, harpsichord, German-flute, hautboy, French-horn, common-flute,*

bassoon and bass-violin (London, 1754; Liverpool, 1754, 1756, 1757, 1758, c.1760).

—— (c.1765), *The compleat tutor for the German flute* (London).

—— (c.1770), *Compleat instructions for the fife* (London).

—— (c.1778), *Euterpe; or, remarks on the use and abuse of music, as part of modern education* (London).

—— (1798), *A treatise on the theory and practical system of music* (London).

—— (c.1816), *Harmonic cards*, tr. Jousse (London).

—— (1818), *The Logierian system ... exploded* (London).

—— (1829), *The young lady's book ... elegant recreations* (London).

—— (1853), *The vocal preceptor or pocket guide to the art of singing* (Glasgow).

—— (1895) *Instructions for teaching staff sight-singing in elementary schools* (London).

—— (1901), *Instruction and duty for the bugle, drum & flute for use in the Royal Navy* (London).

—— [1902], *Violin made easy; or, how to practise the violin ... how to read music at sight* (Liverpool).

—— [1913], *The star easy and progressive pianoforte tutor* (London).

—— (1914), *Tutor for side drum and bugle* (London).

—— (n.d.), *The concertina as a substitute for the violin, by an amateur* (London).

Appleton, E. (1915), *Private education ... young ladies ... to parents, private governesses, & young ladies* (London).

Aprile, G. (c.1791), *The modern Italian method of singing* (London).

Arban, J-B. (1864), *Grande méthode complète pour cornet à pistons et de saxhorn* (Paris).

Asioli, B. (1809; tr. [1825]), *Principi* (Milan), tr. Jousse as *A compendious musical grammar* (London).

Auer, L. (1921), *Violin playing as I teach it* (London).

Avison, C. (1752), *An essay on musical expression* (London).

Bach, C. P. E. (1753, 1762/R1957; tr. 1949/R1974), *Versuch über die wahre Art das Clavier zu spielen* (2 vols, Berlin; Eng. tr. W. J. Mitchell, New York).

Baillot, P. M. F. de Sales (1835; tr. 1991), *L'art du violon: nouvelle méthode* (Paris; Eng. tr., L. Goldberg, Illinois).

Balfe, M. W. (?1850), *The Italian school of singing* (3rd edn, London).

—— (1857), *A new universal method of singing* (London).

Banister, J. (1699; bk. 5 1727), *The compleat tutor to the violin ... plain and easie directions for beginners, with the newest tunes now in use, and a flourish in every key* (London).

Barbella, D. E. (?1763; 1992), *Six duets for two violins* (London), in

Performers' facsimiles No.79 (New York).
—— (1765) *Six solos for a violin and bass or two violins. Composed for gentlemen performers* (London, 1765), in *Late eighteenth-century masters: continuo sonatas for violin*, ed. J. Adas (see 'Collections' below).
Barnett, J. (1845), *School for the voice, or the principles of singing* (London).
Barrow, W. (1802), *An essay on education ... discipline & instruction in our academies* (2 vols, London).
Barthélemon, F. H. (c.1778; 1986), *Six duettos: two for two violins, two for a violin and tenor, and two for a violin and violoncello*, Op.8 (London); ed. R. Stowell (London).
Bemetzrieder, A. (1782), *Abstract of a new method of teaching the principles of music* (London).
—— (?1795), *A new guide to music ... for the use of young beginners* (London).
—— (c.1796), *The art of modulating* (London).
—— (c.1797), *A view of the principles of music* (London).
—— (c.1798), *The cliffs, keys, & time* (London).
—— (1800–1803), *A complete treatise on music* (3 bks, London).
—— (1805), *A new guide to the musical science* (London).
—— (?1809), *The art of tuning our instruments ... dedicated to the amateurs who like to tune occasionally their pianofortes* (London).
—— (c.1813), *Principles of music* (London).
Bennett, J. (1850), *A new vocal method* (London).
Bennett, T. (1807), *An introduction to the art of singing* (London).
Bériot, C.-A. de (1858), *Méthode de violon* Op.102 (Paris).
Bertini, A. (c.1829), *A machine to improve the physiology of the hand ... execution on musical instruments* (London).
Billington, T. (1784), *A fourth set ... a few hints to young vocal performers* (London).
Blagrove, R. M. (c.1822), *An entire new guide to the theory of music* (London).
Borghese, A. D. R. (1790), *A new & general system of music*, tr. J. Gunn (London).
Bottomley, J. (1823), *A dictionary of music* (Sheffield and London).
Bremner, R. (1756; 1762; 1763), *Rudiments of music* (Edinburgh; enlarged 2nd edn; 3rd edn, London).
—— (attrib.) (c.1760, c.1770), *The compleat tutor for the violin* (London; 3rd edn).
—— (1765), *The harpsichord or spinnet miscellany ... beginner to the tolerable performer ... to save masters the trouble of writing for their pupils ... fully & clearly treated* (London).

—— (1777), *Some thoughts on the performance of concert music* (London).
Busby, T. (*c*.1783–1785), *An universal dictionary of music* (London).
—— (*c*.1801), *A complete dictionary of music* (London, *c*.1801).
—— (1818/R1976), *A grammar of music ... music as a science* (London).
Callcott, J. W. (*c*.1792), *Explanation of the notes* (London, *c*.1792).
—— (1798), *Plan of a practical dictionary of music; compiled from the most approved treatises* (London).
—— (1806), *A musical grammar, in 4 parts* (London).
Cartier, J.-B. (1798; [1799/R1977; 1801), *L'art du violon* (Paris; 2nd edn; enlarged 3rd edn).
Catel, C.-S. (*c*.1825), *A treatise on harmony ... pupils at the royal conservatoire ... Paris ... translated into English* (London).
Cazalet, W. W. (1861), *The voice, or the art of singing* (London).
Cellini, L. (1894), *A small treatise on the old Italian method of voice production* (London).
Cherubini, L. (1837), *A course of counterpoint & fugue ... tr. J. A. Hamilton* (2 vols, London).
Clarke, J. (1864), *A catechism of the elements of harmony* (London).
—— (1830; *c*.1849), *A catechism of the rudiments of music ... for the assistance of teachers of the piano-forte* (London; 39th edn).
Coggins, J. (*c*.1815), *The governess's musical assistant* (London).
Corder, F. (*c*.1900), *A plain and easy introduction to music, or, The new 'Morley'* (2nd edn, London).
Corelli, A. (?1710), *XII sonata's or solo's for a violin a bass violin or harpsicord ... Op.5* (London).
—— (*c*.1795), *Twelve solos for the violin with a thorough bass for the harpsichord or violoncello ... Op.5* (London).
—— (1865), *Twelve solos or sonatas for the violin & violoncello, with a thoroughbass for the pianoforte Op.5* (London).
Corfe, J. (1799), *A treatise on singing* (Salisbury).
Corrette, M. (1782/R1973), *L'art de se perfectionner dans le violon* (Paris).
Corri, D. (*c*.1787), *A complete musical grammar* (Edinburgh).
—— (1799), *A treatise on the art of singing* (London).
—— (1810; 1993–5), *The singer's preceptor* (London), ed. C. R. F. Maunder as *Domenico Corri's treatises on singing: a four-volume anthology* (New York and London, 1993–5).
Corri, H. (1826), *The delivery of vocal music simplified* (Dublin).
Corri, M. P. (*c*.1830), *A treatise on the art of singing* (London).
Corri, P. A. (1810), *L'anima di musica* (London).
Costa, M. A. A. (1838), *Analytical considerations on the art of singing* (London).

Crivelli, D. F. (1843), *The art of singing* (London).
Crome, R. (*c.*1740, *c.*1750, *c.*1760, *c.*1765, *c.*1785), *The fiddle new model'd, or a useful introduction for the violin, exemplify'd with familiar dialogues* (London).
—— (*c.*1765), *The compleat tutor for the violoncello* (London).
Crotch, W. (1812), *Elements of musical composition* (Oxford and London).
Curwen, J. (1858; 1905), *The standard course of lessons on the tonic sol-fa method of teaching to sing* (London; 13th edn).
Dancla, (J. B.) C. (*c.*1850), *Méthode élémentaire et progressive pour violon* (Paris).
Danneley, J. F. (1825), *An encyclopedia, or dictionary of music* (London).
—— (1826), *A musical grammar: comprehending the principles & rules of the science* (London).
Dannreuther, E. (1893–5), *Musical ornamentation* (2 vols, London).
Dauprat, L. F. (*c.*1807–8), *Méthode de cor alto et cor basse* (Paris).
Dibdin, C. (*c.*1807–8), *The musical mentor, or, St. Cecilia at school ... to assist the musical education of young ladies at boarding schools* (London).
—— (1808a), *The English Pythagoras; or, every man his own music master* (London).
—— (*c.*1830), *Music epitomized: a school book* (London; 9th edn, rev. J. Jousse).
Diettenhofer, J. (1799), *Proposals ... composition ... counter-point ... thorough bass ... for juvenile scholars, as well as those who are already advanced in this science* (London).
Donaldson, J. (1816), *New system of musical tuition* (Glasgow).
Egestorf, G. H. (?1815), *A practical dissertation on the science of singing* (London).
Eley, Chr. Fr. (n.d.), *Compleat instructions for the bassoon or fagotto* (Dublin).
Falkener, R. (*c.*1773; 1774), *Instructions for playing on the harpsichord* (London; 2nd edn).
Farmer, H. (1903), *Violin Tutor. New edition*, rev. G. Papini (London).
—— (n.d.), *Tutor for the violin*, ed. & rev. H. Tolhurst (London).
Ferrari, G. G. (1818), *A concise treatise on Italian singing* (London).
—— (1827), *Instructions, both theoretical and practical, in the art of singing* (London).
Fisher, J. A. (1773), *Six duettos for two violins* (London).
Flesch, C. (1924), *The art of violin playing*, tr. F. Martens (2 vols, New York).
Fontana, B. (1849), *The music manual, containing both the theory and practice of instrumental and vocal music* (London).

Ford, A[nn] (1761), *Instructions for playing on the musical glasses ... to perform in a few days if not in a few hours* (London).
—— (?1761), *Lessons and instructions for playing on the guitar* (London).
Forsyth, C. (1914; 1935), *Orchestration* (London; 2nd edn).
Franz, O. (c.1880; tr.1902), *Grosse Waldhorn-Schule* (Dresden), tr. T. Busby as *School for the horn both theoretical and practical* (London).
Fuchs, C. (1906), *Violoncello method* (3 vols, London).
Galeazzi, F. (1791–6; 1817), *Elementi teorico-pratici di musica* (2 vols, Rome; 2nd edn).
García, M. (1824), *Exercises and method for singing* (London).
—— (1863), *School of singing* (London).
García, M. P. R. (1847; tr. 1857, 1894), *Traité ...* (Paris); rev. and tr. as *New treatise on the art of singing* (London).
Gardiner, W. (1832), *The music of nature* (London).
Gehot, J. (1785), *Six easy duettos* Op.3 (London).
Geminiani, F. (1749), *A treatise of good taste in the art of musick* (London).
—— (1751; [1952], *The art of playing on the violin* Op.9 (London; facsimile edn; London, c.1777, c.1790; Boston, 1769; Fr. tr., Paris, 1752, 3rd edn, ?1763, rev. edn, c.1803; Ger. tr., Vienna, 1782).
—— (attrib.) (c.1770; c.1790), *The compleat tutor for the violin ... to obtain a proficiency. With some useful directions, lessons, graces, &c. by Geminiani ... airs, marches, minuets, song tunes, & duetts* (London).
—— (attrib.) (c.1775; c.1806), *New and compleat instructions for the violin ... easiest and best methods ... to obtain a proficiency* (London; 4th edn).
Gevaert, F. A. (1885; tr. ?1906), *Nouveau traité d'instrumentation* (Paris); tr. E. F. E. Suddard as *A new treatise on instrumentation* (Paris and Brussels).
Giardini, F. (c.1763), *Sei duetti a due violini* Op.2 (London).
—— (1769; 1990), *Six duos for violin and violoncello* Op.14 (London), ed. L. Vigh (Budapest).
Gibbs, J. (1746), *Eight solos* (London); nos.3 and 5, ed. D. C. Stone and C. Tilney (London, 1974); no.1, ed. L. Salter in *Eighteenth-century violin sonatas*, bk.1 (London, 1975); nos.2 and 4, ed. D. C. Stone and R. Platt (Oxford, 1990).
Goodban, T. (1818), *New game of musical characters adapted for the improvement of beginners* (London).
—— (c.1820), *The rudiments of music ... for beginners ... for teaching in classes as for private tuition* (London and Dublin).
[Graham, G. F.] (1817), *General observations upon music, & remarks on Mr Logier's system* (Edinburgh).

Green, J. (c.1826), *Harmonic cards ... Mr Logier's system* (London).
—— (1827), *A bird's eye view of the rudiments of music ... Logier's system* (London).
Greig, J., ed. (1910), *The musical educator: a library of musical instruction by eminent specialists* (5 vols, London).
Guhr, K. ([1829]; Eng tr. [1915]), *Ueber Paganinis Kunst die Violine zu spielen* (Mainz; Fr. tr., Paris, [1830]; It. tr., Milan, 1834), tr. by S. Novello as *Paganini's art of playing the violin, with a treatise on single and double harmonic notes*, rev. C. E. Lowe, new edn (London).
Gunn, A. (c.1803), *An introduction to music ... musical games* (Edinburgh and London).
Habeneck, F. A. (c.1835), *Méthode théorique et pratique de violon ... notes en facsimile de l'écriture de Viotti* (Paris).
Hallam, S. (1998), *Instrumental teaching: a practical guide to better teaching and learning* (Oxford).
Hamilton, J. A. (1837; rev. 1882), *A dictionary ... musical terms* (London, 4th edn).
—— (1834), *Practical catechism on singing* (London).
—— [1853], *Modern instructions for singing* (London).
Hawkes, W. (1798), *A treatise on the theory & practical system of music* (London).
—— (1805), *The theory of music simplified* (London).
Henley, W. (1905), *The violin: solo playing, soloists and solos* (Strad Library 13) (London).
Hering, C. F. A. (1857; tr. [1909]), *Elementar-Violinschule* (Leipzig; Eng. tr., London).
Heron, L. (1771), *A treatise on the German flute* (London).
Hickson, W. E. (1836/R1984), *The singing master* (London).
Hodges, E. (?1819), *New notation for music* (Bristol).
Howell, T. (c.1813), *A new musical game ... in a much shorter time than that in which they are generally learnt* (Bristol).
—— (c.1825), *Howell's musical arithmetic* (Bristol).
—— (?1826), *Six quartetts for two violins ... to remove the difficulty of playing nicely in tune ... an excellent position of the left hand fingers* (Bristol).
Hoyle, J. (1791) [pseudonym of John Binns], *A complete dictionary of music* (London).
Hughes, T. A. (?1827–9), *Six duetts for two violins ... for the improvement of practitioners, and the use of teachers* Op.4 (2 bks, London).
Hugot, A. and Wunderlich, J. G. (1804), *Méthode de flûte du conservatoire* (Paris).
Hullah, J. (1842/R1983), *Method of teaching singing* (London).

Hummell, F. L. (1822), *The art of singing exemplified* (London).
Joachim, J. and Moser, A. (1902–5; 1959; tr. ?1907), *Violinschule* (2 vols, Berlin; 2nd edn, ed. M. Jacobsen); Eng. tr. A. Moffatt (Berlin and Leipzig).
Jousse, J. (c.1804), *The harmonious tree ... dedicated to the queen* (London).
—— (?1815), *Introduction to the art of sol-fa-ing and singing* (London).
—— (1918), *Arcana musicae ... calculated to facilitate the study of music to young pupils, & save much time & trouble to the master* (London).
—— (c.1829), *A compendious dictionary* (London).
Keeble, J. (1784), *The theory of harmonics* (London).
Keith, R. W. (c.1822–3), *A musical vade mecum ... the whole art of music ... in an easy catechetical form apprehensible to the meanest capacity* (London).
Kemp, J. (c.1821a), *A new system of musical education; being a self-instructor, & serviceable companion to music masters: announced & explained in his lectures* [c.1810–19] (London).
—— (c.1821b), *Upwards of 100 cards ... connected with the new system* (London and Dublin).
King, J. (?1823), *An introduction to the theory and practice of singing* (London).
Kinsey, H. (1954), *The foundations of violin playing and musicianship* (London).
Kollmann, A. F. C. (1796), *An essay on musical harmony* (London).
—— (1799), *An essay on practical musical composition* (London).
—— (1806), *A new theory of musical harmony ... a complete & natural system of that science* (London).
—— (c.1820), *An introduction to extemporary modulation* (London).
—— (1824), *Remarks ... Logier ...* (London, 2nd edn).
Lablache, L. (c.1840), *A complete method of singing* (London).
Langey, O. (1903), *Tutor for the violin* (London).
—— [1908a], *Practical tutor for the B-flat valve-trombone, and the B-flat baritone* (London).
—— [1908b], *Practical tutor for the clarinet in the simple and the Boehm systems, and the corno di bassetto* (London).
—— [1908c], *Practical tutor for the double-bass – with three strings* (London).
—— [1908d], *Practical tutor for the double-bass – with four strings* (London).
—— [1909a], *Practical tutor for the B-flat slide-trombone – in the bass-clef* (London).
—— [1909b], *Practical tutor for the flute in four systems* (London).

—— [1909c], *Practical tutor for the violoncello* (London).
—— [1909d], *Tutor for the side drum* (London).
—— [1910a], *Practical tutor for the French-horn ... with and without valves* (London).
—— [1910b], *Practical tutor for the tenor saxhorn and the tenor cor* (London).
—— [1911a], *Practical tutor for the E-flat bombardon* (London).
—— [1911b], *Practical tutor for the oboe and the cor anglais* (London).
—— [1911c], *Practical tutor for the piccolo in the simple and the Boehm systems* (London).
—— [1912], *Practical tutor for the viola* (London).
—— [1913], *Practical tutor for the B-flat euphonium* (London).
Lanza, G. (1843), *New method of teaching class singing* (London).
Lefèvre, J. X. (?1802), *Methode de clarinette* (Paris).
Lenton, J. (1693; 1702), *The gentleman's diversion, or the violin explained* (London; 2nd edn, as *The useful instructor on the violin*).
Liston, H. (1812), *An essay on perfect intonation* (Edinburgh and London).
Loder, J. D. (1837), *A first set of three duets for two violins, dedicated to his pupils for their instruction* (London).
—— [1911], *The world's tutor ... A new edition of J. D. Loder's celebrated violin school revised and enlarged ... By Robert Fels. The most practical, largest, and best edition published* (London).
Logier, J. B. (c.1813), *A treatise on practical composition & harmony* (Dublin).
Löhlein, G. S. (1774; 1781; 1797), *Anweisung zum Violinspielen* (Leipzig and Züllichau; 2nd edn; enlarged 3rd edn, ed. J. F. Reichardt).
Lowe, C. E. [1903], *Lessons in harmonics for violinists and other musical students* (Novello's music primer 62) (London).
—— (1908), *Hints to young violinists* (Novello's elementary music manual 5) (London).
Lussy, M. (c.1885), *Traité ...* (Paris, 1874), tr. as *Musical expression* (London).
Macdonald, A. (1826), *The notation of music simplified* (Edinburgh, Glasgow and London).
Mace, T. (1676/R1958), *Musick's monument* (London).
Mackintosh, J. (1862), *The music master, for schools and families* (London).
Malcolm, A. (1721), *A treatise of musick, speculative, practical, & historical* (Edinburgh).
Marsh, J. (c.1800), *Hints to young composers of instrumental music* (Chichester and London).

McKerrell, J. (c.1800), *A familiar introduction to the first principles of music* (London).

Miller, E. (c.1817), *Miller's music primer ... dedicated to all parents who have children learning music* (London).

Monti, H. de (1796), *The self-taught musician; a treatise on music* (Edinburgh).

Morley, T. (1597/R1771), *A plain & easy introduction to practical music* (London).

Mozart, L. (1756/R1976; tr. 1948), *Versuch einer gründlichen Violinschule* (Augsburg; 2nd edn, 1769–70, enlarged 3rd edn, 1787/R1956, 4th edn, 1800; Dutch tr., 1766/R1965; Fr. tr., 1770; Eng. tr., E. Knocker, as *A treatise on the fundamental principles of violin playing*, London; 2nd edn, 1951/R1985).

Müller, I. (c.1821), *Méthode pour la nouvelle clarinette et clarinette-alto* (Paris).

Nathan, I. (1836), *Musurgia vocalis* (London).

Novello, M. S. (1856), *Voice and vocal art* (2nd edn, London).

—— (?1860), *Vocal school* (London).

Pasquali, N. (c.1757), *The art of fingering the harpsichord* (Edinburgh).

Philpot, S. [1766], *An introduction to the art of playing on the violin, on an entire new plan ... a regular foundation for young beginners ... easy rules and principles as will enable a scholar to acquire a proper method for performing on that instrument* (London; 2nd edn, 1767).

Pitman, A. (1815), *The miseries of the music-masters ... a serio comick didactic poem* (London).

Place, G. (1856), *A catechism of music for the use of young children* (London).

Playford, J. (1654; 1658), *An introduction to the skill of musick* (London; 2nd edn, 1658; 7th edn, 1674/R1966; 19th edn, 1730).

—— (1669; 1713), *Apollo's banquet for the treble violin...also rules and directions for practitioners on the treble violin* (London; 10th edn).

Prelleur, P. (1730/31/R1965; 1738), *The modern musick-master or, the universal musician* (London; 4th edn) [Part I: Singing; Part II: Flute; Part III: German flute; Part IV: Hautboy; Part V: Violin; Part VI: Harpsichord; A brief history of musick; musical dictionary].

Prescott, O. (1882), *Form, or design in music, instrumental and vocal* (London).

Prout, E. (1889), *Harmony: its theory and practice* (London).

Quantz, J. J. (1752; tr. 1966/R2001), *Versuch einer Anweisung die Flöte traversiere zu spielen* (Berlin; Eng. tr., E. R. Reilly, London and New York).

—— (?1790), *Easy and fundamental instructions ... extempore embellishments or variations ... Translated from a famous treatise on music* (London).

Rameau, J.-P. (1752), *A treatise of musick ... composition ... science. Translated* (London).

Reichardt, J. F. (1776), *Ueber die Pflichten des Ripien-Violinisten* (Berlin and Leipzig).

Reinagle, J. (1800/R1982), *Thirty progressive lessons for the violoncello* (London).

Relfe, J. (c.1817), *Just published, the principles of harmony ... progressively exhibited* (London).

Riemann, C. W. J. H. [1897–1910], *New pianoforte-school/Neue Klavierschule* (12 pts, London).

Rimbault, E. F. (1857), *New instructions on the art of singing ... chiefly selected from the celebrated tutor of Lablache* (London).

Rockstro, W. S. (1879; c.1890), *A history of music for the use of young students* (London; 3rd edn).

Rodwell, G. H. B. (1830), *The 1st rudiments of harmony. To which is added, a short account of all instruments employed in an orchestra* (London).

Rootsey, S. (1811), *An attempt to simplify the notation of music* (London).

Round, H. (1905), *Wright & Round's drum and fife band primer* (Liverpool).

Rowland, A. C. (1876; 1888), *The rudiments of music and class-singing combined* (London; ?2nd edn).

Roy, C. E. (?1825), *Méthode complette pour le flageolet* (Paris).

Rutherford, D. (c.1750, c.1760, c.1765), *The art of playing on the violin ... favourite airs ... agreable lessons in two parts* (London).

Sainton-Dolby, H. (1872), *Tutor for English singers* (London).

Sammons, A. E. (1916), *The secret of fine technique in violin playing ... daily practice for soloists and advanced players* (London).

Sass, A. L. [1909], *The secret of acquiring in a short time a beautiful, clear and penetrating tone (on the violin and violincello [sic]) ...* [including] *The Ševčík method by Paul Stoeving* (London).

Sax, A. [?1850], *Méthode complète pour saxhorn et saxotromba* (Paris).

Schneider, J. C. F. (1828), *The elements of musical harmony & composition ... a compendium for tuition, & a guide for self-instruction. Translated* (London).

Ševčík, O. (1901), *School of violin technic, in 4 parts Op.1* (London).

Shield, W. (1800), *An introduction to harmony* (London).

[Skinner, A.] (1929), *Violin made easy. A diagram for the use of students* (London).

Smith, T. R. (n.d.), *The violoncello preceptor, containing the rudiments of music, with scales* (London).
Spence, S. (*c*.1810), *Introduction to the science of harmony ... 1st practical lessons on the piano forte, the rudiments of thorough bass* (London).
Spencer, C. C. (*c*.1829), *The elements of practical music* (London).
Spohr, L. [1808], *Grande duo pour violon et viola ... Op.13* (Leipzig).
—— (1816; 1963), *Violin concerto no.7, Op.38* (Leipzig); ed. F. Göthel (Kassel).
—— (1820), *Violin concerto no.8, Op.47* (Leipzig).
—— ([1832]/R1960), *Violinschule* (Vienna).
—— (1915), *45 exercises by Louis Spohr (from the violin school)* edited by H. Wessely (London).
Steetz, W. (1812), *A treatise on the elements of music* (London).
Stephenson, R. J. (*c*.1822), *Elementary elucidations ... for general use, vocal or instrumental* (London).
—— (*c*.1824), *2d-series amateur's assistant vocal or instrumental* (London).
Stoeving, C. H. P. [1904], *The art of violin-bowing* (London).
Stretton, A. J. (1903), *Hawkes & Son's unison scale-books for military and brass bands* (London).
Swaine, N. (*c*.1818), *The young musician, or the science of music* (Stourport).
Tansur [or Tans'ur], W. (1746; 1830), *A new musical grammar* (London; 8th edn).
—— (?1767), *The elements of musick display'd ... Book III ... the structure of musical instruments with the scale of musick applicable to each and directions ... bass viol, violin and guittar* (London).
Tartini, G. [1760], *Lettera* [dated 1760] (Venice, 1770; Ger. tr., 1786), tr. C. Burney as *A Letter ... Tartini to Signora Maddalena Lombardini (now Signora Sirmen) ... an important lesson to performers on the violin* (London, 1770/R1967, 2nd edn, 1779).
—— (1771; 1961), *Traité des agrémens de la musique* (Paris; Eng. tr., ed. E. R. Jacobi, Celle and New York).
Taylor, J. (1872), *A manual of vocal music for use in elementary schools* (London).
Tenducci, G. (?1785), *Instruction of Mr. Tenducci, to his scholars* (London).
Tessarini, C. (*c*.1765a), *An accurate method to attain the art of playing ye violin* (London).
—— (*c*.1765), *A musical grammar* (Edinburgh).
—— (1981), *Works for the violin*, ed. G. Banat, *Masters of the violin*, vol.4 (New York).

Thistleton, F. (1913), *Modern violin technique: how to acquire it, how to teach it* (London).
Thomas, E. E. (*c*.1821), *Under the patronage ... Duchess of Kent ... the elements of music, combining instruction with amusement* (London).
Thompson, T. (1801), *A dictionary of music ... young pupils, as well as proficients* (Newcastle-upon-Tyne).
Thomson, J. (1778; 1793), *The rudiments of music* (Edinburgh; 3rd edn).
Tosi, P. F. (1723; tr. 1742/R1926; 1743), *Opinioni* ... (Bologna), tr. and ed. J. E. Galliard as *Observations on the florid song* (London; 2nd edn).
Türk, D. G. (1789; 1802), *Klavierschule* (Leipzig and Halle; 2nd edn).
Vaccai, N. (1834), *Practical method of Italian singing* (London).
Vierling, J. G. (*c*.1828), *An introduction to the art of preluding & of extemporaneous performance in general ... translated ... Hamilton* (London).
Viguerie, B. (1798), *L'art de toucher le piano-forte* (Paris).
Viotti, G. B. (1976), *Four violin concertos*, ed. C. White, *Recent researches in the music of the pre-classical, classical and early romantic eras*, vols 4 and 5 (Madison, Wisc.).
—— (*c*.1785), *Six sonates pour violon et basse, oeuvre 4e* (Paris, *c*.1785), ed. J. Adas, in *Late eighteenth-century masters: continuo sonatas for violin* (see 'Collections' below).
—— [1803], *Three duets for two violins ... Op.18* (London).
—— [1884], *Viotti's six duets for two violins* (London).
Wainewright, H. (1836), *Critical remarks on the art of singing* (London).
Ware, G. (1822), *A dictionary of musical chords ... a scientific instructor* (London and Manchester).
Watson, J. (*c*.1821), *A system of musical notation for use of the blind* (London).
Wessely, H. (1913), *A practical guide to violin playing* (London).
Widor, C.-M. (1904; 1906), *Technique de l'orchestre moderne* (Paris); tr. E. Suddard as *The technique of the modern orchestra* (London).
Williams, J. H. (1902), *The first principles of pianoforte technic* (London).
Winch, C. (attrib.) (*c*.1746, *c*.1756), *The compleat tutor for the French horn* (London).
—— (attrib.) (*c*.1750), *The French horn master* (London).
Woldemar, M. (1798; *c*.1800), *Méthode pour le violon* (Paris; 2nd rev. edn, as *Grande Méthode ... pour le violon*).
—— (1801) *Méthode de violon par L. Mozart rédigée par Woldemar, élève de Lolli. Nouvelle édition* (Paris).

Worgan, T. D. (c.1806), *Harmonic pastimes ... cards ... amusement ... the science* (London).
Wright, T. (?1823), *Musical primer & supplement* (Stockton-on-Tees).

Collections

Little pieces from 18th century violin methods for 2 violins, vols 1 and 2 (Vienna, 1982 and 1985), including works by L'abbé *le fils*, M. Corrette and others.
Late eighteenth-century masters: Continuo sonatas for violin, general editor J. Adas, *The eighteenth-century continuo sonata*, vol.6 (New York and London, 1991), including works by D. E. Barbella, P. Nardini, G. Pugnani, G. B. Viotti, P. Gaviniès and others.

Secondary sources

Allsop, P. (1999), *Arcangelo Corelli: 'new Orpheus of our times'* (Oxford).
Almond, C., ed. (1979), 'The developing violin', *EM*, 7: 155–65.
Anon. (1747), *A general description of the trades ... by which parents ... may with greater ease and certainty, make choice* (London).
—— (1830), 'On musical studies. (From the French)', *Harmonicon*, 8: 144–5.
—— (1831), *Biographical sketch of Nicolo Paganini ... critiques on his first three concerts given at the King's Theatre, Haymarket* (London).
—— (1832), *Memoir of Signor Paganini with critical remarks on his performances* (Liverpool).
—— (1880), *Designs and plans for the construction and arrangements of the new model violin* (London).
Argent, M., ed. (1992), *Recollections of R. J. S. Stevens: an organist in Georgian London* (London).
Arnold, D. (1965), 'Instruments and instrumental teaching elsewhere in the early Italian conservatoires', *GSJ*, 18: 72–81.
Atlas, A. W. (1996), *The Wheatstone English concertina in Victorian England* (Oxford).
—— (1999), 'The 'respectable' concertina', *M&L*, 80: 241–53.
Babitz, S. (1957), 'Differences between eighteenth-century & modern violin bowing', *The Score*, 19: 34–55.
Bacon, R. M. ['Vetus'] (1818–19a), 'On the character of musicians', *QMMR*, 1: 284–94.

—— (1818–19b), 'On the objects of musical education', *QMMR*, 1: 421–8.
—— (1820a), 'Music as a pursuit for men', *QMMR*, 2: 7–14.
—— (1820b), 'The Royal Academy of Music', *QMMR*, 2: 370–400 and 516–26.
—— (1829), Review, 'Hummel's Instructions' [Chron., 1829], *QMMR*, 10: 359–69.
Bailey, P. (1998), *Popular culture and performance in the Victorian city* (Cambridge).
Baines, A. C. (1976), Brass instruments: their history and development (London).
—— (1966), *Woodwind instruments and their history* (3rd edn, London).
Banat, G., ed. (1981), 'Works for the violin: Carlo Tessarini', *Masters of the violin*, vol.4 (New York).
Barbieri, P. (1991), 'Violin intonation: a historical survey', *EM*, 19: 69–88.
Barbour, J. M. (1952), 'Violin intonation in the eighteenth century', *JAMS*, 5: 224–34.
Barnard, H. C. (1961), *A history of English education, from 1760* (London).
—— (1969), *Education and the French revolution* (Cambridge).
—— (1970), *Were those the days? A Victorian education* (Oxford).
Barrow, W. (1802), *An essay on education* (London).
Barry, J. and Brooks, C., eds (1994), *The middling sort of people: culture, society and politics in England, 1550–1800* (London).
Bashford, C. (2000), 'The late Beethoven quartets and the London press, 1836–ca.1850', *MQ*, 84: 84–122.
—— and Langley, L., eds (2000), *Music and British culture 1785–1914: essays in honour of Cyril Ehrlich* (Oxford).
Bate, P. (1969), *The flute* (London and New York).
—— (1975), *The oboe* (3rd edn, London and New York).
—— (1978), *The trumpet and trombone* (2nd edn, London and New York).
Beechey, G. (1983), 'Robert Bremner and his *Thoughts on the performance of concert music*', MQ, 69: 244–52.
Beedell, A. V. (1992), *The decline of the English musician 1788–1888* (Oxford).
Berkenhout, J. (1790), *A volume of letters from Dr Berkenhout to his son at the university* (Cambridge and London).
Bermingham, A. (2000), *Learning to draw: studies in the cultural history of a polite and useful art* (New Haven).
Bevan, C. (1978), *The tuba family* (London and New York (2nd edn, Winchester, 2000)).

—— (1990), *Musical instrument collections in the British Isles* (Winchester).
Bicknell, S. (1996), *The history of the English organ* (Cambridge).
Bie, O. (1889), *A history of the pianoforte and pianoforte players* (London).
Bingley, W. (1814, 1834/R1971), *Musical biography* (2 vols, London; 2nd edn).
Blades, J. (1984), *Percussion instruments and their history* (London, rev. edn).
Blom, E. (1947), *Music in England* (London, rev. edn).
Boeringer, J. (1975), 'Further 19th century accounts of English organs', *MT*, 116: 73–5, 170–72.
Boyce, M. F. (1973), 'The French school of violin playing' (unpublished Ph.D. thesis, University of North Carolina).
Boyd, M., and Rayson, J. (1982), 'The gentleman's diversion: John Lenton and the first violin tutor', *EM*, 10: 329–32.
Boyden, D. D. (1950), 'The violin and its technique in the eighteenth century', *MQ*, 36: 9–38.
—— (1951), 'Prelleur, Geminiani and just intonation', *JAMS*, 4: 202–19.
—— [1952], 'Introduction', Facsimile edn, F. Geminiani, *The art of playing on the violin* (London).
—— (1959), 'Geminiani and the first violin tutor', *AM*, 31: 161–70.
—— (1960), 'A postscript to "Geminiani and the first violin tutor"', *AM*, 32: 40–7.
—— (1965/R1975), *The history of violin playing, from its origins to 1761* (Oxford).
—— (1980), 'The violin bow in the eighteenth century', *EM*, 8: 199–212.
Brewer, J. (1997), *The pleasures of the imagination: English culture in the eighteenth century* (London).
Briggs, A. (1959; 1979/R1994), *The age of improvement 1783–1867* (London, 2nd edn).
Brinsmead, E. (1879), *History of the pianoforte* (London).
Broadhouse, J. [1879]; [1882]; [1889], *Facts about fiddles. Violins old and new* (London; enlarged 2nd edn; 3rd edn).
Brook, D. (1948), *Violinists of today* (London).
Brown, C. (1980), 'The popularity and influence of Spohr in England' (unpublished D.Phil. thesis, University of Oxford).
—— (1984), *Louis Spohr: a critical biography* (Cambridge).
—— (1988), 'Bowing styles, vibrato and portamento in nineteenth-century violin playing', *JRMA*, 113: 97–128.
—— (1993), 'Dots and strokes in late eighteenth- and nineteenth-century music', *EM*, 21: 593–610.

—— (1994), 'Ferdinand David's editions of Beethoven', in R. Stowell, ed., *Performing Beethoven* (Cambridge), 117–49.
—— (1999), *Classical & romantic performing practice 1750–1900* (Oxford).
Brown, H. M. and Sadie, S. (1989), eds, *Performance practice: music after 1600* (London).
Brown, J. D. (1886), *Biographical dictionary of musicians with a bibliography of English writings on music* (London).
Brown, J. D., and Stratton, S. S. (1897), *British musical biography* (Birmingham).
Brun, P. (2000), *A new history of the double bass* (Villeneuve d'Ascq (France)).
Bull, S. C. (1886), *Ole Bull. A memoir* (London).
Burden, M., and Cholij, I., eds (1989, 1993, 1996 and 1999), *A handbook for studies in eighteenth-century English music*, vols 2, 4, 6 and 10 (Edinburgh).
Burgan, M. (1989), 'Heroines at the piano: women and music in nineteenth-century fiction' in Temperley, ed., 42–67.
Burgh, A. (1814), *Anecdotes of music* (3 vols, London; Ger. tr., 1820).
Burney, C. (1876–89), *A general history of music* (4 vols, London; ed. F. Mercer, 2 vols, London, 1935/R1957).
—— (1959), *Dr Burney's musical tours in Europe*, ed. P. A. Scholes (2 vols, London).
Busby, T. (1825), *Concert room and orchestra anecdotes* (London).
Button, S. (1889), *The guitar in England 1800–1924* (New York).
Caldwell, J. (1999), *The Oxford history of English music. Volume II: From c.1715 to the present day* (Oxford).
Campbell, M. (1980), *The great violinists* (London).
Campbell, R. (1747), *The London tradesman ... of all the trades ... for the information of parents and instruction of youth in their choice of business* (London).
Cannon, J., ed. (1997), *The Oxford companion to British history* (Oxford).
Careri, E. (1993), *Francesco Geminiani (1687–1762)* (Oxford).
Carse, A. (1941), 'Text-books on orchestration before Berlioz', *M&L*, 22: 26–31.
—— (1948), *The orchestra from Beethoven to Berlioz* (Cambridge).
—— (1951), *The life of Jullien* (Cambridge).
Cazalet, W. W. (1854), *The history of the Royal Academy of Music, compiled from authentic sources* (London).
Chapman, G. (1773), *A treatise on education* (London).
Charlton, D. (1988), 'Classical clarinet technique', *EM*, 16: 396–406.
Clutton, C. and Niland, A. (1963; 1982), *The British organ* (London; 2nd edn).

Cobbett, W. W. (1910), 'Violin-playing', *Grove 2*, vol.5: 328–31.
Cole, M. (1997), *The pianoforte in the Classical era* (Oxford).
Colles, H. C. (1933), *The Royal College of Music: a jubilee record 1883–1933* (London).
Colles, H. C. and Cruft, J. (1982), *The Royal College of Music: a centenary record 1883–1983* (London).
Colls, R. and Dodd, P., eds (1986), *Englishness: politics and culture 1880–1920* (London).
Collyer, J. (1761), *The parent's and guardian's directory and the youth's guide in the choice of a profession or trade* (London).
Cooper, A. (1989), 'Banks of England: eighteenth-century Engish violin maker Benjamin Banks', *The Strad*, 100: 287–95.
Corder, F. (1922a), *A history of the Royal Academy of Music from 1822 to 1922* (London).
—— (1922b), *Royal Academy of Music centenary souvenir* (London).
Cowgill, R. (2000), '"The most musical spot for its size in the kingdom": music in Georgian Halifax', *EM*, 28: 557–75.
Cox, G. (1993), *A history of music education in England 1872–1928* (Aldershot).
Cox, J. E. (1872), *Musical recollections of the last half century* (2 vols, London).
Cox, H. B, and Cox, C. L. E. (1907), *Leaves from the journals of Sir George Smart* (London).
Crump, J. (1986), 'The identity of English music: the reception of Elgar 1898–1935', in R. Colls and P. Dodd, eds, *Englishness: politics and culture 1880–1920* (London).
Cudworth, C. L. (1966), 'An essay by John Marsh', *M & L*, 36: 155–64.
—— (1967), 'An eighteenth-century musical apprenticeship', *MT*, 108: 602.
Curry, P. B. (1968), 'The François Tourte violin bow' (unpublished Ph.D. thesis, Brigham Young University).
Curwen, J. (1873), *The present crisis of music in schools: a reply to Mr Hullah* (London).
Cyr, M. (1995), 'Violin playing in late seventeenth-century England: Baltzar, Matteis, and Purcell', *PPR*, 8: 54–66.
Daly, W. (1910), 'The violin', in J. Greig, ed., *The musical educator* (5 vols, London).
Davenant, F. (1870), *What shall my son be? Hints to parents on the choice of a profession or trade* (London).
Davey, H. (1895; 1921/R1969), *History of English music* (London; enlarged 2nd edn).
David, P. (1879), 'Geminiani', *Grove 1*, vol.1: 587–8.
—— (1889), 'Violin-playing', *Grove 1*, vol.4: 287–99.

—— (1906), 'Geminiani', *Grove 2*, vol.2: 154–5.
Davidson, J. W. [1877], 'Joseph Joachim', in *The portrait. Photographs and memoirs of men of note* (London).
Davidson, P. (1871; 1880; 1881; 1895), *The violin ... construction, theoretically and practically treated* (Glasgow; 2nd edn, London; 3rd edn; 4th edn).
Davy, C. (1787), *Letters, addressed chiefly to a young gentleman* (2 vols, Bury St Edmunds).
Dibble, J. (2001), 'Grove's musical dictionary: a national monument', in H. White and M. Murphy, eds, *Musical constructions of nationalism: essays on the history and ideology of European musical culture 1800–1945* (Cork), 33–50.
Dibdin, C. (*c.*1791), *A letter on musical education* (London).
Dilworth, J. (1988), 'Lotts of value: the life and work of John Lott', *The Strad*, 99: 800–9.
—— (1994), 'Richard Duke: the grand old Duke of lutherie', *The Strad*, 105: 249–55.
Doane, J. (1794), *A musical directory for the year 1794* (London).
Dodd, P. (1986), 'Englishness and the national culture', in R. Colls and P. Dodd, eds, *Englishness: politics and culture 1880–1920* (London).
Donington, R. (1970), 'Geminiani and the gremlins', *M&L*, 51: 130–55.
—— (1988), Review, G. Moes-Haenen, *Das Vibrato in der Musik des Barock*, *EM*, 16: 571–3.
Dubourg, G. (1836; 1852; 1878), *The violin: some account of that leading instrument and its most eminent professors* (London; 4th edn; 5th edn).
Duckles, V. (1981), 'Musicology', in Temperley, ed., 483–502.
Duffin, E. W. (1839), *Particulars of the illness and death of the late Mr. Mori, the violinist* (London).
Eaton, T. D. (1872), *Musical criticism and biography* (London).
Edgeworth, M. (1801), *Practical education* (3 vols, 2nd edn, London).
Edwards, O. (1968–9), 'English string concertos before 1800', *PRMA*, 95: 1–13.
—— (1976), 'The response to Corelli's music in eighteenth-century England', *Studia Musicologica Norvedica*, 2: 51–96.
—— (1989), 'Espionage, a collection of violins, and *Le bizzarie universali*: a fresh look at William Corbett', *MQ*, 73: 320–43.
Ehrlich, C. (1976; 1990), *The piano: a history* (London; 2nd edn).
—— (1985), *The music profession in Britain since the eighteenth century: a social history* (Oxford).
—— (1995), *First Philharmonic: a history of the Royal Philharmonic Society* (Oxford).
—— and McVeigh, S. (1999), 'Music' in McCalman, ed.: 242–50.

Elbourne, R. (1980), *Music and tradition in early industrial Lancashire 1780–1840* (Woodbridge).
Elgar, E. (1968), *A future for English music and other lectures*, ed. P. M. Young (London).
Ella, J. (1878), *Musical sketches, abroad and at home* (3rd edn, London).
Escott, T. H. S. (1885), *England: its people, polity, and pursuits* (2 vols, London).
Ess, D. H. van (1981), 'Band Music', in Temperley, ed.: 135–43.
Farmer, H. G. (1947; 1970), *A history of music in Scotland* (London; repr. New York).
Father of a family, The (1824), 'Musical tuition', letter to the editor, *QMMR*, 6: 306–9.
Fellowes, E. H. (1846), *Memoirs of an amateur musician* (London).
Fenelon, A. F. de S. de la M. (1750), *Instructions for the education of daughters* (Glasgow).
Ferguson, H. (1975), *Keyboard interpretation from the 14th to the 19th century* (London).
Ferris, G. J. (1884), *Sketches of great pianists and great violinists* (London).
Fétis, F. J. (1829), 'State of music in London', *Harmonicon*, 7: 181–6, 214–20, 241–6, 275–81.
—— (1835–44), *Biographie universelle des musiciens* (8 vols, Paris).
—— (1851; tr. [1852]; 1876), *Notice biographique sur Nicolo Paganini* (Paris), tr. by W. E. Guernsey (London, [1852], 2nd edn, 1876).
—— (1856; tr. 1864/R1964), *Antoine Stradivari, luthier célèbre* (Paris); tr. J. Bishop (London).
Fisher, H. [1888], *The musical profession* (London).
Fiske, R. (1983), *Scotland in music: a European enthusiasm* (Cambridge).
Fiske, R. and Johnstone, H. D., eds (1990), *The Blackwell history of music in Britain: the eighteenth century* (Oxford).
Fleming, J. M. (1883; 1890), *Old violins and their makers* (London; 2nd edn).
Ford, B., ed. (1990), *The Cambridge guide to the arts in Britain*, vol.6 (Cambridge).
Forster, S. A. (1864), *The history of the violin* (London).
Foucher, G. (1894; 1897), *Treatise on the history and construction of the violin* (London; rev. edn).
Fuller, S. (1998), 'Women composers during the British musical renaissance, 1880–1918' (unpublished Ph.D. thesis, University of London).
Fuller-Maitland, J. A. (1902), *English music of the nineteenth century* (London).

Gable, F. K. (1992), 'Some observations concerning baroque & modern vibrato', *PPR*, 5: 90–103.
Galloway, W. J. (1910), *Musical England* (London).
Gane, M. J. (1972), 'Social changes in English music and music making 1800–1870, with special reference to the symphony orchestra' (unpublished Ph.D. thesis, University of London).
Gardiner, W. (1838–53), *Music and friends* (3 vols, London).
Gelrud, P. G. (1941), 'A critical study of the French violin school (1782–1882)' (unpublished Ph.D. thesis, Cornell University).
Gessele, C. M. (1992), 'The Conservatoire de Musique and national music education in France, 1795–1801', in M. Boyd, ed., *Music and the French Revolution* (Cambridge).
Gillett, P. (2000a), *Musical women in England, 1870–1914: 'encroaching on all man's privileges'* (London).
—— (2000b), 'Ambivalent friendships: music-lovers, amateurs, and professional musicians in the late nineteenth century' in Bashford and Langley, eds (2000), 321–40.
Girdham, J. (2002), 'The flageolet player: the ultimate amateur musician', *EM*, 30: 397–409.
Golby, D. J. (1999a), 'Violin pedagogy in England during the first half of the nineteenth century, or *The incompleat tutor for the violin*', in B. Zon, ed., *Nineteenth-century British music studies*, vol. 1 (Aldershot), 88–104.
—— (1999b), 'The violin in England c.1750–c.1850: a case-study in music education' (unpublished D.Phil. thesis, University of Oxford).
Golby, J. M., ed. (1986), *Culture & society in Britain 1850–1890* (Oxford).
Goldsmith, P. (1979a), 'First violin methods using the Tourte bow', *The Strad*, 90: 729–30, 800–802.
—— (1979b), 'Bowing articulation in the transitional period', *The Strad*, 90: 1039.
Goodban, T. (1820), *The rudiments of music* (London).
Gouk, P. (1999), *Music, science and natural magic in seventeenth-century England* (New Haven and London).
Graham, G. F. (1816), *An account of the 1st Edinburgh musical festival ... some general observations on music* (Edinburgh).
Graham, M. (1996), *Britain in old photographs: Oxfordshire at school* (Stroud, 1996).
—— (1977), *Oxfordshire at play* (Stroud).
Grant, K. S. (1983), *Dr. Burney as critic and historian of music* (Ann Arbor, Mich.).
Hadley, D. (1972), 'British musical society in early nineteenth-century England: studies in the history of a profession, 1800–1824' (unpublished Ph.D. thesis, Harvard University, 1972).

Hadow, W. H. (1931), *English music* (London).
Halfpenny, E. (1954), 'Castilon on the clarinet', *M&L*, 35: 332–8.
—— (1964a), 'The earliest English bassoon tutor', *GSJ*, 17: 103–5.
—— (1964b), 'An eighteenth-century trade list of musical instruments', *GSJ*, 17: 99–102.
—— (1965), 'Early English clarinets', *GSJ*, 18: 42–56.
—— (1977), 'The Boehm clarinet in England', *GSJ*, 30: 2–7.
Hamilton, J. A. (1837), *A dictionary of two thousand Italian, French, German, English, and other musical terms* (London, 4th edn).
Harding, R. (1978), *The piano-forte; its history traced to The Great Exhibition of 1851* (2nd edn, Old Woking).
Harris, T., ed. (1995), *Popular culture in England, c.1500–1850* (London).
Hart, G. (1875; 1885), *The violin: its famous makers and their imitators* (London; 2nd edn).
—— (1881), The violin and its music (London).
Harvey, B. W. (1995), *The violin family and its makers in the British Isles: an illustrated history and directory* (Oxford).
Haweis, H. R. (1873; 1881), *Music and morals* (London; 10th edn).
—— (1844; 1898), *My musical life* (London; 5th edn).
—— (1898), *Old violins and violin lore* (London).
Hawkins, J. (1776), *A general history of the science and practice of music* (5 vols, London; facs. repr. of 2nd (1853) edn, with an introduction by Charles Cudworth, 2 vols, New York, 1963).
Haynes, B. (1991), 'Beyond temperament: non-keyboard intonation in the 17th and 18th centuries', *EM*, 19: 356–81.
—— (2001), *The eloquent oboe: a history of the hautboy 1640–1760* (Oxford).
Herbert, T., ed. (2000a), *The British brass band: a musical and social history* (Oxford).
—— (2000b), 'Popular nationalism: Griffith Rhys Jones ('Caradog') and the Welsh choral tradition' in Bashford and Langley, eds (2000): 255–74.
—— and Wallace, J., eds (1997), *The Cambridge companion to brass instruments* (Cambridge).
Herissone, R. (2000), *Music theory in seventeenth-century England* (Oxford).
Heron-Allen, E. (1884; 1885), *Violin-making, as it was and is* (London; 2nd edn).
—— (1890–94), *De fidiculis bibliographia: being the basis of a bibliography of the violin and all other instruments played with a bow in ancient and modern times* (2 vols, London).
—— (1900), *A catalogue of books, pamphlets and miscellanea relating to the violin, forming part of the [RCM] library* (London).

Hickman, R. (1983), 'The censored publications of "The art of playing on the violin", or Geminiani unshaken', *EM*, 11: 73–6.
Higham, C. (1896), *Biographical sketch of Francis Barthélemon* (London).
Highfill, P. H., Burnim, K. A., and Langhans, E. A. (1973–93), *A biographical dictionary of actors, actresses, musicians ... in London, 1660–1800* (16 vols, Carbondale, Ill.).
Hill, W. H., A. F., and A. E. (1902), *Antonio Stradivari: his life and work* (London).
Hodges, E. (1836), 'On the objects of musical study', *MW* 1: 37–41, 85–8, 149–52.
Hogarth, G. (1830), 'Musical literature', *Blackwood's Edinburgh Magazine*, 28: 471–81.
—— (1835; 1838), *Musical history, biography and criticism* (London; enlarged 2nd edn, 2 vols, London).
Holden, J. (1770), *An essay towards a rational system of music* (Glasgow).
Holloway, J. (1996), 'Corelli's op.5: text, act ... and reaction', *EM*, 24: 635–43.
Holman, P. (1993/R1995), *Four and twenty fiddlers: the violin at the English court 1540–1690* (Oxford).
—— (2000), 'The Colchester partbooks', *EM*, 28: 577–95.
[Honeyman, W. C.] [1893]; (1939/R1983), *The violin: how to choose one* (Dundee; 6th edn).
Hopkins, E. J. and Rimbault, E. F. (1855; 1887/R1972), *The organ: its history and construction* (London; 3rd edn).
[Horncastle, F. W.] (1822), 'Plan for the formation of an English conservatorio', *QMMR*, 4: 129–33.
Howes, F. (1966), *The English musical renaissance* (London).
Hueffer, F. (1889), *Half a century of music in England, 1827–1887. Essays towards a history* (London).
Hughes, M., and Stradling, R. (2001), *The English musical renaissance 1840–1940: constructing a national music* (2nd edn, Manchester).
Hullah, J. (1865), *A course of lectures on the third or transition period of music history, delivered at the Royal Institution of Great Britain* (London).
Humphries, J. (1998), 'The Royal Academy of Music and its traditions', *Brass Bulletin*, 101: 42–52.
—— (2000), *The early horn: a practical guide* (Cambridge).
Hyde, D. (1998), *New-found voices: women in nineteenth-century English music* (3rd edn, Aldershot).
Irving, H. (1999), *Ancients and moderns: William Crotch and the development of Classical music* (Aldershot).

Jackson, W. (1791), *Observations on the present state of music in London* (London).

Jacoby, R. J. (1980), 'The role of technique in violin playing' (unpublished Ph.D. thesis, University of Aberyswyth).

Jarrold, T. (1819), 'On education. Letter VIII', *Monthly Magazine*, 47: 11–14.

Johnson, E. (1994), 'Good vibrations – without vibrato', *The Strad*, 105: 554–5.

Johnston, R. (1996), 'Concerts in the musical life of Belfast to 1874' (unpublished D.Phil thesis, Queen's University of Belfast).

—— (2000), '"Here we will sit": the creation of the Ulster hall', in Bashford and Langley, eds: 215–32.

Johnstone, H. D. (1996), 'Yet more ornaments for Corelli's Violin Sonatas, op.5', *EM*, 24: 623–33.

Kappey, J. A. (*c*.1894), *Military music: a history of wind-instrumental bands* (London).

Karp, C. (1986), 'The early history of the clarinet and chalumeau', *EM*, 14: 545–51.

Kassler, J. C. (1972), 'Burney's "Sketch of a plan for a public music-school"', *MQ*, 58: 210–34.

—— (1976), 'Music made easy to infant capacity 1714–1830. Some facets of British music education', *Studies in Music* (Australia), 10: 67–78.

—— (1979), *The science of music in Britain, 1714–1830. A catalogue of writings, lectures and inventions* (2 vols, New York and London).

—— (2001), *Music, science, philosophy: models in the universe of thought* (Aldershot).

Kidd, R. R. (1968), 'The sonata for keyboard with violin accompaniment in England (1750–1790)' (unpublished Ph.D. thesis, Yale University).

Kollmann, A. F. C. (1812), 'A retrospect of the state of music in Great Britain, since the year 1789', *Quarterly Musical Register*, 1: 6–28.

Kolneder, W. (1972; 1993; tr. 1998), *Das Buch der Violine* (Zurich; 5th edn); Eng. tr. and ed., R. G. Pauly as *The Amadeus book of the violin: construction, history, and music* (Portland, Ore.).

Komlós, K. (1995), *Fortepianos and their music: Germany, Austria, and England, 1760–1800* (Oxford).

Kruse, S. L. (1986), *The viola school of technique: etudes and methods written between 1780 and 1860* (Ann Arbor).

Langford, P. (1998), *A polite and commercial people – England 1727–1783* (Oxford)

—— (2000), *Englishness identified: manners and character (1650–1850)* (Oxford).

Langley, L. (1983), 'The English musical journal in the early nineteenth century' (unpublished Ph.D. thesis, University of North Carolina at Chapel Hill).
Langwill, L. G. (1965), *The bassoon and contrabassoon* (London and New York).
Lasocki, D. (1982), 'Professional recorder playing in England 1500–1740', *EM*, 10: 22–9.
Lawson, C., ed. (1995), *The Cambridge companion to the clarinet* (Cambridge).
—— (2000), *The early clarinet: a practical guide* (Cambridge).
Lawson, C., and Stowell, R. (1999), *The historical performance of music: an introduction* (Cambridge).
Lawson, J. and Silver, H. (1974), *A social history of education in England* (London).
Leppert, R. (1985), 'Music teachers of upper-class amateur musicians in eighteenth-century England', in *Music in the Classic period: essays in honor of Barry S. Brook*, ed. A. W. Atlas (New York), 133–58.
—— (1988), *Music and image: domesticity, ideology and socio-cultural formation in eighteenth-century England* (Cambridge).
Long, N. (1959), *Music in English education* (London).
Lyle, A. (1977), 'John Mahon's clarinet tutor', *GSJ*, 30: 52–5.
McArtor, M. E. (1951), 'Francesco Geminiani, composer and theorist' (unpublished Ph.D. thesis, University of Michigan).
McCalman, I., ed. (1999), *The romantic age: British culture 1776–1832* (Oxford).
Mackerness, E. D. (1964), *A social history of English music* (London).
McVeigh, S. (1983), 'Felice Giardini: a violinist in late eighteenth-century London', *M & L*, 64: 162–72.
—— (1989a), *The violinist in London's concert life 1750–1784: Felice Giardini and his contemporaries* (New York and London).
—— (1989b), 'The professional concert and rival subscription series in London, 1783–1793', *RMA Research Chronicle*, 22: 1–135.
—— (1993), *Concert life in London from Mozart to Haydn* (Cambridge).
—— (2000), 'The society of British musicians (1834–1865) and the campaign for native talent' in Bashford and Langley, eds: 145–68.
Mainzer, J. (1848), *Music and education* (London and Edinburgh).
Marsh, J. (1796; 1955), 'A comparison between the ancient & modern styles of music', *Monthly Magazine*, 2: 981–6; ed. C. Cudworth as 'An essay by John Marsh', *M & L*, 36: 155–64.
Matthew, C., ed. (2000), *Short Oxford history of the British Isles: nineteenth century* (Oxford).
Matthews, B. (1984), *By God's grace: a history of Uppingham school* (Maidstone).

May, T. (1996), *An economic and social history of Britain 1760–1990* (London).
Middleton, R. (1981), 'Popular music of the lower classes', in Temperley, ed. 63–91.
Milligan, T. B. (1983), *The concerto and London's musical culture in the late eighteenth century* (Ann Arbor, Mich.).
Milnes, J., ed. (2000), *The British violin: the catalogue of the 1998 exhibition, '400 years of violin & bow making in the British Isles'* (Oxford).
Monosoff, S. (1985), 'Violin fingering', *EM*, 13: 76–9.
Montagu, J. (2002), *Timpani & percussion* (New Haven and London).
Morgan, K. O., ed. (1984), *The Oxford illustrated history of Britain* (Oxford).
Mori, N., ed. [1832], *The Musical Gem, a souvenir for MDCCCXXXII* (London).
Morris, W. M. (1904; 1920), *British violin-makers* (London; 2nd edn).
Moser, A. (1966–7), *Geschichte des Violinspiels* (Berlin, 1923, 2nd rev. edn, Tutzing).
Musgrave, M. (1995), *The musical life of the Crystal Palace* (Cambridge).
—— (2000), 'Changing values in nineteenth-century performance: the work of Michael Costa and August Manns' in Bashford and Langley, eds, 169–91.
Nelson, C. (2000), 'Tea-table miscellanies: the development of Scotland's song culture, 1720–1800', *EM*, 28: 596–618.
Nettel, R. (1944), *Music in the five towns 1840–1914* (Oxford).
—— (1945–6), 'The influence of the industrial revolution on English music', *PRMA*, 72: 23–40.
—— (1946), *The orchestra in England: a social history* (London).
Neumann, F. (1982), 'The use of Baroque treatises in musical performance', in F. Neumann, *Essays in performance practice* (London), 1–9.
—— (1991), 'The vibrato controversy', *PPR*, 4: 14–27.
—— (1993a), 'Dots and strokes in Mozart', *EM*, 21: 429–35.
—— (1993b), *Performance practices of the seventeenth and eighteenth centuries* (New York).
Newsome, R. (1998), *Brass roots: a hundred years of brass bands and their music (1836–1936)* (Aldershot).
Norman, P. (1986), 'Two organ guides from late 18th-century England', *MT*, 127: 637–43.
Olleson, P. (2000), 'Samuel Wesley and the music profession', in Bashford and Langley, eds, 23–38.
Otto, J. A. (1833), *Treatise on the construction, preservation, repairs,*

and improvement of the violin, and all bow instruments, tr. T. Fardeley (London).
—— (1848; 1860; 1875), A treatise on the structure and preservation of the violin, tr. J. Bishop (London; 2nd edn; 3rd enlarged edn).
Palmer, F. M. (1997), Domenico Dragonetti in England (1794–1846): the career of a double bass virtuoso (Oxford).
Parke, W. T. (1830/R1970), Musical memoirs ... 1784, to the year 1830 (2 vols, London).
Pearce, J., jun. (1866), Violins and violin-makers (London).
Philip, R. (1992), Early recordings and musical style (Cambridge).
Phillips, H. (1864), Musical and personal recollections during half a century (London).
Phipson, T. L. (1877), Biographical sketches and anecdotes of celebrated violinists (London).
—— (1898), Voice and violin (London).
Pickering, J. M. (1990), Music in the British Isles 1700–1800: a bibliography of literature (Edinburgh).
Pine, R., and Acton, C., eds (1998), To talent alone: the Royal Irish academy of music 1848–1998 (Dublin).
Pitts, S. (2000), A century of change in music education: historical perspectives on contemporary practice in British secondary school music (Aldershot).
Pleasants, H. (1961), The musical journeys of Louis Spohr (Norman, Okla.).
Pleasants, V. (1985), 'The early piano in Britain (c.1760–1800)', EM, 13: 39–44.
Pollens, S. (1995), The early pianoforte (Cambridge).
Potter, J. (1762), Observations on the present state of music and musicians (London).
Potter, J., ed. (2000), The Cambridge companion to singing (Cambridge).
Poulin, P. L. (1990), 'A view of eighteenth-century musical life and training: Anton Stadler's "Musik Plan"', M & L, 71: 215–24.
Powell, A. (1996), The keyed flute by Johann George Tromlitz (Oxford).
—— (2002), The flute (Princeton, 2002).
Prout, E. (1897), The orchestra (2 vols, London).
Pulver, J. (1920–21), 'The viols in England', PRMA, 47: 1–21.
—— (1923–4), 'Violin methods old and new', PRMA, 50: 101–27.
R., J. (1824), 'Outline of a rational system of education', letter to the editor, Gentleman's Magazine Vol.94, No.1: 504–7.
Rainbow, B. (1967), The land without music (London).
—— (1981), 'Music in education', in Temperley, ed., 29–45.

—— (1989a), 'The rise of popular music education in nineteenth-century England', in Temperley, ed., 17–41.
—— (1989b), *Music in educational thought & practice: a survey from 800BC* (Aberystwyth).
—— (1990), *Music in the English public school* (Aberystwyth).
Raynor, H. (1972), *A social history of music* (2 vols, London).
Relfe, J. (1819), *Remarks on the present state of musical instruction; with the prospects of an improved plan* (London).
Rendall, F. G. (1941–2), 'A short account of the clarinet in England', PRMA, 68: 55–86.
—— (1954; 1971), *The Clarinet* (London; rev. 3rd edn by P. Bate).
Rensch, R. (1969), *The harp: its history, technique and repertoire* (London and New York).
Rice, A. R., (1984), 'Clarinet fingering charts, 1732–1816', GSJ: 16–41.
Riley, M. W. (1954), 'The teaching of bowed instruments from 1511 to 1756' (unpublished Ph.D. thesis, University of Michigan).
—— (1958), 'A tentative bibliography of early wind tutors', *Journal of research in music education*, 6: 3–24.
Rimbault, E. F. (1860), *The pianoforte: its origins, progress and construction* (London).
Ringer, A. (1970), 'Beethoven and the London Pianoforte School', MQ 56: 742–58.
—— ed. (1990), *The early Romantic era* (Basingstoke).
Ripin, E., et al. (1989), *Early keyboard instruments* (London).
Ritchie, W. [1916], *Chats with violinists, or how to overcome difficulties* (London).
Robison, J. O. (1982), 'The *messa di voce* as an instrumental ornament in the seventeenth and eighteenth centuries', MR, 43: 1–14.
Rohr, D. A. (1983), 'A profession of artisans: the careers and social status of British musicians 1750–1850' (unpublished Ph.D. thesis, University of Pennsylvania).
Rose, A. (1895/R1995), *Talks with bandsmen: a popular handbook for brass instrumentalists* (London).
Rosenblum, S. (1988), *Performance practices in classic piano music: their principles and applications* (Bloomington, Ind.).
Roth, H. (1997), *Violin virtuosos from Paganini to the 21st century* (Los Angeles.
Rowland, D., ed. (1998), *The Cambridge companion to the piano* (Cambridge).
—— (2001), *Early keyboard instruments: a practical guide* (Cambridge).
Royal Academy of Music (1838), *A list of pupils received into the Academy* (London).

Royle, E. (1997), *Modern Britain: a social history 1750–1997* (2nd edn, London).
Ruff, L. M. (1970), 'The social significance of the 17th century English music treatises', *Consort*, 26: 418.
Russell, D. (1987; 1997), *Popular music in England, 1840–1914* (Manchester; 2nd edn).
—— (2000), 'Musicians in the English provincial city: Manchester, *c*.1860–1914', in Bashford and Langley, eds, 233–53.
Sadie, S. (1958–9), 'Concert life in eighteenth-century England', *PRMA*, 85: 17–30.
Sainsbury, J. S., ed. (1824/R1966), *A biographical and historical dictionary of musicians from the earliest times* (2 vols, London).
Saint-George, H. (1896; 1909), *The bow: its history, manufacture and use* (London; 2nd edn).
Samson, J., ed. (2002), *The Cambridge history of nineteenth-century music* (Cambridge).
Sands, M. (1943–4), 'The teaching of singing in eighteenth-century England', *PMA*, 70: 11–34.
Sandys, W., and Forster, S. A. (1864), *The history of the violin and other instruments played on with the bow* (London).
Schlesinger, K. (1910), *The instruments of the modern orchestra & early records of the precursors of the violin family* (2 vols, London).
Scholes, P. A. (1934), *The puritans and music in England and New England: a contribution to the cultural history of two nations* (London).
—— (1947), *The mirror of music 1844–1944. A century of musical life in Britain as reflected in the pages of the Musical Times* (2 Vols, London).
Schonberg, H. C. (1970/R1989), *The lives of the great composers* (London).
Schott, H. (1985), 'From harpsichord to pianoforte: a chronology and commentary', *EM*, 13: 28–38.
Schueller, H. M. (1960), 'The quarrel of the ancients and the moderns', *M & L*, 41: 313–30.
Schwarz, B. (1958), 'Beethoven and the French violin school', *MQ*, 44: 431–47.
—— (1984), *Great masters of the violin* (London).
—— (1987), *French instrumental music between the revolutions (1789–1830)* (New York).
Scott, D. B., ed. (2000), *Music, culture, and society: a reader* (Oxford).
—— (2001), *The singing bourgeois: songs of the Victorian drawing room and parlour* (2nd edn, Aldershot).
—— (2002), 'Music and social class' in Samson, ed., 544–67.

Scott, H. A. (1938), 'London concerts from 1700 to 1750', *MQ*, 24: 194–209.

Seletsky, R. E. (1996), '18th-century variations for Corelli's Sonatas, op.5', *EM*, 24: 119–30.

Sharpe, C. (1999), 'An annotated bibliography of early English violin tutors published 1658–1731 ...', in *A handbook for studies in 18th-century English music*, ed. M. Burden and I. Cholij, 10: 1–50.

Shaw, G. B. (1932), *Music in London, 1890–1894* (3 vols, London).

Shelton, E. [1892], *The violin and all about it* (London).

Sheppard, L. (1971), 'The English Tourte', *The Strad*, 81: 579–80.

Simpson, A. (1966), 'A short-title list of printed English instrumental tutors up to 1800, found in British libraries', *RMA Research Chronicle*, 6: 24–50.

Small, C. (1977), *Music – society – education* (London).

Snedeker, J. (1992), 'Joseph Meifred's Méthode pour le cor chromatique ou à pistons', *Historical Brass Society Journal*, 4: 304–33.

Society for the Encouragement of Arts, Manufacturers, and Commerce (1866), *First report of the committee ... on the state of musical education at home and abroad* (London).

Sorensen, S. and Webb, J. (1986), 'The Harpers and the trumpet', *GSJ*, 39: 35–57.

Spohr, L. (1860–61; tr. 1865/R1969; 1878), *Selbstbiographie* (2 vols, Kassel and Göttingen; abridged tr. as *Autobiography* (London; 2nd edn).

Spring, M. (2001), *The lute in Britain: a history of the instrument and its music* (Oxford).

Stafford, W. C. (1830), *History of music* (Edinburgh).

Standage, S. (1989), 'Haydn seek', *The Strad*, 100: 367–9.

Stanhope, P. D., 4th Earl of Chesterfield (1775), *Letters* (4 vols, 6th edn, London).

Stolba, K. M. (1968–9/R1979), *A history of the violin etude to about 1800* (Hays, Kan.).

Stone, W. H. (1879), 'Clarinet', *Grove 1*, vol.1, 361–4.

Stowell, R. (1978), 'The development of violin technique from L'abbé *le fils* to Paganini' (unpublished Ph.D. thesis, University of Cambridge).

—— (1984), 'Violin bowing in transition; a survey of technique as related in instruction books *c*.1790–*c*.1830', *EM*, 12: 317–27.

—— (1985), *Violin technique and performance practice in the late eighteenth and early nineteenth centuries* (Cambridge).

—— (1988), '"Good execution and other necessary skills": the role of the concertmaster in the late 18th century', *EM*, 16: 21–33.

—— (1991), 'Leopold Mozart revised: articulation in violin playing during the second half of the eighteenth century', in R. L. Todd and

P. Williams, eds, *Perspectives on Mozart performance* (Cambridge), 126-58.
—— ed. (1992), *The Cambridge companion to the violin* (Cambridge).
—— ed. (1994), *Performing Beethoven* (Cambridge).
—— (1998), *Beethoven: Violin Concerto* (Cambridge).
—— ed. (1999), *The Cambridge companion to the cello* (Cambridge).
—— (2001), *The early violin and viola: a practical guide* (Cambridge).
Straeten, E. S. J. van der (1911), *The romance of the fiddle* (London).
—— (1915), The history of the violoncello (2 vols, London).
—— (1933/R1968), *The history of the violin* (2 vols, London; New York).
Street, O. W. (1915-16), 'The clarinet and its music', *PRMA*, 42: 89-115.
Strict timeist, A. [pseudonym] (1823), 'On the time devoted to the study of music', *QMMR*, 5: 304-5.
Strong, R. (1998), *The story of Britain: a people's history* (London).
Swanwick, K. (1994), *Musical knowledge: intuition, analysis and music education* (London).
Taruskin, R. (1995), *Text & act: essays on music and performance* (Oxford).
Temperley, N. (1958-9), 'Domestic music in England 1800-1860', *PRMA*, 85: 31-47.
—— (1959), 'Instrumental music in England, 1800-1850' (unpublished Ph.D. thesis, University of Cambridge).
—— ed. (1981), *The Blackwell history of music in Britain: The Romantic age 1800-1914* (London).
—— (1984-7), *The London pianoforte school, 1766-1860*, 20 Vols (New York and London).
—— ed. (1989), *The lost chord: essays on Victorian music* (Bloomington and Indianapolis).
—— (1999), 'Xenophilia in British music history', in B. Zon, ed., *Nineteenth-century British music studies*, vol.1 (Aldershot), 3-19.
Thistlethwaite, N. (1990), The making of the Victorian organ (Cambridge).
Thistlethwaite and Webber, eds (1998), *The Cambridge companion to the organ* (Cambridge).
Thomson, H. B. (1857), *The choice of a profession: a concise account and comparative review of the English professions* (London).
Tilmouth, M. (1857-8), 'Some early London concerts and music clubs, 1670-1720', *PRMA*, 84: 13-26.
—— (1960), 'Nicola Matteis', *MQ*, 46: 22-40.
Timotheus [pseudonym] (1807), 'On the moral effects of music', *The Director*, 2: 1-24.

Todd, R. Larry, ed. (1990), *Nineteenth-century piano music* (New York).
Toft, R. (2000), *Heart to heart: expressive singing in England 1780–1830* (Oxford).
Towse, R. (1993), *Singers in the marketplace: the economics of the singing profession* (Oxford).
Trevelyan, G. M. (1944; new illustrated edn, 1978/R1985), *English social history: a survey of six centuries from Chaucer to Queen Victoria* (London).
Turnbull, H. (1974), *The guitar from the renaissance to the present day* (London).
Turner, G., and Turner, A. W. (1996), *The trumpets will sound: the story of the Royal Military School of Music, Kneller Hall* (Tunbridge Wells).
Tyler, J. (1980), *The early guitar* (Oxford).
Walden, V. (1998), *One hundred years of violoncello: a history of technique and performance practice, 1740–1840* (Cambridge).
Walker, E. (1907; 1952), *A history of music in England* (Oxford; 3rd edn).
Walls, P. (1984), 'Violin fingering in the eighteenth century', *EM*, 12: 300–15.
—— (1986), '"Ill-compliments and arbitrary taste"? Geminiani's directions for performers', *EM*, 14: 221–35.
—— (1990), 'The influence of the Italian violin school in 17th-century England', *EM*, 18: 575–87.
—— (1996), 'Performing Corelli's Violin Sonatas, op.5', *EM*, 24: 133–42.
Warner, T. E. (1967), *An annotated bibliography of woodwind instruction books, 1600–1830* (Detroit).
Waterhouse, W. (1999), 'The double flageolet: made in England', *GSJ*, 52: 172–82.
Watson, F. (1909), *The beginning of the teaching of modern subjects in England* (London).
Weber, C. M. F. E. von (1827), 'On the expectations & prospects of a musical professor', *Harmonicon*, 5: 106–7.
Weber, W. (1975), *Music and the middle class: the social structure of concert life in London, Paris and Vienna 1830–1848* (London).
—— (1989), 'London: a City of Unrivalled Riches', in N. Zaslaw, ed., *The classical era: from the 1740s to the end of the 18th century* (London), 293–326.
—— (1992), *The rise of musical classics in eighteenth-century England: a study in canon, ritual, and ideology* (Oxford).
Weliver, P. (2000), *Women musicians in Victorian fiction, 1860–1900* (Aldershot).

Wetherell, E. (1998), *Albert Sammons – violinist* (London).
Whatley, G. L. (1981), 'Music theory', in Temperley, ed., 474–82.
White, C. (1992), *From Vivaldi to Viotti: a history of the early classical violin concerto* (Philadelphia).
Wilson, J., ed. (1959), *Roger North on music: being a selection from his essays written during the years c.1695–1728* (London).
Wollenberg, S. (2001), *Music at Oxford* (Oxford).
Woodward, L. (1962), *The age of reform: England 1815–1870* (Oxford).
Worgan, T. D. (1819), *An address to the Philharmonic Society … musical education* (London).
—— (1829), *The musical reformer* (London).
Wylde, ? [1882], *Art training in music, a series of four lectures delivered by Professor Wylde … at Gresham College … 1882* (London).
Young, P. M. (1994), 'The transition from Baroque to Romantic: a study in English provincial music-making', in M. A. Parker, ed., *Eighteenth-century music in theory and practice* (New York), 263–87.
Zaltsberg, E. (2002), 'Autumn flowering [Adolf Brodsky]', *The Strad*, Vol. 113 (May): 524–9.
Zaslaw, N. (1976–7), 'Toward the revival of the classical orchestra', *PRMA*, 103: 179–87.
—— (1979), 'The compleat orchestral musician', *EM*, 7: 46–57.
—— (1980), 'The orchestral musician completed', EM, 8, 71–2.
—— (1989), *The Classical era* (London).
—— (1991), 'Vibrato in eighteenth-century orchestras', *PPR*, 4: 28–33.
—— (1996), 'Ornaments for Corelli's Violin Sonatas, op.5', *EM*, 24: 95–115.
Zon, B. (2000), *Music and metaphor in nineteenth-century British musicology* (Aldershot).

Index

academic styles, 55, 56, 61, 63
Academy of Ancient Music, 106
accessibility, 11, 53, 57, 87, 93, 101, 105, 122
Ackermann's Repository of Arts, 136
adagio, 190
adult education, 58
advertisements, 93, 101
Aeolina, 238
airs, 115, 119, 134
Albert, Prince, 69n., 109, 257
Althaus, B., 264
Amateur Musical Society, 209
amateur/professional divide, 4–6, 7, 9, 21, 26, 38, 43, 46, 63, 77, 80, 267, 268
    Europe, 13–17
    provincial, 12–13
    violin, 108
amateurs, 4, 11, 25, 26, 33, 38, 66, 76, 107, 250, 257, 260
    bands, 227
    consumers, 7, 12, 19, 121, 161
    foreign, 13–14, 15–16, 17
    native, 203, 208, 211
    performers, 12
    standards, 6, 40, 50, 78, 79, 82, 86, 156, 209, 229, 269–70
    training, 102
    tuition, 96, 103, 140
    violin, 147–8, 203
    see also amateur/professional divide; gentleman amateurs
ambition, 6, 14, 44, 46, 87
Ancient Concerts *see* Concerts of Ancient Music
'ancient' style, 61–2, 63, 106, 109, 151, 163, 208
andante, 187
Anderson, Mrs, 222
appoggiatura, 189, 190
appointments, 20, 91
apprenticeship, 25, 89–92, 210

Arban's cornet treatise, 230
Arbos, F., 256
aristocracy, 15, 16, 45, 46n., 65, 148, 215, 241, 243; *see also* upper classes
Arne, Thomas, 90, 227
'art' music, 29, 40
artisans, 19, 25, 254
artists, 23, 74, 75
arts, 74–7
    education, 18
audiences, 5, 6
Avison, Charles, 62, 204

Bach, C. P. E., 109, 224
Bach, J. C., 104
Bacon, Richard Mackenzie, 25, 45, 78, 79, 90, 241, 246
Baillot, P., 138, 154, 166, 179, 184, 185, 200, 242
Baltzar, Thomas, 146
bands, 39, 49, 86, 87, 225, 227, 229, 234, 237, 254, 258, 259, 260; *see also* brass bands; military music
Barbella, 196, 199
Barnett, John, 97
Barrett, W. E., 82
Barthélemon, F. H., 61, 96, 120–21, 159, 160, 171, 180n., 181, 187, 189, 196
bassoon, 226
Bates, T. C., 133
Bath, 99, 131
Beethoven, Ludwig van, 197, 221–2
    string quartets, 24
    Violin Concerto, 107, 201, 207, 209
beginners, 122, 138, 140, 200, 234
bel canto, 57, 142
Belfast, 13
Bemetzrieder, A., 54, 187, 189, 220
benevolent funds, 23

Bennett, Sir William Sterndale, 24, 224, 261, 262
Beringer, Oscar, 222
Berlin, 15
Berlioz, H., 238
Bertini, 238
Billington, T., 57
binaries, 41–2
Birmingham, 13, 205
Bishop, John, 71, 126–7, 131, 162n., 172, 247, 248
Blagrove, Henry G. (1811–72), 152, 160–61, 205, 247, 248
Blagrove, Richard Manning, 214, 237, 248
blind people, 72
boarding schools, 31, 251, 252
Boccherini, 62
Bochsa, N., 236, 243
Boehm system, 228
Borsdorf, 232
Bottesini, 215
boys, 8, 21, 31, 49, 58, 102, 245, 251, 263
brass bands, 9, 11n., 32, 35, 36, 73, 83, 87, 212, 227, 231, 232, 237
  standardization, 230
  trainers, 234
brass instruments, 24, 38, 49, 84, 229–35
  conservatism, 233, 235
  keyed, 230, 231
  new technology, 230–31
  practical tuition, 229–30
  social factors, 235
  style, 234
  treatises, 233–4
  valved, 230–31, 232, 234
brass players, 13, 225, 232, 234–5; *see also* brass bands; brass instruments
Bremner, Robert, 12n., 119, 123, 180, 186, 188, 191, 192, 193
Brewer, J., 42
Bristol, 12n., 99, 130
Britain, 18
  low standards, 14, 16, 20
  musical ideal, 203–4
  regional differences, 11–12
  violin playing, 108
Broadwood piano, 221, 223

Broderip, R., 223
Brodsky, Adolf, 207, 258
bugle, 230, 231, 233, 234
Bull, Ole, 153
Burghersh, Lord, 243, 247
Burney, Charles, 5, 51, 55, 61, 62, 77, 90, 94, 104, 120, 150, 180, 192, 233
Burrowes, 103
Busby, Tom, 51, 122, 232

Cambridge University, 253
Camden, Archie, 229
Camidge, 223
Campagnoli, B., 129–30, 133, 138, 168, 169, 171, 179, 181, 185, 195
  Metodo, 184
Carrodus, J. T., 136, 204, 205–6
Carter, Thomas, 107
cathedrals, 12, 89
Cazalet, W. W., 244, 245n., 246, 248
cello, 46, 49, 215–16
Cervetto, Giacobbe, 215, 216
Cervetto, James, 215
Challoner, N. B., 71, 124, 131, 133, 134, 137, 160, 176, 181, 184–5, 207, 223
chamber music, 34, 213
Chappell & Co., 139
charity, 30
cheap editions, 37, 73, 101
cheap instruments, 11, 37, 39, 73, 87, 263
Chesterfield, Earl of, 4, 44–5, 51, 75, 78, 251
children, 21, 29, 31, 53, 66, 67, 72, 122, 135, 139, 212, 254, 263
choral music, 31–2, 58, 59, 64, 86
choral societies, 11n., 32, 39, 68, 86
Choron, 58
chromatic scales, 170, 171, 195
church, 21, 30, 32, 56, 58, 59, 67, 86, 89, 240
  bands, 227
  organists, 92n., 224
Clare, John, 212
clarinet, 226, 227–8, 259, 260
Clarke, J., 121
class, 3, 8, 20, 27, 28, 42, 55, 59, 84, 86, 221, 250, 265, 267

clavicors, 231
Clement, Franz, 201n.
Clementi, M., 220, 222, 223, 224
closed shop, 94, 101
Cobbett, W., 129
Cobham, 160
Cocks & Co, 229, 233, 234
College of Organists, 225, 258, 264
College of Violinists, 103, 205, 264
commodities, 3, 8
communities, 9, 12, 27, 86, 87, 91, 226, 269
competition, 9, 24, 36, 59, 77, 85, 91, 92, 94, 244
   fear of, 22, 23, 80, 93, 96
composers, 53, 55
composition, 51, 53, 95
concertina, 235, 236–7
concerto, 198, 201
concerto grosso, 6
concerts, 5n., 13, 34, 35, 72, 205, 213; *see also* public concerts
Concerts of Ancient Music, 34, 63, 79, 255
congregational singing, 31, 58
conservatism, 8, 20, 32, 60–65, 71, 90, 105, 106, 111
   brass instruments, 233, 235
   violin playing, 126, 132, 142, 148, 156, 159, 195, 203, 207, 208
   wind instruments, 227
conservatoires, 15, 26, 241–50, 255–60; *see also* music colleges
consumerism, 3–8, 9, 11, 12, 19, 32, 37, 73, 85, 96, 221, 238, 255
consumers, 4, 7, 8, 10, 26, 70, 121, 140, 161, 203, 219, 220, 265, 266
control, 31, 38, 39, 42, 47
Cooke, T., 160
Corder, F., 238, 242
Corelli, A., 5, 61, 105, 109, 117, 127, 134, 150, 152, 155, 156
   method, 119
   repertoire, 198
   significance of, 108
   style, 62–3, 64, 108, 149, 190, 204
cornet, 230, 234
Cornopean companion of scales, The (1836), 234

Corri, Domenico, 57, 97, 107
Corri, P. A., 223
Corri family, 12n., 141, 223
counterpoint, 51, 53
courts, 15, 19, 91
Covent Garden, 259
Cox, G., 69
Cramer, Franz, 151, 160, 246, 248
Cramer, J. B., 222, 224
Cramer, Wilhelm, 4, 150, 151, 159, 184
'Cramer' bow, 163
critics, 11, 63, 72; *see also* music criticism
Crome, R., 114, 117, 123, 134, 165, 178, 188, 216
Crosdill, John, 215
Crotch, William, 22, 52, 62, 72, 77, 97, 109, 244, 253
Croydon Conservatoire of Music, 205
Crystal Palace, 35, 36, 72, 212
culture, 10, 12, 16, 18, 19, 74
   consumption of, 4, 106
Curwen, J., 31, 59, 68, 69, 70
Cutler, 103
Czerny, 198, 223

Dale, J., 237
Danby, J., 223
Dando, Joseph, 160, 161, 263
David, Ferdinand, 128, 154, 155, 185
David, Paul, 154, 156, 161, 198, 204, 261, 262
Davies, Fanny, 222
de Bériot, 197
Dean, J., 133
dedications, 20, 45
demand, 7, 8, 10, 11, 17, 27, 32, 33, 35, 36, 37, 38, 39, 41, 49, 73, 85, 91
   amateur, 19, 26
   eighteenth century, 52, 84
   instrumental music, 87, 98
   tuition, 96, 101, 121
   violin training, 203
   vocal music, 58, 59
Dibdin, C., 72
Dickens, Charles, 82, 236
dilettantism, 108, 116, 117, 118, 258

discipline, 28, 31
display *see* virtuosity
Distin family, 73, 227, 231
Dodd, John (Kew), 163
Dodd, Thomas, 189
domestic music, 28, 30, 86, 106
double bass, 133, 214–15
Dragonetti, D., 214
Dublin, 13, 130, 258
Dubourg, George, 81, 99, 127, 147–8, 153, 160, 174, 197, 198, 247, 248, 249
Dubourg, Matthew, 159
duets, 82, 134–5, 137
Duke, Richard, 162
Duke of Edinburgh, 209
duos, 196–7, 233
Duport brothers, 215
Dussek, J. L., 111, 223, 224, 238

Eager, 72, 103
early music, 65
ear-training, 60
Eck, Franz, 151, 152, 204
Edinburgh, 12, 99
education, 8, 18, 27, 30, 31, 42, 43, 50, 67, 68, 112
   vocal training, 58–60, 66
   see also music education; schools; universities
Education Act (1870), 69, 243, 261
Ehrlich, C., 37, 95, 241
eighteenth century, 4–5, 41–65, 170, 175, 238, 239
   arts, hierarchy of, 74
   foreign influences, 104
   gender, 43–9, 50, 53–5, 59, 60
   old and new styles, 61–5
   private tuition, 93–5
   progress, 77, 78–9
   teaching materials, 112–20, 122, 130, 137, 140, 146, 166, 169, 172, 175, 180, 195
   vocal music, 56–60
elementary schools, 39, 59, 60, 66, 70, 97, 104, 212, 250, 252, 255, 260, 261, 263
Elgar, 206, 207
Eliot, George, 82
elites, 15, 17, 19, 20, 21, 30, 35, 40, 46, 64, 105, 267

Ella, John, 33, 34, 91, 157
embellishments, 188, 189, 190
emotions, 62, 74, 153, 203
employers, 29, 30, 254
England, 14, 17, 72
   conservatoire plans, 241
   piano, 223–4
   treatises, 116, 17
   violin school, 113
enjoyment, 38
entertainment, 58, 59, 85
euphonium, 233
Europe, 13–17, 82
   training, 102, 240–41ff.
examinations, 247, 258, 263
exclusivity, 6, 19
Exeter Hall, 68
Exeter Music College, 254
expectations, 7, 9, 43, 100, 265
experimentation, 56, 62, 71
expression, 108, 142, 150, 195–6, 203, 204

factory schools, 253
families, 21–2, 24, 42, 44, 91, 94, 124; *see also* parents
Farmer, Henry, 138, 200
Farmer, John, 263
fashion, 25, 44, 45, 85
fees, 90, 96–7, 245, 256
Fellowes, E. H., 79, 102
Festing, Michael, 119, 159
Fétis, F. J., 16–17, 70, 72, 223, 245, 246
fiddle, 146–7, 148, 212, 213
Field, John, 222
financial rewards, 8, 9, 22, 24, 43, 85, 87, 90, 96–7, 101
fine arts, 74–7
finger activity, 168
fingerboard charts, 115, 119
Fischer, J. C., 225
Fisher, H., 100
flageolet, 226
flute, 46, 49, 72, 87, 96, 116, 226
   treatises, 120
folk music, 39
foreign musicians, 4, 5, 34, 35, 54, 79, 104, 214, 215, 240
   brass, 232
   competition from, 24

critics and, 105–11
and RAM, 247
superior status, 18, 19, 20, 21
treatises, 125
violin, 24, 146, 149–59
Forster, William, 69, 162, 243
fortepiano, 223
France, 14, 16, 18, 109, 111, 146, 163, 232, 242–3, 259
freedom, 7, 38
French violin school, 16, 146, 151, 204, 242
Fuchs, Carl, 258
function, 92

Gainsborough, Thomas, 52, 74, 77, 149, 150
Galliard, 57, 141, 142
García, M., 57, 141, 142
Gehot, J., 120, 170, 181, 186, 187, 189, 238
Geminiani, F., 19–20, 24, 61, 109, 110, 114, 133, 151, 159, 194, 195, 203, 204, 207
  Art, The, 187, 188
  Compleat Instructions, 169–70, 189
  Opus 7 concertos, 62
  Treatise of good taste, 188
  violin treatise (1751), 94, 114, 117–19, 125, 126, 129, 134, 149, 165, 166, 168, 175–6ff., 183, 191, 193, 203, 208
gender, 6, 42, 43–9, 50, 53–5, 59, 60, 80, 229, 265, 267
  instruments, 48, 49, 71, 84, 87, 106, 107
  popular music, 84, 85, 86
genteel society, 3, 8, 19, 20–21, 121, 232, 233
gentleman amateurs, 4, 5, 20, 25, 28, 44–6, 50, 51, 52, 78, 102, 112, 113, 115, 117
  and 'good taste', 61
  private tuition, 94
  and singing, 57
  wind instruments, 225, 226
Germany, 14–15, 18, 52, 109, 111, 171, 185, 232
Giardini, F., 94, 150, 159, 196, 220

Gibbs, Joseph, 149, 199
girls, 49, 76, 85, 99, 103, 210, 211, 251, 252, 257, 260, 261, 263
Glasgow, 99
glee clubs, 57
Glover, S., 59, 68, 252
Goldschmidt, Otto, 222
'good taste', 19, 60–61, 62, 105–11, 141, 157, 188, 194, 224, 234
Goodban, T., 71, 131, 133, 176, 186, 207, 223, 254
governesses, 99, 101
Graham, G. F., 80
grammar schools, 49
gramophone, 36, 86
Greg, Samuel, 73
Griffiths, Samuel, 259
group performance, 9, 31, 57
group tuition, 23, 91, 102–4
Grove, Sir George, 33, 55, 72, 257
Grove's *Dictionary*, 18, 71, 261
Guest, Jane Mary, 222
Guhr, K., 126, 171
Guildhall School of Music, 205, 208, 214, 235, 256–7
guitar, 72, 210, 235–6
Gunn, John, 215, 226

Hack, R., 124, 133, 137, 176, 181, 186, 200
Haddock, E., 129, 133
Hall, Marie, 211
Hallé, Charles, 13, 258
Hallé, Lady *see* Norman-Neruda, Wilma
Hallé Orchestra, 235, 258
Hamilton, J. A., 71, 123, 130, 131, 133, 136, 225, 238
  Catechism, 133, 137–8, 162n., 197
  double bass treatise, 133
  'Modern instructions', 223
  violin treatise, 123, 168, 171, 177, 181, 184, 186, 198
Hammond, J., 223
Hancock, C., 131, 133
handbooks, 99, 111
Handel, G. F., 5, 32, 61, 62, 63, 66, 104, 105, 109, 233
  Messiah, 64
harmonica, 238

Harmonicon, 80
harmonium, 225
harmony, 51, 53, 169, 170–71
harp, 210, 235, 236
Harper family, 231, 234, 235
harpsichord, 106, 219, 221
Harvey, B. W., 148, 161
Haweis, H. R., 27, 31, 32, 147, 149, 207
Hawker, 72, 223
Hawkins, J., 51, 61, 163, 192, 233
Haydn, F. J., 62, 63
Heron-Allen Collection, 145n.
hierarchy, 3, 19, 51, 63, 109
Hill, Henry, 213
Hodges, E., 54, 109
Hogarth, George, 30, 51, 56, 62, 80, 82, 151, 152, 153, 160, 197, 198, 204
Holmes, Alfred, 161
Holmes, Henry, 125, 126, 127, 128, 129, 155, 161, 171, 172, 175, 183–4, 194, 198, 204, 247
Honeyman, W. C., 128–9, 130, 134
Hook, James, 22, 222
horn, 230, 231, 232
   duos, 233
   tutors, 234
Howell, James, 214
Howell, Thomas, 12n., 71, 99, 131, 134, 135, 196, 199, 223
   violin treatise, 124, 130, 136, 137, 160, 167ff., 172, 177, 182–3, 186, 187, 189, 194, 207
Hughes, Samuel, 235, 259
Hughes, William, 58
Hullah, John, 31, 58, 68, 69–70, 252
Hullah-Wilhelm system, 20, 58, 68, 252
Hummel, 223, 224
Hyde, F., 233
Hyde, John, 231

Iles, John Henry, 73
immorality, 21, 27
impresarios, 4
'improving' music, 29, 79
improvisation, 188
incentives, 10, 85, 87, 90, 110
Incorporated Society of Musicians, 256

individuals, 25, 70–73, 77, 84, 91, 103
industrialization, 3, 10, 29, 37, 86, 110
innovation, 5, 56, 63, 65, 70, 77, 105–6, 108, 111, 224
institutions, 18, 26, 102, 103, 204
   amateurism, 241, 249–50, 255
   eighteenth century, 239, 240
   foreign, 240–41, 242–3, 246, 247
   funding, 244–5, 246
   see also conservatoires; music colleges; schools; universities
instrument makers, 4, 10, 221
   foreign, 161
   native, 161–2, 163–4
   violin, 161–4
instrumental music
   amateur, 4, 5
   backwardness, 10, 50, 73–4, 267, 270
   demand for, 7–8, 87
   eighteenth century, 44–5, 50, 52
   Europe, 13, 15–16, 17, 107
   and gender, 59–60, 106, 107
   instruction, 104, 255
   and middle class, 28, 93, 96
   moral aspects, 28, 29
   new style, 62
   private tuition, 92–102
   schools, 261, 262, 263
   and social class, 59–60
   technical demands, 5
   treatises, 57, 71–2, 141–2
   and vocal music, 56, 57, 141–2
instrumentation, 238
intellectualism, 5, 28, 29, 38, 50, 51, 55, 57, 61, 62, 75, 81, 115, 154, 172, 267
intelligentsia, 10, 83, 106
interpretation, 206
Ireland, 72
ISM, 79
Italy, 14, 15, 91, 111, 117, 146, 241

Jackson, Enderby, 73
Jackson, William, 63
James, W. N., 120
Joachim, J., 102, 110, 128, 158–9, 185, 201, 202, 203, 205, 208, 256, 262

journals, 15, 21, 33, 39, 49, 73, 80, 108, 127, 131–2, 148, 198, 238
Jousse, J., 71–2, 99, 111, 120, 131, 149, 151, 162, 163, 198, 243
　piano treatise, 223
　violin treatise, 123, 133–4, 135, 166, 168, 170, 173, 176, 181, 184, 185, 187, 189–90, 193, 195, 207
Jullien, Louis, 35, 72, 81

Kassler, J. C., 80, 241
Kay, James, 58, 67, 68, 254; *see also* Kay-Shuttleworth, Sir James
Kay-Shuttleworth, Sir James, 31, 58
Keith, R. W., 72, 99, 131, 133, 173, 176, 181, 193–4, 223
Kelway, Joseph, 104
Kemp, J., 71, 72, 80, 254
keyboard instruments, 48, 106, 107, 219–25
　development of, 4
　private tuition, 95, 96
　technique, 223
　texts, 57, 72, 99, 100, 104, 121
　see also harpsichord; piano
Kiesewetter, 160, 174
Klose, 228
Kneller Hall, 68, 103, 235, 258–60
Kollmann, A. F. C., 54, 71
Kreutzer, R., 134, 242

L'abbé *le fils*, 170, 171, 176, 179, 180
Lafleur & Sons, 228
Langey, O., 71, 131, 234
Lazarus, Henry, 228, 234, 258, 259–60
lectures, 25, 34, 71
Leeds, 13
legato, 111, 187, 224
leisure, 37; *see also* recreation
Lenton, 177
liberal arts, 51, 253
liberal education, 25, 45, 241, 243
Lind, Jenny, 62
Lindley, Robert, 105, 215–16
literacy, 53
literature, 74, 75, 110, 121, 148
Liverpool, 13, 35
Locatelli's Caprices, 156

Locke, John, 44
Loder, J. D., 71, 128, 130, 131, 134, 135–6, 168, 182, 194, 196, 204, 205, 207, 208, 248
logic, 80, 109
Logier, J. B., 23, 54, 72, 97, 103, 222, 254
　chiroplast, 72, 103, 223
　gamut-board, 72
Löhlein, 134
Lolli, A., 63, 150, 153, 174
London, 3, 11, 12, 14, 22, 35, 37, 93, 96, 97, 105, 214, 221
London College of Music, 257
London Piano School, 110, 221, 223
lower-classes, 9, 10, 11, 18, 25, 36, 38–9, 53, 65, 73, 82, 221, 226, 266, 268
　demand from, 72, 83, 203
　group instruction, 103
　instrumental music, 29, 49, 59, 87
　music education, 91–2, 250, 252
　violin, 212–13
　vocal music, 58
　see also popular music movement; working-class

McArtor, M. E., 192
McVeigh, S., 18
Mainzer, J., 31, 252
Manchester, 13, 35, 235
Manchester College of Music, 258
Mandel, Carl, 259
Mannheim school, 15, 151, 204
markets, 4, 7, 11, 37, 38, 73, 74, 82, 85, 121, 256, 266
Marlborough College, 262
marriage, 8, 46, 85, 211, 219
Marsh, John, 51, 61
mass-production, 37, 230, 263
'master', 23, 90, 93, 99, 123–4, 125, 127, 128, 132, 134, 136, 223
　and pupil, 117; *see also* pupil–teacher relationship
mathematics, 51, 115
Matteis, Nicola, 146
Mawkes, 248
mechanics' institutes, 27, 58, 254, 264
Mell, Davis, 146
men, 8, 22, 35, 43–6, 49, 55, 83, 84,

97, 100, 115, 209, 225, 226, 229
control by, 47, 50
middle-class, 4, 28, 39
professional training, 6
teachers, 98
voyeurism, 211
working-class, 7, 9, 25, 32, 38–9, 59, 87, 235, 269
see also gentleman amateurs
Mendelssohn, Felix, 20, 32, 109, 110, 149, 157, 158, 262
Elijah, 64
Violin Concerto in E minor, 201, 202, 207
Violin Concerto in D minor, 202
Methodism, 31, 64
metre, 186
middle-classes, 3, 4, 9, 11, 25, 26, 78, 79, 110, 212, 255, 266, 268
active role, 12
conservatism of, 64, 235
education, 66, 70, 251
Europe, 13, 15, 16
men, 4, 28, 39
morality, 28, 31, 32
music appreciation, 33–4, 35, 36
self-improvement, 68
wind instruments, 226
women, 7, 11, 28, 32, 38, 39, 53
military music, 68, 225, 226, 227
bands, 232, 238, 259
training, 92, 258–60
Millington, William, 229
Molique, Bernard, 158, 205, 237
Monday Popular Concerts, 35
Moralt, Sophia Dussek, 104
Mori, Nicolas, 160, 202, 246, 247
Morley, T., 50
Moscheles, I., 16, 110, 222, 223, 224
mouth organ, 238
Mozart, Leopold, 118, 119, 134, 138, 165, 176, 178, 179, 180, 183, 190, 191, 192, 195, 227,
Versuch (1756), 115
Mozart, W. A., 107, 197
Müller's *Méthode*, 228
music
ambivalence to, 5, 26, 30–31, 65, 105, 266
as art, 50, 54

growing interest in, 7, 10, 36, 37, 48, 77
inherent value of, 8, 9, 10, 17, 70, 270
low standards, 7, 42, 66, 86
moral aspects, 10, 17, 27–33, 47, 57–8, 59, 61, 62–4, 67ff., 78–9, 86, 102, 149, 210ff., 252, 255, 265, 267
political aspects, 18, 19
social value, 10, 11, 30, 31, 73, 78, 86, 251–2, 253, 265, 267
status of, 11, 14, 21, 27, 42–3, 46, 49, 63, 77–8, 83, 270
music colleges, 101, 103, 106, 210, 211, 254, 256–60, 264; see also conservatoires
music criticism, 33, 51, 72, 105, 107–11, 136–7
music education, 6–7, 20, 35, 60, 80, 83, 102, 251–2, 269–70
eighteenth century, 43
Europe, 14, 15
female, 85
lower classes, 91–2, 252
popular, 84–8
professional, 23–4, 25, 26
state role, 66–70
theory and practice, 50–56
see also apprenticeship; conservatoires; music colleges; schools; teaching materials; training; tuition; universities
music festivals, 36, 73, 86
music societies, 4, 6, 12, 36
musical appreciation, 8, 11, 23, 25, 26, 33–6, 72, 80, 88, 103, 121, 147
Musical Institute of London, 34, 55
musical instruments, 20, 22, 24, 33, 37, 65, 72, 81, 106–7, 237–8
changes in, 111
and gender, 48, 49, 71, 84, 87, 107, 210
hire, 101
technology, 230–31
tuning, 101
see also instrument makers
Musical Times, 82
Musical Union (1845–81), 34, 91, 213

Musical World, 80, 238
musical writings, 33–4, 51, 55, 71–2, 80–81, 99–100
  histories, 65
  see also teaching materials; treatises; tutor books

Naples, 14, 241
Nathan, Isaac, 57, 141
National Training School, 136, 205, 256; *see also* Royal College of Music
nationalism, 18, 40
native musicians, 13, 18, 34, 105, 260, 265
  amateur, 203, 208, 211
  brass, 234–5
  employment, 21, 22
  low status, 18–24, 26, 79, 95, 240
  professional, 203, 205–7, 209, 211, 213, 214
  and RAM, 247–8, 249
  social status, 4, 5–6, 12
  success of, 24
  teaching, 96
  treatises, 116, 135, 136
  violinists, 98, 159–61, 203, 208, 211
  vocal, 141–2
New instructions (1780), 233
new music, 5, 61, 65
New Musical Fund, 23
new technology, 40, 86, 230–31
nineteenth century, 5, 27, 65–88, 204
  private tuition, 95–102
  teaching materials, 119, 120–41, 147–8ff., 166
Nolens volens (1695), 113–14, 115
Nonconformists, 58, 67
Norman-Neruda, Wilma, 211
North, 62
Novello, 37, 139

oboe, 24, 114, 120, 225, 226
opera, 31, 36, 43
ophicleide, 230, 235
opportunities, 9, 10, 33, 49, 65, 83, 96, 221
oral instruction, 14, 117
oratorios, 32, 36, 59, 86
orchestras, 15, 35
  amateur, 13, 15, 85
  school, 263
orchestration, 238
organ, 58, 62, 221, 224–5
organists, 25, 224, 251, 253
organology, 106, 111
ornamentation, 115, 187–94, 234
Ouseley, F. G., 253
Owen, Robert, 73, 254
Oxford University, 253

Paersch, 232
Paganini, N., 63, 109, 110, 126, 127, 152–3, 154, 155, 162, 170, 171, 184
Paine, J., 122, 123, 167–8, 173, 182, 186, 190, 200, 207
painting, 74, 75, 76
pamphlets, 99, 112
parents, 99, 100, 124, 139, 235
Paris, 13, 16
Paris Conservatoire, 16, 169, 207, 216, 242–3, 246, 260
Parke, John, 225
Parke, William, 105
Parsons, Sir William, 22, 75
participation, 7, 8, 9, 10, 13, 17, 37, 49, 51, 53, 65, 72, 148
part-songs, 57
Pasquali, Francis, 215
Pasquali, N., 12n., 220
passions, 109, 203
'pasticcio' tradition, 111
patronage, 13, 21, 45, 148, 241, 254
pedagogy, 5, 8, 11, 14, 33, 39, 50, 52, 53, 54, 71–2, 80–81, 99, 131, 138, 140
  method, 100, 104, 203
  see also teaching materials
People's Concert Society, 35
percussion, 237–8, 260
performance, 34–5, 40, 80, 81, 87, 110, 132, 229
  low status, 52, 101, 147
  moral qualities, 62–4
  theory of, 51
performers, 4, 5, 6, 14, 53, 204, 222
  amateur, 12
  low status, 55–6
  male, 44
  women, 44, 80

see also violinists
philanthropy, 11, 31, 35, 37, 59, 73
Philharmonic Society, 34, 64, 76, 79, 135, 154, 159–60, 241, 244, 248
philistinism, 29
Philpot, Stephen, 45, 119–20, 123, 129, 132, 133, 134, 165, 166, 169, 170, 176, 180, 189, 191, 193
Phipson, Dr T. Lamb, 209
physiology, 54, 55, 140, 141
piano, 11n., 20, 39, 87, 104, 106, 210, 238, 263
   academies, 254
   development, 110–11
   group tuition, 103 style, 223–4
   teachers, 222, 223
   treatises, 220–21, 222–3
   women and, 219, 220–21, 222
Piano-forte magazine, 221
Piatti, Alfredo, 216
Platt, Henry, 232
Playford, J., 5, 50, 111, 113, 120, 146, 186
Pleyel, Ignaz, 62, 197
plucked strings, 235–7
pocket scores, 34
poetry, 32
popular music movement, 7, 9–10, 18, 27, 29, 30, 31, 36, 38–9, 40, 43, 84–8, 225–6, 237; *see also* brass bands; lower-classes; working-class
popular song, 58
portamento, 174, 175, 206
potential, 7, 9, 10, 16
Potter, C., 153, 172, 222, 237, 238
power, 3, 4, 7; *see also* control
practical instruction, 7, 8, 12n., 71, 72, 80, 81, 83, 95, 100, 123, 203, 230, 252, 254; *see also* tuition
practice, 50–56, 80, 119, 120
Pratten, Robert Sidney, 105
Prelleur treatise (1731), 108, 115, 118, 119, 175, 238
   part V, 114, 117, 133, 137, 138, 165, 168, 178, 186, 188, 189, 199
Prince of Wales, 46

private tuition, 20, 23, 92–102, 115
   eighteenth century, 94, 95–6
   Europe, 102
   fees, 96–7, 101
   nineteenth century, 96, 96–102
   standards, 97–8
   women, 94, 100–101
   written materials, 99–100
producers, 18, 27
professional musicians, 4, 9, 10, 11, 12, 34, 40, 55, 244
   brass, 225
   employment, 19–21, 22
   foreign, 203, 207, 215
   in Europe, 13, 14, 15, 16
   lack of support for, 21, 23–4, 70–71, 79, 240
   low status, 17, 18ff., 26, 42, 46, 66, 78, 102
   male, 22
   native, 203, 205–7, 209, 211, 213, 214
   provincial, 12, 13
   regulation of, 79, 90, 101, 102
   repertoire, 5
   singers, 56, 57
   supply of, 37
   support for, 25–6
   wind, 225
programme notes, 33, 34
Prout, E., 55, 238
providers, 66, 78
provincial towns, 3, 12–13, 37, 93, 99, 130–31
public concerts, 4, 14, 106
public schools, 59, 251, 253, 261–3
publishers, music, 4, 10, 12n., 35, 139
Punto, 233
pupil–teacher relationship, 99, 117, 121, 135, 221
Purcell, Henry, 146
puritanism, 27, 29, 59, 65

qualifications, 79, 103, 264
quality versus quantity, 77, 85, 100
Quantz, J. J., 95, 116, 227
Quarterly Musical Magazine and Review, 80, 81, 132, 241
Queen's Hall, 35

radio, 36, 86
Radley College, 251
Raikes, A. H., 263
Rainbow, B., 41n., 66, 241
reason, 109
recitals, 34
recreation, 10, 30, 32, 102, 269
Reed, 130
refinement, 63, 105, 224
Regondi, Giulio, 237
Reinagle brothers, 215
Relfe, J., 80, 97, 121
religion, 31, 58; *see also* church
repertoire, 5, 36, 48, 61, 64, 146
    violin, 196–203
respectability, 26, 27, 28, 75, 77,
    139, 140, 224
Reynolds, William, 74, 75
Richardson, Joseph, 105
Rode, 126, 133, 134, 135, 162, 174,
    181, 184, 185, 187, 195, 196,
    201, 242
Rohr, D. A., 18, 42n., 93
romanticism, 51, 111
Royal Academy of Arts, 74, 75, 76,
    241, 244
Royal Academy of Music (RAM), 55,
    75, 91, 131, 206, 208, 209,
    214, 216, 242
    amateur bias, 6, 241, 250, 255
    aristocratic elements, 243, 249
    conservatism, 65, 71
    examinations, 247
    failures of, 247–8
    finances, 244–5, 246
    foreign musicians, 247
    foundation of, 79, 243
    native musicians, 247–8, 249
    non-musical instruction, 241, 245
    professional musicians, 243, 250
    violin teaching, 245, 246–7, 248
    women, 210
Royal College of Music, 145n., 206,
    247, 256
Royal Irish Academy, 245, 258
Royal Military School of Music, 103,
    258; *see also* Kneller Hall
Royal Musical Association, 34, 55
Royal Navy School of Music, 260
Royal Society of Musicians, 23, 210
Rudolphus, 126, 127

Rutherford, 114, 165, 175, 178, 188

Sacred Harmonic Society, 65
St James's Hall, 35
Sainton, P., 201, 202, 205, 256
Salisbury, Lord, 69n., 221n.
Salomon, J. P., 4, 133, 151, 159
Salvation Army, 229
Sammartini, G.-P., 24, 150, 225
Sammons, Albert, 205, 206–7, 215,
    264
Sauret, Emil, 205, 208, 256
scholars, 25, 63
scholarships, 256
school inspectors, 69, 82
schools, 14, 25, 27, 30, 35, 49, 69,
    83, 93, 100, 250–52, 260–63,
    264
    instrumental music, 104
    piano, 222
    singing, 59, 60, 68, 86
    see also elementary schools;
        grammar schools; public
        schools; secondary schools
science, 50–56, 76, 111, 172
Scotland, 12n., 72, 130, 215
sculpture, 74, 75
secondary schools, 8, 55, 60, 70, 73,
    104, 251, 252, 255, 260, 261,
    263
secularism, 12, 21, 28, 29, 32, 240
self-esteem, 87
self-expression, 28, 51, 53
self-improvement, 68, 78, 84, 111,
    157, 212, 266, 270
self-instruction, 92, 95, 99, 100, 112,
    116, 117, 123, 138
semi-professionalism, 4n., 8, 9, 11n.,
    13, 22, 23, 77, 79, 83, 85, 90,
    96, 222, 257, 268
semitones, 171, 172
sensuality, 28, 49, 57
sentimentality, 49
Ševčík, 208, 211
sex, 211
sheet music, 101
sight-singing, 57, 59, 86, 105, 263
sin, 210; *see also* immorality
singers, 25, 30, 56–7, 59
    Italian, 56
    native, 105

singing, 31, 68, 210
   high status, 56–7, 59
   house, 77
   and religion, 58
   teachers, 97, 254
Smart, George, 22, 55, 62, 141, 222
Smart, Henry, 62, 224
social reformers, 10, 29, 32, 37, 250
social status, 3, 7, 11, 14, 16, 18–24, 26, 28, 102, 221, 250, 251, 265, 266
   and low standards, 86
   native musicians, 4, 5–6
   private tutors, 95
   and violin, 147
Society of Arts report (1865), 257
Society of British Musicians, 55, 247
solo music, 5, 107, 197–9
sonatas
   accompanied, 48, 106–7, 220
   solo, 107, 198
sostenuto, 187
Spagnoletti, 160, 246
specialization, 24, 103, 120, 125, 264
Spohr, Louis, 72, 109–10, 111, 149, 153, 207
   bowing, 177, 179, 183ff.
   character, 152
   Fourteenth Violin Concerto, 155
   'Gesangsszene' Concerto, 154, 202
   harmonics, 171
   influence of, 98–9, 126–30, 133, 154–5, 156–7, 158, 159, 203, 204, 205, 208
   left-hand technique, 174–5
   Octet, 160
   ornamentation, 188, 190–91
   repertoire, 197, 201, 202–3, 247
   style, 64, 111, 152, 154, 158, 195, 204, 205
   as teacher, 98–9, 246–7, 248
   vibrato, 194
   violin treatise, 98, 124–6ff., 135, 149, 166, 167, 171ff., 204, 208, 247
sport, 77, 269
staccato, 187
Stamitz, J., 151
standards, 11, 16, 17, 26, 40, 45, 99, 229, 269
   improving, 7, 34, 35, 36, 46, 49, 78, 87, 156–7
   low, 6, 7, 8, 21, 86, 93, 101, 115, 116, 146–7, 244
   popular music, 9
   private tuition, 97–8
   state, 14, 16, 20, 32, 66–70, 102, 243, 257, 260
Stevens, W. S., 96, 223
Stewart, J., 167
Straeten, 190
Stretton, Arthur, 260
string instruments, 49, 260; *see also* cello; viola; violin
string quartets, 34
Strutt, John, 73, 254
students, 245, 246, 247, 256, 257
styles, 5, 6, 19, 73, 81, 110, 111
   brass, 234
   old and new, 61–5, 106, 149
   piano, 223–4
   violin, 108–10, 126, 128, 149–50ff., 167, 187, 195–6, 203–4, 208, 209
   vocal, 57
Suffield, Lord, 45
Sugden, D. H., 102n.
Sullivan, Sir Arthur, 76, 259
Sullivan, Thomas, 259
superficiality, 62, 81, 109, 240
supply, 10, 11, 17, 24, 27, 36, 37, 38, 41, 85
Symphonium, 238

tambourine, 237
Tartini, G., 120, 134, 150, 155, 180, 195, 198–9
   'Devil's Trill' sonata, 190
Tashanberg, 121, 181
taste, 32, 51, 65, 73, 82, 106, 108, 110, 111, 117; *see also* 'good taste'
Tattershall, W. D., 58
Tavistock Violin Academy, 264
Taylor, Edward, 25
Taylor, Franklin, 222
teachers, 4, 6, 7, 14, 23, 43, 68, 93, 100–101, 123ff., 127, 225, 226, 228, 258
   cello, 215–16
   demand for, 96, 100

native, 247-8, 249
registration, 101
social status, 95
training, 257
vocal, 97, 254
women, 7, 8, 10, 37, 43, 48, 85, 94, 96, 100
see also 'master'; teaching
teaching, 9, 17, 20, 22, 23
   eighteenth century, 94-5
   financial rewards, 96-7
   see also teachers; teaching materials
teaching materials, 12n., 23, 37, 39, 52, 80, 81, 99-100, 264
   advanced, 117, 118, 120ff., 126, 136, 138, 140, 208
   demand for, 96, 101, 121, 139
   dual-purpose, 100
   eighteenth century, 112-20, 122, 130, 137, 140, 146, 166, 169, 172, 175, 180, 195
   elementary, 114, 131, 132, 138, 139, 140
   foreign, 132, 133, 140, 149
   general musical, 131-2 native, 135, 136, 139, 140, 177, 195
   nineteenth century, 120-41, 147-8ff., 166
   provinces, 130-31
   reviews of, 131, 136-7
   role of teacher, 123-4, 125, 127, 128, 132, 134, 136
   vocal, 141-2
   youthful beginners, 122
   see also treatises; tutor books
technique, 116, 124
temperament, 52, 115, 120, 169, 172
Tertis, Lionel, 214
Tessarini, 134
texts *see* treatises
theme and variations, 120
theory, 34, 50-56, 61, 80, 81, 100, 115, 119, 120, 123
Thomson, A., 123, 130, 168, 184
thorough-bass, 53, 107, 119
Thring, Edward, 49, 55, 261-2
timpani, 237-8
tonic sol-fa, 58, 69, 86, 260
Tosi, 57, 111, 141, 142

Tours, B., 130
Tourte bow, 162, 163, 176, 181, 182, 199
Tovey, D., 55
training, 23, 24, 80, 82, 87, 90, 91, 92, 229, 239, 257
   apprenticeships, 89-92
   Europe, 102, 240-41ff.
   see also tuition
translations, 57, 100, 111, 125, 132, 215, 216
transport, 4, 12n., 100
treatises, 55, 107, 110
   brass, 233-4 cello, 216
   conservatism, 203, 207, 208
   foreign, 116, 207, 208, 242
   frontispieces, 175, 176
   general, 238
   harp, 236
   instrumental, 57, 99, 100, 113-41
   keyboard, 99, 220-21, 222-3
   native, 207-8
   significance of, 203-4
   violin, 108, 113-31, 133-9, 165ff., 203-4ff.
   vocal, 57-8, 141
   wind, 227, 228-9, 233
   see also teaching materials; tutor books
tremolo, 194
trills, 189-90, 234
Trinity College, 256
trios, 197, 198
triviality, 54, 62
trombone, 230
Tromlitz, 227
trumpet, 230, 231
   slide, 231-2, 233, 234
tuba, 233
tuition
   self-instruction, 92, 95, 99, 100, 112, 116, 117, 123, 138
   sources, 89
   see also private tuition; teaching materials; training
Tully, Charles, 233
Türk, D. G., 222, 224
tutor books, 52, 53, 55, 71-2, 99, 111, 112
   guitar, 236
   horn, 234

instrumental, 112–17, 122
keyboard, 100, 104, 121
text in, 117, 137, 165
wind, 225, 226
see also treatises

Union of Graduates in Music, 79
United States, 17
universities, 51, 59, 63, 253, 264
upper classes, 3, 11, 20, 21, 26, 31, 63, 77, 78, 102, 148, 209, 242
   see also aristocracy
Uppingham School, 49, 261
urbanization, 9, 29, 30
utilitarianism, 10, 27, 29, 59, 68, 83, 255, 268

valved instruments, 230–31, 232, 234
vibrato, 191–4, 234
Vienna, 13, 15–16, 17
Vincent, Thomas, 225
Vincent family, 24, 90
viola, 170, 213–14
violin, 11n., 46, 48, 49, 72, 81, 95, 107, 242, 245, 246–7, 248, 261, 263, 264
  amateur, 147–8
  articulation, 187
  bow, 118, 120ff., 162–3, 175–85, 198, 199
  difficulty of, 145–6, 156, 157
  duets, 134–5, 137, 196–7
  expression, 195–6, 204–5
  Geminiani grip, 166
  harmonics, 170–71
  hold, 165–8
  intonation, 173, 193
  left hand, 165–6, 168–75
  low status, 102, 146
  moral qualities, 210, 211, 212
  ornamentation, 187–94
  portamento, 174, 175, 206
  private tuition, 94
  repertoire, 196–203
  right hand, 182–3, 196
  shifting, 172, 173
  Stainer model, 162
  standards, 99, 146–7
  styles, 108–10, 126, 128, 149–50ff., 167, 187, 195–6, 208, 209

  technique, 124, 127, 137, 154, 164–96, 204
  tempo, 186–7
  tuning, 186
  vibrato, 191–4
  see also fiddle; treatises; violin makers; violinists
violin makers, 161–4, 263
violinists, 107, 201, 202–3, 204–7
  foreign, 146, 149–59
  native, 146, 147, 148, 158–61, 169
  perceptions of, 212–13
  tuition, 98–9
  women, 84, 148, 209–11, 213
Viotti, G. B., 19–20, 64, 109, 126, 151, 159, 160, 162, 163, 184, 204, 208, 246
  duos, 196–7, 198
  violin concertos, 107, 199, 201, 242
virtuosity, 61, 62, 63, 64, 106, 108, 109, 110, 111, 127, 164, 195, 204
virtuosos, 5, 159, 201
Vivaldi, 62
vocal music, 11n., 56–60, 141–2, 252, 267, 270
  education, 58–60, 66, 68, 69, 83
  foreign styles, 141
  moral aspects, 31, 56, 57–8, 59
  popularity of, 59, 63–4
  texts, 57–8
  women, 57, 86
  see also choral music; singers; singing
voluntary schools, 25, 70, 250

Wales, 13
Walmisley, T. A., 75, 253
wealth, 3, 6, 11, 12, 14, 35, 42, 98, 250
Weichsel, 159
Weist-Hill, T. H., 256
Wesley, Samuel, 22, 224
Wessely, Hans, 129, 175, 194, 195, 204, 208, 256
West, W. H., 133
Widor, 238
Wilhemj, A., 128, 158, 256
Willman, T. L. A., 228
Winch, 233

wind instruments, 24, 49, 84, 87, 163
  popular, 225–6
  teaching, 225, 226, 228, 258
  treatises, 227, 228–9, 233
  women, 229
women, 6–7, 8, 13, 28, 30, 57, 76, 82, 83, 131, 216
  education, 85, 251, 256, 257
  eighteenth century, 46–8, 84
  instruments, 71, 84
  middle-class, 7, 11, 25, 32, 38, 39, 53
  opportunities for, 49
  organists, 224
  performers, 44, 80
  piano, 219, 220–21
  plucked strings, 235–6
  private tuition, 94, 97, 99, 100–101
  singers, 57, 86
  string orchestras, 213
  tambourine, 237
  teachers, 7, 8, 10, 37, 43, 48, 79, 85, 94, 96, 100, 268

violinists, 84, 148, 209–11, 213
wind players, 229
working-class, 39
Wood, Henry, 206
Wordsworth, William, 67, 68, 243
Worgan, T. D., 54, 80
working-class, 27, 33, 35, 73, 77, 86, 212, 266, 268–9
  brass instruments, 233
  education, 69n., 253–4
  men, 7, 9, 38–9, 87, 235, 267
  and morality, 29–30, 31
  and new music, 65
  self-improvement, 68
  women, 39
Wragg, J., 120
writers, 29, 71, 80, 81–2
Wybrow, S. H., 133, 138, 176

Young, 80
youth, 43, 122
Ysaÿe, E., 206, 256

Zeiss, Carl, 259

For Product Safety Concerns and Information please contact our EU representative GPSR@taylorandfrancis.com
Taylor & Francis Verlag GmbH, Kaufingerstraße 24, 80331 München, Germany

www.ingramcontent.com/pod-product-compliance
Lightning Source LLC
Chambersburg PA
CBHW050428240426
43661CB00055B/2311